THE NEW CHINESE
DOCUMENTARY
FILM MOVEMENT

THE NEW CHINESE DOCUMENTARY FILM MOVEMENT

FOR THE PUBLIC RECORD

EDITED BY CHRIS BERRY, LU XINYU, AND LISA ROFEL

香港大學出版社
HONG KONG UNIVERSITY PRESS

Hong Kong University Press
14/F Hing Wai Centre
7 Tin Wan Praya Road
Aberdeen
Hong Kong

© Hong Kong University Press 2010

Hardcover   ISBN 978-988-8028-51-1
Paperback   ISBN 978-988-8028-52-8

British Library Cataloguing-in-Publication Data
A catalogue record for this book is available from the British Library.

Secure On-line Ordering
http://www.hkupress.org

This digitally printed version 2010

Table of Contents

List of Illustrations

Contributors

Chris Berry is professor of film and television studies in the Department of Media and Communication, Goldsmiths, University of London. His research is focused on Chinese cinemas and other Chinese screen-based media. His publications include (with Mary Farquhar) *Cinema and the National: China on Screen* (2006); *Postsocialist Cinema in Post-Mao China: The Cultural Revolution after the Cultural Revolution* (2004); (edited with Ying Zhu) *TV China* (2008); (editor) *Chinese Films in Focus II* (2008); (edited with Feiyi Lu) *Island on the Edge: Taiwan New Cinema and After* (2005); (edited with Fran Martin and Audrey Yue) *Mobile Cultures: New Media and Queer Asia* (2003); and (translator and editor) Ni Zhen, *Memoirs from the Beijing Film Academy: The Origins of China's Fifth Generation Filmmakers* (2002).

Yomi Braester is professor of comparative literature at the University of Washington, Seattle. He is the author of *Witness against History: Literature, Film, and Public Discourse in Twentieth-Century China* (2003) and *Painting the City Red: Chinese Cinema and the Urban Contract* (2010).

Chao Shi-Yan is a doctoral candidate in cinema studies at New York University. Having published various articles in Chinese, Chao is currently completing a dissertation on Chinese *tongzhi*/queer media representation. His recent article, "Performing Gender, Performing Documentary in Postsocialist China" is in Yau Ching, ed., *As Normal As Possible: Negotiating Sexuality and Gender in China and Hong Kong* (Hong Kong University Press, 2010).

Cathryn Clayton is assistant professor in Asian studies at the University of Hawai'i at Manoa. Her recently published monograph, *Sovereignty at the Edge: Macau and the Question of Chineseness* (2009) is an ethnography of the intersections between sovereignty and Chineseness in Macau during its transition from Portuguese to Chinese rule. Her recent translations include a number of

Chinese stage plays and opera librettos, including "Under the Eaves of Shanghai," "Cheng Ying Rescues the Orphan," "The Jade Hairpin," and "The Fan Family Library."

Lu Xinyu is professor in the School of Journalism, Fudan University, Shanghai. A prolific author on media topics, she is best known for her groundbreaking book *Documenting China* (2003), on the New Documentary Movement. With a Ph.D. in Western aesthetics from Fudan University, she is also the author of *Mythology • Tragedy • Aristotle's Art of Poetry: A New Concept in the Poetics Tradition of the Ancient Greeks* (1995).

Seio Nakajima is assistant professor of sociology at the University of Hawai'i at Manoa. His research has appeared in *From Underground to Independent*, edited by Paul G. Pickowicz and Zhang Yingjin (2006) and *Reclaiming Chinese Society*, edited by Ching Kwan Lee and You-tien Hsing (2009).

Bérénice Reynaud teaches film theory, history, and criticism in the School of Critical Studies and the School of Film/Video at the California Institute of the Arts and is co-curator of the Film/Video series at the Roy and Edna Disney/ CalArts Theater (REDCAT). She is the author of *Nouvelles Chines, nouveaux cinémas* (1999) and *Hou Hsiao Hsien's "A City of Sadness"* (2002). Her work has been published in periodicals such as *Sight & Sound*, *Screen*, *Film Comment*, *Afterimage*, *The Independent*, *CinemaScope*, *Senses of Cinema*, *Cahiers du Cinéma*, *Libération*, *Le Monde diplomatique*, and *CinémAction*. She is currently working on a book on the Chinese martial arts film.

Luke Robinson is a lecturer in film and TV studies at the Institute of Film and TV Studies, University of Nottingham, UK. He is currently working on a book manuscript about "liveness" and independent Chinese documentary.

Lisa Rofel is professor of anthropology at the University of California, Santa Cruz. She has written two books and co-edited several volumes on a range of topics about China, including *Other Modernities: Gendered Yearnings in China after Socialism* (1999), *Desiring China: Experiments in Neoliberalism, Sexuality and Public Culture* (2007), and co-edited with Petrus Liu a special issue of the journal *positions: east asia cultures critique*, *Beyond the Strai(gh)ts: Transnational Chinese Queer Politics* (2010).

Jia Tan is a Ph.D. candidate in critical studies at the School of Cinematic Arts, University of Southern California. She is also a research assistant in the Getty Research Institute.

Paola Voci teaches at the University of Otago, New Zealand. She is the author of *China on Video: Smaller-Screen Realities* (2010), a book that analyzes movies made and viewed on smaller screens (i.e. the DV camera, the computer monitor — and, within it, the internet window — and the cell phone display). Her work also appears in several edited collections of essays and she has published in *Modern Chinese Literature and Culture, Senses of Cinema, New Zealand Journal of Asian Studies,* and contributed to the *Encyclopedia of Chinese Cinema.*

Yiman Wang is assistant professor of film and digital media at the University of California, Santa Cruz. She has published in *Quarterly Review of Film and Video, Film Quarterly, Camera Obscura, Journal of Film and Video, Literature/Film Quarterly, positions: east asia cultures critique, Journal of Chinese Cinemas, Chinese Films in Focus: 25 New Takes,* edited by Chris Berry (2003), *Cultural Identity, Gender, Everyday Life Practice and Hong Kong Cinema of the 1970s,* edited by Lo Kwai-cheung and Eva Man (2005), and *Stardom and Celebrity: A Reader,* edited by Sean Redmond et al. (2007).

Wu Wenguang was a primary school teacher and then a journalist for Kumming Television and China Central Television (CCTV), before making his first independent documentary, *Bumming in Beijing: The Last Dreamers* (1990), which is widely seen as inaugurating China's New Documentary Movement. In 1991, he founded the Wu Documentary Studio and in 1994 he co-founded The Living Dance Studio with his partner, the dancer and choreographer Wen Hui, with whom he often collaborates. Between 1996 and 1997, he published a desktop magazine, *Documentary Scene,* then founded and edited the independent monthly art magazine *New Wave* (2001). He has written three books inspired by his videos, and edited a three-part collection of critical texts entitled *Document.* In 2005, Wu and Wen established the Caochangdi Workstation, where Wu co-ordinated the *China Village Self-Governance Film Project,* a collection of ten documentaries in which villagers record the introduction of grassroots democracy in China. He continues to train young filmmakers at Caochangdi and has recently completed a second installment of the *China Village Self-Governance Film Project.*

J. X. Zhang is a painter-etcher, freelance art critic and translator.

Part I

Historical Overview

1 Introduction

Chris Berry and Lisa Rofel

If you turn on Chinese television today, you may be surprised. News reporting outside China often gives the impression that the country is still a tightly controlled propaganda culture. Yet, you will find dozens if not hundreds of different television channels, with a spontaneous, free-flowing style of reporting. Ordinary citizens are interviewed on the street and express their opinions in a sometimes stumbling and therefore clearly unrehearsed manner. Reporters do not speak as representatives of the Communist Party and government line, but as independent journalists. With hand-held cameras, they breathlessly investigate social issues and follow stories. While certainly monitored by the state and at no time oppositional, China's most popular medium adopts a more spur-of-the-moment style than many foreigners would expect. And if China's reputation for a rigorously policed internet limits your expectations, the local equivalent of YouTube — Tudou.com — may surprise you, too. Here a vibrant amateur version of the same on-the-spot style found in television reporting also dominates the scene. All kinds of videos stream off the screen, from personal videos and reflections on home life to oral history and recordings of local events — some of them contentious.[1]

However, this wholesale transformation of public culture has been relatively ignored by academic work to date. Outside China, that may be because these kinds of materials do not circulate internationally as readily as blockbuster feature films or contemporary art. Inside China, that neglect began to change in 1997, with the publication of our co-editor Lu Xinyu's article on the "Contemporary Television Documentary Movement," followed by her 2003 book on the "New Documentary Movement" in general.[2] This work traced the major transformations that had occurred in all kinds of actuality-based visual culture — from television news to the internet — back to the beginning of the 1990s, and in particular to documentary film and video production. Not only had the topics, style, and production circumstances of documentary changed in China, but also the new documentary aesthetic has been at the cutting edge of changes elsewhere in Chinese film, television, and video production. What you see today on Chinese television and at Tudou.com was pioneered by the New Documentary Movement from the early 1990s on.

Therefore, any attempt to understand China's visual culture today must start from an understanding of the New Documentary Movement. With this anthology, we attempt to follow Lu Xinyu's lead into the world of English-language Chinese film studies. So far, significant discussion of China's New Documentary Movement in English has been largely confined to articles and book chapters.[3] Here, we bring together work by some of the main scholars writing on the topic to create a sustained focus on Chinese independent documentary in English for the first time. In this introduction, we will discuss the significance of the New Documentary Movement in two ways. First, we will try to indicate why it has taken such a central role in Chinese audio-visual culture over the last two decades. Second, we will consider it in its more recent digital form as a contribution to the debates about what cinema is in the digital era, and argue that this new Chinese digital cinema treasures immediacy, spontaneity, and contact with lived experience over the high levels of manipulability associated with the special effects culture of mainstream cinema. The history of the movement is outlined and analyzed in Lu Xinyu's first chapter for this volume, which follows on from this introduction. Looking back from today, she not only traces the development of the movement but also questions many of the assumptions that have been made about it so far. This introductory chapter, along with Lu Xinyu's historical overview and a chapter by Wu Wenguang, considered by many as the initiator of the New Documentary Movement, comprise Part I of this volume, which is meant to offer a broad introduction to the movement.

What is the New Documentary Movement and why has it been so important in China's visual culture? Before 1990 all documentary was state-produced, and took the form of illustrated lectures. Television news was delivered by newsreaders who spoke as the mouthpiece of the Communist Party and the government. There were no spontaneous interviews with the man (or woman) on the street, and no investigative reporting shows. Independent film production was impossible in an era where all the studios were nationally owned and controlled. The internet did not exist, and even the constitutional right to put up "big character posters" (*dazibao*) had been abrogated in 1978 in response to the Democracy Wall movement.[4] However, the 1980s had witnessed a flourishing of independent thought and questioning of the status quo in response to both the disillusion with Maoism following the debacle of the Cultural Revolution (1966–1976) and the changing nature of relationships with the West that had followed.[5] In 1990, former television station employee Wu Wenguang produced a no-budget independent documentary using borrowed equipment. Called

Bumming in Beijing: The Last Dreamers, it is analyzed in detail in Bérénice Reynaud's chapter in this volume, and noted in nearly all the others. *Bumming in Beijing* is a video film about artists who, like Wu, were struggling to survive independently outside the state system. This is now frequently cited as the first independent documentary to be made in China. Not only was the topic one unlikely to be covered by the relentlessly optimistic state studios and television stations. Furthermore, Wu used a hand-held camera, no artificial lighting, synch sound that was often unclear, and shot things as they happened. This spontaneous style was so unprecedented that it came to have a name of its own: *jishi zhuyi*, or on-the-spot realism, not to be confused with *xianshi zhuyi*, the type of highly orchestrated realism associated with socialist realism.

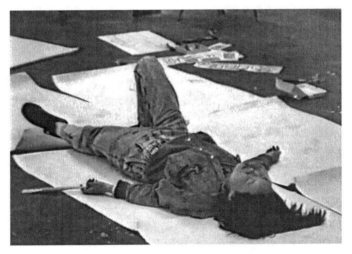

Figure 1.1. Zhang Xiaping's nervous breakdown in Wu Wenguang's *Bumming in Beijing*.

This nitty-gritty and low-budget *jishi zhuyi* style of realism became the hallmark of independent documentary in China, which took off rapidly through the 1990s. In her historical analysis of China's New Documentary Movement in this volume, Lu Xinyu notes that most scholars writing on the topic have only included independent films like Wu's in the New Documentary Movement. However, she questions this, noting that many of Wu's friends and former colleagues working inside the state-owned television system were also beginning to experiment with a more spontaneous mode of documentary at around the same time. In other words, strikingly original though it was, *Bumming in Beijing* did not come out of nowhere. In her chapter, she locates its emergence in a larger cultural context that also encompasses documentary photography and the new "Sixth Generation" of feature filmmakers, some of whom also took part in the New Documentary Movement.

Lu also notes that the term "New Documentary Movement" first appeared in 1992, a little while after the first films began to appear. This places the origins of the movement between two crucial dates in Chinese history: 1989 and 1992. Nineteen eighty-nine is the year of the Tiananmen Democracy Movement and its suppression. Nineteen ninety-two is the year that Premier Deng Xiaoping made his famous "Tour to the South," in the course of which he called for increased development of the market economy. As we argue in our chapter in this volume, the 1989/1992 conjuncture shapes the cultural and artistic practices that have developed outside the new state-corporate hegemonic culture of China today. The former date signaled the suppression of a public oppositional movement while the latter presaged the commercialization of culture.

Maoist socialism had ended with the Chinese Cultural Revolution, but until the early 1990s, some still believed in the basic tenets of socialism — the official phrase was "socialism with Chinese characteristics"; meanwhile intellectuals analyzed forms of socialist alienation without rejecting socialism in its entirety. But many were disillusioned by the destruction they experienced through class struggle and continuous revolution, two basic tenets of Maoist socialism. After the Cultural Revolution, the Chinese state introduced reforms, hoping to stave off a potential crisis of legitimacy posed by this disillusionment. Economic reform eventually entailed a rejection of collective enterprise, the gradual promotion of a market economy, and the steady move toward privatization. These reforms were and are built on the premise of a continuity in the political system of governance coupled with a discontinuity in the state's promotion of radical marketization and privatization.[6] It would be misleading then to characterize the market economy in China as in opposition to the state.

Economic reform in the rural areas was somewhat distinct from urban reform. Rural reform, which occurred first between 1978 and 1984, entailed de-collectivization of communes, the partial decentralization of power to local governments, and the development of rural markets. Rural reform had certain unanticipated results: widespread corruption in the transfer of resources and an enormous tide of rural migrants who swept into the cities in search of work. Urban reforms entailed an analogous devolution of power to local governments and managers of state-run enterprises. As in the rural areas, the transfer of resources reorganized social relations, advantages, and interests. The small minority who benefited most visibly, including some managers but also diverse government cadres, eventually formed a new capitalist class.[7]

These reforms created new historical conditions: the marketization of power, inequalities in distribution and rent-seeking behavior, increasingly polarized income levels, the abolition of security in employment, and lack of reforms in social benefits. The reforms had contradictory effects: they enhanced ordinary people's sense of new possibilities but also increased frustrations with the new social inequalities that soon emerged. The Tiananmen demonstrations of 1989 were a response to these contradictions. The state's violent suppression of the 1989 protests led, paradoxically, to a widening of the reforms. For the first time, the state began to encourage foreign direct investment in China. By 2002, China had surpassed the United States as the favored destination for foreign direct investment. In turn, China began to invest in other countries, as both government and private entrepreneurs searched for the natural resources that China's growing economy demanded. An emphasis on consumer and mass culture began to dominate urban life. Over the next decade, a majority of state-run enterprises were allowed to go bankrupt and massive numbers of urban workers, who thought they had garnered the "iron rice bowl" of lifetime employment, found themselves permanently unemployed.[8]

This rapidly changing historical context, with its stark contrasts, provides the impetus and the rationale for the New Documentary Movement, in the political, social, and technical senses of the term "movement." It addressed new political themes, filmed social subjects marginalized by mainstream and official media, and transformed audio-visual culture in China, including not only independent documentary and amateur work on the internet but also broadcast television and fiction feature film production.

The people making independent documentaries were friendly with former colleagues in television stations, and in many cases they themselves were continuing to work in those stations. New TV series such as *Oriental Horizon*, a Chinese news magazine show in the mode of the famous American CBS show *60 Minutes*, pursued many elements of on-the-spot realism. Combined with investigative tendencies, the results were immediate hits with audiences.

Other independent documentarians had friends who were young filmmakers, some of whom were also striking out on their own outside the state-owned industry. For them, on-the-spot realism also provided a signature style different from what had gone before. They felt a need to mark themselves out from two earlier tendencies. On the one hand, there was the socialist realist tradition, which had the glossy aspirational look of Hollywood but narratives driven by class struggle rather than individualized psychology. On the other hand, there were the highly stylized works of the Fifth Generation, which had marked themselves out from socialist realism by use of unusual angles, virtuoso visual design, and settings in the exotic border areas or the past. The so-called Sixth Generation, who started working in the 1990s, used on-the-spot realism to create their own signature style, along with contemporary urban settings. Even Zhang Yimou himself picked up the observational documentary trend in the opening sequence of *The Story of Qiu Ju* (1992), placing a heavily disguised Gong Li among the rural crowds and filming her with hidden cameras.[9]

Zhang Yimou's adoption of the New Documentary Movement style in *The Story of Qiu Ju* is early evidence of its wide impact. If you ask the average Chinese citizen about Wu Wenguang and *Bumming in Beijing*, or indeed most of the other films and filmmakers discussed in this volume, they will probably have no idea what you are talking about. But they certainly will know *Oriental Horizon*, and the makers of *Oriental Horizon* know Wu and the other documentary independents. In other words, the core films and filmmakers of the New Documentary Movement are an avant-garde. Like avant-gardes all over the world, they often set the pace and are best known in their field; while the general public might well recognize the innovations they have introduced, they would less likely be able to name artists and works.

In China, the public's knowledge of these works is further complicated by their unofficial nature and resulting difficulties of access. China's system of cultural production continues to bear the traces of its Maoist heritage in certain ways. In the Maoist era, the Communist Party and the state not only controlled cultural production but also set the agenda. Just as entrepreneurship has been encouraged in the wider economy now, so too, cultural producers initiate their projects rather than waiting for instructions from the state. However, it remains the case that nothing can be broadcast without approval from the censorship apparatus, and no film can be shown commercially in movie theaters without similar censorship approval. As a result, these works circulate through other channels. As well as pirate DVDs, legal ones exist of some films, because the DVD censorship authority is separate from that for films or broadcasting. Screenings occur in art galleries, university classrooms, and at other informal venues, as discussed further in our chapter and in Seio Nakajima's chapter in this volume. And, of course, many films can be downloaded. This means that while they may not be reaching a general public, they may be more easily found and seen in China than outsiders might expect. This cirulation also helps to explain the ongoing wide cultural impact of the movement.

When the mini DV camera was introduced in about 1997, both the New Documentary Movement and its low-cost style received a further boost. The impact of the mini DV was remarkable. First, it changed the mode of filmmaking. The small camera made one-person filmmaking possible. In his chapter translated for this volume, Wu Wenguang himself celebrates his experience of the DV camera as a personal transformation and even a salvation. This is not because of the technical properties of DV, but because he feels it enables him to break through the barrier between the filmmaker and their subjects, creating a communal experience rather than a hierarchical one.

Another important transformation enabled by DV was the proliferation of the movement. Affordable to most middle-class people, relatively easy to use, and easy to edit for anyone with a home computer, the DV camera could be taken up by people with no professional training or experience. In the early days, it was possible for a visitor to know all the Chinese independent filmmakers and see their films. After the introduction of DV, even the leading filmmakers had difficulty keeping track of the scope and range of production. Jia Zhangke, who has continued to make independent documentaries at the same time as his feature films have won awards at festivals like Venice (*Still Life*, 2006), hailed the post-DV era in China as the "age of the amateur."[10]

This intersection of on-the-spot realism in its various guises and the digital age makes China's independent documentary movement more than the key force in China's visual culture. It also makes it an important and different contribution to the international debate about digital culture and its impact upon what we call "cinema" today. In the People's Republic of China, there was no earlier development of independent or amateur film culture with either 16mm or 8mm film. Therefore, when DV arrived in China soon after the upsurge of independent production, it not only enabled the growth of independent production, but also led to the identification of DV with the independent and amateur movement in its on-the-spot realism form. Around the turn of the century, China's bookshops featured various titles on what was called the DV aesthetic, all of which also emphasized the idea of independent filmmaking and on-the-spot realism.[11]

This Chinese understanding of the essence of DV stands in stark contrast to the common understanding in the United States and elsewhere in the West. This distinction can be exemplified by the contentions put forward by Lev Manovich in *The Language of New Media*. Here, Manovich notes that DV introduces the ability to manipulate the image at the level of the pixel. Whereas Chinese filmmakers and commentators valued DV's ability to capture what was happening around them in a direct and unmediated way, Manovich emphasizes the ability to manipulate what is recorded in an almost equally direct manner. On this basis, he argues for a reconsideration of the history of cinema. Instead of the indexical or direct recording of reality as a watershed moment in which cinema marks itself out from painting, the digital and the possibility for the artist to manipulate every pixel provides cinema with a new lineage that once again places it within the long history of painting.[12]

Given Hollywood's embrace of digital's ability to be used for spectacular special effects, it is hardly surprising that many other authors have also focused on similar aspects in their writings on DV.[13] But this alternative appropriation of DV in the People's Republic should alert us to the fact that DV has no single essence, but already means different things in different places according to local circumstances.

Of course, the local significance of the New Documentary Movement in China goes beyond filmmaking, and is more fundamentally rooted in its commitment to record contemporary life in China outside any direct control of the state. That is, the New Documentary Movement filmmakers self-consciously fashion themselves as committed to a social practice that they hope will open up new public spaces for discussion of social problems and dilemmas in the post-socialist era. They have forged a novel space of social commentary and critique, not simply in the reception of the films by audiences but much more in the actual process of producing the documentaries. Most notably, this production process includes long-term relationships developed between filmmakers and subjects, in which the filmmaker might spend several years living with those being filmed, more in the manner of an anthropologist than of an investigative journalist. The social and political commentary of the film develops organically out of this relationship. These independent documentaries have the potential to craft a unique public space.

This striking manner of crafting documentary builds from a set of assumptions distinct from common understandings of documentary film in English-language academic writing. Film and video in general are considered to be a "representation" of reality. In consequence, many discussions of documentary ethics proceed from the assumption that the key issue for documentary is how to represent reality as accurately as possible. They ask how to minimize the impact of the documentary-making process on the reality that it is meant to represent. In the case of studies of activist documentary, the focus is on reception after the production of the film rather than its social engagement during production.

However, the independent documentary practice that has developed in China works from completely contrary assumptions. It understands documentary making as a part of life, not a representation separate from it. Furthermore, the documentarians see their work as part of the lives of their subjects, and they are concerned that their documentary making should be a social practice that helps those people.

Thus, many of the chapters in this volume join the move beyond the purely textual focus that continues to dominate mainstream film studies to address the social practices embedded in the films. The questions these chapters address include: Given the difficulties with independent filmmaking in China, can this practice provide an unexpected opportunity for ordinary citizens to make themselves heard? How do these documentarians as well as their subjects grapple with the way power is at once open to contest and resistant to change? How do they articulate in the film- or video-making the production of politics, inequality, difference, and community? To what extent can we say that these documentarians are oppositional activists? How do they operate within specific institutional, historical, sociological, and ideological constraints? And how do the documentarians as well as the subjects within the documentary produce specific identities (national, regional and trans-regional, class, gender), cultural and ideological perspectives, and aesthetic values?

The chapters in Part II of the book, "Documenting Marginalization, or Identities New and Old," address one of the most important features of the movement: attention to those hitherto neglected in China's media. This aspect of the movement cannot be over-stressed. The suppression of public dissent after Tiananmen did not lead to a withering away of critical voices and the New Documentary Movement is a central place where they can be found. Due to the nature of these documentaries — the lack of voiceover and thus the seeming absence of ideological framing, coupled with the fact that the "common folk" speak in their own voices — the state has found it difficult to respond with direct intervention. Thus, the movement presents both implicit and explicit social and political critique. It also offers a sense of the contradictory emergence of new subjectivities as a result of the market economy and its transnational imbrications. In her magisterial chapter on Wang Bing's *West of the Tracks*, Lu Xinyu examines the significance of his decision to look at the death of a heavy industry district that once symbolized the triumph of socialism. She argues that the film demands attention to the price being paid for marketization, in terms of both personal upheaval and the abandonment of socialist ideals. The film stands as a monument to the otherwise undocumented destruction that accompanies the more frequently celebrated construction that is going on in other parts of China. On the other hand, Chao Shi-Yan's chapter focuses on social identities that have emerged with marketization, namely gay and lesbian sexual identities. He compares two films about lesbians, one produced by a self-proclaimed heterosexual woman, the other by a lesbian. Chao argues that while observational documentaries have addressed certain important political questions of representation in China, they raise other sorts of contradictions when questions of identity come into the picture. By identifying with lesbians, the filmmaker Shi Tou is able to experiment with styles of filmmaking that do not concern themselves with observational distance or objectification.

In the third part of the book, "Publics, Counter-Publics, and Alternative Publics," we turn to the spaces the films circulate in, the spaces documented by the films, and the spaces they create. Independent films in China are shown in a wide variety of spaces, including film clubs, university classrooms, and private homes. Seio Nakajima answers the often-raised question of whether and where these "independent" and therefore "underground" productions are screened in China, by conducting an ethnographic investigation of the film clubs of Beijing and their role in the circulation and discussion of the new documentary films. In his study he found at least four different types of film clubs in Beijing: (1) "politically oriented film clubs," (2) "commercially oriented film clubs," (3) "'art for art's sake' film clubs," and (4) "artistic, commercial film clubs." Nakajima goes on to analyze the kinds of debates that occur in these spaces about the films that are screened. These debates address not only the distinctions between documentary and fiction film but also the influence of the West on Chinese filmmaking practices. Paola Voci examines the Beijing of the New Documentary Movement in "Blowup Beijing: The City as a Twilight Zone." With allusions to Michelangelo Antonioni and the eponymous television series of the 1960s, Voci examines what she argues is a central feature of Chinese documentaries: their tendency to highlight the barely visible locations of Beijing's marginal inhabitants. Unlike the conventional images of Beijing, these films make accessible an unofficial, unconventional, and unlikely Beijing. Finally, Berry and Rofel turn to the complicated question of the social and political status of these films. Rather than label them as "oppositional," "underground," or "resistance" films, we argue that "alternative," understood in a specifically Chinese context, is the most appropriate nomination of the movement.

The chapters collected in the final section of the book, "Between Filmmaker and Subject: Re-creating Realism," return to investigate in more detail some of the formal features of documentary film discussed at the beginning of this introduction. While many have noted the distinctive visual quality of the new documentary films, their aural qualities have been less frequently examined. Bérénice Reynaud rectifies this lacuna with detailed analysis of the voice and its complex deployments in *Bumming in Beijing*. In his chapter, Luke Robinson interrogates the often-noted turn to "private" filmmaking with the arrival of the DV camera, and, through analysis of key works, asks if this turn really means a retreat from the social or another way of approaching it. Finally, both Yomi Braester and Yiman Wang are interested in the ethical issues that have been coming to the fore with the development of the New Documentary Movement. Braester challenges the presumption of cinematic objectivity in the movement. He focuses on the many instances of intrusion by the filmmaker into the scene, including prodding subjects into action. Analyzing four films in detail, Braester not only raises questions about intrusions into others' seemingly private lives but also demonstrates how these intrusive films rely on a notion of auteurship that implicitly highlights the inherent theatricality behind the supposedly spontaneous interactions in other documentary films. Wang examines "personal" documentaries made with the benefit of DV technology and the redefinition of documentary ethics that proceeds from them by configuring new relationships between the documentary maker and the subjects. She addresses two apparently contradictory statements by personal documentarians — an identificatory "I am one of them" and a theatrical "they are my actors" — to analyze the relations between experiencing, witnessing, and performance.

We hope that the chapters here will begin to draw the attention that China's New Documentary Movement deserves in the international English-speaking world. Furthermore, we hope and believe that this volume will stimulate further debate, not only on the movement itself, but also on the wider culture that it has pioneered. There is an even more notable lack of work on the protean textual output of internet and amateur visual culture in China today, especially work that goes beyond issues of ownership and control to actually engage with the texts themselves. We hope this anthology will help to provide a springboard for more work of that nature. We would like to take this opportunity to thank all the filmmakers and the authors of the volume, as well as our editors and readers at Hong Kong University Press. We also thank the Pacific Rim Research Program of the University of California for funding that enabled our research for this volume.

2 Rethinking China's New Documentary Movement: Engagement with the Social

Lu Xinyu, translated by Tan Jia and Lisa Rofel, edited by Lisa Rofel and Chris Berry

The rise of the New Documentary Movement is one of the most important cultural phenomena in contemporary China. The definition of this contemporary film movement has not reached a consensus, as the movement itself is heterogeneous. However, it is clear that the movement arose in the historical, political, and social context of the 1980s and 1990s and must be understood within that context. One common characteristic of the New Documentary Movement filmmakers is their rebellion against the old, rigid aspects of Maoist utopianism and established political ideologies in China. They presented a challenge especially to the hegemonic notion of "reality" and how it should be represented in film. One can discern this challenge even across the differences between the two distinct phases of the movement; the first phase from the 1980s to the mid-1990s and the second phase roughly from the mid-1990s onward. Second, it cannot be so easily asserted that the movement was wholly separate from official sites of media production. Finally, while the content of New Documentary Movement films is diverse, they tend to focus on marginalized subjects. They highlight the experiences of marginalization within a market economy. Thus, the power of the New Documentary Movement is to reveal new, and often painful, forms of reality.

In 2003, I published *Documenting China*, which described the main characteristics of the New Documentary Movement. In this chapter, I would like to rethink several commonly held assumptions about the New Documentary Movement that have become pervasive since I published that book.

First, there is the assumption that a clear line can be drawn between "independent" documentary films that comprise the New Documentary Movement and television programs. Against this assumption, I argue that some television programs should be included in the New Documentary Movement. Second, against the assumption that individualization (*gerenhua*) in documentaries appeared with the use of digital video (DV), I argue that although the appearance of DV facilitated individualization in documentaries, it was part of the New Documentary Movement before the widespread use of DV. Finally, I question the common assumption that there has been a retreat from engagement with social and political issues since DV and individualization. Rather, the form of engagement has changed.

What's New about the New Documentary Movement?

During the late 1980s and throughout the 1990s, documentary filmmaking in China was in a continuous state of development. The New Documentary Movement as a concept was first brought up in a casual meeting, attended by about a dozen people, at the then independent feature and documentary filmmaker Zhang Yuan's home in 1992. Zhang Yuan is one of China's Sixth Generation filmmakers. His major works include *Beijing Bastards* (1993) and *East Palace, West Palace* (1996). According to those in attendance, the meeting focused on the independence of documentary, at both a practical and conceptual level. No manifesto or schema was proposed at this meeting (though the participants were encouraged to keep in touch with and support each other). Yet the idea of a New Documentary Movement began with rebellions both inside and outside the dominant media system, especially against the "special topic program" (*zhuantipian*), the model of traditional Chinese television propaganda program. This is why the movement is labeled as "new."

The special topic program is a product of the Chinese television industry, but its history dates back to the heyday of cinema in socialist China. Before the general adoption of television, newsreels under the series title *News Highlights* were projected right before feature movies. These started with *News Clips (Xinwen jianbo)* in the 1950s, and were later turned into a series named *New Look of the Motherland (Zuguo xinmao)*. They were produced by Central Newsreel and Documentary Film Studio. These and other scientific or educational films produced by other domestic film studios were generally called documentaries. Guided by the aesthetic of "socialist realism," the social function of these documentaries was to inspire socialist consciousness in the people and to serve the mainstream political ideology of the state using the Leninist method of "political visualization."

The influence of these journalistic films spread to television during the 1980s. Today, the highest rated program on China Central Television 1 (CCTV1) is still *News Headlines (Xinwen lianbo)*, which grew out of *News Clips* and *New Look of the Motherland*. The most important divisions in China's television industry during the early 1980s were the News Division and the Special Topic Division. While *News Headlines* was produced by the News Division, other news programs regarding specific issues were produced by the Special Topic Division.

The model of producing film documentaries was followed not only by special topic programs on television but also by several special topic television series that offered political commentary. Both of these genres appeared during the mid-1980s. In these two genres, explanation was more important than image, and voiceover narration guided the interpretation of the images. One famous example is *River Elegy* (1988). This six-part documentary series offered a negative portrayal of Chinese culture, arguing that China was a land-based civilization that had been defeated by maritime civilizations.[1] Certain Chinese Communist Party leaders supported the airing of this documentary, to lend ideological support to the rapid development of an export-oriented market economy. But the series became controversial once other party leaders accused it of being one of the primary elements triggering the Tiananmen demonstrations of 1989.

Beginning in the early 1980s, television sets became more popular in the home. Therefore, going to the movies went into decline, leading to decreased production of film newsreels and documentaries.[2] As I explain below, this coincided with the beginnings of the turn away from Maoist socialism, a period known as "economic reform" (1984–1991) that gradually introduced a market economy into China. Television programs consciously tried to distance themselves from the kinds of film documentaries previously shown in movie theaters, because of their association with a certain kind of socialist propaganda linked to Maoism. Hence, the term "special topics" was used to refer to programming that resembled documentaries. The term "documentary," however, fell into disuse because of its association with socialist realist ideology and politics.

Thus, by the time Wu Wenguang, known as one of the founders of the New Documentary Movement, began shooting *Bumming in Beijing: The Last Dreamers* (1990), he claimed that he had no concept of documentary.[3] Gradually, however, following Wu's lead, the shared pursuit of a new kind of documentary emerged. These new documentarians created a vision of "reality" in contrast to what they viewed as the fake, exaggerated, and empty characteristics of not only the old socialist realist documentaries but also the more recent special topic programs. They viewed their documentaries as a challenge to, and a rebellion against, the officially sanctioned special topic programs. Therefore, in this rebellion, the term "documentary" was rediscovered in opposition to the special topic programs. New Documentary Movement filmmakers had a common object of opposition. As a result, in the search for a new documentary form, groundbreaking documentarians such as Wu Wenguang, Duan Jinchuan, Jiang Yue, Zhang Yuan, and others began to perceive the need for new representations of reality. The rebellion became collective and the movement took shape. The filmmakers who began to forge what became known as the New Documentary Movement were very idealistic about their work, especially in the 1980s and

1990s. They believed that the search for a new kind of reality in their films would generate new social meanings and therefore new ways of dealing with social problems. This profound transformation can only be understood in the context of the social, economic, political, and ideological changes that started in China in the 1980s.

Most important, a sense of disillusion had followed the aftermath of the Cultural Revolution (1966–1976). When it was launched, the Cultural Revolution addressed class antagonisms. Mao's desire to challenge a new and privileged social elite of political cadres who had emerged under socialism drove his early calls for youth to experience revolution by overthrowing this elite. But the Cultural Revolution quickly devolved into violent struggles, including the use of class warfare tactics to pursue personal antagonisms. To end this urban warfare, Mao ordered urban youth, the main protagonists of the Cultural Revolution, to go to the countryside and learn from the farmers. Some went idealistically, not realizing how difficult official policy would make it for them to return to their homes in the city. As the Cultural Revolution wound down, many of these youth lost their idealism to a new view of the Cultural Revolution: that it was the result of power struggles among top leaders who had merely used them in their schemes. Corruption — using unofficial means to gain privileges that were otherwise hard to obtain — also became endemic and obvious. Thus, the end of the Cultural Revolution, which essentially ended with Mao's death in 1976, left Maoist socialism in tatters.

Those who eventually became part of the New Documentary Movement were therefore part of a larger search for new ideals and meaningful goals. This search began in the early 1980s and, one could argue, continues to this day. During the early 1980s, official policy promoted economic reform, a rejection of Maoist socialism, and the gradual promotion of a market economy. The new leader, Deng Xiaoping, advocated "seek truth from facts" to impart the sense that ideology would not be used to mask reality, whether that reality be the economic need for development or the need for scientific expertise not driven by socialist ideals. Both official and popular practices groped their way toward building a strong China, even as new forms of inequality emerged as a result.[4]

In the first years after the Cultural Revolution, cultural producers were encouraged to continue working with a sense of social responsibility, something that had been emphasized under socialism. Many intellectuals and other cultural producers embraced this sense of responsibility, even when they did not always agree with official ideology. Today, some members of the younger generation of directors tend to interpret this sense of social responsibility as an oppressive concept. But in my understanding, it means that directors use their own style to maintain a dialogue with society. This dialogue includes investigation of social problems, interpretation of the reality of those problems, and intervention through public exposure in documentaries. In a transitional society such as China's, which is developing a market economy while trying to maintain a socialist government, if one makes a conscious effort not to blindfold oneself, one will discern how social changes enter people's consciousness. In fact, for many of us who are intellectuals and cultural producers, it is difficult to cut ourselves off from these social transformations. They force us to re-examine our own social role. For Chinese documentary directors, sensitivity toward the enormous social changes taking place in China is virtually unavoidable, for they live in the same society.

The first creative works to appear in the New Documentary Movement spanned the 1989 Tiananmen Incident.[5] The Tiananmen events in 1989 were crucial as they made certain Chinese filmmakers begin to realize the necessity of understanding social reality from the bottom up. The Tiananmen Incident shocked them. How could such a thing occur? What was its significance for China's past, present, and future? They discovered that they understood little about what China actually was. They felt the need to begin a new understanding of Chinese society. During the 1980s, they had examined China from on high. Now they felt the need to go to the grassroots, and to understand China's changes and their causes from this other vantage point.

As a result, the New Documentary Movement reflected the weight of that historical moment, with a distinctive and shared mode of thinking and expression. In its earliest phase, the first group to use independent modes of production was Wu Wenguang, Wen Pulin, Duan Jinchuan, Jiang Yue, Zhang Yuan, Bi Jianfeng, Lu Wangping, Lin Xudong, Shi Jian, Hao Zhiqiang, Wang Zijun, Chen Zhen, and Fu Hongxing. They went on to have a major influence on the movement. Most of them were located in Beijing; one could say Beijing was the "headquarters" of independent documentary production. This group of Beijing documentarians shared collective aims and influenced and encouraged one another. The most influential works by this first group include *Bumming in Beijing: The Last Dreamers* (Wu Wenguang, 1990), *Tiananmen* (Shi Jian and Chen Jue at CCTV, 1991), *I Graduated!* (SWYC Group, 1992), *Catholics in Tibet* (Jiang Yue, 1992), *The Sacred Site of Asceticism* (Wen Pulin and Duan Jinchuan, 1993), *Tibetan Theater Troupe* (Fu Hongxing, 1993), *1996, My Time in the Red Guards* (Wu Wenguang, 1993), *Big Tree County* (Hao Zhiqiang, 1993), *The Square* (Duan Jinchuan and Zhang Yuan, 1994), *At Home in the World* (Wu Wenguang, 1995), *The Other Bank* (Jiang Yue, 1995), and *No. 16 Barkhor South Street* (Duan Jinchuan, 1996). These works were not only shown at international film festivals but also in unofficial venues in China. They mainly used television equipment as the medium for documenting realities that were being left out of mainstream media. The subject matter they addressed was very broad. If one were to summarize, one could say that they were efforts to establish a new self-awareness and a different societal awareness at a distinctive historical moment. The funds for making these films derived largely from the directors' own resources, but many of them were also able to find ways to borrow equipment from television stations.

During this period, they had various private and formal relationships with the television stations. Many were actually working within the television system. Chinese television is state-owned and controlled, although then it was still largely state-funded whereas today it is funded by advertising and driven by ratings. Today, there is a plethora of stations run by provincial, municipal, and township governments as well as the central government. But at that time, the pre-eminent station was China Central Television (CCTV), and it was undergoing thorough reform. It was the golden era of television development in China, and this group of documentary filmmakers had a profound influence on documentary within the television system. Therefore, the roots of the New Documentary Movement can be found both inside and outside the system. On the one hand, this was because television workers had more direct contact with society than feature filmmakers, and so they were more sensitive to social change. On the other hand, television production cost much less than filmmaking. Documentary is not a form that belongs in the ivory tower or among elites, and so the emergent New Documentary Movement benefited from this affordability.

Many people contributed to the development of television documentary at this time. Among them was Chen Meng, who launched China's first daily short documentary television program, *Life Space (Shenghuo kongjian)*, in 1993. The program focused on "the people's own stories," an approach that influenced and even defined television documentary at the time. The group, who in 1993 created Shanghai Television's first program to use the term "documentary," *Documentary Editing Room*, focused on the fate and circumstances of ordinary people in the midst of Shanghai's momentous transformations. Kang Jianning, then at Ningxia Television Station, made a long documentary entitled *Yinyang* (1994).[6] This documentary, about a geomancer in an impoverished and remote village, made evident the immense labor that goes into documenting China's reality from the perspective of those in the lower social strata. In the first period of the New Documentary Movement, there was plenty of interaction between the inside and outside of the system. But after the commercialization of Chinese television in the 1990s with television's rising dependency on advertising revenue, this situation gradually dissipated.

However, the tidal wave of documenting realism did not recede in the 1990s. In the second period of the New Documentary Movement (as detailed further below), the so-called Sixth Generation of Chinese feature filmmakers began to adopt the new realist style of the New Documentary Movement. At the same time, DV became accessible, thus making possible a different mode of "individualization" (*gerenhua*) of filmmaking practice, which had already begun in the first phase of the documentary movement but, as I discuss below, continues in a different form in the second phase. In this second period, many young students studying in film schools started joining the creative community of documentarians with their own digital videos. By this time, it was almost the beginning of the twenty-first century.

The New Documentary Movement was thus part of social developments in China. But it was also part of a historical movement. The mass mourning for Zhou Enlai in Tiananmen Square in the late 1970s and the Tiananmen Incident in the late 1980s marked the beginning of documentary photography and documentary television in China respectively.[7] At the end of the 1970s, Chinese citizens only had still photography cameras. When faced with these momentous social transformations, they used these still cameras to witness them. By the end of the 1980s, China had entered the television era. Filmmakers could use television equipment to focus on society. By the late 1990s, the Sixth Generation feature filmmakers had emerged with clear realist aesthetics.[8] Thus, from a broader point of view, these three events in different historical periods should be related together for further discussion, as they constitute part of the historical context of the Chinese New Documentary Movement. As I detail below, the new crop of documentaries was dramatically different from the old special topic programs in terms of topics, concepts, aesthetics, and style. Their perspective on contemporary society was unofficial and their interpretation distinctive. Independent productions gained a higher reputation while informal productions such as home-made videos also exploded in number because of the widespread adoption of DV. Therefore, almost ten years after I had started researching the movement, I formally named it the New Documentary Movement in my book *Documenting China: The New Documentary Movement in China*.

In the following sections, I detail the relationship between the New Documentary Movement and film theory; the television industry; the different phases of documentary filmmaking in contemporary China; and the specific themes of geographic difference, humanism, and the relationship between the market and the state. Throughout, I emphasize the focus of the New Documentary Movement on the marginalized social strata of contemporary China. In the first section, "The New Documentary Movement and Film Theory," I argue that while various film theories have influenced the New Documentary Movement, the movement used these theories in order to resolve certain practical as well as ideological questions filmmakers faced in their commitment to a new version of reality that would enable them to film society from the bottom up. In the next section, "The Rise of the New Documentary Movement Outside (and Inside) the Official System," I argue that while the common emphasis has been on how the New Documentary Movement developed outside the mainstream system, I want to emphasize overlooked links and connections with documentaries made inside the state-owned television system. Rather than portraying a strict opposition between the New Documentary Movement and the official television system, I propose it might be better to perceive the relationship as a series of overlaps and interactions. "The Late 1990s: A New Phase of the New Documentary Movement" describes the distinctive characteristics of the second phase of the movement. In terms of subject matter, the second phase is an extension of the first phase. However, the documentarians use such techniques as performative and reflexive filmmaking in which they eschew the purely observational stance prevalent in the first phase. The last two sections, "Documentary China: Dual Perspectives from the City and the Countryside" and "The Rise of Humanistic Documentaries: Narratives of the Market and the State" address the various themes of recent documentaries. I end with a warning about the recuperation of nostalgic views of Chinese culture and the fetishization of Chinese culture that stultify our understanding of the complexities of modern Chinese history.

The New Documentary Movement and Film Theory

The New Documentary Movement began with no effective theoretical background except its own practices. Significantly, Western film theories were first introduced to academic film studies in China in the early 1980s. These included the theories of André Bazin and Siegfried Kracauer, as well as the Italian neo-realists.[9] They were popular among the Fourth Generation filmmakers, such as Wu Yigong, Xie Fei, Zheng Dongtian, Zhang Nuanxin, and Wu Tianming, because the theorists' emphasis on "reality" extended and stretched traditional socialist realism. The legacy of socialist realism meant that realism was the only officially acceptable aesthetic form in China at that time. Therefore, these neo-realist theories, as a branch of humanism, assisted filmmakers of the Fourth Generation in their legitimate break with the model of filmmaking that had been practiced throughout the Cultural Revolution (1966–1976). However, the whole aesthetic of realism was abandoned in the mid-1980s as the ideology it was based on was also abandoned. One might say that Fourth Generation filmmakers deconstructed socialism in the name of realism while Fifth Generation filmmakers deconstructed and emptied the revolutionary narrative model in the name of revolutionary romanticism. For instance, movies made by the Fifth Generation such as *Yellow Earth* (Chen Kaige, 1984) and *One and Eight* (Zhang Junzhao, 1983) reworked revolutionary themes. *Yellow Earth* tells the story of a cultural worker from the Yan'an-based Eighth Route Army, prior to the socialist revolution, and his interaction with a local farming family. The film is a searing critique of the way Communist Party cultural workers, instead of fully working with the farmers, opportunistically used local cultural knowledge for their own revolutionary ends while ignoring the pressing needs of the suffering farmers. *One and Eight* tells the story of how a political instructor of the Eighth Route Army is unjustly accused of being a traitor. Subsequently, he inspires the criminals he is imprisoned with to sacrifice themselves for the cause of national liberation in the Anti-Japanese War.

By the time the Fifth Generation filmmakers appeared, the theories of Bazin and Kracauer were much criticized in the field of film studies. It was no longer felt that the achievements of the Fifth Generation had to be explained theoretically through realism, even though their use of the camera was in accordance with Bazin's theories emphasizing the long take and the long shot. This forgotten legacy of realism was made explicit after the emergence of the Sixth Generation led to Wang Xiaoshuai's *Beijing Bicycle* (2001), which paid homage to the classic Italian neo-realist movie *Bicycle Thief* (1948).

The New Documentary Movement arose, developed, and thrived during the evolution from the Fourth to the Sixth Generations. The documentarians unconsciously inherited the Fourth Generation directors' narrative search for ethics and values. They were also inspired by the Fifth Generation's cinematic aesthetics. But even more important were their own explorations in response to certain problems. While the Fifth Generation directors abandoned realism, the New Documentary Movement started to redefine what realism meant. And this was passed on to the Sixth Generation. While Bazin's theory of realism was criticized in film studies,[10] it was nevertheless appreciated in the television industry.[11] However, when the New Documentary Movement started, it was not theoretically driven but rather interested in rethinking television documentary practices. Most discussion among the first group of New Documentary Movement filmmakers back then was restricted to the establishment of technical methods, such as choosing the point of view and camera position. The use of on-camera, in-person interviews, synchronized sound, and long takes became symbols of truth in documentary. Naturally, these documentary methods were defined as "realist."

Yet by the mid-1990s, marking the beginning of the second phase of the movement, these filmmakers challenged the relationship between reality and representational realism again. This was because the realist techniques they had been using were being appropriated by television genres other than documentary. Therefore, they no longer sufficed to define truth in documentary. The question went back to the ontology of documentary, and New Documentary filmmakers realized that the notion of "reality" actually included questions regarding ideas and values determined by ideologies.[12] This rethinking of the relationship between reality and representational realism began in the later part of the first phase of the movement, thereby initiating the second phase.[13] The first phase of the movement was reacting against the special topic programs. Filmmakers in this first phase used techniques such as synchronized sound, long shots, and follow shots to distinguish their way of capturing reality from that of the special topic programs. The second phase of the movement began to use performative and reflexive techniques. In general, there was greater diversity in the techniques used, as the filmmakers in the second phase wanted to move beyond the kind of documentary filmmaking of the first phase, which had been more committed to pure observation. They also wanted to distinguish themselves from the various television programs that had adopted the techniques of synchronized sound, long shots, and follow shots.

In less than a decade, filmmakers and critics in China went through the most important keywords from the past one hundred years of Western documentary — Direct Cinema, *cinéma vérité*, and the concepts of performative and reflexive documentary. Direct Cinema and *cinéma vérité* are two types of documentary that used lightweight equipment to go directly into the world without rehearsal or setting up. Direct Cinema was an American form that developed in the 1960s and was purely observational, without voiceover narration, extra-diegetic music, or interviews. The French *cinéma vérité* differed by including on-the-spot interviews. These two models were very powerful in the early days of the New Documentary Movement in China. "Performative" and "reflexive" are two of the modes of documentary defined by American scholar Bill Nichols in his various writings.[14] The former refers to films which foreground the subjective experience of the filmmaker and the latter to films that acknowledge their constructedness and the absence of any direct access to truth.

These ideas were introduced to China in the 1990s. Together with responses to their own work, this led the filmmakers to adopt the notion of individualization. Individualization appeared in both phases of the movement. However, in the first phase the emphasis was on the individual position (as distinct from official position) of the filmmaker, while in the second phase the emphasis was on individualism as a form of expression. In other words, in the first phase filmmakers in the movement saw themselves as taking up an "individual" position because they were filming from the point of view of the bottom up rather than the official perspective of looking at society from the top down. This distinction made them view themselves as having an "individual" as opposed to official position. Their goal was to film "others" who had not had a voice in representations of themselves. Their approach was not to include themselves in the film but to use a purely observational position. They nonetheless viewed their filmmaking as "individualistic." An example of this kind of individualization in the first phase is Wu Wenguang's *Jiang Hu: Life on the Road* (1999). Wu Wenguang used a purely observational positioning from which to film migrant performers, allowing them to voice their views in the film, without adding a voiceover to tell the audience how to view these subjects. In the second phase, filmmakers used performative and reflexive techniques to make themselves into the subjects of their own films. An example of individualization in this second phase is Zhang Hua's *The Road to Paradise* (2006). Zhang Hua, also discussed by Yiman Wang in this volume, had originally been the subject of Li Jinghong's documentary on her failed attempts to run a beauty parlor. Zhang Hua then took up a DV camera and began to film women like herself, who try to establish their own small businesses, although their failures mean they cannot extricate themselves from the poverty-stricken margins of society. This not only continued the challenge to official realism but also, in acknowledging the standpoint of the individual filmmakers, questioned the purely observational model that had developed in the early stages of the movement.

However, the relationship between the question of reality and individualization in documentaries requires some clarification. First, the concept of individualization also implies that every individual being is, at the same time, a social being surrounded by social values. An individual who can escape the restrictions of the dominant ideology cannot necessarily give up his/ her own ideological position, or be immune to morality and self-reflection. Specifically, Chinese new documentaries are responding to a reality they depict in contradistinction to dominant ideological versions of reality, which means that they are required to clarify their own ideology. This is the meaning as well as the power of the movement. Here, the individualized standpoint is defined against the restrictions placed on individuals by the system.

Yet, while individualization was important, it did not negate the sense of a collective pursuit by these filmmakers. That is, these filmmakers realized that their emphasis on individualization was something they shared across their different films. This was the greatest strength of the movement at this time, its key characteristic, and, as already indicated, the primary force behind the movement's emergence. One of the techniques they used in the first phase of the movement to express this individualization was Direct Cinema. Looking back, a key question is why, at the end of the 1980s and the beginning of the 1990s, China's New Documentary Movement developed a sympathetic identification with the concept of Direct Cinema. Duan Jinchuan's *No. 16 Barkhor South Street* is an example. This film was explicitly influenced by Frederick Wiseman, who was welcomed in China, and his filmmaking was discussed a great deal. Duan made his film after viewing Wiseman's work but before he came to

China in 1997. (Wu Wenguang introduced him to CCTV, who interviewed him on the program *Life Space*.) In his film, Duan uses Direct Cinema techniques to film Tibetans and government officials meeting together. He does not add commentary, nor does he put himself into the film.

Figure 2.1. American documentary filmmaker Frederick Wiseman in China. Squatting in the foreground left is Duan Jinchuan, and right is Wu Wenguang. The author is the woman standing in the middle of the picture.

The new domestic role of the New Documentary Movement also appears in its impact on feature filmmaking. While the Fifth Generation filmmakers were busy recreating cultural symbols of "feudalism" in China prior to the socialist revolution, the Sixth Generation filmmakers, up to and including Jia Zhangke, introduced a refreshing new realism.[15] Like the New Documentary Movement, they focused on contemporary Chinese reality rather than the ancient past. Furthermore, many of them shot documentaries themselves, and the themes, styles, and aesthetics of their features have genealogical connections with documentary filmmaking. Jia Zhangke and Zhang Yuan are representative examples. All of their feature films reflect the influence of documentary filmmaking themes, style, and aesthetics. For example, Jia Zhangke's *Xiao Wu* (1997) is a feature film that juxtaposes two young men who used to be friends and fellow pickpockets. One of them continues in his "profession" while the other becomes a successful, small-town capitalist by using virtually the same techniques as a pickpocket but in a legal, capitalistic manner. In this film, which won numerous prizes at international film festivals, Jia Zhangke uses a realist documentary filmmaking style to show contemporary China's social inequalities. For example, he uses non-professional actors, his actual home town rather than a fictional one, and even uses some real names of the non-professional actors playing some characters. Zhang Yuan, another internationally known filmmaker, emphasized the observational approach in his early films such as *Beijing Bastards* and *Sons* (1996). Like Jia Zhangke, he used non-professional actors and actual locations to reflect the vast social transformations taking place in contemporary China.

In a discussion of the rise of the New Documentary Movement, it is important to emphasize that this movement did not arise in isolation from other visual art forms. I have therefore emphasized its relationship to the Fourth, Fifth, and Sixth Generation filmmakers.

I would like to end this section with a few words about documentary photography because it broadens our understanding of the context in which the New Documentary Movement arose. The same questions about reality were being raised in both photography and cinema, demonstrating that the pursuit of a new realism had broad social roots. Thus, another place where one can see the domestic importance of documentary filmmaking is in the broader context in which visual documentation gained force in China. For example, the documentary photographer Zhang Xinmin's series shot between 1990 and 1998, *Besiege the City by the Country*, is based on ten years moving back and forth between cities and the countryside. His method was no different from the documentary filmmakers at that time. He wanted to place his photographs within the historical context of China's last half century. Most important was Mao's famous reliance for victory in the socialist revolution and the winning of national power on farmer warfare, including the ability of the farmer-based Communist army to descend from the Communist base areas in the countryside to surround the cities at the end of the civil war in 1949. Zhang Xinmin's photography series asks the question: what is the historical logic and relationship between that history and the waves of today's rural residents who enter the cities? For today's rural migrants are much disdained by urban residents and even the government considers them to be illegal residents of the city.

Documentary photographs such as *Besiege the City by the Country* and documentary landscapes shared the same approach to representing reality as Sixth Generation films. The underclass has borne the brunt of a painful social transition. But the portrayal of this transition is beyond the scope of the mainstream media, and the subjectivity and physical existence of this underclass are only revealed by the New Documentary Movement and allied endeavors by documentary photographers and Sixth Generation feature filmmakers.

Some photography theorists in China argue that realism in the West is outdated, so therefore realist photography in China is also outdated.[16] However, in the history of world cinema, every crucial social transition has also sparked new realisms. Grounded in social reality, the New Documentary Movement filmmakers point a critical finger at reality, but also allow the power of reality to enter into their films and thereby exceed their subjective will as filmmakers. Objective reality exceeds any theories of modernity or postmodernity. The New Documentary Movement breaks out of the enclosed circles of mainstream discourse, and puts us in touch with Chinese reality.

The Rise of the New Documentary Movement Outside (and Inside) the Official System

Most of us who have written on the New Documentary Movement have emphasized its development outside the official system. But here I want to emphasize overlooked links and connections with documentaries made inside the state-owned television system. In the early 1980s, CCTV generated a craze for big-budget "special topic" series. One prominent type featured omniscient, humanistic commentaries that accompanied footage of natural environments. A typical example is *Yangtze River* (1983). The other genre was politically oriented, for example the famous *River Elegy* (1988). All of these series were first written and then images were found to match the script. The special topic program boom in the 1980s was part of the intellectual elite's search for cultural roots amidst the new era of social reform. Natural environment and folk cultures formed the basis for the re-examination of national identity and the nation-state. Patriotism was the main theme of such series. Geographical sites charged with ethnic symbolism were the focus of the most influential special topic series, such as *Silk Road* (1980, CCTV), *Ancient Road of Tangbo* (1985, CCTV), and *Thousand Miles of Coastline* (1988, CCTV), all of which echoed the national economic policy of "opening up" to the outside world (*kaifang*). These films about ancient China showed different historical interactions with the West over land and sea, revealing (and justifying) the evolution of China's contemporary policy.

The 1980s began with praise for the "mother river" in the series *Yangtze River*. But the decade ended with another river with a long history, the Yellow River, being used to symbolize the tragic downfall of Chinese civilization in the series *River Elegy*. Both series embodied the search for cultural roots, but they led to quite different conclusions. The fact that one rejected the Yellow River while the other embraced the Yangtze River reflected internal disputes among the country's intellectual elite. In the end, these disputes led to the exceptional era of the 1990s: the era of the market economy.

When production started for the television series *Odyssey of the Great Wall* (CCTV/Tokyo Broadcasting System) in January 1990, the television industry had not yet been fully subsumed into the market economy. This interim period facilitated a short but golden age of television documentaries that lasted for less than a decade but produced numerous new concepts, programs, and series. For example, *Odyssey of the Great Wall* had first been in production earlier, in late 1988. In 1989, the primary production team decided unanimously to reject the script that had been commissioned with a lot of investment from the government.[17] This was a risky and provocative move. But in the end, the team was authorized to establish the themes by themselves. The final version was not shown until after the 1989 Tiananmen Incident. It was aired at virtually the same time that Wu Wenguang made his *Bumming in Beijing*. Every individual production sub-group established a realist style of filming: the use of interviews, synchronous sound, long shots, and so on. This opened up the state-run media system to a realist aesthetic. Within the context of the television programs of that time, even the most basic realist methods were very new and fresh. With the old special topics documentaries, there was no synchronous sound, and the main subjects were all leaders or heroes. But in these new documentaries, ordinary people became the main interviewees.

When the censors passed and legitimated such programs, it was a breakthrough related to the larger social context. First, in accordance with the policy of "opening up" to the outside world, television production methods were adopted from abroad. Documentaries on China by filmmakers such as Joris Ivens and Michelangelo Antonioni were shown and discussed in public and private. Second, *Odyssey of the Great Wall* was a co-production with Japan's Tokyo Broadcasting System (TBS). The Japanese production crew so impressed their Chinese colleagues that they became models for them. After extensive discussion, the main producers of the series started to take up the outdated notion of "documentary" once again, and used it to replace the then popular term "special topic programs." In this way, *Odyssey of the Great Wall* was labeled as a new genre of television programming, and documentary was rediscovered within the mainstream system.

In addition, a set of documentaries from Japan was highly influential at the Shanghai International Television Festival (established in 1989). Again, this was virtually at the same time that Wu Wenguang began making his *Bumming in Beijing*, though he did not finish it until after the 1989 Tiananmen Incident. In other words, both those we think of as the founding filmmakers of the New Documentary Movement and some of those making related kinds of documentaries for television began exploring these techniques at the same time in the late 1980s. The makers of these documentaries followed the main characters and lived their everyday lives with them. The popularity of the films eventually led to the establishment in 1993 of a television program called *Documentary Editing Room* in Shanghai, which achieved an audience share of 36 percent at its peak.[18] Various programs focusing on the daily lives of ordinary Shanghainese were produced. In them, the everyday was made to echo the changing times and speak to the larger historical context.

Also in 1993, institutional reforms at CCTV led to the creation of *Life Space* as a segment of *Oriental Horizon*. This was also a so-called producer-centered program. In other words, it was the era when CCTV instituted the producer system, in which the producer was the main decision maker in the creation of a program. On air eight minutes a day, its slogan "telling common people's own stories" (*jiangshu laobaixing zijide gushi*) was extremely popular among Chinese audiences because it purported to show an unmediated view of people's everyday lives.

Since the mid-1990s, an increasing number of similar programs have been created at local television stations. Focusing on the socially marginalized has become a trend, and "humanistic concern" has since become the most popular term in the realm of documentary theory.[19] Here, one of the most important effects of the New Documentary Movement is the legitimacy conferred on the development of documentary programs on television. This legitimacy has ensured the survival of documentaries in the official media system, facilitated their connections with the most overlooked groups in society, and established the foundation for reaching a broader audience. The two programs that started in 1993 — CCTV's *Life Space*, which "told ordinary people's stories" and Shanghai's *Documentary Editing Room* — both focused on ordinary people and won good ratings in the 1990s. In fact, in China, a lot of excellent documentary makers have been working inside the system all over the country, but they also use every opportunity to produce their own documentaries outside the official media system. Their hard work consolidated the development and success of the New Documentary Movement.

Much of the New Documentary Movement has had strong connections to television. This is a very important phenomenon. Shooting on video makes the movement mobile, convenient, and cheap compared to the previous documentaries shown in movie theaters. This allows it to have greater democratic significance: as television employees, the documentary makers can also make more direct and sensitive contact with Chinese society.

Early independent documentary makers denied the label of "underground," which implied opposition to the official media system. Furthermore, since the 1990s, documentary production within the system has become more diverse and less constrained. Moreover, some independent producers have been willing to cooperate with the system in the drive to give themselves more opportunities, so long as they do not have to sacrifice their fundamental principles. For instance, the main funding for one of the best known works by Duan Jinchuan, *No. 16 Barkhor South Street*, came from CCTV.[20] Since there were no private foundations funding cultural activities in China in the early 1990s, independent documentary makers usually made their living by working for television stations. Therefore, they were employees of the state, even as they took advantage of their positions to make independent documentaries not necessarily aired on television.

The system has also benefited from the presence of these filmmakers. For example, independent filmmaker Jiang Yue played an important role in the initiation of *Life Space*, by creating the first documentary for the program. CCTV's earliest documentary producer, Shi Jian, is now a powerful figure in the CCTV system. In the early days he took advantage of his position inside CCTV to make the independent documentaries for which he is well known. Even those special topic programs and historical documentaries made from an official perspective about figures who were leaders nonetheless absorbed other new documentary elements to the extent that they could. Furthermore, if a television documentary won a prize at international film or television festivals, it affirmed the station's professionalism and world standards. This motivated the provision of funds for documentaries on topics suited to festivals, regardless of profit.

In the 1980s, special topic programs were not well received by foreign audiences. Therefore, the producers in the international divisions at the television stations were forced to experiment with new genres inside the official system. For example, *Documentary Editing Room*, the program from Shanghai, was produced by the International Division at Shanghai Television Station. Interestingly, most of the earliest documentary makers worked in the international divisions of various television stations.

Without government funding, resources for independent production were very limited. Nevertheless, besides self-funding, all kinds of collaborations with television stations were possible. Television stations provided the major resources for most documentaries in China back then. As mentioned, filmmakers within the system used the funding and equipment to produce their own independent films while working simultaneously on official programs. From the very beginning, there was less of an opposition between the New Documentary Movement and the official television system and more a series of overlaps and interactions, where the liveliest and most creative documentary making happened alongside experiments within the television system.

As already mentioned, commercialization and reliance on ratings constricted this experimental space within television from the mid-1990s, but even today, television continues to find room for more challenging documentaries. For example, *Factory Director Zhang Liming* was directed by Li Xiao in 2000 for

Shanghai Television's *Documentary Editing Room* series. It portrays a factory director's efforts to save a state-owned company from bankruptcy and his eventual failure to do so. This film has a quality of black humor to it. Factory director Zhang's character has comic elements, but comedy has tragedy as its underside. A good person wants to do a good deed. As a result, his life becomes entangled with a state enterprise and its workers. But the situation of a state enterprise in today's society dooms Zhang Liming to failure, for the state is actually shutting down most state enterprises, forcing them to privatize or declare bankruptcy. But Zhang Liming still wants to gamble with his destiny and that of this era. The more he is unwilling to admit defeat, the more we find the final failure deeply moving. In the end the factory is demolished by explosion. Zhang Liming's motivations and behavior are righteous and proper. What then does this failure signify exactly? This is no longer Zhang Liming's tragedy alone.

In sum, the significance of the emergence of the New Documentary Movement lies in its perspective from the bottom up on the status of different social classes under current political, economic, and social transformations in China. The movement was a supplement and correction to the dominant ideology and it opened up opportunities for ordinary people to be included in the writing of history. The convenience, mobility of television crews and camera and editing equipment, and accessibility of television make the medium a more democratic one. The production crew in the television industry is directly and sensitively connected to Chinese society, providing a democratic base. It therefore represents a social democracy.

The Late 1990s: A New Phase of the New Documentary Movement

Jiang Yue's work *The Other Bank* (1993) is a watershed moment in the transformation of the positions, perspectives, and methods of the New Documentary Movement. It presages the second phase of this movement. *The Other Bank* follows the production of an avant-garde play. But its focus moves from the play itself to the young actors. They have come from faraway provinces to Beijing to pursue their dreams. But when the play's run is over, their dreams are extinguished. They have to face cruel reality and start all over again. In this sense, Jiang Yue sympathetically depicts those who will comprise some of the second phase filmmakers, that is, those who come to Beijing but who are not accepted as filmmakers through the conventional routes and therefore must rely on other means. The documentary communicates the director's reassessment of the utopianism of the 1980s.[21] There were several utopian trends in the 1980s. One was to take the West as a utopian model of what China could strive for. The other, in reaction to modernization and urbanization, was to search for utopianism in the countryside or among minorities, with their presumably simpler, more natural and untouched way of life. These utopian trends were torn down in this work, showing how the 1980s search for utopia had failed. However, the counter-impulse — the search for a new utopia — is also embedded in the film in the final scenes: one of the migrant performers returns to his home village with a group of actors to put on one of their plays. The villagers watch without understanding all the postmodern references in the play. However, at the very end, the actors invite the villagers to participate in pushing an old tractor forward. This final action signifies a possible utopia of collective action toward a better future.

Figure 2.2.   Jiang Yue's *The Other Bank*.

By the mid-1990s, Chinese society had gone through tremendous changes. Compared to the previous decade, the idealism that grew from challenging authoritarianism was encountering its major enemy: commercialism. Both television and independent documentaries also faced this challenge. In the 1980s those of us who cared about China's future imagined that the West and modernization would be the sources for a post-socialist utopia. But this imagined utopia evaporated as the gap between the rich and the poor widened with the rise of the market economy in the 1990s, setting the scene for the second phase of the New Documentary Movement from the mid-1990s to the present.

Today's independent productions are made inexpensively and in a wide variety of styles. Especially since the appearance and popularization of mini DV technology, various experimental works have appeared, leading to even more spaces for new developments. With the elimination of burdensome ideological pressure, a number of important independent works have revitalized the movement. Starting with the popularization of DV, documentary production has entered a phase of multiple developments. On the one hand, the popularity of documentary television shows has fallen dramatically under the onslaught of more commercial television. Influenced by Western entertainment documentary television channels such as the Discovery Channel, Chinese television documentaries have also begun to adopt market principles and pursue dramatic narratives. Furthermore, the new generation of independent filmmakers is living in a totally different social environment, where the impulse to resist authority is no longer primary, and social and political values are less important for them. Television stations are no longer so crucial to the new independent documentary makers, either. Today, low-budget independent productions are made by all kinds of companies, organizations, and individuals. For example, CNEX, or "Chinese Next," is a non-profit organization founded by a group of professionals from mainland China, Taiwan, and Hong Kong, who are passionate about the portrayal of Chinese culture. It is devoted to the production and promotion of documentaries related to the Chinese people.[22]

Many documentary makers during the second phase are no longer only based in television. Many have also come from avant-garde art circles, educational film institutions, fine art, and multimedia, or are just young people hoping to express themselves. They have brought an experimental avant-garde spirit and exploration of film language into the production of documentary, imbued with a resistant and subversive impulse in both form and topic. These documentaries are intensely, if not aggressively, focused on marginalized groups such as sexual minorities, ethnic minorities, the disabled, low-income groups, miners, sex workers, farmers, low-paid laborers, and substance abusers. For example, *The Box* (Ying Weiwei, 2001), discussed elsewhere in this volume by Chao Shi-Yan, is a film that addresses the lives of lesbians, without treating them as a spectacle. On the contrary, it tries to show the poetry in their emotional existence, making their lives appear normal by showing their beauty. *The Garden of Heaven* (Ai Xiaoming and Hu Jie, 2007) takes a feminist approach. It follows the difficult pursuit of justice by the mother of a young teacher killed by her boyfriend after an attempted date rape. *Voice of the Angry River* (Shi Lihong, 2004) looks at the impact of dam building on the local populations in southwest China. The film follows the residents of an area where a dam is planned, on a visit to a site where a dam has already been built; the residents at that site are now obliged to live by scavenging at a garbage dump.

In terms of subject matter, the second phase is an extension of the first phase. However, most films during the first phase were observational, borrowing their techniques from the 1960s American Direct Cinema, such as Frederick Wiseman's works, and from Japanese social issue documentaries of the same era, such as Ogawa Shinsuke's films. These earlier observational documentaries had also focused on the lives of the underclass and had a great impact on society. Such observational methods were directly connected to the motivations of the New Documentary Movement, which were to interpret contemporary Chinese society from the bottom up. While many works continued this tradition, others in the second phase were self-reflexive or performative explorations. They created a new era dominated by personal images, deploying documentaries to express their individuality by putting themselves in the films, and producing a different relationship between documentary and art. For example, Hu Xinyu's *The Man* (2003) describes the lives of three young men. Hu Xinyu puts himself in the film as one of its subjects. Analyzed further in this volume in Luke Robinson's chapter, the film does not simply record their daily lives. Rather the young men re-enact — and therefore perform — their lives in front of the camera. It records their feelings of failure to express a successful masculinity.

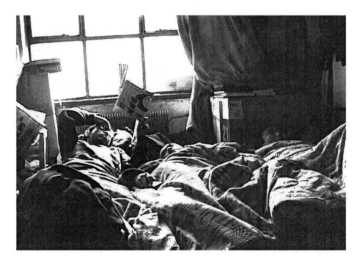

Figure 2.3.   Hu Xinyu's *The Man*.

The filmmakers from the first phase were born in the 1960s or early 1970s. They are from the generation who went to the streets and protested in pursuit of their ideals, such as democracy and an end to government corruption. They preferred to be identified as "artisans" to distinguish themselves from the elitist contemporary art establishment. Their works had a different spirit from those of the newer generation. Filmmakers from the second phase, in contrast, emphasize their individuality through self-reflexivity and share a commitment to artistic exploration. In an era of depoliticization, individual experiences have become the premise for all artistic creation. In resistance to the absurdity and meaninglessness of life, they use the authenticity of the individual and his or her soul in everyday life to articulate the fate as well as the redemption of humanity caught up in the process of modernization, presenting us with a new opportunity to discuss art and reality in contemporary China.

Documentary China: Dual Perspectives from the City and the Countryside

Originally, I thought Duan Jinchuan's *No. 16 Barkhor South Street* signaled the end of the search for utopia in distant places. For this film, which Duan made after living in Tibet for a number of years, neither romanticizes nor mysticizes Tibetan life but rather depicts ordinary Tibetans in their ongoing engagements with the Chinese government. Yet I have discovered that this utopian impulse never really ended but has continued under new conditions. Tibet still serves as a symbol of distant lands and as the sign of difference from modern civilization. Its significance has not waned, and it continues to provide a reverse-shot perspective. In 1993, Ji Dan followed in the footsteps of Wu Wenguang when he went to Xinjiang, and those of Duan Jinchuan when he went to Tibet in the 1980s, by also searching for utopia in distant lands. She lived together with ordinary Tibetans, and learned the Tibetan language. *Gongbu's Happy Life* and *The Elders* (both 1999) are the results of her pilgrimage. They describe Tibetans' ordinary lives, which Ji Dan, full of admiration, judges to be "happy." By the time these documentaries received their first public screenings in 2003 at the first Yunnan Multi Culture Visual Festival (Yunfest), a decade had already passed since she began filming.

"Happiness" appears to have become a keyword in several other films in this second phase of the New Documentary Movement. For example, Jiang Yue called his film about workers' lives at a train station under the pressures of potential unemployment *This Happy Life* (2002). Jiang redefines the meaning of happiness and a happy life. In a vision that corresponds to his own beliefs, it seems that no matter how stressful life is, so long as there is hope there is happiness. Happiness is not giving up; it is having this mentality forever. Happiness lies in how someone relates to their psychological world.

The quest for meaning in life and happiness also characterizes the repeated turn to the countryside in films by the new generation of directors, and this quest has become stronger than ever before as we are swept up into globalization. Even in a film by veteran Fifth Generation filmmaker Tian Zhuangzhuang, *Delamu* (2004), we can see a certain approval of cultures that have not yet been invaded by modern civilization. *Delamu* is about the lives of people living in the Nujiang

River Valley along the ancient caravan route, the Tea Horse Road, which runs between Yunnan Province and Tibet. Tian, who also directed the feature film *The Blue Kite* (1993), documents a caravan trip taking raw materials to a modern construction site, and interviews people who have lived along the route all their lives.

Delamu, *Gongbu's Happy Life*, and *The Elders* all turn away from the city and modernity as sources of utopia. We can see premonitions of this turn in Wu Wenguang's documentary, *Bumming in Beijing*, made shortly after the 1989 Tiananmen Incident and an indirect commentary on it. The film describes five artists — the "last dreamers" — who come from the provinces to Beijing, China's most central of cities, searching for their dreams. The destruction of those dreams propels them out into the world. While no direct mention is ever made in the film about the Tiananmen Incident, the viewer infers that Tiananmen is the direct cause of the destruction of these artists' dreams. In Wu's follow-up film, *At Home in the World* (1995), we see these artists transfer their unrealized dreams from Beijing to the West. With one exception, all of the artists have migrated to the United States or Europe. Yet the film concludes with their disillusion with the idea that utopia can be found in the West.

Wu Wenguang's later film, *Jiang Hu: Life on the Road* shatters another idealization of urban utopias, this time from the perspective of ordinary rural residents. The film depicts a group of migrant performers from the countryside who try to make a living by singing pop songs. The film shows a mismatch between their rural sensibilities and their hopes of success through popular culture. There is a painful sadness to the film as the viewer absorbs the contradiction between the songs' contents and the lives of these struggling performers, and the film becomes an indirect critique of mass culture and the kind of unrealistic utopia it proffers.

In view of the critique of modern ideals by a range of cultural critics in China, including the filmmakers just discussed, many of the new generation of documentary filmmakers have embraced nostalgia. Nostalgia has become both a kind of refusal of but also a reflection on modernity, thus giving modernity an unintended prolonged significance. This is part of the frequent theme of searching for utopia in the countryside, which itself picks up on a tendency also present in the 1980s. One can discern it, as I have just mentioned, in Tian Zhuangzhuang's *Delamu*. Other filmmakers also pay homage to the dignity and value of those people who live in the countryside under harsh conditions. A good example would be Sha Qing and Ji Dan's *Wellspring* (2002), which is about a family coping with a dying son and the difficult decisions they have to make about his medical care. It won the Grand Prize at the 2003 Yunfest. As the festival jury commented: "It displays a deep understanding and compassion for people's hardships. It shows the strength of love among people on the lower rungs of society. Its respect for life and death shows poetic radiance. It has a terse, temperate, and clean beauty that is pure gold." The themes of these types of films are distinctive, and their styles vary, but all express a poetic affirmation of human life and emotional strength against the backdrop of the harsh existence of the underclass, as the religions and customs of traditional societies once again become objects of inquiry.

Yet the city has not disappeared entirely in the documentary films from the second phase of the New Documentary Movement. Not least, this is because a central theme is the relationship between the city and the countryside in the modernization process. Starting with Jia Zhangke's feature film *Xiao Wu*, in which a small town in China was explored, the entanglement of city and countryside has become a metaphor, which also signifies the imbrications between China and the world as well as the overlap between the coast and inland. For instance, Guangzhou, one of China's first coastal cities to be modernized, and Sanyuanli, a village swallowed up into Guangzhou, represent this close interconnection between urban and rural. Guangzhou was China's largest trading entrepôt during the late Qing dynasty; it was the region where the Qing Empire and the West had direct encounters. When the British Empire dumped opium into China, it was from here that they entered China's hinterland. It was here that Commissioner Lin Zexu banned and destroyed opium. In the First Opium War of 1841, the greatest resistance to the British occurred in Sanyuanli. At the time it was merely a hamlet on the northern outskirts of Guangzhou, and the resistance leaders came from the village school.

Today, over one hundred years later, the expansion of the city has turned Sanyuanli into a "village within the city," which means it retains a village structure, farmers' land, and the rural residence permit system. As the construction from modernization surrounded it on all sides, it became a village in the midst of a city. As urban real estate rose in value, the farmers built dense multi-story buildings on their own land, with the aim of renting them out and making profits. In addition, Guangzhou's railway station is located there. It is the busiest in all China, and a major hub for migrant labor. This also makes it a place of encounter between the urban and the rural. Its population and structure are complex; it has well-developed drugs, crime, and sex industries, and it is the most chaotic district in the city. Taking all these factors together, it can be seen that Sanyuanli thus bears the weight of China's entire modern history.

The significance Sanyuanli holds for encounters between China and the West, and the city and the countryside, is expressed in the documentary *Sanyuanli* (Ou Ning and Cao Fei, 2003). The film has neither main characters nor a traditional dramatic narrative. Instead, it is in the city symphony mode, using a montage of black-and-white images to show how history has shaped the topography of the city. Quite different from traditional documentaries, this is the result of avant-garde artists joining China's New Documentary Movement. Ou Ning's creative work is part of a collective: Ou Ning and Cao Fei are the main artists in U-thèque, an alternative film and arts organization. If Wu Wenguang launched the New Documentary Movement by documenting avant-garde artists' lives in *Bumming in Beijing*, I take *Sanyuanli* as a continuation from the second phase of the movement. It repeatedly emphasizes the problematic relationship of art, reality, and history. It was made by a collective of avant-garde artists rather than by a single filmmaker. Also, it uses some avant-garde techniques in its filmmaking styles. For example, the beginning of the film has music but no people and no voiceover. It starts by filming the water from a boat as it approaches the city, then gradually moves to the city and then to Sanyuanli, all visual images accompanied by avant-garde music.

Figure 2.4. Ou Ning and Cao Fei's *Sanyuanli*.

The New Documentary Movement in China, especially in its second phase, is a thoroughly avant-garde form of art, which totally goes against the commercialization or Hollywoodization of the Chinese film industry. Millions of dollars have been invested in the latter to create ahistorical, apolitical, and delocalized works that are proclaimed as representative examples of "national cinema." In contrast to these empty and expensive visual spectacles in commercial cinema, the significance of the New Documentary Movement becomes more obvious. In the booklet publication that bears the same title as the film *Sanyuanli*, director Ou Ning uses the line "the debt of history" in the preface.[23]

Huang Weikai, director of *Floating* (2005), is also a member of the U-thèque collective. *Floating* is the story of a busking guitar player who has come from a village in Henan Province to Guangzhou. It depicts his loves, life, and views on the contemporary era, as well as how his fate is bound together with it. Huang himself was born in this new era, and when he turned his lens on the city he had grown up in, his original idea was to film a love story. But in the process, he stumbled across the structural violence of an unknown but solid system lying beneath the more familiar images of his city. The film ends with the main subject being picked up by the police and sent back to his hometown far from Guangzhou. The director picks up his DV camera and chases after the police van, offering the busker money to take care of himself. However, another person not depicted in this film but who also came to Guangzhou from the provinces was not so fortunate. He died after being taken into police custody. This is the famous case of Sun Zhigang. Sun was a university student, and his death was a sensation that stirred up pressure to eliminate such police practices. The Sun Zhigang case occurred just three days after *Floating* was filmed. Behind the film's title are the anonymous crowds pouring into the cities; they are the hidden subjects of this film.

Figure 2.5.   Huang Weikai's *Floating*.

Houjie (Zhou Hao and Ji Jianghong, 2002) is another documentary that tackles the complexity of urbanization in south China's economically advanced Pearl River Delta Region in southern Guangdong Province. Houjie itself is a street in Dongguan, a famous manufacturing town. Most people in the neighborhood of Houjie are farmers who have come from remote rural areas, particularly the western province of Sichuan, to work in the factories. The film was produced after 9/11 when global trade was declining. Having lost their jobs, they face the choice of struggling on in Houjie or leaving. This documentary shows how a disaster in the United States can influence the fate of farmer-workers in small-town China during the era of globalization. The film describes this group, how they gather together from different places, the contradictions in their daily lives, their emotional entanglements, gang fighting, and their different values.

The Pearl River Delta was where economic reforms first took off. It has thus become the place that bears the burden of witnessing China's most intense and dramatic history. Yet another documentary about the fate of one of the Pearl River Delta villages caught in the process of modern urbanization is *Taishi Village* (Ai Xiaoming, 2005). Using traditional folk music to structure the editing of the images, it offers a deeply tragic story of modernity. The villagers had a violent confrontation with local government officials over the loss of their land. This village, like others, was eventually swallowed up by the city, but it left behind questions that move us.

Sanyuanli can represent the process of urban expansion or the swallowing up of rural lands that has occurred in many Chinese cities. These areas usually become the location of the city's lowest social strata. In Zhao Gang's *Winter Days* (2003) we see another relationship between urban expansion and farmers' loss of land. In this case, it happens under the rubric of "democracy." Over the past decade, China has instituted democratic elections at the village level. The farmers in *Winter Days* lose their struggle to reclaim their land, because the representative they have democratically chosen has sold out their interests. The village has named itself after the famous classical poet, Su Dongpo, but in the film, this nostalgic-sounding name serves as an unintended irony. With the urbanization of Dongpo village, the village residents disappear; none of the promises made to them are fulfilled. They are afraid and anxious; they want to choose a capable person who will protect their interests. They engage in fortune telling, which reminds them that fate is not really in their hands, but is an external power. In the face of this inability to control fate, everyone tends to feel powerless. This raises the question of how a transplanted democracy can be localized and how villagers' interests can be truly protected. Democracy should proceed according to trial and error. But villagers only have voting rights; they do not have supervisory or recall power. A system with no means to rectify mistakes cannot be called a democracy. As a result, the villagers pay an unbearable price. In the documentary, one can see that villagers' enthusiasm for the elections is quite high, because it concerns their interests and their very lives. But lower-level democratic elections are never simply a question of the lower level; it is a social structural question. Lower-level democracy cannot resolve things on its own. What this documentary shows us is that the lowest level villages, in entering the democratic process, end up paying the biggest price. These farmers who have lost their lands will quite likely migrate to "villages in the city" like Sanyuanli or other areas where the urban poor live.

Alternatively, they will enter dangerous underground coal mines, as documented in *Mine No. 8* (Xiao Peng, 2003) and depicted in the feature film, *Blind Shaft* (Li Yang, 2003). The former focuses on daily life in just such a mine. *Blind Shaft* tells a story of two con artists who lure young men into the mines and then rob and kill them, making it look like a mining accident. They then say the victim is a relative and claim compensation from the mine owners. The main visual impact of both films, however, is in the working conditions in the mines and the desperation of men from rural areas to make a living, which drives them to risk their lives by working in them. With modernization, the village has become internal to the city and internal to modernity. If China's urbanization results in vast numbers of farmers who have lost their lands having no choice but to move to the cities or enter dangerous work like mining, then the rural crisis will become an urban crisis. How we understand China's countryside will determine our comprehension of China's cities, and vice versa.

Many urban residents in China believe their lives are completely separate from those of farmers in rural areas. They do not see that their urban advantages connect them to the work of those farmers who migrate to the cities. In fact, China's urbanization developed with industrialization during the Maoist era. The urban-rural hierarchy has existed since the residence permit system was established by the government in the 1950s. This system is not the origin of the advantages that urbanites enjoy, as they would believe, but the result of the rapid urban industrialization policies the government adopted then and has maintained ever since. Although urbanites often blame farmers for the ills facing Chinese society or for the farmers' own marginalization, within this historical context, we can see that the blame should lie with the policy emphasis on developing urban advantages at the expense of the countryside.

The city's many advantages, however, come with a price. The energy crisis and environmental pollution, for example, are unavoidable "historical debts" now demanding repayment. This is why there has suddenly been so much documentary photography and video work, as well as so many independent feature films, focusing on coal mines as key sites where skyrocketing demands for energy in China also lead to environmental problems. The global energy crisis has resulted in an unprecedented increase in the price of coal just as China is privatizing its coal resources. The mine boss in *Blind Shaft*, for example, is a private owner. Even though central government directives stipulate that the mines should be state-owned, local government lust for profits leads them to privatize this resource, resulting in a continuous rise in China's coal prices. The central government's repeated injunctions have failed to stop this trend. The mine workers who have died in accidents are mainly migrant workers from the countryside. They have become the subjects of contemporary China's biggest tragedy, with their lives a sacrificial offering to China's urbanization. What swallows them into the bowels of the earth is modernization's hunger for energy. This reveals another rarely seen perspective on the collision of rural China with China's modernization and urbanization.

Another zone of conflict in the modernization process is the western part of China, where China's numerous ethnic minority groups are heavily concentrated. *A Student Village* (Wei Xing, 2002) was shot in a remote mountainous village in western Yunnan Province. Most of the residents there belong to the Bai and Lisu ethnic groups. Quite a few documentaries focus on this area, but *A Student Village* is particularly touching because it portrays the optimism of the poor and shows respect toward them. Upon finishing the film, Wei Xing brought it back and showed it in the village. Villagers from miles away walked to the screening and shared in the festival-like atmosphere. The documentary received great feedback after it was broadcast on television. A lot of people donated money for the village and as a result its situation was greatly improved.[24] This case shows that documentary can be powerful and can change reality.

However, under the belief that knowledge can transform life, the children in *A Student Village* think tireless studying is the only way they can change their lives. But what kind of "knowledge" is this? What is the future for those village children who leave the mountains and enter the cities? And what of those children who cannot leave? This film cannot answer these questions for us, but it does provide a starting point for thinking about them.

Everyone faces challenges in this era when everything that used to be stable is changing. One of the most dramatic transformations has been the flooding of a vast area of farming villages following the building of the Three Gorges Dam. *Before the Flood* (Li Yifan and Yan Yu, 2004), one of the most important of contemporary Chinese documentaries, panoramically records the submerging of the small town of Fengjie due to the Three Gorges Project, and the lives of the residents there. Fengjie is famous for a poem written by Li Bai, one the greatest poets from the Tang dynasty (618–907); it has become a symbolic location for nostalgic responses to the relentless penetration of modernization. The directors of this documentary spent eleven months on site. Subtle details make the film leave a deep impression. For example, the filmmakers describe the ancient town gate, which we see whole at the beginning of the film, and its symbolic importance in the lives of the townspeople. But at the end of the film we see the town gate in ruins because of the flooding that resulted from the building of the dam. The Three Gorges Project is driven by modernization's demand for power and electricity, but this documentary reveals the pain of the underclass and the uncertain fate of countless people that lies behind it.

The Rise of Humanistic Documentaries: Narratives of the Market and the State

At present, documentary television programs about social reality are declining, and a new genre of humanistic documentaries is flourishing. The style of these documentaries strongly echoes the special topic programs of the 1980s. Despite the twenty-year gap, the traumatic divide between the 1980s and 1990s owing to the 1989 Tiananmen Incident and the subsequent marketization of China has generated an impulse to return to the 1980s, not for the sake of returning to the past, but for the sake of representing the present. Recently, there has been a trend to reshoot serial documentaries from the 1980s, such as the historical series *Forbidden City* (Xinying Studio, 1987), which was recently remade as *The Forbidden Palace* (CCTV, 2005). This popular series is now widely available on DVD. It details the long historical journey that made Beijing the capital of China, by focusing on the building, destruction, and rebuilding of the Forbidden Palace, the English name for the imperial government's residence.

In the 1980s, the emphasis was primarily on cultural heritage of this sort that symbolized the nation in patriotic narratives. However, today the meanings of local images are more commonly emphasized. This can be seen from the titles of documentary series such as *Jiang Nan* (CCTV, 2002), referring to the area south of the Yangtze River; *Hui Prefecture* (CCTV, 2003), which is the name of a former prefecture in Anhui Province; *Merchants of Hui* (CCTV, 2005); and *Merchants of Jin County* (Shanxi Television Station, 2003), which was broadcast by CCTV. The meaning of these humanistic documentaries can be summed up with the phrase, "to salvage lost commercial civilizations." They look back into history from the perspective of the market economy, and resonate with debates about the sprouting of capitalism in Chinese history.

Culture was the key word of the 1980s, whereas humanism has become the key word since the "humanistic spirit" debates of the 1990s.[25] In opposition to the concern about the demise of the humanistic spirit, humanistic documentaries have become one of the most popular genres in the television industry, while humanistic geography has become a hot tourism trend in China. Humanistic geography means historic locations that seem rich in humanistic endeavors such as art and ancient history, in contrast to locations that emphasize their natural beauty.

Above all, these humanistic and geographical documentaries are driven by a need to handle the relationship between space and time. One trend is to disregard where things are headed and focus on subjects that are disappearing. Yet, in this case, as we see in the documentaries mentioned above, the changing of these subjects over time is absent, as is the socio-political context behind those changes. What is left is the momentary existence of the subject, a somehow superficial existence that depends on the camera's fetishization. This means cleansing all the modern destructive factors away, leaving only that which symbolizes humanity's beauty and warmth — in other words, finding sustenance in the remains of "objects" from a spiritual homeland, with all the modern factors understood as a kind of disturbance. "Humanity" turns into "cultural objects": sterilized, decontaminated, and set apart, they are museumized.

At the time of its broadcast in the late 1980s, *River Elegy* expressed anxieties resulting from modernization through a thorough critique of China's culture and tradition. Today, China's economic development has once again led to a search for China's own civilization. Therefore, today's humanistic documentaries are reversing the treatment of tradition found in *River Elegy*, and expressing a passionate interest in a filtered reality and a frozen past. Just as in the 1980s, they have an extra-diegetic and omniscient narrator who transcends both history and the present, and they rely on the logic of the script rather than the images themselves to drive the narrative forward. When power over the narrative is exercised in such an overdetermined manner, however, are we still capable of reflecting on the origins of and limits to our own historical perspective?

Questions about narrative in documentaries, especially the use of the logic of the script to decide images, first appeared in the debates about special topic programs in the late 1980s. People asked, who are we, how do we narrate, and why do we narrate?[26] These questions deserve further consideration. Are there alternatives? Is it possible for these elite humanistic documentaries to open up to multiple perspectives, incorporating the lives of ordinary people into the narrative of history? These questions go beyond filming technique itself to encompass historical perspective. In past official narratives, history was a closed loop and now it is narrated in an ahistorical way. Both of these approaches are problematic. How can we understand how people and things together manifest the passage of history? Where is humanism's reflexive standpoint located? The New Documentary Movement is precisely concerned with the relationship between history and the lives of ordinary people in the midst of radical transformation.

How can the "objects" of history and reality emerge through documentary images? Although a documentary depends on the director's subjective views and own construction, the director and "objectivity" have an impact on one another. As far as documentaries are concerned, the creator's own intentions must always confront the challenges of history and reality. This is the source of their significance and appeal. This is also why the question of documentary realism is always complex. Recording is an action on the part of the director, but it is impossible to have absolute unity between the director's intention and what is being filmed. This results in the complex nature of documentary images. For example, the director's intentions have been heavily critiqued in the cases of both Joris Ivens's *How Yukong Moved the Mountains* (1977) and Leni Riefenstahl's *Triumph of the Will* (1935), but the images themselves are worthy of further discussion precisely because they cannot be totally controlled by the director. The significance of documentary is that a gap exists between its thinking and its images, a gap that cannot be entirely closed, unlike drama films that submit to the director's will.

As part of the decline of the special topic program in the late 1980s and the rise of the New Documentary Movement in the 1990s, realist humanistic themes were widely accepted in the movement and the grand narrative of the nation was strongly challenged by individualistic narratives. Yet today, national narrative is being revived under a new cover, suggesting the beginning of a new national identity project. The government has begun to support historical cultural documentaries, such as those aided by the "Chinese Cultural Essence Project," which is jointly funded by the central government and various local governments in order to promote Chinese culture. Today, many empty cultural symbols are endlessly produced by the market. But, paradoxically, they seal off the liveliness and richness of history, and close off the unceasing circulation between the past and the present. This is why New Documentary Movement filmmakers, and those of us in dialogue with them through our scholarship, want to break up the monopoly of the dual discourse of the state and the market.

Today in China, television documentaries' use of closed narrative models, as influenced by the Discovery Channel and National Geographic, is clearly motivated by the market. The logic, as borrowed from these global channels, is that complex reality and locality have to be sacrificed to the simplification of themes that can generate profit. Historical complexity and contingency are sacrificed to this logic. Thus, the state-supported media industries in China are also going global, having borrowed this logic.

On the independent documentary scene, historical films are still too rare. Yet for a traumatic period in history, such as the early land reform campaigns of the new socialist government in the 1950s, serious and careful historical documentaries are very important. Duan Jinchuan and Jiang Yue, who are among the most important first generation New Documentary Movement filmmakers, have produced just such a film on the land reform. Entitled *The Storm* (*Baofeng zhouyu*, 2005), it experiments with oral history, archival materials, interviews, and more. It examines the construction of the discourses on land reform in socialist China and the historical motivations behind those constructions from various perspectives, and not just from the official perspective that has offered a linear narrative of straightforward embrace of the land reforms by the farmers. The complexity of history shows there is room for interpreting the land reforms on multiple levels. These filmmakers' reflections on historical consciousness itself make *The Storm* one of the most inspiring documentaries on historical themes in the New Documentary Movement.

Figure 2.6.   Duan Jinchuan and Jiang Yue's *The Storm*.

Thus, the New Documentary Movement faces various challenges as it continues to forge documentaries that confront mainstream views. The commercialization of history and culture, the adoption of global aesthetics, and the nostalgic interest in recovering cultural objects from the Chinese past offer new challenges for filmmakers in the New Documentary Movement. They will need to continue to examine how representations of reality, aesthetics, and their individual positionings can challenge both state- and market-sponsored representations of the past and present.

Conclusion

This chapter has sought to elucidate the heterogeneity of the New Documentary Movement. This heterogeneity lies in themes, approaches to politics and history, and modernity and marginalization, as well as relationships with the official media system. Yet the New Documentary Movement distinguishes itself by sharing the effort to open more space for image-based reflections that are not included in official or mass media.

One of the contributions of the New Documentary Movement is the emphasis on the constructive function of images themselves. This includes not only revealing the role of the camera in image construction by making it part of the film, but also the concealment of the camera for conveying more "objective" values. Today, many works by directors from the new generation break the boundary of the inside and outside of images by making themselves the object of the film. Such a performative method is practiced by these filmmakers even though they may not articulate it theoretically. This chapter has reflected on questions of voiceover, narrative, point of view, and camera positions in documentaries of the New Documentary Movement in order to open more space within history and reality, so as to resist closure and authoritarianism.

Nowadays, China is full of commercialism, which is accompanied by the invisible closures of factories and the painful lives of marginalized migrant workers and farmers losing their land. However, documentary makes these invisible issues visible and also reminds us that such issues should not be neglected because they are the price paid for modernization. In conclusion, the New Documentary Movement will hopefully open up more perspectives on history and self-identity, and bring about more possibilities, which will allow us to reflect on our own condition and understand the present.

3 DV: Individual Filmmaking

*Wu Wenguang, translated by Cathryn Clayton**

Two years ago, in May 1999, in a place in Shanxi Province called Guxian, I spent some time with a traveling performance troupe called the "Far & Wide Song and Dance Troupe." This was an underground group that traveled around from place to place, performing under the big tent they carted around with them. The boss, a fiftyish man named Liu, came from a small village in the Pingdingshan region of Henan Province. His two sons, their girlfriends, and some of his nieces and nephews were all in the troupe. Counting all the actors and crew members, there were probably about thirty people, all of them around twenty years old, and most of them from rural Henan. I had been spending time with this group since the previous year; I had first met them when they were performing by the side of the South Fourth Ring Road in Beijing. Ever since then, I had tagged along on their performances in suburban Beijing and Hebei and Shanxi Provinces, filming them with a small digital video camera. Here I do not want to talk about what material I filmed or what I discovered about the "lower rungs" of society or that kind of thing. Rather, I would like to talk about how the feel of this project was totally different than the very "professional" kind of documentary filmmaking I had done before. With this project, I just carried the DV camera with me like a pen and hung out with the members of the troupe. Every day my ears were filled with the rough sounds of Henan dialect; evenings were spent lying on the stage under the big tent, surrounded by the sleeping forms of the roadies, the air filled with the stink of feet and the smells of the wilderness while the stars glittered through the holes and cracks in the tent's roof. Getting up in the mornings, I would pull on my shoes, walk out of the tent, and take a piss in the wilderness, the air incomparably clear and fresh and perfectly silent. A young roadie would

* Previously published in *Cinema Journal*, 46, no. 1 (2006): 136–40. Originally published in Chinese as "DV: Yige ren de yingxiang," in *Jingtou xiang ziji de yanjing yiyang* (Shanghai: Shanghai Yishu Chubanshe, 2001), 257–63.

be squatting not far off, taking a shit; we would greet each other: "You're up." At times like those, Beijing felt really far away. All that modern art — really far away.

Before that, for me, documentary filmmaking was not such a casual, individual activity. It was the kind of thing that entailed a bunch of people carrying big cameras on their shoulders — very conspicuous, even from a long way off. But in 1995, after I finished *At Home in the World*, I felt like I had some serious problems. The problems were not just with that film itself; I felt that all my documentaries were mired in a fundamental dilemma. This dilemma was that, on the one hand, in making documentaries I was working from individual motivations, so that I would shoot whatever I wanted and do whatever I wanted with what I shot, rather than conforming to the dictates of television or distribution networks. But on the other hand, the filming and editing techniques I was using were the usual ones, techniques that required money. At the very least, before even beginning to film you had to have a little money to rent the camera equipment. But the resulting films usually had very little commercial appeal. This approach, of "taking money to play with ideas," meant that even the people who were interested in giving you money soon stopped daring to play along with you, and your own wallet was never thick enough to support you, so it was impossible to sustain for long. Then I thought that maybe "use film, not video" was the way to go. At that time I was surrounded by a group of people talking about using the medium of film to make documentaries, reasoning that only in this way could a work be considered a "professional documentary film." I was an enthusiast of this approach, also because my experiences at film festivals had led me privately to feel that using film rather than video would allow me access to more competitions, awards, art-house cinemas, and distribution networks. Once I started thinking this way, I began to disdain video; I then had excellent reason to lie around in bed and talk about how, once I found the money, I would make one of those earth-shattering documentaries which would also circulate widely.

This was my way of thinking in 1995. At the time, I felt that this was perhaps the right way to go, but some other people who also thought this way were already running into problems. So I decided to stop completely, and do nothing at all. Then in 1997, I spent some time in the United States. During that trip I spent two weeks in Boston, in Frederick Wiseman's studio. Of all the documentary filmmakers of that generation, Wiseman is the one I respect the most. For more than thirty years he has been using his own unique style to record all different levels of American society. And he has made a film every year — something unheard of, not only in the United States but anywhere in the world. While all the other documentary filmmakers in the world talked about how incomparably difficult it was to make documentaries, there was this guy just making them, one after another. This raised some serious doubts for me. In the space of two weeks, I did not manage to clarify these doubts, but I did discover the source of my problems. During that time Wiseman and I spent day and night together in his Boston home. In the daytime, I sat behind him in his studio as he worked at the editing board cutting his new film *Belfast, Maine*, and occasionally he would turn around and chat briefly with me. In the evenings, we would make dinner together at his house, talking while we ate, and then after dinner we would usually take a walk for an hour or so. The next morning at nine, when I was just getting up, Wiseman would have already left for the studio. Most of the time our conversations had nothing to do with documentary filmmaking; we talked about family, friends, hobbies, what kinds of novels we liked, and so on, but as I came one step closer to understanding the simple, everyday life of this individual who was a major figure in the world of documentary filmmaking, I felt that what I saw in Wiseman resembled an author far more than any of the film people I was accustomed to dealing with. This discovery came upon me suddenly one day as I sat behind him, watching him spooling back and forth through foot after foot of film, like he always did. I believe this was the most important discovery I made in the four years I had known this man: not some easy insights into his documentary approach or technique, but an insight into the spirit hidden behind this approach. It is impossible to articulate exactly what this spirit is; it can only be intuited. The most direct way to express this intuition is: now I know what it is that I most sorely lack.

Through the years that I have been getting to know documentary film, two people have directly inspired me in this way. The first was Japan's Ogawa Shinsuke, who, in the course of film screenings and discussions in his studio in 1991, led me to understand that documentary should not be simply about film or art — it should have a direct relationship with the reality that we live in every day, a direct relationship with social work. From this it follows that one person making a documentary film is not important; what is important is many people working together for its sake. In 1997, in Wiseman's studio, I discovered that there is no direct relationship between the word "independent" and video or film; it is a lifestyle, something that is under your skin and in your blood. I was very fortunate that, soon after I made these discoveries, small digital video recorders became widely available; or perhaps it was that the changes I had undergone had primed me to be able to grasp almost immediately the advantages of this format. Later, I took one in my hands and just followed it, allowing it to change me into the way I am today: having abandoned the notions of themes and plotlines, abandoned the idea of pursuing, like a hunter, a single target; instead, I ramble around by myself, mini-cam in hand, distancing myself ever more f professional filmmakers.

Sometimes I ask myself exactly what it is that I am doing. Other people ask me this kind of question too. Once in a small town in Shanxi Province, the troupe was accused of "staging obscene entertainment." The local police sealed off the big tent, hauled the boss and all the actors down to the station for questioning, and then fined them for having a "substandard performance license." I was there for the whole thing (though of course I could not film any of it), and I was also questioned as to what I was doing. The two answers I could come up with — "I'm making a documentary" or "I'm an author" — sounded strange even to me, and made my questioner obviously uncomfortable. Three days later, when everything that had been confiscated from the tent was returned to the troupe, they loaded it all onto a truck and moved to another small town, reassembled the tent and the stage, and the sound of music and singing once again filled the air. That day, in order to celebrate, and because the troupe members had not seen a piece of meat in days — the wok had gone all rusty — I went to the butcher's shop in town and bought ten catties of pork, came back, picked up a ladle, and cooked up a big wokful of my specialty, *hongshao* braised pork. The cooking stove was right next to the stage where a performance was in full swing, so the aroma of braised pork wafted out into an atmosphere already full of song and dance. Everyone backstage crowded around the stove; as the actors finished their parts and came off stage they made straight for the wok, and when it was their turn to go back on stage they went directly from stove-side to center stage; while someone was singing on stage, the rest of us would be echoing them off stage. It really felt like a festival, everyone was in high spirits. In my right hand I held the ladle, and

Figure 3.1. *Jiang Hu: Life on the Road.*

in my left the DV camera, kidding around and randomly recording stuff; after a while someone else took the camera, and then countless hands snatched it back and forth, filming each other.

It has been two years since then, and there are a lot of people and things I have forgotten, but those days I spent with the troupe remain with me. Now, even though the film *Jiang Hu: Life on the Road* (1999) and the book *Report from the Jiang Hu (Jianghu baogao)* are long since done and published, I still cannot leave the "big tent."[1] What I mean is that I am no longer able to disappear from the scene as soon as the shooting is done, like the "professional documentarian" I used to be. I cannot stop myself from keeping in touch with members of the troupe. Some of them have left the troupe and joined other troupes, and some new people have joined. From time to time I go to stay with them in the tent or in their home villages, and each time I go I bring along my DV camera, casually recording stuff here and there. I do not know if I will ever use this material, and at the moment I am not too worried about whether I will or not. I am just following my own sensibilities, following life itself.

In the three years since I began filming Jiang Hu, I have roamed around in other places with my DV camera as well. I have two DV cameras, one big and one small. The big one is a Canon XL-1, with interchangeable lenses, and the small one is a Sony 100E Handycam; which one I use depends on the environment and what I want to film. One after another, people and things enter my lens; I do not go looking for them with the idea of making a movie, they just naturally happen in the course of my life. For example, a young guy from rural Shandong once brought me a script he wrote about his struggles to get into filmmaking in Beijing; he wanted me to make a film based on his script. I did not make his film; what I did do was follow him around with my DV camera as he talked to all kinds of film and video production companies, investors, and directors, which ended up drawing out all kinds of people and issues related to cinema. For another example, I videotaped the wedding of some friends of mine from Shanghai, which later developed into the possibility of a poignant love story. An art exhibit, a rock concert, a dinner party with friends, or just walking along the street … all kinds of people and things, entirely without theme, intention, or plot, crowd together onto the DV tapes. After two or three years, maybe some of this material could be worked into a long-form documentary, some of it could make a ten-minute short, some of it could be worked into multimedia material I have made for theater or dance performances. Of course most of it is comprised of "paragraphs" or fragments of everyday life, which may not have any connection to great plots or profound intentions, and will forever be just a series of digital frames and sounds recorded on tape, but they are still a part of my "visual diary."

I would like to talk a bit now about the editing of my films. To match my style of DV shooting, I have set up an "individual non-linear workstation," which is really just a regular personal computer with a video card and pretty big hard drive. It cost a total of 20,000 yuan [approximately US$2,500], but it allows me to work comfortably and freely at home. "Just five steps from bed to computer editing board" — that pretty much describes my very personal mode of filmmaking. I am very happy not to have anything to do with editing rooms and post-production, and I am especially glad that there is no voice from behind my shoulder telling me to do this or not to do that.

Having removed myself from the usual orbit of "a bunch of people eating, drinking and working together for the sake of the film," I have become an individual with a DV camera, filming anything I please that happens to wander into my line of vision, whether or not it has anything to do with the "theme" of the film. I then edit the material however I like, rather than having to follow a careful plan. Finally, when the film is finished, I have a few screenings and discussions in universities, bars, film festivals, libraries, and so on. Because this approach does not cost much money, I do not really care whether or not it turns a profit. Maybe this is what is meant by "individual filmmaking." The result of this way of doing things is that I have moved farther and farther away from "professionalism," television, film festival competitions and awards, but I find that I have moved closer and closer to myself, my own inner world. As a result I have finally come to understand that "independent filmmaking" and "free cinema" are not just so-called standpoints that can be realized through "manifestos" or "position statements," or the attitude that you can live off one or two films for the rest of your life. Given the "investigative" and commercial imperatives that filmmakers are surrounded by these days, if I brag emptily about "independence," you can be sure that it is just talk. So today, when I talk about my relationship to documentaries, I can only speak about DV. I should also say that I want to thank DV: it was DV that saved me, that allowed me to maintain a kind of personal relationship to documentary making, and made it far more than just an identity.

Part II

Documenting Marginalization, or Identities New and Old

4 *West of the Tracks*: History and Class-Consciousness

Lu Xinyu, translated by J. X. Zhang*

> We wanted to create a world, but in the end this world collapsed.
>
> — Wang Bing, director of *West of the Tracks*[1]

After watching *West of the Tracks* (2003), the long take at the beginning remains unforgettable. The camera stares from the cabin of a small goods train moving slowly through snow-muffled, abandoned factories. A few ghostly figures flit under a gloomy sky. The only sound in a silent landscape is the creak of its wheels. These three minutes are like a rite of passage into history. We are entering another world, one that has already been destroyed: a ruin of industrial civilization.

Tiexi — "West of the Tracks" — is a district of Shenyang, the city once known as Mukden. For fifty years it was China's oldest and largest industrial base, a fortress of the socialist planned economy. The origins of the zone go back to the 1930s, when Japan seized Manchuria and constructed a military-industrial complex for its further advance into China. Factories were built in the south of Mukden, producing weaponry for the Kwantung Army and machinery for large-scale military enterprises, and workers' housing grew around them. After liberation in 1949, the USSR supplied China with additional industrial equipment dismantled from Germany at the end of the war, in what was known as the 156 Investment Projects of Soviet aid, most of which were located in the northeast. Favorably situated close to Russia, and building on the industrial foundations left by Japan, Tiexi became a pioneer example of Soviet-style planning in a region that served as an engine of socialist modernization for the country as a whole. As late as 1980, around a million workers were employed in the plants of Tiexi, and even today the state owns three-quarters of the assets in the province of Liaoning, of which Shenyang is the capital.[2]

---

* Originally published in an abridged form as "Ruins of the Future: Class and History in Wang Bing's Tiexi District," *New Left Review*, no. 31 (2005): 125–36.

In the reform era, as China's path of development shifted from a planned to a market economy, Deng Xiaoping's open-door policy concentrated investment first in the south's Pearl River Delta and then around the Lower Yangtze, with a special focus on Shanghai-Pudong. But while south and central China were shifting to market mechanisms, the northeast still depended on command planning, with a high proportion of its output of steel and machinery transferred out of the area at low prices to the state, and its enterprises subject to heavy taxes. Fifty years of the PRC's planned economy were made to bear the cost of the twenty years of its market economy. By the early 1990s, some of the plants in Tiexi were already starting to decline, and by the end of the decade most of its factories had closed. In 2002, the 16th Congress of the Chinese Communist Party announced that market reforms would rejuvenate the northeast industrial region, transforming it into an area of high-tech, capital-intensive enterprises. But the central government is neither willing nor able to shoulder the investments necessary for such a change, hoping instead that foreign capital will step into the breach. The reality is that Chinese industrial development is heavily dependent on the import of capital goods, which now account for two-thirds of total investment in fixed assets. No ready solution to the plight of the northeast is in sight. The region's oil and coal reserves are seriously depleted. In Liaoning Province alone the jobless number some 2.5 million; labor protests and street demonstrations have multiplied as mass unemployment becomes an acute social problem.[3]

It was into this scene that Wang Bing arrived in late 1999. He had studied photography at the Lu Xun Academy of Fine Arts in Shenyang from 1991 to 1995, and then undertaken postgraduate studies at the Beijing Film Academy. But he had never made a film before. Wandering around Tiexi in somewhat low spirits, he rented a small DV camera. A year and a half later, he had shot three hundred hours of footage about the district.[4] Out of this material he created a monumental trilogy. *West of the Tracks* is a documentary that runs for a total of nine hours, divided into three parts of descending length — 4:3:2 — whose English-language titles are "Rust," "Remnants: Pretty Girl Street," and "Rails." It is without question the greatest work to have come out of the Chinese documentary movement, and must be ranked among the most extraordinary achievements of world cinema in the new century. Out of the dense maze of plants in Tiexi, with a purpose-built industrial railroad winding through them, Wang Bing picked three to film. The first was the Shenyang Foundry, built by the Japanese under the puppet Manchukuo state in 1934, which remains the most famous factory in Tiexi. The foundry has three huge chimneys, the first dating from the 1930s, the other two from the 1960s, that were long a virtual icon of the industrial northeast. When Wang Bing started shooting, it was still in normal operation. The second plant he chose was the Electric Cable Factory, which produced vital equipment for China's power-supply system, also first built by the Japanese and then reconstructed by the Russians. By 1999, 90 percent of its workers were already off-post — the official euphemism for "temporary" unemployment on reduced pay — with only middle-level cadres and above still at work. The third factory was the Shenyang Steel Rolling Mill, which, like a number of others in Tiexi awaiting formal approval for bankruptcy, was virtually abandoned, with only a few people remaining on site as guards.[5]

By the time he finished shooting, all three plants had closed. Wang Bing captured the precise moment at which the Shenyang Foundry received its death sentence. He was filming a worker lying on a bench during a break and talking about his experiences, from the time he went to primary school till he was sent to the countryside in the late 1960s. The worker is recounting his life story, his relations with society, and his view of himself, quite unaware — as was the director — that within minutes his destiny was about to change. Suddenly a supervisor walks in and announces that the factory has been closed. The scene, caught live, made a profound impression on Wang Bing. But though *West of the Tracks* conveys an unforgettable sense of working lives in northeast China, the true protagonist of its first part, in Wang Bing's words, is the factory itself, as an industrial reality and social ideal. Wang Bing, who was born in the late 1960s, explains *West of the Tracks* as follows:

> We wanted to create a world, but in the end this world collapsed. I filmed the life of the mainstream population, their relation to society, and traces their lives had left behind. If you see my film together with things from the last few decades, you can see what people have been doing over the decades in this country, what they have been dreaming of, and if their dreams have come true. This is a very important issue, because it tells us how we might live in the future.[6]

Here "the mainstream population" refers to China's working class. The working class and its history in the Third World socialist countries are different from that in the developed capitalist countries. This difference is what we need to clarify. What exactly does Third World socialist revolution and modernization mean? This question is unavoidable and urgent. It will help to shape the self-consciousness of China and the Chinese people, which itself is being formed through the struggle between other various different forces. This is the most important thing that *West of the Tracks* shows us.

"Rust"

> Inasmuch as industry sets itself "objectives" — it is in the decisive, i.e. historical, dialectical meaning of the word, only the object, not the subject of the natural laws governing society.
>
> — Georg Lukács, *History and Class Consciousness*[7]

> The factory is my protagonist.   — Wang Bing[8]

The first part of *West of the Tracks* is called "Factory" in Chinese, but interestingly it is translated as "Rust" in English. In this way, Chinese industry is renamed in the historical context of Western industry. This reminds us that Chinese industrialization cannot be separated from Western industrial history, but was an episode in a worldwide process. The furnaces of Shenyang implied the pre-existence, and legitimacy, of the evolutionary atlas of Western industrial civilization — which would also, it might be said, predetermine their fall. For does not today's Tiexi merely repeat the decline of the rustbelt in the American Midwest or of the Ruhr in Germany? The same historical rationality appears to unfold remorselessly across space and time, and no one can escape its compulsion. As Lukács puts it in the quotation at the beginning of this section, in a dialectical and historical sense industry is the object of a social-natural law. It is in the spirit of this objectivity that Wang Bing constructs a narrative of the factories of Tiexi. How have they developed and lasted? What have they been through? These are the key questions. In Wang Bing's film, the factories are transformed from objects into subjects. There are no characters or intrigues threading through "Rust" as in traditional movies. The Refinery, the Steel Mill, and the Electric Cable Factory — these three factories established in 1934 become the protagonists of the film. The process of production itself becomes the main plot of the film. The film offers an extremely detailed analysis of the factories through observing, entering, selecting, progressing, balancing, and realizing. "Rust" has the most complex structure among the three parts comprising *West of the Tracks*. It was filmed according to factory routines, and edited according to the work process.

First comes copper. We see the rough smelting of electrolytic coppers, their loading, electrolysis, and then return to rough smelting, revolving, and refining. Next, lead: from welding in a workshop, to the lead tower and another workshop for processing, then on to the workers' break room, and exit from the factory at the end of the day. After that comes the now idle Electric Cable Plant — and back to the previously omitted process of lead electrolysis and lead casting, before returning to the lead-tower again. This completes a narrative that makes up the first two hours of the film. The next two hours depict the closing down of the factories. The camera starts again from the copper section of the foundry. Halfway through, it jumps to the workshops for zinc, cutting off when they are due for closure, before going back to copper, where electrolysis — which we saw at the very beginning of the cycle — becomes the last section to shut down. With every workshop now empty, a few workers take a final shower. The entire foundry — in which so many people spent so much of their lives — has been closed.

Figure 4.1.   *West of the Tracks*. The factories.

After the story of copper, the film doubles back to finish the narrative of lead. Once the foundry has closed, lead workers are dispatched to a country hospital twenty miles away for detoxification. One of them drowns in a pond nearby. In the Electric Cable Factory, where even caretakers have been forced to take long leave since no heating expenses can be afforded, people are shoveling half-metre-thick ice in a freezing workshop. The film now turns to depict the demolition of the Steel Rolling Mill. It ends by following a worker — whom we have seen at the start of the film having his hair cut in the break room of the copper-smelting workshop — going home on the factory train through the snow-bound wilderness of a now derelict industrial district. Step by step, the film thus completes two interwoven narrative cycles — the cycle of production within the factories, and the life cycle of the factories themselves, closing in icy silence and stillness. For Wang Bing, "the factories, with their hugeness and realism, form a kind of attraction, which seems like a person's past ideal."[9] Now, the factories have become the ruins of that ideal.

For Wang Bing, each sequence is linked together in the narration cycle of "Rust," but each one is also multifaceted. Each one narrates not only the work and the event, but also the workers' thoughts and feelings. There is something that will appeal to each individual viewer. A former worker from one of the factories will see the entire factory that was once so familiar to him. A person interested in industry research will see the complete industrial process, from raw materials to final products. A thread among all the stories is people: workers, their work and their lives.

However, in "Rust," although the workers are important, they do not have the leading roles, but the supporting roles. The factory has its own rhythm of life. The steel and iron machinery, the smelting furnace, the conveyor belt, the crane, move and roar like so many automatic giants, their huge mass making the human beings beneath them seem tiny and insignificant. The workers appear to be mere appendages of this vast complex. This is what the film then explores: the relationship between the individual lives of the workers and the various industrial routines they face, the inner truths laid bare in the most exterior textures of daily existence. We see workers in a break room, listening to a radio announcement about joint-stock reform, and then discussing their prospects of unemployment, their wages, and their pensions. They chat, play cards, eat meals, shower, brawl, swear, tell dirty jokes, and watch porn movies. In the break rooms their work and their outside lives are both joined and held apart. Wang Bing's focus is highly specific: on a particular set of relationships, in a particular span of time, in a particular country. "Rust" does not, on the whole, individuate the workers it follows. They wash in the same showers, wear the same clothes, use the same lunch box, talk about the same things.

Although some may tell their life-stories, here they are not otherwise identified: they compose a collective humanity whose destiny forms another polyphonic structure within the film, contrasting and echoing the fate of the factories themselves. What seems trivial, boring, or fragmentary in their existence is integrated into an overall narrative in which the idea of the factory is counterpointed with elements of human life, as individual experiences are overwhelmed by the flow lines of history. This comprehensive sense of a common fate finds its most shocking expression in the repeated scenes of bathing and showering in the factory, as different workers expose their bodies to the camera with the same numbed gaze. The human form is reduced to an object of indifference. The limp, naked genitals figure its castration. Such exposure has nothing to do with the standards or otherwise of any civilization. Civilization and desire have vanished. All that is left is the impotent human body, emasculated by the formidable factory machine, and the instinct that can no longer be realized by it. The workers sent for detoxification sit without the slightest show of feeling in front of erotic scenes of coupling in a pornographic film. Reified, the human body has become alien.

Wang Bing has remarked that a director's first work is often particularly sensitive to the world, as an unfamiliar landscape in which much still remains to be recognized or understood.[10] At times the imagery of "Rust" recalls the aesthetic of the machine in Michelangelo Antonioni's *Red Desert* (1964), where the nameless fear in the heart of the heroine is like the unbanishable ghost in an industrial civilization. In the visual metaphors of *West of the Tracks*, we may sense a similar feeling of loss and despair. When we enter an enormous, empty factory and a crane suddenly roars into life and rises threateningly into the air, it is as though we were walking through an ominous valley and were startled by the cry of some strange bird ascending from its floor. But what if, confronted with the vast objectivity of world history, such a shock was the beginning of our salvation? What are the consequences of the appearance of industry for the history of humanity?

The secret of the Industrial Revolution is that human wealth henceforth no longer relies on the union of land and labor as it did in traditional agriculture and handicraft — in which it was based on renewable natural resources such as organic fertilizer, labor, solar energy, and wind, water, and animal energy. Human modernization since the Industrial Revolution has relied on non-renewable mineral resources as the resource for wealth. The magic of capitalism is based on the depletion and alienation of nature. In this process capital depletes humanity in the same way it does a mine. When Karl Marx says that "capital is not a thing, but a social relation between persons which is mediated through things," he profoundly underlines capital's enslavement of humanity by means of social alienation.[11] However, when capital places labor as the only source of value, it gives labor a position higher than nature. This separation between humanity and nature is the premise of Enlightenment thought. This conceals the deep structure of human enslavement and the depletion of both men and things, namely that capital acts in this way on humanity in the same way that it acts on other natural forces. Labor is nothing but a form of natural force. The enslaving of labor entails separating the farmer from the land, which is similar to extracting minerals from stone — these are both conquests over natural forces. Marx observed from his time that capital relied on the enslavement of labor to complete its primitive accumulation, and therefore he gave labor higher status than natural forces.[12] Also, Hegelian historical dialectics had pre-designated the historical subjectivity of the working class as satisfying the demand for a subject to drive history. However, the union of the working class and the most advanced productive forces has not been guaranteed or realized. On the contrary, the contemporary working class is being rejected by the most advanced productive forces. Capital-

and technology-intensive forces have replaced labor; science and technology have become the productive forces; and employed labor has been rejected, because science and technology have proven that it is machines not men that can produce quicker capital appreciation. Science and technology transform natural forces into means of production and capital by accelerating the consumption of global energy and natural resources.

Productive force is the capacity to transform natural resources into capital, but the price is the serious global ecological crisis. This explains why the earliest labor movements started with the smashing of machines. Hatred toward machinery results from capital's rejection of men. Machines are anti-human. When machines replace men, men are transformed, and the world is inevitably reified. The workers' revolt against machines is the revolt against the reification of men by capital. Because machinery does not need labor time to sustain labor reproduction, when machinery becomes the first driver of the Industrial Revolution and ever more quickly transforms natural resources into capital as commodities, humanity loses its importance as an instrument. Because capital does not need to bear the costs of the reproduction of natural forces for the huge consumption of coal, petroleum, and all the other mineral resources of the earth, machinery becomes the perpetual engine of the industrial civilization. For the realization of surplus value, commodities need to be consumed as quickly as possible. Therefore, the process of capital appreciation means the transformation of natural resources belonging to all human beings on the earth into private property. This process of transformation is the biggest secret of contemporary capitalism.

In the shift from classical political economy to modern economics, the most significant change is the disappearance of "things." Marginal utility theory, arriving as an analysis model of modern economics, emphasizes the influence of subjective factors upon economic activities. Its starting point is human desire and its satisfaction.[13] Consumption, distribution, price, market, and so on are the core of the theory. Capital seems to have lost its physical attribute. Modern economics has completed its concealment of capital's materiality and become psychology, discussing the edge effect. The study of economics shifts from social existence as physical existence to social psychology. Concentration becomes an economic problem, while natural and social ecology is not an economic problem. The capitalist knowledge system cannot reveal but only conceal the relation of capital to the reification of nature. Therefore, in the end, postmodernist theories interpret the consumer-society as a society of signifiers.[14] The source of the commodity is concealed in the consumer-society. Signifiers have been cut off from their connection to objects, the signified disappears, and the signifiers remain alone. Marxist political economy has been turned into a political economy of empty signifiers, where theories have been disconnected from objects and history. In such a political economy of empty signifiers, the "thing" becomes signifier and information, culture becomes a carnival of signifiers, capital becomes wealth, and currency becomes a capital market in empty signifiers. This is how the bubble of the capital market is formed. The "thing" itself has perished forever in the knowledge system of capitalist societies. In this sense, Lukács is right when he points out that capitalist ideology is unable to overcome its own antinomies.[15] To achieve its abstract eternal dominance, the formation of capital must extract the real materiality and conceal its origin. However, no commodity can eliminate its physical body, just as no human can eliminate their flesh — it is this physical body that demands the right to exist. Plastic bags, a white pollution all over the world, appear as signifiers of commodities, yet do not disappear along with the consumption of the commodities. Similarly, human beings as unprofitable "things" are rejected by capital, yet these "things" demand the right to exist. When the subject is sealed up in the symbol system, it becomes a subject without a material or physical body. This means the cancellation and extermination of the subject — the extermination of humanity. For the working class, this means unemployment, the logical result of the fact that human beings as "things" cannot be transformed into commodities. Capital abandons workers in the same way as it abandons a hollowed mine; capital has defined the meaning of the existence of things. Anything that cannot be transformed into a commodity has lost its existential value and is consigned to the darkness of history. Places abandoned by capital become rubbish yards of industrial civilization. Social alienation is unimaginable without the premise of natural alienation.

When the commodity is understood as emerging magically under the charm of capital, and when the laborer is no longer the productive force but science and technology are, a simple truth is concealed: wealth awakened from underground by capitalism is nothing but a thing transformed from natural resources, wealth is still material, and currency itself cannot create wealth. But the price of the consumer society is the future, namely the limit of nature, and the limit of unrenewable energy. Is it true that it is only after becoming the victim of transformation that humanity can become aware of its status as a "thing"? The environmental pollution of land, water, and air, the ecological crisis, as well as all kinds of labor movements and social movements, all insistently demonstrate the subjectivity of the world and society.

Objective facts will in the end deny the historical narrative of neo-liberalism, in other words the claim that the history of humanity is nothing more than the history of production and reproduction of capital or the history of market expansion. When Marx measured value with abstract labor time, he opened a back door for the ideological subjectivity of capital, enabling capital to hide its plundering of the laborer as a human being and natural resources as material.[16] As Theodor Adorno points out, any transformation is a kind of forgetfulness.[17] It is the time to resume in dialectics the status of the subjectivity of things as the subjectivity of history. In this sense, I still place myself in the perspective of the historical dialectics of Marxist materialism. The deviation in the labor theory of value is the re-encounter with Marx's theory of alienation. The world is material and capital is the transformation of material, the transformation of nature, and the deprivation and alienation of nature. During this process, the working class and even all humanity are the victims of transformation.

In this sense, we need to re-think the working class and its destiny. Awareness of transformation is the self-consciousness of the working class, but this consciousness will lead to unprecedented connections — with farmers losing their land, the bankrupt Korean farmer killing himself in Cancun in a protest against the WTO,[18] the black Civil Rights Movement, and all forms of environmental protection movements. Only on the basis of the most widespread real connections can the overall historical dialectics show its power and the working class have its self-consciousness identified and reconstructed. In this sense, *West of the Tracks* manifests not only the Chinese workers' history and their class-consciousness, but also the history and class-consciousness of Third World socialist countries. This process itself is an intrinsic part of the history of humanity.

In contemporary China, the ideology proclaiming the working class's role as protagonists of a socialist country has become hypocritical. The theory of true value as determined by labor input, which dominates China's official socialist ideology, has become an insurmountable dilemma in market socialist theories. The working class has lost the significance it once had under socialism. In the context of the market economy, unemployed workers can no longer be called upon by national ideology. The working class is losing its subjectivity and failing to become a part of the material world. Therefore, it is the working class itself — its factual existence — that demands subjectivity and legitimacy, but this can only be realized with the reconstruction of its class awareness. How can the contemporary Chinese working class restore its self-consciousness? Does negative dialectics imply that only when the working class resumes objectivity can we return to subjectivity?

The declining class-consciousness of the contemporary Chinese working class and the loss of class-consciousness of the Chinese farmer class are different manifestations of our transformed world. Capital's dispossession of farmers, though morally condemned by Marxist theory, has been justified by historical dialectics. Therefore, neither capital's dispossession of farmers nor farmers' revolts against capital can be included in the modern Marxist historical narrative.

Classical Marxism's denial of the class-consciousness of peasants can be regarded as the premise for the loss of class-consciousness of the contemporary working class. The absence of the class-consciousness of farmers in modern theories results from the fact that capital needs to base its development upon the rejection of traditional agricultural means of production. This is the constraining subconscious of modern theories. It is also a major issue that needs to be reconsidered in the critique of today's modern theory. The self-consciousness gained by the working class in its union with capital loses its material base when capital extracts wealth directly from natural resources and natural forces. Capital's rejection of employed workers is based on the same logic as its rejection of traditional farmers. Therefore, the fate of the working class and that of the farmer class ought to be treated in a common historical context. This is an urgent issue in contemporary China. The Chinese working class is once again a proletariat, the bankrupt farmers are exposed daily to the world market, and millions of migrant laborers are compelled to leave their land. The destinies of these populations are historically connected together in an unprecedented manner. Being transformed and rejected by capital is the common destiny of Chinese workers and farmers. Therefore, the liberation of the working class cannot be obtained alone. The reconstruction of the working class's self-consciousness cannot be realized without the farmer class resuming its consciousness first. This is exactly what we have learned from the defeat of the socialist modernization experiment undertaken with China's planned economy since 1949.

"Remnants: Pretty Girl Street"

> In the ruin, history has physically merged with the setting. And in this guise history does not assume the form of the process of an eternal life so much as that of irresistible decay. Allegory therefore declares itself to be beyond beauty. Allegories are, in the realm of thoughts, what ruins are in the realm of things.
>
> — Walter Benjamin, *The Origin of German Tragic Drama*[19]

The second part of *West of the Tracks* is entitled "Remnants: Pretty Girl Street." The name of the street comes from a legend that the maidservant of a rich family was buried here, so it was called Housemaid's Grave. Later the name changed to Pretty Girl Street, implying it was a haunt of prostitutes. In keeping with this allusion to women of low social position, the local residents were typically marginal people. From the 1930s to the 1950s, most were workers who had migrated from the south to find employment in Japanese factories. In the late 1970s and early 1980s, some sent-down youths returning from the countryside also settled there. At the end of the 1990s, the majority of its inhabitants were workers from plants in the Tiexi district. As Wang Bing's camera tracks along the street, we see nothing but low, dilapidated shacks, inside which crouch sick mothers, exhausted or disoriented fathers, aged grandparents, and restless youngsters. This shabby, formless landscape, without depth or elevation, lacks any of the dramatic shapes or colors, let alone scale, of the factories in Part One. We are as if in their underside.

Figure 4.2. *West of the Tracks*. The residential neighborhood.

But reversing the structure of "Rust," amidst these deteriorated dwellings "Remnants" focuses on expressions of human vitality. Its first half follows a group of seventeen- or eighteen-year-olds who have finished school, but not found jobs, as they loaf around a neighborhood littered with snow and rubbish. Their youthful impulses, desires, quarrels, and laughter bring a touch of bright color to the gloomy background. Still embodiments of life and hope, they represent the most energetic element in a declining area. According to the director's own account, they offered the director himself a certain mirror to his own past, as well as a set of troubling questions about their future. Watching these children wandering around the street all day long, the viewer is bound to wonder, as does Wang Bing: what will become of them? Their vague longings — born out of instinct or intuition, without any knowledge of the world — are touching, but also disquieting. For what chance have any of them of realizing their dreams? Are they even in a position to formulate some? An exchange between two of the boys runs as follows:

- I don't know either. You ask me what to do. I don't know what to do.
- No dreams at all, just like me.
- So why are you having a go at me?
- Just like me, no dreams at all.
- What dreams?
- Fuck you!
- What dream?
- What dreams, what dreams?
- I'm trying to chat with you.
- Can we get food from chatting?
- What dreams?

The boy who says he has no dream does so, in Wang Bing's words, with an "extremely charming smile: like a flower briefly blooming in the frost." The most popular girl in the group is abandoned by all the boys after she breaks up with her boyfriend: a prolonged shot shows her standing alone, after everyone else has left, as if youth itself were deserting her. In the last scene of "Remnants," which is also the last shot of the entire film, the street is banked up with thick snow, and most of the houses have already been demolished. Under the dim street light, a boy comes out from a house and looks aimlessly into this wasteland, once familiar but now utterly silent.

"Pretty Girl Street" is translated into "Remnants" in English. The second part of the film observes the death of the street, as the closure of factories in Tiexi is followed by demolition of the neighborhood where its workers live, to make way for commercial development. Such clearances are uprooting communities of the laboring poor all over China today, where urban speculators or local authorities — there is often no clear line between them — are flattening traditional neighborhoods and pockets of popular life to build malls and high-rises. The old ones have been demolished, but where are the new ones? For the workers of Tiexi, the demolition means the total disintegration of public and daily life. Workers are sent off by uncontrollable forces to far frontiers and lose contact with each other. When the working class has lost its self-consciousness, it has also lost its voice.

In fact, what Tiexi witnessed at the beginning was not China's socialism but the expansion and invasion of Japanese militarism in the guise of capitalism. Because of Tiexi's unique geopolitical location in Asia, it became post-revolutionary China's socialist industrial base, aided by the Soviet Union, with machinery confiscated from defeated Nazi Germany. World history made Tiexi a witness of both hot and cold wars in the twentieth century, as well as a battlefield of industrialization where socialism confronted capitalism. The northeast was the most treasured place of the Qing dynasty, the battlefield where the allied armies fought against Japan, the birthplace of the first generation of steel workers and petroleum workers in the People's Republic of China, and the place where volunteer troops valiantly crossed Yalu River to aid Korea and resist the United States. Because of the demolition, people have discovered in Tiexi a large number of rusty shells left behind by the Japanese as well as underground constructions suspected to be army hospitals.

The appeal for modernization that prioritizes industry over agriculture in order to resist the global hegemony of plundering capitalism has created in Third World socialist countries a working class whose history and class-consciousness are different from those in Western countries. In the 1960s, China's working class was symbolized by Wang Jinxi, son of a poor peasant and one of the first generation of oil well drillers in New China. His spirit was "sharing the country's sufferings and making every effort to win honour for the nation."[20] Because the first step in China's industrial modernization was to solve the problem of energy and steel — the most essential things for modern industry — it is no surprise that petroleum workers and steel workers become the role models of the Chinese working class. The sense of themselves as masters refining oil and smelting steel for their own country shaped the consciousness of the working class. As in other Third World socialist nation-states, the consciousness of the working class was realized in relation to the establishment of the nation's industry. Therefore, when today's Chinese working classes cherish the memory of Mao Zedong's time, they are not praising dictatorship, but calling for Third World nationalism to resist the hegemony of Western capitalism. This consciousness enabled the Chinese working class to found and develop its own country with great initiative. When the oppressed have experienced being masters, they could and should never forget it. This is the undeniable heritage of today's socialism.

The destiny of the Chinese working class has been closely tied to the process of China's modernization. Because China's appeals for modernization had learnt a lesson when confronted by the armies of imperialism, it is no wonder that early modernization movements such as Westernization start with the war industry. This demonstrates a historical logic: in order to become a nation-state, China was doomed from the beginning of its modern history to develop industry, and especially heavy industry. This logic pre-existed and became the historical motive for the prioritization of heavy industry in the People's Republic of China. China's appeals for industrialization and a nation-state are both products of modern history. China's modernization is not an invention of Chinese Marxists alone, because after the Opium War in the mid-nineteenth century, China was already caught up in the globalization of capitalism. As a semi-colonial country, it was impossible for China to rely on a "free" market to modernize its national economy. In the 1930s, when China's agriculture and national industry fell deeply into crisis, Chinese intellectuals debated about modernization, industry, and agriculture. Most people then believed that national salvation was dependent upon catching up in industry, especially heavy industry. However, as the liberal Hu Shi clearly realized, the most important thing for China's modernization was national sovereignty, for neither industrial nor agricultural modernization could be realized without it.[21] In 1949, when Mao Zedong proclaimed the founding of the People's Republic from Tiananmen Gate, he said, "The Chinese people have stood up." The significance of this statement is that the concept of the people can only exist within the framework of modern nation-states.

Just as Tiexi's history is deeply marked by the Soviet brand, China's revolution and socialist construction were closely tied to the Soviet Union. The similarity between post-revolutionary China and the Soviet Union has not received enough attention. Both began with farmer movements, and both were built on the dispossession of the farmer. The Chinese working class are the children of farmers. In contrast, socialist revolutions have never matured in developed capitalist countries where the working class is powerful. The appearance of socialism in the Soviet Union and China resulted from failed national capitalism. History certainly gave China and Russia the opportunity to develop market capitalism, but this development led to social schism. When capitalism excludes and plunders the farmers, they rebel against it and social crisis ensues, leading to socialism as an alternative modernity. In countries with successful national capitalism, socialism has failed. The United States has witnessed worker movements yet no socialism, because it has no farmer revolution or an agricultural civilization with thousands of years of history to resist capitalism. This may explain why the French Revolution is the most brutal of Western bourgeois revolutions. The old France was actually overthrown by Britain, which had experienced both industrial and political revolution. This created a domino effect in world revolutions. In France, the most wealthy absolutist country with the most powerful traditional agriculture on the European continent, farmers amounted to more than 80 percent of its population. Therefore, the French Revolution's relation to modernity is still a complex and significant question today and its historical significance is far from being exhausted. As Immanuel Wallerstein points out in *After Liberalism*, in the French Revolution, liberalism and socialism were closely related, for socialism is nothing but radical liberalism.[22] We appreciate now that the French Revolution and the Russian October Revolution ought to be compared. They do not meet Marx's expectation that the working class from the most developed capitalist countries would stand up and overthrow capitalism with anti-capitalist revolutions in capitalist countries. Rather they are the old world's rebellion against emergent capitalism. These revolutions succeeded under the flag of socialism and socialist countries have resulted from farmer movements instead of worker movements. However, in these socialist countries, it is the subjectivity of the working class that was assigned as the motor of history by Marxist historical dialectics. This ideological prioritization of the working class has the dispossession of the farmers as its premise and price. Although farmers pushed forward the revolution to victory, they became the exploited. What a historical paradox! The historical mission of a nation-state is to develop capitalism and modernization with the power of the nation. Therefore, the primitive accumulation of capital required by modernization and industrialization is always based on plundering farmers and agriculture. Whether it is capitalist Britain or socialist China and the Soviet Union, the same applies.

Post-revolutionary China was short of capital. To develop capital-intensive heavy industry, it could not rely on the market but had to squeeze farmers and agriculture. This has opened up ever deeper schisms between city and village, industry and agriculture, and they have resulted in China's most serious social crises today. However, these are not simply crises of socialism, but the logical result of China being compelled to accept the concept of the modernized nation-state in the framework of globalization today. Consequently, the "Three Great Differences" — the gaps and inequalities between industry and agriculture, town and country, and mental and manual labor — were not overcome in Mao's time, but have increased in today's market economy. The town and country split has always been a serious problem in China's modernity. Mao Zedong, though born in a peasant family and with great sympathy for the lower classes, had to depend on state power to establish a system dividing town and country in order to guarantee the industrialization of the nation-state. He tried to overcome the "Three Great Differences" through ideological mobilization. His tragedy, as well as that of China's socialist experiment, are rooted in the history of globalization and modernization, and therefore cannot be understood within Chinese socialism alone. Mao's socialist road was actually the Chinese version of socialist primitive accumulation and "Industrial Revolution." The gain and loss of the self-consciousness of the Chinese working class are both related to this history. In fact, the turn to the market economy in the 1980s is nothing but another national plan to continue modernization. The legitimacy of political power in the People's Republic of China depends upon modernization. This is an irresistible destiny once the nation-state is established. The "Great Leap Forward" in Mao's time has a historical logic similar to today's acceleration to modernize. In China today, the introduction of foreign capital and industrialization targets have become criteria for judging official achievement. As a result, the history of statistical fraud repeats itself, with the "Great Leap Forward" appearing again in a different historical time.

Furthermore, also appearing again is the paradox of China's modernization, namely social crisis in the form of "migrant laborers" and worker protests. The tragedy of today's Chinese working class in the market economy is a modern socialist tragedy. The historical paradox lies in the fact that the self-consciousness of the working class has collapsed after the socialist nation-state finished its "industrialization" with the help of the planned economy. The working class is no longer the creator of value, but the exile of capital. The time of the capitalist market economy has arrived. But, as many researchers point out, without thirty years of highly intensive accumulation through Mao's planned economy, it would have been impossible for Deng Xiaoping to implement his policy to realize the market economy. Behind this highly intensive accumulation are the broad masses of Chinese workers and farmers who have paid an enormous price for the country's modernization. Under the market economy, this price has not been compensated, but written off. "Modernization" has become an alien power to them.

Today, the decline of industry in northeast China means the end of the historical mission of the socialist planned economy. Tiexi, a place that suffered the development of heavy industry in a Third World socialist nation-state, a place with the working class constrained by the narrative of today's market economy, has been burnt into our memory by the documentary *West of the Tracks*. Why did we build such big factories? Why did this become the dream of an entire age? Why did the entire country sacrifice everything else to realize it? Why did we want to create a world, and why did this world collapse in the end?

"Rails"

> The iron road ... whose embankments and cuttings, bridges and stations formed a body of public building beside which the pyramids and the Roman aqueducts and even the Great Wall of China paled into provincialism, was the very symbol of man's triumph through technology.
>
> — Eric Hobsbawm, *The Age of Revolution*[23]

Since their invention for the coal mining industry, railroads have been closely related to the Enlightenment belief in the progress of human history. Trains have become a symbol of history and human destiny. As a result, the traditional interpretation of the world and time has changed dramatically. The belief in the cycle of life and the experience of time developed from observation of the growth of grain have disappeared and agricultural civilization has declined. The age of industrial civilization arrives with the whistle of trains and the white fog of steam engines, giving an unprecedented shock to humanity. History has become the reinforced concrete sleepers under the steel bodies of trains, cold and glittering, extending to the infinite distance. Objective existence appears in the form of steel and iron. Those who submit prosper; those who resist perish.

As Benjamin indicates in *The Origin of German Tragic Drama*, in this age when the resources of mysterious nature have been taken at any cost, the ancient Greek god of time and the ancient Roman spirit of the crops have become death, the grim reaper. The sickle in his hand no longer slices crops but humans.[24] The flow of time is no longer the annual cycle of sowing, harvest, and winter fallow, but life's irretrievable stride toward death. Originally, history is just like seeds scattered on the earth, but now we scatter the seeds sadly on the fallow earth. This is what Benjamin means by allegories. Allegories are the combination of nature and history. When the world of gods disappears, allegories preserve the world. Allegories are indeed ruins, occurring when history declines. Observed from the structure of allegories, objects appear fragmentary, incomplete, and imperfect, like ruins. The details and fragments the allegories refer to are the objects settled into the intentionally constructed ruins. Benjamin has re-narrated the history of modernity by means of allegories.

West of the Tracks faithfully renders Benjamin's allegories with its giant images of ruins. This astonishing conjunction gives us new trust in and comprehension of the existence and meaning of art in this world. I named the introduction of my book discussing the rise of documentaries in China since the late 1980s "On the Ruins of Utopia — China's New Documentary Movement."[25] In a society undergoing huge transformation, the documentary movement attempts to expose oppression and exploitation. Under history's iron logic, art strives to find a place for humanity's survival and feelings. This is how art establishes its relation to time and society and becomes a force questioning the logic of history, a force that can redeem humanity.

In *West of the Tracks*, Wang Bing composes many different types of places and people after he has considered their narratives and metaphorical significance. He constructs the film through factories, streets, and rails that complement each other and make the entire film stable and objective. *West of the Tracks* reveals the decline of materiality in this world, the decline of humanity, the disappearance of spirit, and the decay of this age. The film creates a strange but startling effect, without any cheap or unproved optimism and, resisting the temptation to please the audience, it has rejected any light or easy approach. Every single shot of the nine-hour-long film has been strictly handled with reason and sobriety, pointing directly at reality and the innermost truth. The length of the film has its own reason as a work of art has its own vital rhythm. Wang Bing said, "I truly wish that I could confirm the value of life, but in the face of reality, I feel so powerless and have become more and more sceptical towards life."[26] He has turned this suspicion into powerful images. During the one-and-a-half-year shooting process, Wang always tried to keep his mind calm and clear in order to observe and understand reality. When an avalanche of events occurred during the shoot, Wang Bing was deeply touched and realized that he had not reflected upon these things enough before. For the filmmaker as well as the audience, *West of the Tracks* is a difficult experience.[27] Wang Bing believes that the importance of a work does not depend upon who makes it but upon its ability to be meaningful for the viewer. If the viewers relate to the film's concerns, then they will pay attention.

The film ends as it began, with the train still moving slowly through Tiexi. Historically, the locomotive was a ubiquitous symbol of dynamism in the optimistic documentaries made by avant-garde directors between the wars, extolling modern industry and the progress it represented — works like John Grierson's *Industrial Britain*, Walter Ruttmann's *Berlin, Symphony of a City*, or Dziga Vertov's *Enthusiasm: Donbass Symphony*. Ruttmann also started his film with a train, traveling through open fields in the early morning. With wires skipping on both sides and rails opening and closing underneath, we speed into the awakening city and its industrial districts. The sequence is a heady celebration of a new age. In the metropolis, every kind of machinery gradually starts into motion. Human beings spring into action with increasing rapidity, as if driven by some magic power. Watching *West of the Tracks*, I was repeatedly reminded of this great work from another time. But here, the train has become the opposite of its image in the classic documentary. The small industrial wagons rumble drearily through a wasteland of decayed factories, over and over again, until the railroad itself becomes no more than a memento of a rust-ridden past. The plants have been closed down, but the train still wanders through the empty, absurd space of their debris. The factories and people are gone, but the railroad persists like the dead soul of the ruins around it. In this snow-covered land, surrounded by buildings in decay, its journeys no longer symbolize the progress of history or humanity. They have become a ceremony of mourning for their decline.

In the dark night of history, how do we affirm our own lives? What is a real life? "Rails" raises these questions through the depiction of a group of people making their living on trains. They spend every day on the train traveling through the meaningless and absurd factories. Each person, puzzled with his own problems and limited by reality, vainly seeks pleasure in life, longing for a change, or something that can make time meaningful. They do not know how to escape the situation in which they are trapped but upon which they depend. Willingly or unwillingly, each person in this country is bearing and experiencing such a destiny. The fate of individuals is struggling within the larger fate of the nation. The nation, buried under the allegories of vast rusty steel and material, has its prosperity and decline decided by powers beyond its control. The struggle of individuals contains the strength of life itself. Wang Bing believes that, if by such destiny one gets to understand oneself and reality, then one might be awakened even in the middle of this destiny — and awakening is the premise for redemption.

Compared with the first two parts of *West of the Tracks*, "Rails" has a striking difference: people as individuals are illuminated against the dim background. Du Xiyun and Du Yang are a father and son whose lives depend on the trains. They are not employees of the railroad, and have no official relationship to it. Like many others in contemporary China, they are marginals drifting below the surface of the social order, of no fixed abode and on no household register, seeking a precarious, sub-legal foothold in the crevices of the system. One-eyed Du and his son survive by doing menial jobs for the railwaymen who have come to tolerate them, and by selling coal picked up or stolen from the train. The father owns nothing in the world, but hardships have strengthened him and given him a certain cunning. He has his own view of society and those around him, and makes a great effort to create a minimal space for himself and his child in the unstable eddies of life. But his seventeen-year-old son, whose mother went off when he was very young, is withdrawn and silent, visibly the product of an abnormal environment that has left him highly vulnerable to the outside world.

In the course of Wang Bing's filming, the father was arrested for stealing coal and sent to a detention center. What follows is an astonishing sequence of *cinéma vérité*. Left alone at night in the little hovel where they live, the son finds a package wrapped in plastic bags. When he opens it, we see a pile of photos: one of the whole family, another of his mother when she was young, leaning against a haystack and smiling warmly at the world. Suddenly a clock on the wall strikes eleven times, and the camera swings slowly away from the photos toward it. When it swings back, tears are glittering on the son's face. The next day, we follow his desperate journey to the detention center to release his father. In a heart-rending scene, the old man is finally allowed to go, and the two return together to their tiny, bleak room, alone in the world again. At the end of the film, the train is still traveling through the blurred shadows of the factory district. As if in the white night of the century, desolate buildings emerge and recede as in a dream, farther and farther away. We look out at the railroad gradually extending behind us. At this moment, snowflakes start to fall silently on the camera lens, in a shade of grey somewhere between light and darkness. The sky and earth become obscured. It is the twilight before history is clarified. As it journeys on through this ambiguity, to what kind of future is the train taking us?

5 Coming out of *The Box*, Marching as Dykes

*Chao Shi-Yan**

In the 1980s and early 1990s the People's Republic of China saw the blossoming of independent documentary filmmaking. Wu Wenguang, Duan Jinchuan, Zhang Yuan, and Jiang Yue launched a wave of documentary filmmaking commonly referred to as the Chinese New Documentary Movement.[1] Until the mid-1990s, this movement was monopolized by men. Starting with Li Hong's *Out of Phoenix Bridge* (1997), a number of women filmmakers emerged. Female documentarists like Liu Xiaojin, Yang Lina, and Tang Danhong have focused their cameras on the turmoil and uncertain destiny faced by individuals in post-socialist China. What connects these contemporary women filmmakers, in film scholar Zhang Zhen's view, is their focus on issues of social change particularly from the perspective of their effects on women. This approach diverges from that of their male peers in general and, in particular, the epic and idealistic perspective advocated by Dziga Vertov through his concept of "kino-eye," and film classic *The Man with a Movie Camera* (1929). For these reasons, Zhang labels these women documentarists "women with video cameras."[2]

This chapter focuses on two independent documentaries made by women: *The Box* (2001) and *Dyke March* (2004). While *The Box* was produced, directed, shot, and edited single-handedly by a woman, Echo Y. Windy (Ying Weiwei), *Dyke March* was a collaborative work by a lesbian couple, Shi Tou and Ming Ming. Echo Y. Windy graduated from the Department of Chinese Literature at Liaoning University. She had worked as an editor for several newspapers and magazines before she started her television career as a writer-director in 1999. In August 2001, Windy completed her first independent documentary, *The Box*, which is also known as the first documentary from the People's Republic that features lesbian subjects. *The Box* depicts the past experiences and current life of a lesbian couple in China.

* I would like to thank the editors of this anthology, as well as Zhang Zhen, Charles Leary, Shi Tou, Cui Zi'en, Kiang Mai, and my partner, Bennett Marcus, for their generous comments and assistance.

Whereas *The Box* is the first lesbian documentary from China, *Fish and Elephant* (2001), directed by Li Yu, is considered China's first lesbian feature film. Premiered in the Venice International Film Festival in 2001 and winner of their Elivra Notari Prize, *Fish and Elephant* was thereafter invited to show in several other international film festivals, including the 2002 lesbian and gay film festivals in New York and San Francisco.[3] As one of the lead actresses in *Fish and Elephant*, Shi Tou also accompanied the film and toured both cities. It was during her stop in San Francisco that Shi Tou seized the opportunity to shoot the raw footage of *Dyke March*. Co-edited by her girlfriend Ming Ming, *Dyke March* chronicles the lesbian parade that took place in San Francisco on June 28, 2002. It is noteworthy that before Shi Tou made this documentary, she had been known as a talented female artist from Yuanmingyuan in Beijing, the first artists' village in China. Her multimedia creations include paintings, photographs, and videos, and have been shown in various art exhibitions at home and abroad.[4] As the first self-identified lesbian who came out to discuss same-sex relationships on national television, Shi Tou is arguably also the most noted lesbian activist in China. She has been deeply engaged in various LGBT/Q-related activities for a decade or so.[5] *Dyke March* illustrates Shi Tou's status as both an artist and a lesbian activist.

Although *The Box* and *Dyke March* both choose lesbians as their subjects, they differ in their approaches to production and their political concerns. In comparing these two works, this chapter examines the imbrication of technique with content (particularly the use of digital video), and the issue of "objectivity" in documentary filmmaking. It further raises the question of producing knowledge about social others. What are the links between knowledge and politics? Arguing that a tension exists between the knowledge/power scheme associated with *The Box* and a LGBT/Q-oriented politics, I then turn to *Dyke March* to contrast its sensitivity to the socio-political specificities of its subjects, as well as its political activist responsibility for its subjects. I conclude this chapter by introducing two more recent lesbian documentaries from China, tentatively pointing to a trend currently developing in Chinese lesbian documentary filmmaking: independent production that emphasizes both collaboration and the specificity of a lesbian identity.

Identity Politics and Production Methods

Opening with the official manifesto of the San Francisco lesbian parade, *Dyke March* presents a blatant political appeal. The film's overt lesbian standpoint, as noted, is associated with Shi Tou's background as a veteran lesbian activist. *The Box*, by contrast, adopted a feminist angle from the very beginning of its production. In her statement "Hezhong qiri" (Seven days in the box), Windy said that she wanted to make *The Box* because, "In today's patriarchal society, women still remain underprivileged."[6] She found her subjects through the following internet post: "I am a woman. I am a documentary director. I am making a documentary with women as my subjects. If you are willing to face my camera, please contact me."[7] In light of these words, we may infer that the making of *The Box* was, in some measure, motivated by a feminist consciousness.

Such a "feminist" stance notably implies a liberal overtone. It diverges from the traditional, Chinese state feminism — the officially sponsored project of women's liberation (*funü jiefang*). The latter was based on the premise of a naturalized and essential sex difference. It manipulated the concept of gender equality to construct and regulate gender behavior and sexual practice "in support of the [state] project of social control and economic development."[8] Under such an official discourse, both men's *and* women's energies "were to be channeled into working for the collective benefit."[9] Since the 1980s, though, such a state-oriented discourse has been widely challenged by many with the idea that women should define their own needs and create their own subject positions in society. With a strong appeal to women's own interests and underprivileged social status, Windy's feminist stance represents this challenge to party-state appropriation. Although Windy herself is a straight woman, she expands her concern for women to lesbians, who presumably are more disenfranchised than straight women generally. In this regard, Windy's feminist approach presents a perspective that is largely absent from the mainstream (straight) feminist agenda.

Not only are *The Box* and *Dyke March* predicated on different political foundations, they also take disparate approaches to production. Although both films were shot on digital video (DV), different attributes of the DV camera were emphasized. In Wu Wenguang's opinion, the advent of DV in China in the late 1990s signified the birth of "a sort of personal writing" that is most representative of the "civilian standpoint." And, by making it "something really personal," DV emancipates the "imagery of reality" from the mass and the system.[10] To Windy, the portable and relatively affordable DV equipment further represents "a liberation of women,"[11] allowing female filmmakers to work independently of the male-dominated system. In particular, DV enabled her to make a documentary single-handedly with a comparatively low budget. However, *The Box* registers long takes and static camera positioning, while the portable facility of the DV camera is more vividly rendered by the dexterity of the camera framing in *Dyke March*. Shi Tou moved around and along with the crowd, capturing various arresting moments as the parade unfolded.

Moreover, like a talking-heads documentary, *The Box* includes lengthy interviews with the lesbian couple, who remain anonymous and are referred to only as A and B. Interspersed among the interviews are several observational, slice-of-life sequences. The film begins with a sequence of interviews with A and B. In this eighteen-minute-long segment, A and B separately address their individual life experiences before they knew each other. The second and third sequences are each about nine minutes long; they portray moments of their daily life together. The second sequence depicts the mundanities of the couple's morning routine: they wash their faces, brush their teeth, comb their hair, put on contact lenses, and tend to the plants. The third sequence documents their evening life: their protracted embrace upon B's arrival home from work (which alone lasts for about one hundred seconds) and their playful wrestling on the bed at night. These two sequences, as a whole, portray the intimacy between A and B through their hugs and romps, as well as some more detailed physical interactions like A wiping B's face, B combing A's hair and wiping her sweat. The next (i.e., the fourth) sequence unfolds around the fact that there was once a woman, named W, who came between A and B. This segment may be considered the turning point of the film's narrative. In terms of its formal approach, this twenty-six-minute sequence consists of both interviews and observational footage.

Despite the fact that lengthy interviews are incorporated into *The Box*, the questions posed to the interviewees, along with the interviewer's bodily presence, are deliberately excluded from the film. Except for a few moments during the second half of the film, we do not find Windy conversing with either A or B.[12] This documentary technique creates the illusion that the interviewees are merely doing monologues or confessions. The effacement of the interviewer's presence corresponds to the formal consideration of the slice-of-life sequences in the film. Untampered as they seem to be, those segments reflect the documentary aesthetic known as Direct Cinema, whose practitioners assume that a filmmaker/camera can observe the events unraveling in the scene without any involvement with, or intervention in, what is occurring in front of the camera. The practitioners of Direct Cinema, in other words, believe they can employ a fly-on-the-wall stance and approach reality with objectivity. This self-effacing stance that Windy adopts is further evinced in the intertitles deployed in *The Box*. In addition to the title card and the closing credits, four inserts are employed throughout the film. They read in sequence, "Many years later he visited me," "After that I found myself pregnant and had an abortion," "On Mooncake Festival, the year 2000, we got to know each other through the internet," and "Once between us there was a woman called W." Note that the filmmaker selects "I" (instead of B) for the first two intertitles and "we/us" (rather than A and B) for the next two. This demonstrates precisely Windy's intent to tell the story from her subjects' first-person perspective, excluding her own viewpoint.

If an attempt to maintain the boundary between filmmaker and subjects is discernable in *The Box*, that very boundary is blurred — intentionally and otherwise — by Shi Tou and her subjects in *Dyke March*. Several times we hear murmurs or whispers from behind the camera, implying that the camera is not a transparent or objective presence. Moreover, those in front of the camera sometimes talk directly to Shi Tou, or even chat with her and her friends. For instance, a white male excitedly communicates to Shi Tou, adding emphasis with hand gestures, "I saw your film [*Fish and Elephant*]. It's great!" In another scene, a policewoman amiably asks Shi Tou where she is from. As the activities unfold in front of us, we twice witness Shi Tou putting the camera in the hands of her friends. She spontaneously enacts a "coming out" in front of the camera, crossing the boundary between filmmaker and her subjects.

Figure 5.1. *Dyke March*. Director Shi Tou enacts a "coming out" before the camera, obliterating the boundary between filmmaker and her subjects.

Shi Tou is more than a passive observer of the march; she is instead an active participant in the event. If the impulse permeating *The Box* and the observational sequences in particular invokes the realist style of Direct Cinema or, to borrow Bill Nichols's categorization, the observational documentary, then *Dyke March* may be regarded as a rendition of the "participatory documentary."[13] According to Nichols, observational documentary, with Direct Cinema as its major expression, conveys to the viewers "a sense of what it is like to be in a given situation but without a sense of what it is like for the filmmaker to be there."[14] The participatory documentary filmmaker, by contrast, "steps down from a fly-on-the-wall perch, and becomes a social actor (almost) like any other," giving viewers "a sense of what it is like for the filmmaker to be in a given situation and how that situation alters as a result."[15]

Of course, a discussion of the differences between observational and participatory documentary should not neglect their relative significance in the context of 1990s China. The major formal constituents of *The Box*, namely Direct Cinema's realist approach and the interview format, both possess particular appeal for independent documentary filmmakers in post-socialist China. Contemporary Chinese independent documentarists reject the official tradition of newsreels and *zhuantipian* — literally, special topic films. Special topic films are characterized by images compiled in accordance with pre-written scripts and a manner of directly addressing the audience from a top-down perspective. In their pursuit of reality, filmmakers from the New Documentary Movement highlight instead a sense of immediacy — "being 'here' and 'now'," as well-known documentary filmmaker Wu Wenguang succinctly puts it.[16] As Chris Berry notes, they strive for an "unscripted spontaneity."[17] In addition, as Lu Xinyu has argued, they show a deep concern for "civil society" from a "personal standpoint."[18] Contemporary Chinese documentary filmmakers thus try to distance themselves from official approaches in their efforts to document the lives of ordinary people, especially those on the margins of society.[19] Direct Cinema likewise contains a heightened "reality effect" with, as Nichols states, its "directness, immediacy, and impression of capturing untampered events in the everyday lives of particular people."[20] When this production mode was introduced to Chinese documentary filmmakers in the early 1990s, it had a profuse resonance among them. At the same time, many documentary filmmakers started to realize the potential reality effect implicated in the interview format. By compiling diverse, even mutually contradictory, points of view from various interviewees, they strategically offset or debunked official discourses.[21]

Embedded in this post-socialist milieu, Windy's formal choices are politically salient. Through them, Windy expresses a feminist approach of blending the personal content into the political. In so doing she contests a prevalent attitude in China that dismisses women writers, artists, and filmmakers for merely "personalizing" issues. Nonetheless, I suggest that the static camerawork and prolonged takes in *The Box*, together with Windy's erasure of her own voice in the film, also conversely reflect the heightened awareness of a boundary between the filmmaker and her subjects. Windy confesses that before she made *The Box*, she knew little about the world of lesbians.[22] If so, the boundary between Windy and her subjects coincides with the difference between their identities along the axis of sexual orientation. Windy's retention of the demarcation between her status as a straight woman and her lesbian subjects, in a sense, shows her discretion about, and even her respect for, that difference.

By contrast, Shi Tou chooses not to distance herself from her subjects in *Dyke March*. The simple fact that Shi Tou marches with the crowd reflects the fact that the filmmaker does not want to be an unattached bystander but an active participant in the event. Through mobile framing and a vivacious rhythm to the editing, the film sensually weaves the viewers into the scene, affectively engaging us with the parade. Blurring the boundary between the filmmaker and her subjects simultaneously evokes a sense of intersubjectivity between the two parties. The filmmaker's participatory approach corresponds to her political identification: I am a lesbian too! I am standing by you all!

Bringing out Lesbianism in Contemporary China

As many have pointed out, between 1949 (the founding of the PRC) and the 1970s, "homosexuality" was totally absent from public and scholarly discussions. Although homosexuality was not explicitly prohibited, or even described, in Chinese law, same-sex behavior between men might incur punishment under such rubrics as "hooliganism" or disruption of social order. Same-sex behavior was understood to mean sodomy or gender transgression, but not the identity category of homosexuality. This picture began to change only in the 1980s, with China's redevelopment of a market economy and the reintroduction of certain aspects of Western culture. "Sex" was no longer taboo but actually became a prominent discursive formation that was exploited for commercial enterprise,[23] while the taxonomy of homosexuality surfaced in public and scholarly discussions. However, the majority of those published texts, according to Tze-lan Sang, simply rehashed early Western sexological theories of homosexuality as gender reversal and psychological abnormality.[24] Stereotypes about homosexuality thus proliferated in literature and medical treatises.

Some progress in the Chinese *tongzhi* (GLBT/Q)[25] movement finally came at the turn of the millennium. The state's Criminal Law deleted the category "hooliganism" in 1997,[26] and the health authorities removed homosexuality from the list of mental disorders in 2001.[27] Still, the larger society remains mostly uninformed about or prejudiced against lesbians and gay men. Most Chinese women and men who engage in same-sex acts still encounter tremendous difficulty becoming active and visible, even though many of them have already developed lesbian or gay identities, as well as knowledge of global lesbian and gay cultures.[28]

Unable to embrace their identities fully or display them in public, the majority of lesbians and gay men have been forced into leading closeted or double lives. To some degree, my comparison of *The Box* and *Dyke March* also underlines this dilemma. One can see this dilemma reflected in the film locations. Except for two segments, *The Box* was mostly shot inside the house of A and B. Shooting indoors coincides with the imagery of confinement, to which the film's title alludes. On the other hand, the decision to shoot in the home might have been to preserve some level of anonymity for A and B, by not revealing their locale to the general public. The film's *mise-en-scène* points to the oppressive forces, visible or not, of the larger society and the system.

Dyke March, however, takes a detour, showing some aspects of the lesbian and gay movement taking place overseas. In particular, it provides the domestic *tongzhi* audience with scenarios of what they, too, might someday enjoy, that is, an increased public visibility, having access to the public sphere, and even taking over public spaces. China's metropolitan areas in the 1990s saw the development of a semi-public culture of gay cruising zones, unadvertised gay bars and restaurants, and gay corners in discos. At the same time, a substantial number of works depicting homosexual existence in contemporary China have also been produced by local and transnational Chinese journalists, sociologists and activists, who were later joined by international scholars and activists. Even so, the majority of such works and projects, according to Sang, feature "the gay man — and, more specifically, the gay man in metropolitan Beijing."[29] The lack of public and scholarly accounts of lesbianism in China reflects the fact that lesbian activities and subculture, compared with their male counterparts, have even less visibility. It also mirrors the situation that lesbianism in China has remained mostly unknown to the general public.

Against this backdrop, we must first acknowledge that to enhance lesbian networking and social visibility a series of efforts have been made by numerous dedicated individuals from within the *tongzhi* community, such as Xu Bin, Shi Tou, Cui Zi'en, and Wan Yanhai, among others. They have worked shoulder-to-shoulder with homophile professionals, such as China's leading sexologist Li Yinhe and AIDS researcher Zhang Beichuan. To some degree, *The Box* can also be understood as an attempt to bring out lesbianism, initiating a dialogue between the straight populace and (female) *tongzhi*. Like many new documentary films aimed at getting Chinese audiences to learn about, understand, and feel sympathy for those on the margins of society, *The Box* is arguably addressed to mainstream audiences in China.

Several of the interviews in *The Box*, for example, unwittingly form a complicit relationship with mainstream discourses about homosexuality. During the first sequence in the film, A and B talk separately about their families and their experiences growing up. B, the more extroverted one of the couple, says that she grew up in an ordinary family, while A confesses that she has been afraid of her parents since her childhood. A adds that when growing up she not only "lacked maternal love," she also had a father "who hated the family" and an elder sister who seemed "like a boy." A then draws a conclusion, "In retrospect, I assume they more or less have contributed to my loving girls." In a subsequent discussion about their early sexual experiences, A confesses that she had been sexually harassed by men, including her cousin and her own father. B reveals her tumultuous experience with her ex-boyfriend, including becoming pregnant, getting an abortion alone in a clinic, and eventually being deserted by him.

It seems clear that, even though the above remarks come from A and B, they do not mean to challenge mainstream ideas about same-sex desires. Taking the form of "confessions," they somehow reinforce the public imagination of homosexuality: it is a product of dysfunctional families and frustrated heterosexual relationships. Symptomatically, several articles that discuss *The Box* indeed interpret lesbianism in a way that is patronizing and patently biased. They summarize A and B and the "cause of [their] homosexuality:"[30] "One was hurt by her family; the other by a man. Eventually they choose to escape [from the straight reality]."[31] With such an unapologetic misunderstanding in mind, some commentators even praise the film for having "sociological significance."[32] However, to borrow Michel Foucault's insight from *The History of Sexuality*, we should be aware of how the dominant discourse of sexuality in a society produces human subjects and their knowledge about sex: by encouraging them to "talk" about and "confess" their sex. In so doing they produce the "truth" about human sexuality, which conversely solidifies the power/knowledge structure or "regime" (as Foucault puts it) of society.[33]

To put it another way, remarks by members of a sexual minority do not automatically forge a challenge to the dominant discourse. To assess a film like *The Box*, we have to pay special attention to the *power relations* in which the film is embedded. On one level, we may wonder, for instance, how the interviews were conducted. What exactly were the questions that Windy presented to A and B? Furthermore, who has the right to pose questions or, rather, who has the right to study and question social others? What kind of power structure does the knowledge thereby produced serve or reflect?

In addition to such possible methodological concerns regarding the interviews, we find that some elements of the film are also meant to give the impression to the viewers that the misfortunes of A's and B's pasts are somehow connected to their current lesbianism. The strategy of comparison plays an essential role here. Other than the thematic comparisons like past/present, misfortune/happiness, single/couple, and straight/lesbian, we notice that when A and B talk about their troubled experiences growing up, the entire sequence is shot in black-and-white. But after the insert indicating the beginning of their relationship, the footage changes to color. It seems clear that the contrast between black-and-white and color conveys the message that the couple's current life is a form of redemption from their grim histories. Moreover, the sequence in color begins with a medium shot of the green plant at the window, which is then replaced by a close-up of the same plant. Whilst the greenery tellingly signifies the couple's life reborn, the change of the lenses punctuates such a message in the viewers' minds. In other words, what we get from *The Box* is not as objective as some may assume. The various comparisons in this film encourage the impulse to make sense of these lesbians as social others. In particular, the impression that lesbianism in *The Box* is explicable through each woman's past coincides with the public belief that wants to make sense of same-sex eroticism as an aberration.

What other assumptions subtend *The Box*, as well as the idea that lesbianism is something that needs to be explained? In her own statement, Windy reveals why she chose A and B as her subjects. The reason, according to the director, had to do with the fact that A adores Pedro Almodóvar's *All about My Mother* (1999). This piece of information convinced Windy that A is "a person of high cultural taste, so I immediately decided to videotape them."[34] Interestingly, not only does *The Box* include a sequence where A is painting and B is playing guitar and singing, but during the film we repeatedly hear Western classical music in the background. Further, the film ends with a sequence featuring A and B reciting poems, which again seems to verify that A and B possess "a spiritual world of elite qualities,"[35] to paraphrase two critics. Although the music played in the scene was determined by A and B[36] and the poems were actually written by A, implicit in the filming is the imbrication of cultural taste, class, gender, and sexuality.

An issue pervasive in public discussions in post-Mao China is the "quality" (*suzhi*) of the populace. This discussion derives from concerns about population control and desired kinds of children, centering on the constitution of Chinese subjects who are capable of accumulating wealth for their families in this post-socialist economy. The idea of *suzhi* also promotes proper bourgeois subjectivities, which are, to varying degrees, demarcated by broad-ranging variables, such as class-inflected cultural tastes,[37] levels of education,[38] and the division between urban and rural.[39] It seems to me that the emphasis on a lesbian couple's *suzhi* functions as an ideological lever which counterbalances their higher level of cultural taste and class against the lesbian couple's "failure" to conform to women's supposed destinations of the heterosexual family and reproduction. In addition, the film's emphasis on the couple's *suzhi*, along with its stress on the spiritual aspect of their life, helps the subjects skirt the stigma associated with their carnal desire.

Not unlike early gay activism in the United States that adopted a conformist strategy and pleaded for social tolerance, *The Box*'s portrayal of low-profile lesbian subjects with decent cultural taste could also be a political strategy. That is, an affective appeal to the largely straight audiences might have been anticipated as a part of the film's discursive effect, in which respect for and acceptance of these socially marginalized subjects are solicited from the non-*tongzhi* viewers.

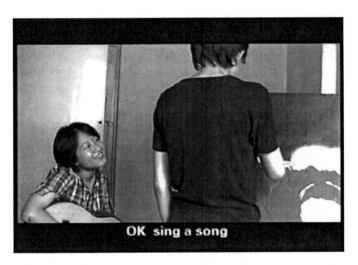

Figure 5.2.   *The Box*. A and B enjoy their shared moments painting, playing guitar, and singing.

I appreciate Windy's contribution to increasing the visibility of Chinese lesbianism in a socio-cultural environment that is ignorant of, yet paradoxically hostile to, *tongzhi* groups. While I recognize Windy's discretion and her respect for the identity difference between herself and her lesbian subjects, I am also concerned about the power relations associated with this documentary film. What I see behind the filmmaker's ostensibly disengaged approach to her subjects is the tension among three perspectives: the filmmaker's expansive feminism, the film's intended non-*tongzhi* audience, and the standpoint of a more radical queer politics. In part because the filmmaker herself was an outsider to lesbian socio-cultural networks, and in part because non-*tongzhi* people were the target audience, this documentary film does not challenge the dominant discourses about homosexuality. Instead, the priority seemed to be the revelation of a largely invisible social group to heteronormative society.

In her own statement, Windy uses such phrases as "pure," "beautiful," and "fragile" to describe "the world of A and B."[40] Though I find the world represented in the film to be earnest, I do not consider it especially "pure" or "fragile." Doesn't the existence of W between A and B attest that the couple's relationship is not utterly "pure," while the very perseverance of that relationship, even with W's intervention, goes against the "fragility" perception? There seems to be a distance between the represented subjects and the picture the filmmaker had in her mind. I assume this distance partly indicates the filmmaker's deep empathy with her subjects. I also wonder if those terms echo a sort of idealized yet intangible sentiment associated with some utopian world, some "all-women's world" that a straight feminist filmmaker overly sympathized with and unwittingly projected onto a lesbian couple.[41]

This utopian imagination, coincidentally or not, underlines the higher level of "cultural taste" and "spiritual world" enjoyed by A and B. The result is ambiguous: by de-emphasizing the carnal desire of the couple, it looks away from the homophobic stigma imposed on lesbians by the dominant society. While it garners a stronger affective appeal from the largely non-*tongzhi* audience, it also, paradoxically, de-specifies A and B's relationship as a lesbian one.

Perhaps due to Windy's lack of familiarity with lesbian culture, and perhaps also due to her conception of the film as a personalistic one about women, *The Box* does not emphasize the significance of a lesbian identity in relation to the social and the political. By this, I do not mean to deny the political tenor of the work. In fact, Windy's choice of techniques — i.e., observational documentation and the interview format, the effacement of the filmmaker's own voice, the inserts — are themselves informed by the socio-politics of the larger cultural ambience. Likewise, the filming location, along with the film's emphasis on the personal, hints at the way the personal is blended into the political. The political commitments of *The Box* are not invisible, but they are rendered in an indirect way. Still, lesbians in present-day China encounter various practical issues that are marginalized in, if not completely absent from, *The Box*. These include the tension between identifying as lesbian and dealing with one's natal family, the difficulty of finding acceptance in the workplace and among friends, the pressure to marry, and finally, life among the emerging lesbian (sub)culture and community. All of these issues are significant to contemporary Chinese female and male *tongzhi*. Even the topic of "coming out," arguably the most thorny issue encountered by Chinese *tongzhi*, is not treated as an issue at all. We do not know the extent to which A's and B's family members know about their sexual orientation, let alone how they view it. Interestingly, in the segment in which B talks about having had an affair with W, B mentions at one point that her sister tried to talk her out of it. That is, B's sister should have known B's lesbian identity even back then. This fact, however, is not discussed further anywhere else in the film.

In sum, as a documentary film, *The Box* seems to promise an "objective" view and knowledge of Chinese lesbianism by virtue of its seemingly disengaged approach to its subjects. However, due to Windy's lack of familiarity with lesbian culture, her conception of the film as personalistic and about women, and the targeted non-*tongzhi* audience, *The Box* is nonetheless imbricated in discourses mediated by heterosexual-oriented thinking. Although obviously made with good intentions from an expansive feminist standpoint, *The Box* contains an unresolvable tension in relation to a more radical *tongzhi*/queer politics.

Lesbians with Video Cameras

In Foucault's view, "power and knowledge directly imply one another."[42] Of course Foucault meant not only to challenge the seemingly "repressive" mainstream, but he wanted to question all discourses that establish identities in the name of sex, including those that appear in the name of gay liberation. If the knowledge about lesbianism produced by *The Box* unwittingly speaks to a heteronormative discourse about sexuality, we must likewise pay attention to the power/knowledge of *Dyke March*. Whereas in *The Box* Windy utilizes an observational approach and a non-hierarchical attitude to her subjects, Shi Tou establishes an identification with the people she films through the use of a participatory method. She constructs an identification based on a lesbian identity that simultaneously crosses national/cultural boundaries. By means of such a nation- and culture-crossing identification, a form of knowledge about lesbianism is invoked. This knowledge informs and is informed by power.

There is no doubt that to some lesbians in China, the kind of knowledge and politics represented by *Dyke March* is not easy to digest. While *The Box* speaks to a largely non-*tongzhi* audience in China, *Dyke March* speaks to a particular queer audience. This queer audience is arguably more urban than rural and fashions itself as cosmopolitan enough to care about queer people in other countries. If we take the dyke march at face value, we must at least acknowledge that there are many lesbians, even in the United States, who do not feel comfortable participating in such a march or who feel that it is not relevant to their lives. In contrast to the power/knowledge associated with *Dyke March*, other ways of being lesbian are reflected in *The Box*. The latter, for example, captures precisely the sense of being isolated and closeted. Nevertheless, to numerous lesbians in China, particularly those who are relatively cosmopolitan, being equipped with the kind of positivist knowledge associated with *Dyke March* can be enabling. It brings them an uplifting vision of collective identity and self-identification. It affirms the idea that they are not alone, that they should also have the right to be proud of themselves and their partners, that they can also pursue the right to adopt children and form (same-sex) families, and that from a *tongzhi*'s perspective they can be equally concerned about various political and human rights issues, ranging from resisting capitalism to liberating Palestine, and decriminalizing prostitution (as seen during the parade in the film). In other words, even though it documents an event that takes place overseas, *Dyke March* also encourages female and male *tongzhi* at home to strive for their own rights, in the hope of obtaining a more promising future.[43]

In *Dyke March* the filmic techniques and representations inform each other; they simultaneously invoke and reify a positivist politics and knowledge about being lesbian. In terms of the camerawork, for instance, Shi Tou chooses to portray the motorcycles leading the parade with several long shots from a lower camera angle. Through this angle the scale (and movement) of the bikes is moderately magnified, while the long shot treats the cheering public in the background as of equal import to the "dykes on bikes," as they are known. The subjects and the surroundings thereby reach a balance, while the dynamic between them is brought to the fore. The jubilant atmosphere highlights the pride of being a lesbian.

Several times throughout the film Shi Tou chooses a higher position as her vantage point, along with panning and zooming, to portray the marching crowd. At an early moment in the film, for example, Shi Tou dexterously uses a high-angle shot and a zoom-in to direct our attention to the group gathered under the banner "Asian Queer Women's Services." Arguably, it is with these queer-identified Asian women (as opposed to lesbians without Asian ethnic/cultural heritages) that a high percentage of Chinese lesbian viewers will more easily establish identification. At a later moment, Shi Tou's camera, likewise adopting a high-angle framing, slowly pans to the right and zooms in to show us the far end of the street packed with people marching by. She then deploys a zoom-out and pans to the other end of the street. Without a cut but through framing and reframing only, this forty-second take tellingly portrays the crowd's magnitude, conveying the collective power of lesbians marching shoulder to shoulder. As noted earlier, the cinematography of *Dyke March* is characterized by the DV camera's easy mobility. As the filmmaker marches with the crowd, her identification with her subjects is vividly inscribed in her camerawork.

Moreover, *Dyke March* pays special attention to the section of the parade that features lesbian parents and their children. During post-production, Shi Tou and Ming Ming applied the format of split screen exclusively to that footage. The Chinese characters translating the signs that read "Our family" and "I love my two moms" appear at the bottom on the left side of the screen. As the images in both frames proceed side-by-side and are given equal importance, the split-screen device seems to punctuate the very doubleness and equality of these families' core members. Notably, the Chinese characters here are tinted with the colors of the rainbow pattern, while the rainbow pattern itself forms a central motif of the whole film: rainbow patterns are seen on flags, top hats, suspenders, neck cords bearing whistles, leis, whirligigs, and a pet dog. The rainbow pattern is also applied to certain captions imposed on the imagery, and is the chief design of the film's opening. If the rainbow pattern has become a symbol of or *lingua franca* for queer identification, such a political identification is seen not only in the film's San Francisco subjects but is also eagerly expressed, in post-production, by the filmmakers from China. Through Shi Tou and Ming Ming such a queer identification forms an organic part of *Dyke March*.

Figure 5.3. *Dyke March*. The split-screen device, with captions "Our family" and "I love my two moms" in a rainbow pattern, punctuates the very doubleness and equality of the core members of the same-sex families in the dyke march.

Here I must emphasize that, even though *Dyke March* provides the domestic *tongzhi* audience with a glimpse of San Francisco's lesbian parade, the significance of this documentary in the context of the Chinese *tongzhi* movement does not reside in an open call for a full-scale transplantation of the political tactics and ideas of the gay rights movement from the West. Nor do I believe that Shi Tou and Ming Ming wholeheartedly embrace the universality of a global gay identity. To assess the specific meaning of this film, I propose we look beyond the rigid thinking that presumes the local and the global to be two polarized and mutually impermeable entities. Additionally, we have to acknowledge the importance of imagination in the configuration of human subjectivities.[44] We may assume that when *tongzhi* audiences in China watch the dyke march taking place overseas, they are stimulated to imagine the legitimacy of their own identities, and to strive for their equal rights. In fact, global flows of queer-themed information (e.g., various gay civil rights debates overseas) and media representations (e.g., pirated copies of the TV series *The L Word* [2004–2009], and Ang Lee's *Brokeback Mountain* [2005]) have become an indispensable component in the formation of local *tongzhi* subjectivity. With the rapid circulation of ideas and transnational media, they have already constituted the trans-local and "glocal" dimension of *tongzhi* subjectivity.[45] Notably, even though this *tongzhi* subjectivity is influenced by global flows, it is by no means a direct copy of a gay identity developed in the "West."[46] As Arjun Appadurai points out, globalization is not merely a reductive and homogenizing process; it is instead full of differences and disjunctures.[47] In her book *Translingual Practice*, Lydia Liu also stresses that any ideas entering a culture from overseas can only be made sense of in terms of the existing cultural conditions and conventions; she thereby foregrounds negotiation and local agency.[48] In "Qualities of Desire: Imagining Gay Identities in China," Lisa Rofel pays special attention to the role indigenous cultural belonging (or "cultural citizenship") plays in the configuration of local (male) *tongzhi* identities. Her concept of "transcultural practices" precisely describes the intricate process that resists any "interpretation[s] in terms of either global impact or self-explanatory indigenous evolution."[49]

The part that *Dyke March* plays in such transcultural practices is to raise consciousness, engaging Chinese female/male *tongzhi* in performing and negotiating their identities. As mentioned above, while *The Box* lays emphasis on a personalized portrayal of a lesbian couple, it offers an indirect critique of the socio-political environment that keeps lesbians from public visibility. In comparison, *Dyke March*, by taking a detour abroad, encourages *tongzhi* to envision a scenario in which they have obtained access to public locales and the public sphere. After all, to enhance public visibility and to partake in public affairs are imperative for *tongzhi* communities to further their civil rights.

Essential to the consciousness-raising function of *Dyke March* is the sense of queer performativity engendered in the *tongzhi* audience through their viewing. By "queer performativity" I mean the sense of subversion animated by such acts and performances that voluntarily challenge the heteronormative reiterations configuring our subjectivity, and that in effect transform the signification of "shame."[50] Like the rainbow pattern, public bodily exposure also forms a central motif of *Dyke March*. Shi Tou's camerawork frequently directs our attention to those women who publicly expose their breasts or proudly exhibit their unclad torsos. To the domestic *tongzhi* viewers, such public bodily exposure and other forms of bold behavior are beyond the merely exotic or erotic; they are endowed with a sense of queer performativity. They challenge the imaginary of being *tongzhi*/queer in today's China in (at least) four respects. First, they directly challenge the socio-politics that discipline women's bodies in terms of gender, class, and sexuality. The very fact that these women expose their bodies in public contradicts the bourgeois concept of decorum. As the women's bodies on display are meant for other women and not for men, they also contest the economy of the heterosexual male gaze as well as patriarchy. Second, these self-identified lesbians challenge the division of the public/private vis-à-vis sexuality. By making lesbianism visible in public, they challenge the oppressive puissance that tries to keep queer behavior/identities out of the public sphere, transgressing, as Lauren Berlant and Elizabeth Freeman put it, the "categorical distinctions between sexuality and politics, with their typically embedded divisions between public, private, and personal concerns."[51] Third, because of the constricted political sphere in today's China, all acts involving a mass group or publicly visible marginalized group inevitably confront state politics. The state is undoubtedly heteronormative. Thus, if a dyke march, along with an array of queer performances, poses a strong challenge to the heteronormative policing of the public/private division, such activities in China must at one and the same time contest China's restricted political circumstances. Queer performativity, in China's case, is imbricated in and meant to break through this larger political oppression. Fourth, by dint of transcultural imagination and practice, the lesbian parade with its emboldening queer behavior delivers to local audiences a message that taunts efforts to make homosexuality equivalent with shame. In this context Shi Tou's presence in front of the camera is especially meaningful, for her participatory performance exerts a strong impact on the audience that is informed by a shared sense of wish-fulfillment and queer performativity.

Conclusion

I appreciate Windy's endeavors to create a dialogue between the non-*tongzhi* public and *tongzhi* groups through *The Box*. From the standpoint of *tongzhi* politics, however, I am more touched by the example of Shi Tou and Ming Ming. With some adjustment to Zhang Zhen's term "women with video cameras," I would like to dub filmmakers like Shi Tou "lesbians with video cameras." By "lesbians with video cameras," I mean those filmmakers who are, or who at least politically identify with, lesbians, who must be highly aware of the varied experiences and issues associated with being a lesbian, and who express this political concern in their work.

My call for "lesbians with video cameras" echoes Thomas Waugh's notion of the "committed documentary." As Waugh asserts, committed filmmakers are "not content only to interpret the world but [are] also engaged in changing it."[52] Committed films, accordingly, "must be made not only *about* people directly implicated in change, but *with* and *for* those people as well."[53] What cannot be overemphasized in my concept of "lesbians with video cameras" is, then, a commitment to changing the social status of Chinese lesbians premised on a sensitivity to the socio-political conditions specific to them. At the same time, I sense a trend developing in the fledgling Chinese lesbian documentary filmmaking scene: the call for collective creation from within the community. Corresponding to Waugh's idea about making films "with" and "for" the underprivileged, this development sees its United States counterparts in anti-racist, feminist, and lesbian and gay documentary film of the 1970s and onward, as well as AIDS videomaking from the late 1980s, where filmmaking has become an efficacious extension of the activism and consciousness-raising of various civil rights and minority liberation movements.[54]

When I completed the first version of this chapter, *The Box* and *Dyke March* were the only documentaries available that were either about or by Chinese lesbians. I concluded that article with an urge for more "lesbians with video cameras" to join them.[55] Since then, three other documentaries featuring Chinese lesbians or issues of same-sex eroticism have come to my attention. They are entitled *Women Fifty Minutes (Nüren wushi fenzhong*, 2006), *The Girls That Way (Bieyang nühai*, 2005), and *Gender Game (Shang hua*, 2006). The first, also by Shi Tou and Ming Ming, offers a panoramic view of the changing lives of Chinese women not only in metropolitan Beijing but also in the developing regions of Tibet, Qinghai, and particularly Guizhou, the couple's home province. From a lesbian perspective, the filmmakers pay attention to the affections, intimacies, and same-sex eroticism between women, who do not necessarily identify as lesbians but who, in some cases, share lifelong emotional commitments to one another.[56] The second film, *The Girls That Way*, focuses on a group of young, Beijing-based lesbians, while the third, *Gender Game*, follows a "T," a tomboy or butch lesbian, living in the Shanghai metropolitan area. To my knowledge, the filmmakers themselves are insiders (*quannei ren*): they are self-identified lesbians, and/or they befriended the subjects before shooting.

Perhaps because the filmmakers are insiders, a sense of shared understanding, along with a sense of group participation, are evident between those behind the camera and those before it. If *The Box* unwittingly downplays the specificity of lesbianism, *The Girls That Way* and *Gender Game* take on a variety of issues intimately concerned with being lesbian in the urban (rather than rural) areas in today's China. In *The Girls That Way*, directors Zhang Shadow and Tian Jude, assisted by a three-person production team (Sun Maxwell, Wei Tina, and Zhang Ekyo), address such topics as same-sex relationships (including a subject's soured experience with a bisexual girl), the experience of coming out, work and life philosophy, looks (e.g., some T's strong rejection of wearing skirts since childhood), and the difficulty some T's may encounter when entering women's restrooms. In *Gender Game*, directed by Ni Tracy (a.k.a. Zhi Zibai), and labeled the first work presented/produced by PeriUnion Studio (*Meihao Tongmeng*), a lesbian-identified organization based in Shanghai, several issues specific to being a T in a big city are addressed. *The Girls That Way* further provides a view of a functioning alternative family (*jiazu*) that consists of six core members who are all lesbians except for one lesbian's twin sister. They got acquainted with each other through the internet, and have since hung out together, calling one another "brothers" or "sisters." Through appropriated familial terms, these lesbian subjects manifest their collective agency from within the emerging lesbian community in Beijing.

When *The Box* lays stress upon the intimate and the individual, it takes recourse in "personalized writing," a rhetorical and creative strategy popular in China in the 1990s. *Dyke March*, *The Girls That Way*, and *Gender Game*, by contrast, further appeal to lesbianism as political identification and collective belonging through both their content and their production approaches. That is, to many Chinese lesbian individuals at this historical moment, unity and community are equally important, if not more so, than the pursuit of individuality pervasive in the larger society. A differentiated collectiveness must be underscored. Whereas *The Box* is characterized by the seeming disengagement of Windy from her subjects, *Dyke March*, *The Girls That Way*, and *Gender Game*, with a sense of commitment, emphasize the political consciousness and social function of documentary filmmaking. Involving themselves with social reality in a more politically positivist way than *The Box* does, the makers of *Dyke March* and the participants of *The Girls That Way* and *Gender Game* define themselves through documentary filmmaking, illuminating the experience and collective agency of the emerging female *tongzhi* communities.

Part III

Publics, Counter-Publics, and Alternative Publics

6 Blowup Beijing: The City as a Twilight Zone

Paola Voci

Beijing Documentaries

The title of this chapter reflects two main traits of Beijing documentaries — their tendency to blow up or highlight the city's marginal inhabitants while also emphasizing their often barely visible locations. Unlike the fast-growing capital that shines in the bright daylight or in the neon lights of its nightlife, the "twilight zone" refers to a symbolic dusk — a moment of partial visibility when an unofficial, unconventional, and unlikely Beijing becomes accessible. "Blowup Beijing" is a reference to Michelangelo Antonioni's contested documentary *Chungkuo-Cina* (1972), which also zoomed in on the periphery of the official discourse about China, while "Twilight Zone" alludes to the homonymous 1960s American television series, in which unexpected things happen in a space between reality and unreality.

The renewal of Chinese documentary is generally traced back to Wu Wenguang's *Bumming in Beijing: The Last Dreamers* (1990). Equally ground-breaking was the eight-episode 1991 series *Tiananmen*, produced for CCTV, though never broadcast on national television. The series was written by Shi Jian and Chen Jue, and produced independently by a group of filmmakers who called themselves the "Structure, Wave, Youth, Cinema" Experimental Group (SWYC Group). In both works, the city of Beijing plays an important role in defining the scope and style of what came to be referred to as the New Documentary Movement. Since then, Beijing has been one of the preferred, although by no means the only, location for independent documentarians and therefore also their visual explorations.[1] The de-facto existence of a Beijing-branded documentary was also officially recognized and commodified through the funding of Beijing Channel Zero Media (2001), one of the first and — certainly among the most visible and active — privately run companies specifically targeting documentary production and distribution. Besides being a main location for both the production and distribution of documentaries, Beijing is also often featured as a protagonist, not just as backdrop. For instance, in Wang Wo's *Outside* (2006) and *Noise* (2007) Beijing itself becomes the main subject of a revived *cinéma vérité* that attempts to capture the city as it speaks to us, with no added commentaries — not even intertitles — from either its inhabitants or the documentarian.

In this chapter I explore the trope of Beijing within contemporary Chinese documentary. In particular, I argue that by zooming in on the avant-garde, the rebellious, and the discriminated against, Beijing documentaries show the city as an ultimately opaque space. This opacity is the result of the tension between the visible and legitimate Beijing that was the focus of most pre-1990s documentaries and the concealed, unendorsed, and even illicit status of the marginal people who have become the subjects of many Beijing documentaries since the early 1990s.

In Beijing documentaries, one does not find the bright and shiny capital that has been part of the rhetoric of both socialist realist films and the neo-socialist/capitalist realist celebrations of China's modernization and economic reforms.[2] Because of the marginality of their subjects, Beijing documentarians have consistently roamed around the periphery, decentering Tiananmen Square and expanding their investigation of the city to less central locations and a multiplicity of inarticulate and indecipherable places.[3] Beijing thus becomes a twilight zone where urban realities are only partially visible, neither fully belonging to daylight nor simply confined to nightscapes. As they become exposed under the documentary's discreet spotlight, their acquired visibility is defined as unavoidably limited, both temporally and spatially.

By focusing on *Swing in Beijing* (1999), *Night Scene* (2004), and *Paper Airplane* (2001), I examine the relationship between performance and dissent and the development of contested realism as the visual mode for the unfitting. By emphasizing subjectivity as a defining trait of a new type of contested realism that pursues a sincere acknowledgment of its own limitations in capturing an uncensored and yet necessarily partial and critical version of reality — rather than an unachievable and ultimately deceptive objectivity — these Beijing films point to documentary's limits and unexplored potentials. In my analysis, this contested realism is understood not as a shift away from authenticity, but as a response to both the ideologically driven socialist realism of earlier documentaries and the tell-to-teach style of the controversial and much-analyzed 1988 television series *River Elegy*, which were less concerned with showing and more preoccupied with narrating and explaining. In contrast, in the documentaries analyzed in this chapter, Beijing is revealed in bits and pieces and thus defined as a fragmented and elusive location, an illogical reality, and an abstract construct where the unlikely and the absurd can and do happen. Beijing documentaries' focus on the city as a twilight zone, where marginal communities seek alternative ways to become visible and thus "real," is also a metaphor for a journey into the documentary genre. On the one hand, by exposing the many marginal communities that populate Beijing, the documentaries function as cultural critiques of the inequities of China's reforms and embody an urban uneasiness that is captured in all its unexplained contradictions. On the other hand, these documentaries also function as a critique of realism and suggest that what is real does not shine in the bright sun, but rather barely flickers in the dark. Documentary realism itself is therefore defined as a twilight zone where real people and real issues can only be evoked and subjectively reinterpreted on screen.

From Bumming to Swinging: Performing Dissent in Beijing

In *Bumming in Beijing*, Wu Wenguang's decision to film a group of artist friends was an accidental choice mostly dictated by convenience. However, in the subsequent development of Chinese documentary, the link between performers and authenticity strengthened. In the Beijing documentary, the connection between performance and marginalized communities was developed in films such as Jiang Yue's *The Other Bank* (1995), Wu Wenguang's *Life on the Road* (1999), Wang Shuibo's *Swing in Beijing*, and Wu Wenguang's *Dance with Farm Workers* (2001). As the camera follows the lives of professional and amateur musicians, artists, and actors, the city of Beijing becomes a stage rather than a shooting backdrop, while the documentary engages in the same performative practice as its recorded subjects. Performance itself thus becomes a key to displaying marginalized realities, including those of the documentarian.[4]

Chris Berry discusses the connection between marginality and performance in relation to the "staging of gay life" in Zhang Yuan's *East Palace, West Palace* (1996) as a means to access public discourse.[5] In Berry's analysis, performativity contrasts with Judith Butler's understanding of the stage as a location for a critical re-enactment of realities aimed at undermining established social meanings. Berry argues that what is at stake in Zhang's dramatization of the hidden gay subculture is more the ability to perform publicly than the possibility of acting identities differently. Possibly with an even higher degree of exigency, the same quest for public space takes place in the documentaries focusing on performers, where the need to express oneself creatively is shown as inseparable from the necessity of reaching an audience. Not only the existence of their unconventional identities, but also their physical survival depends on them becoming publicly visible.[6] The search for visibility, however, leads to uneven and contradictory outcomes.

Wu's and Jiang's works specifically focus on stage performers who can only find a temporary space in the city of Beijing. The students directed by experimental theater director Mou Sen (*The Other Bank*), the traveling entertainers singing and dancing in a circus-like tent (*Life on the Road*), or the Sichuan farm workers performing in a former textile factory (*Dance with Farm Workers*) are all clearly defined as *waidi ren* (outsiders) who struggle to put their roots down in the city. In contrast, Wang's documentary, *Swing in Beijing*, includes a broader variety of performances — from punk musicians' concerts to experimental artists' exhibitions — and includes excerpts from films, gallery installations, and theater productions. Unlike the other documentaries, *Swing in Beijing* does not construe the city as a remote or inaccessible location where *waidi ren* are ostracized, exploited, or expelled. On the contrary, Beijing seems to be the fitting, and possibly only, location for the artists who live and work there.

Although in some instances Beijing is portrayed as a decaying city literally demolished by modernization, and even dismissed as "not being real China," the documentary seems to suggest that the disturbed and troubling city also allows openness to non-mainstream choices. While this is often the result of popular indifference or inefficient censorship rather than acceptance, marginalized communities are nonetheless allowed not only to exist but, more importantly, also to become publicly visible. For instance, one of the interviewees, experimental artist Jiang Jie, points out how in "non-official galleries you can show almost anything." Theater and film director Meng Jinghui notes that "restrictions stimulate creativity" and that, despite censorship, 25,000 people in Beijing came to see his adaptation of a Dario Fo play. It is *Swing in Beijing*'s sense of belonging and ambivalent optimism that I would like to explore in more detail.

At the time the documentary was produced, Wang had already left China for almost ten years.[7] Wang can be considered as one of the *mangliu* (vagabonds) who bummed in Beijing and then left to find "a home in the world," to pun on the titles of two Wu Wenguang films.[8] *Swing in Beijing*'s ambivalent optimism is anchored in its diasporic nature and the corresponding sense of nostalgia. It is a Beijing documentary that does not officially belong to the New Documentary Movement. Wang's insider look at Beijing's artistic life is paradoxically that of an outsider.

Immediately after a black screen with the title "Swing in Beijing," the documentary begins with a slightly overexposed medium shot of an alley framed by some trees on the left, a wall on the right, and a bicycle riding in between. After a short musical introduction played over a series of shots of two main tourist attractions — the Forbidden City and Tiananmen Square — a male soloist starts singing: "Leave me alone; no more words, no more people. It seems I am far away from society. I am smiling at nature and shouting to the mountains. I can only hear the wind and my own echo."[9] As the camera zooms in on the famous portrait of Chairman Mao hanging over Tiananmen Square, the singer repeats: "No more words, no more people. It seems I am far away from society." At this point, the camera zooms out to include people walking in front of the gate while the beat accelerates, drums roll, and the soloist forcefully continues: "Then, let me blow up myself completely." The shot fades into a medium close-up of two red flags — that of McDonald's and the national one. The lyrics are disturbed by some loud unidentifiable urban noise, and only the subtitles can clarify the unintelligible words: "I am going to throw all my blood on the flag and shit on it!" A cut to a close-up of the flags fluttering in slow motion is accompanied by the repetition of the refrain. This introductory scene ends with some long shots of Beijing streets in daylight, crowded with cars, buses, and bicycles, as the instrumental part of the song continues until it stops with a cut to two consecutive close-ups of young men, each introducing themselves: "My name is Gao Xing, I'm the singer of Underbaby" and "My name is Shen Yue, the lead singer of The Bad Boys of Anarchism."

Figure 6.1. *Swing in Beijing.* "Then, let me blow myself up completely."

The ensuing interviews clarify that Gao Xing and Shen Yue are big fans of British and American punk bands and want to use punk music to express rebellion and non-conformity. The two singers openly acknowledge their debt to Western music. In fact, they mention that they began their musical careers by simply imitating Western bands and only later developed their own style.

The daylight interviews carried on in a bar or on the streets are intercut with shots of nightlife in Beijing, images and sounds of live concerts, and the MTV video of the opening song. The two musicians outline their life philosophy based on a pragmatic view of life, with "not much ambition, not many dreams." They just try to get by, smoking marijuana (as it is easy to find and "harmless" while "other drugs make you stupid") and enjoying the new economic freedom that allows them to produce CDs and even make some profit.

As the documentary moves to each set of non-mainstream people, the opening song's instrumental part is played again, often accompanied by a long shot of Beijing's avenues. Thus, even though the documentary does not go back to the irreverent young singers, their music becomes the city's soundtrack and acts as a commentary on each of the interviewees' self-proclaimed resistance to mainstream culture. From the hedonist and disenchanted punk musicians we swing to the sophisticated world of avant-garde art and the more articulate opinions of several experimental artists.

Among them, Wei Dong specifically talks about the loss of old Beijing and the pain of seeing its *hutong* alleyways and its memories being destroyed.[10] He also notes that unfortunately his work has not been shown in Beijing, but mostly in Hong Kong, Europe, and the United States, where he thinks the audiences' responses can only be superficial because "they don't understand Chinese culture." He wishes to have Chinese people see his paintings because, he thinks, *they* would understand.

Zhang Wang also comments on the destruction of old houses in Beijing and its inevitability.[11] Rather than stopping the irreversible process of decay and the unstoppable growth of the new, Zhang sees the role of art as recording this painful transition and commenting on it. He locates the houses where the residents refused to leave and begins to repaint these ruins, restoring some pieces before the bulldozer comes to tear them down. He then goes back and takes photographs while big buildings such as the Beijing Hotel are being built. Zhang notes that "Beijing needs to be modernized, as an artist I can't change this transformation," and he goes on to point out how McDonald's and Coca Cola are changing China and how powerful American popular culture is.

Sixth Generation filmmaker Jia Zhangke further develops the idea of Beijing as a staged city, a media creation, and an unreal city.[12] He states that Beijing does not represent China: "Real China is my hometown, Fenyang." He openly blames the economic reforms for the loss of friendship and loyalty, and in his films he wishes to show the impact of these losses on "ordinary people, living at the bottom, because they are the real China." His interest in reaching out to the Chinese people was frustrated by the fact that, although he had already won six prizes, his films were not released in China.[13]

Several other artists are showcased, briefly introduced by the instrumental intermission of the Underbaby song. The last interviewee is Meng Jinghui. He begins by mentioning June 1989. But rather than recalling the event itself, he relates it to a shift in his personal life, as a moment that changed him forever and made him an adult. Yet, despite the reference to one of the saddest and most disturbing episodes in recent Chinese history, Meng is probably the most optimistic speaker. His passion for his work and his confidence are obvious in his words: "If you do experimental theater, you should have a clear mind. You should not be afraid that the Western bourgeoisie won't care or Beijing common people won't understand, or that your senior colleagues will try to put you down." He acknowledges the limitations imposed by censorship, but adds that it is not as bad as it used to be. He notes that "Chinese restrictions stimulate creativity. We just need regulations to become slightly loose. We are still not creative enough, provocative enough. We all, including me, have a big problem: we pre-censor ourselves." He goes on to describe how he managed to bypass censorship and reinvent Dario Fo's *The Accidental Death of an Anarchist* to make it fit the Chinese context. Meng expresses his faith in laughter as a powerful force that can work across language and cultural divides.[14] His statements are visually reinforced by the play's comically bitter ending, which is shown from an angle that includes not only the stage but also the laughing and clapping audience.

During the various interviews, *Swing in Beijing* distances itself from the raw punk rockers and the more sophisticated artists, so that none of them is eulogized as the new hero of Chinese counterculture.[15] Yet, *Swing in Beijing*'s optimism can be inferred throughout the documentary, especially in Meng Jinghui's positive words about the city's opportunities and the slow-motion shot of the theater filled with a clapping audience, which ends the documentary. To underscore such ambivalent optimism, as the final credits roll, another Underbaby song is played over a montage of Beijing nightlife shots. The lyrics offer an equally disconcerting but less angry response than the more aggressive opening song. The documentary starts out with the provocative lyrics of the punk rocker asking to be left alone so he can blow himself up and throw blood on the flag. During the documentary, the destructive force of the song's words is softened through its recurrent use as a simple instrumental intermission. At the end, the soloist sings, "I can't see the sea, I can't see the sky. I can't see the real or the evil side of this world. I have no illusions, no happiness. I don't have the slightest idea of what's real life," while the refrain forcefully repeats "I only have music." This suggests that an alternative to blowing oneself up can be found. With all its unanswered questions, the city can at least offer a twilight zone in which to perform dissent.

Improper People and the Opaque City

In this section, I look at documentaries which deal with a different set of marginalized people. Arguably among the most out of place, even in Beijing's twilight zone, these are the communities living at the limits of legality and, in fact, in many instances considered criminals by the law. Cui Zi'en's *Night Scene*, on male prostitutes, and Zhao Liang's *Paper Airplane,* on drug addicts, explore the world of the not merely improper but actually unacceptable. Abnormality does not derive from artistic aspirations or intellectual dissent but is defined as an irrepressible desire, either the result of personal behavior or the very defining trait of one's identity. In these documentaries, again, Beijing only appears as a trace. We are not shown internationally known iconic locations, but rather places that can be familiar only to those who have lived in Beijing. In *Night Scene*, the city fragments include a park, a street market, sidewalks, and entrance gates to apartment blocks — locations that can evoke Beijing only to those who have been there. Among the more recognizable locations (for a relatively small group of insiders) are meeting points for the gay community and the areas surrounding the Beijing Film Academy. In *Paper Airplane*, Beijing is initially introduced through a panoramic shot of anonymous buildings and later appears in a handful of shots of sidewalks where pirated tapes are sold in daylight, and streets where the camera records drug exchanges in the night. The captions also evoke the city through a series of off-center locations: 100 Flower Lane (Baihua Shenchu), White Cloud Road, Xizhimen Hospital, Wei Gong Cun district, unidentified "outskirts of the city," Xinjiekou Police Station, and the urban suburb of Bali Zhuang.

    Night Scene is one of the few Cui Zi'en films he himself considers a "documentary."[16] However, the video retains very little of the observational style still prevalent in the documentaries previously analyzed and openly stages most of its scenes. In fact, students, professional actors, and real gigolos all appear on screen without revealing their different backgrounds.[17] *Night Scene* can therefore be better defined as a hybridized docu-drama with the flavor of a film essay. While it makes many small revelations about the whereabouts and the backgrounds of the subjects, the video is the negation of the "exposé" mode that places its emphasis on uncovering hidden truths. In *Night Scene*, the camera never captures unaware subjects. Instead, the subjects and the documentarian himself willfully expose themselves and get to choose what to reveal and what to hide. The documentary does not provide any in-depth exploration of either the social phenomenon or the individual identities. Instead, Cui parodies the investigative report format by including inconclusive and fragmented opinions on the topic of male prostitution from unidentified experts.[18] As for the gigolos themselves, their motives and inner feelings are often staged rather than spontaneously conveyed.

The opening sequence begins with a couple of fish swimming in a tank, followed by an out-of-focus shot of a different fish tank completely filled with red fish.[19] As the camera quickly zooms out, it cuts to a medium close-up of a young man behind a fish tank, partially covered by one big fish swimming in the foreground. The first interview plunges straight in, as the young man begins to talk about his first oral sex experience and how he felt sick and cheap. As the monologue continues, the fish often covers most of the speaker's face and one suddenly realizes that a different gigolo has started talking. The next few shots introduce many other young male prostitutes who make brief statements about themselves while looking straight into the camera. Whether indoors or out, they are mostly shot in daylight. In only two instances are the speakers shown in a slightly darker environment, but still their faces and bodies are well lit. Four minutes into the documentary, the title "Night Scene" appears, superimposed on a fish tank — this time in focus — where several fish swim calmly. In contrast to the title, the following shots are all daylight, open space scenes of young men meeting in parks or on the streets.

As the first encounter takes place, one immediately realizes that the "actors" are performing. Rather than observed or spied on by an unobtrusive camera, the young men are facing the camera and clearly following a script. The two young men chat briefly in the park, and then move to an empty university classroom where they stage a surreal lecture on the meaning of love. Next, in the documentary's first night scene, they are shown walking past a series of food stands, eating corn on the cob. However, the illusion of authenticity is disturbed by synthesizer music, which connects the scene with the previous one.

As the documentary continues to follow the stories of these and other young men — students and prostitutes — the tension between supposedly spontaneous interviews and performed docu-drama is never resolved and in fact intensifies.[20] Not only are several of his subjects shown dancing on-stage for money or singing for fun, but some of the interviewees' statements are obviously scripted and recited. For instance, in one scene (again shot in daylight), a group of young men face the camera performing a statement about themselves together. The first begins with "we have nothing," the second continues with "we push the limits," the next one adds "and we become lost," and finally the first speaker concludes "so we have nothing."

In *Night Scene*, the city is never shown via any of its famous landmarks, yet the documentary can definitely be branded a Beijing documentary. A significant portion of the video is shot in the gay bar or in the gigolos' living quarters, and the city is also staged in many of its less famous but equally recognizable locations (especially to Beijing residents). Furthermore, as in *Swing in Beijing*, even though most of the speakers are not Beijingers by birth, they all convey a sense of belonging to the city. Many refer directly to the city as the place they came to in order to be able to live out their homosexuality. Beijing's twilight zone thus seems to offer the only possibility of happiness for people whose living choices, while not illegal, remain socially unacceptable.

Figure 6.2. *Night Scene*. "We have nothing."

Positioned between documentary and art video, Zhao Liang's representations of Beijing are often explicitly manipulated. *Paper Airplane*, co-directed with Fan Junyi, is a more conventional documentary. It begins with a long sequence showing a young man and a young woman in a small room. The man is squatting, getting ready to shoot up. Throughout the preparation process, he repeats that this will be his very last time as he really wants to quit. A third friend arrives. As he enters, he turns toward the camera, mildly surprised: "Oh, you are making a show today?" and then continues to interact with the others, ignoring (or pretending to ignore) the presence of the observer.

As the documentary progresses, other friends are introduced and we follow their lives over two years. No voiceover narration is used. Brief captions inform us of the names of each new subject to appear, but no other information is added. Occasionally, an intertitle indicates a change in time and gives a brief update about the unrecorded gap. For instance, we are informed that six months have gone by, one friend has disappeared for a while, another has been arrested, and another has stayed clean. The camera records the youths while they buy and take drugs, escape police raids, pack and move, return after being detained, are hospitalized after attempting suicide, play and listen to music, and fight with their parents.

Although the documentary is shot in the observational style, it is clear that the documentarian is more than a simple observer. Sometimes, we hear Zhao Liang's voice responding to the speakers. Furthermore, the intertitles often use the pronoun "we," which clearly includes the documentarian within the group. Zhao's personal involvement becomes overt in the final scene, which is shot in black-and-white. This is one of the few technical interventions in the documentary, which has previously only used a couple of slow-motion shots and elaborate camera movements, such as the shot in which the little table used for drug preparation is shown spinning around. The scene is introduced with a brief caption: "In September of 2000, we had news of Wang Yinong. Years of heroin and a recent overdose had left him hospitalized and in a serious condition. He was diagnosed with massive kidney failure." A medium shot then shows the same young man who was getting ready to shoot up in the opening scene now lying in hospital and throwing up into a bag held by an unseen nurse. After a few seconds, there is a cut to a medium close-up of Wang Yinong, who turns toward the camera and asks: "So, do you have a name for your film yet?" At this point, the documentarian's off-screen voice begins to talk with him, first replying that "no, [he has] not yet come up with a title" and then, after Wang suggests that the title should be "paper airplane," asking "Why?" A paper airplane can only fly once, Wang explains, but it goes through a lot of crashes and hardships for that

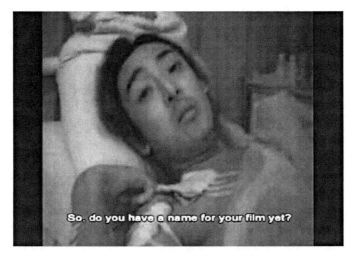

Figure 6.3. *Paper Airplane*. "So, do you have a name for your film yet?"

one flight. Immediately after these words, the title is shown on a black screen, followed by the credits. The short dialogue about choosing of title reinforces the idea of a collaborative project in which the director, although unseen, is far from being the "big brother watching," as he shares the same cultural and emotional space as those on screen.

Like Cui Zi'en's *Night Scene*, *Paper Airplane* has a high level of complicity between the recording subject and the recorded subjects. The documentaries also represent the city similarly as somewhere in which the unaccepted and even illegal can find some space. Although clearly defined as a marginalized community, the protagonists of *Paper Airplane* are oddly integrated into the city. As in *Night Scene*, the improper people are shown not only in their own indoor communal space but also in outdoor environments.

Furthermore, whereas in *Night Scene* the gigolos only actively interact amongst themselves, in *Paper Airplane* one can occasionally witness a direct contamination between the anomalous and the ordinary. In a couple of scenes the youths are at their parents' places. In one instance, Fang Lei is shooting up in the foreground while, through an open door, in the background we can see his father sitting on a chair. In another instance, Liang Yang's mother expresses all her frustration. Liang Yang angrily asks the mother to stop nagging her and to leave her alone.[21] Both Fang Lei's father and Liang Yang's mother are also interviewed separately about their children. Several broken links are thus established between those who use drugs and those who do not. The documentarian himself can in fact be considered the only active link, as he seems located outside the addictive cycle of drugs, and yet has an insider position within the group of friends.

Zhao's exploration of the city has been further developed in his more experimental work that has often appeared in video art installations.[22] In a series of short videos (lasting an average of ten minutes each and all shot in Beijing in 1998), Zhao exposes unnoticed abnormalities and makes them shockingly visible. In these videos, he abandons any attempt to achieve realism or authenticity and in fact uses special effects including filters, masks, superimposed color, images looking like a film negative, and fast- and slow-motion shots to dehumanize and manipulate reality, making it surreal and abstract.

Good Morning, Beijing shows the exercises of a group of Falun Gong practitioners. After a series of observational shots, Zhao obsessively repeats shots of movements such as head rotations and hands clapping on buttocks or legs, intercutting them with scenes of caged animals such as a panda, a cheetah, and monkeys. At one point he inserts still shots of an analogue editing machine's buttons: "All Stop," "Black," "Color BKGD," "Key2 Select," "Mask," and "Power." Then, he literally rewinds and fast-forwards the scenes, while close-ups of a hand using the editing machine pop in. Natural sounds are also accelerated and slowed down, and mixed with the editing machine's rewinding and fast-forwarding noise.

In *A Social Survey*, Zhao uses a series of long takes, all filmed with a hand-held camera, to record crowds of people who are either walking toward the camera or standing and sitting alongside, while he walks around Beijing's streets, shops, and subways. Zhao adds a surreal detail to this seemingly *cinéma vérité* video. In the left corner of all shots, we see a gun pointed toward the people encountered by the camera; it looks as though the gun is actually placed on the camera itself. Everybody seems to ignore the gun, and, for that matter, the camera. The "survey" ends when someone reacts to the "shooting" and looks angrily at the camera/gun.

In *How Long Can You Stand It?*, a close-up of a man's face immersed in water (shot from underneath) is intercut with shots of fish in a tank. The number of fish increases with every shot and the fish tank is eventually completely filled with so many fish that they struggle to survive in the little water left. Other shots from a crowded Beijing bus are mixed and superimposed on the images of the fish. In the background, one can hear the sound of bubbling water.

Witness shows the slaughter of a cow and a goat, with extreme close-ups of their open throats bleeding and their wide-open eyes. The scenes are mixed with images of city life, people walking, riding bikes, and driving cars. We also see soldiers on motorcycles, women pushing baby carriers, and someone in a wheelchair. Other manipulated images pop in. Trees are cut along the streets; Zhao adds bright red rings around their trunks, which clearly remind us of the broken and bleeding throats of the slaughtered animals. President Clinton and President Jiang are talking on TV; Zhao hides their faces using one of those masks used to protect anonymity in television interviews.

From these descriptions of Zhao's short videos, a different and expressionist way of documenting Beijing comes into view. Subjectivity here defines authenticity, rather than negotiates with it. Unlike the documentarian described by Joris Ivens who, standing in the middle of reality, "[a]t every occasion, only chooses to interpret part of that reality," Zhao clearly manipulates reality to show its hidden, true meaning.[23] His camera-gun is a punk version of Dziga Vertov's socialist kino-eye. Vertov's ideological motivations and his — problematic but nonetheless official — insider status within the Soviet film industry contrast with Zhao's individualistic position and outsider condition.[24] However, for both directors, the goal is to find and possibly create hidden meanings. In both cases, the camera emphatically points to the selective and manipulative presence of the viewing subject.

The inclusion of *Night Scene* and Zhao Liang's short videos in my discussion of Beijing documentaries raises the larger issue of what defines documentary as a non-fiction genre. Documentary has been analyzed through topic-related and mode-based categories like the electronic essay, the docudrama, the ethnographic film, the autobiographic documentary, the subjective documentary, television documentary journalism, and many others. Deciding to which documentary subgenres Cui's quasi-documentary and Zhao's experimental videos belong could undoubtedly lead to a better understanding of how, in China too, documentary is indeed a contested and unstable mode of visual representation. However, I prefer to take it as a fluid and inclusive category.[25] What interests me in the context of the present study is Cui's and Zhao's not-quite-documentary take on Beijing's twilight zone as a location that is better defined by contested realism. Their deployment of openly staged scenes and scripted dialogue (Cui) or manipulated shots (Zhao) points to the limits of realism as a means for capturing Beijing's unofficial side and exposing the tension between those who live outside social norms but inside the city.

Documentary as a Twilight Genre

I hope my analysis has shown how, as a direct result of the documentary's own self-reflexive interventions, marginalized communities and counterculture proponents are uncovered, both truthfully and mercilessly. Because of the intrusive nature of their explorations or, in some cases, the personal connections between the recording and the recorded subjects, Beijing documentaries are often the incongruous result of a complex negotiation between subjectivity and authenticity, and empathetic and distancing practices.

While targeting different topics and experimenting with different filming and recording approaches, Beijing documentaries' narratives intercept each other's paths. Not only do they share the same shooting location, but they also revolve around marginalized communities or anomalous individuals who are either excluded from mainstream culture or deliberately choose to distance themselves from it. While all living at the margins, these people are unable or unwilling to connect with each other. What segregates the farmers who perform in Wu Wenguang's *Dance with Farm Workers* from the male prostitutes captured in Cui Zi'en's *Night Scene* is a gap just as wide as the one separating them from the mainstream. As these disconnected communities are implicitly brought together on screens, Beijing documentaries also initiate a process of mutual legitimization through which those who record and those who are recorded, despite their dissimilar needs and even different levels of engagement, all participate in the making of an alternative cultural sphere.

By roaming around Beijing, documentarians have exposed a consistency of traits among marginalized communities including urban punks, avant-garde artists, gays, drug addicts, and immigrants, and demonstrated how central rather than marginal these communities are in shaping the cultural and social space of the city. In a China where the educated classes have monopolized the cultural debate, there are many people who have given up any hope for or interest in a dialogue within or against mainstream culture. Chinese documentaries have begun to show those who do not talk the talk and yet have something to say.

Beijing's urban space as the location of multiple and competing cultures is characterized by unsolved tensions between naïve ideals and stark pragmatism, between honesty and hypocrisy. However, what is under scrutiny is not the corrupting and corrupted quality of the city as it has been analyzed — in China as elsewhere — in various configurations of literary and filmic urban alienations and inhuman fast-paced modernities since the beginning of the twentieth century.[26] Beijing's twilight zone is a postmodern, or more appropriately, post-socialist, construct and its role in displaying alternative cultural strategies makes it closer to the notion of disappearance as described by Ackbar Abbas in his analysis of Hong Kong cinema.[27] According to Abbas,

> The very process of negotiating the mutations and permutations of colonialism, nationalism, and capitalism would require the development of new cultural strategies. Where then can these strategies be found? They will have to be found in the new Hong Kong cinema, in certain kinds of writing, in ways to understand the urban space, in theoretical and empirical discourses on Hong Kong.[28]

Starting from the 1990s, documentary representations of Beijing have introduced and developed the notion of urban uneasiness and exposed some of the conditions that derive from it. Beijing documentaries have moved away from the focus on immorality and developed the notion of a Beijing malady to describe the decay that has affected not just people, but Beijing and its buildings. At the same time, the documentaries suggest that the city might not be well but is still alive.

The representation (or non-representation) of the city in Beijing documentaries also exemplifies an important shift in the definition of cinematic realism. Chinese documentarians have used a combination of interview format and observational style, which emphasized the unobtrusive attempt to capture life from a witness perspective. The New Documentary Movement rejected realism (*xianshi zhuyi*) as too ideologically driven and emphasized authenticity (*zhenshi*). A new style, "on-the-spot-realism" (*jishi zhuyi*), reflected this authentic approach to the real, and the striving to "bear witness to *their realities*."[29] Not only do the Beijing documentaries discussed in this chapter "bear witness to their realities," but they are also makers of these realities.

The conceptual and visual shift in the understanding and representation of urban modernity as ultimately a subjective space brings the Chinese experience surprisingly close to the broader international debate on the nature and scope of documentary filmmaking, which hit a turning point with the first of the Visible Evidence conferences in 1993.[30] In the "Visible Evidence" debate, documentary was acknowledged as being closely linked to the idea of the witness. Unlike fiction films that can venture into the invisible by visualizing temporal, spatial, and psychological locations that are out of any observer's reach, documentary chooses to show only what one can identify with the explicit or implicit presence of a witness. At the same time, documentary's referentiality was also exposed as no different from all other cinematic indexicalities, and the blurring between fiction and non-fiction was recognized as an established fact and indeed a necessity. Moving beyond the "bounds of a rigorously enforced reality principle, which is where documentary theory has too often relegated its object," Michael Renov advocated for the inclusion of interpretative categories (e.g., the unconscious and the scopophilic pleasure associated with it), traditionally associated only with fictional films.[31] In other words, it is the witness's perspective that frees documentary from objectivity and allows for subjective interpretations. After all, a witness is not infallible. At best, a witness can simply offer a very partial (subjective) perspective on the real; at worst, a witness can be biased and unreliable. Once the complicity between the camera and its holder is acknowledged, the focus shifts from the abstract utopia of the *kino-eye* to the physical temporality of the man with the movie camera.[32]

Since the pioneering works *Bumming in Beijing* and *Tiananmen*, Beijing documentaries have emphasized the person with the camera and have pointed to subjectivity as a main defining trait of their representations. Their epistephilic motivations do not exclude or preclude other desires. One should not take the impulse toward authenticity as being the sole concern of the renewed Chinese documentary. Such an impulse certainly directs works like Li Hong's *Out of Phoenix Bridge* (1994) and Du Haibin's *Along the Railroad Tracks* (2000) or *Under the Skyscraper* (2002). These Beijing documentaries also focus on the lives of the out of place. But, unlike Cui or Zhao's works, they seem to embrace a more conventionally defined idea of documentary's authenticity that rejects any overt manipulation or fictionalization of the subject matter. Yet, I believe that, even in the earlier stages of the development of new Chinese documentary, subjectivity was never discarded and in fact was reclaimed as a crucial component, both from the formal and content points of view.[33] Beijing's visible evidences have never claimed to be objective and, in fact, have often openly disclosed their interpretative alterations. While authenticity defines the recording impetus, what is captured is not reality itself, but a series of performed realities, unscrambled mosaic tiles, or manipulated interpretations. The tension between spontaneity and staging is mirrored by the hybridization of non-fictional with fictional techniques. From words to music, from speech to noises, from first-person narration to laconic captions, Beijing documentaries' exploration of the city as a twilight zone is a metaphor for the journey into documentary itself as a twilight genre, precariously and provocatively located at the juncture of feature film and art video.

7 Watching Documentary: Critical Public Discourses and Contemporary Urban Chinese Film Clubs

*Seio Nakajima**

The past several years have seen a surge of interest in Chinese documentary films. A quick search on the internet returns numerous results on Chinese documentary film screenings both in China and abroad. With this rising interest, important academic research has begun to appear on the topic.[1] However, most, if not all, of the existing studies focus on documentary film as "text," and detailed analyses of the social context of production, distribution, and exhibition remain sparse. Highly informative works on how documentary films are produced, utilizing interviews with film directors, have appeared, and these studies provide important insights into the social context of the production of Chinese documentary.[2] Nevertheless, research that deals with the issue of how Chinese documentary films are actually circulated, exhibited, watched, and discussed by Chinese audiences is virtually non-existent. In this chapter, I attempt to fill this gap by presenting an empirical study of documentary film consumption and audiences in contemporary urban China.[3]

From February 2003 to August 2004, I conducted an ethnographic study of "film clubs" in Beijing, where a group of audiences watch independent films including Chinese documentary works.[4] I participated in and observed a variety of activities organized by film clubs, as well as interviewed the organizers and the members/participants, which included a fair number of documentary filmmakers. With this empirical data in hand, I ask two key research questions.

* I would like to thank the film club participants whom I interviewed and spent time with for their kindness in inviting me into their activities. I also would like to thank the participants of the Asia Group Lunch Meeting at the Department of Sociology, University of Hawai'i at Mānoa, for their spirited and constructive critique. Last but not least, I would like to thank the editors of this volume, Chris Berry, Lu Xinyu, and Lisa Rofel for an incisive set of suggestions and their patience.

First, what kinds of topics are discussed and what types of opinions are expressed by the documentary audiences in urban Chinese film clubs? Second is a theoretical question inspired by Jürgen Habermas's discussion of what he calls the "public sphere": Given the continuing existence of restrictions on and (self-) censorship of independently produced documentary films in China, to what extent do the film clubs approximate the Habermasian ideal type of "public sphere," which consists of voluntary associations outside the spheres of the state and the economy? By closely comparing the Chinese reality with Habermas's ideal type, I attempt to elucidate the distinctive characteristics of the urban Chinese film clubs under the specific historical and institutional conditions existing in contemporary Chinese society.[5]

Habermas's Concept of the Public Sphere

What does Habermas mean by the term "public sphere"? According to Habermas, public spheres "had a number of institutional criteria in common."[6]

> *First*, they preserved a kind of social intercourse that, far from pre-supposing the equality of status, disregarded status altogether. The tendency replaced the celebration of rank with a tact befitting equals. The parity on whose basis alone the authority of the better argument could assert itself against that of social hierarchy and in the end carry the day meant, in the thought of the day, the parity of "common humanity" ("bloss Menschliche"). *Les hommes*, private gentlemen, or *die Privatleute* made up the public not just in the sense that power and prestige of public office were held in suspense; economic dependencies also in principle had no influence. Laws of the market were suspended as were laws of the state.[7]

> *Secondly*, discussion within such a public presupposed the problematization of areas that until then had not been questioned.[8]

> *Thirdly*, the same process that converted culture into a commodity (and in this fashion constituted it as a culture that could become an object of discussion to begin with) established the public as in principle inclusive.[9]

In sum, Habermas defined the concept of public sphere with the three institutional criteria of (1) *disregard of status*, (2) *problematization of the status quo*, and (3) *inclusiveness*. In addition, implicit in the description of the first criterion above is that the public sphere exists (4) *outside the spheres of the state and the economy* ("Laws of the market were suspended as were laws of the state"). Moreover, as developed more fully in Habermas's later writings on his theory of communicative action, conversations that take place in the public sphere aim at creating (5) *consensus and agreement* rather than discord and disagreement through debate.[10]

I will refer to the above definition of the public sphere as I proceed to the empirical examination of film clubs in Beijing in the following sections.

Constellation of Film Clubs in Beijing and the Case of Studio Z

There exist a variety of film clubs in Beijing. Some of them use the term "film club" in their names (e.g., Film Club 8), while others use alternative names such as Studio Z.[11] I use the term "film clubs" generically here to refer to the wide-ranging types of entity that organize or host cultural and social activities related to documentary film.

My previous study has shown that there are at least four different types of film club in Beijing: (1) "politically oriented film clubs," (2) "commercially oriented film clubs," (3) "'art for art's sake' film clubs," and (4) "artistic, commercial film clubs."[12]

The first type, the "politically oriented film club," is characterized by its willingness to talk explicitly about politics and to aim at having direct social impacts beyond the confines of the world of film. As one of the core members of a well-known film club told me:

> We really had a clear sense of social responsibility ... We had cultural ideals, and we wanted our club to have social implications and social impact beyond the film world. We wanted to change something in society, and that was really the main purpose of our activity.[13]

Another frequent participant to the film club corroborated the point:

> They had a very high profile political orientation. Often the discussion was heated and touched on big issues like the future of Chinese society and politics as well as the role of film in that future.[14]

The second type of film club, the "commercially oriented film club," can be characterized by its direct connection between film-related activities and its economic function. For example, one notable "commercially oriented" film club charges 30 yuan (approximately US$4) for a film screening and a complimentary drink. The money generated by film screenings is an important source of income for the club.[15]

The third type of film club, the "'art for art's sake' film club," can be characterized by its focus on the screening and promotion of avant-garde, lesser-known film works such as short experimental documentaries produced by art school students. Many of the after screening Q & A sessions of one such club I attended leaned toward the issue of aesthetics rather than the politics or economics of films. The discussion often included such "art for art's sake" questions as "What is your theory of art?" and "How do you define beauty?"

The fourth type of film club, the "artistic, commercial film club," is characterized by its delicate, at times fragile, combination of commercial and "art for art's sake" orientation. On the one hand, its existence is supported by various forms of economic income obtained by charging fees for film-related activities including film screenings. On the other hand, with the economic resources secured by its commercial activities (such as sometimes even showing Hollywood blockbusters), it screens and promotes lesser-known films including a number of independently produced Chinese documentary films.

The constellation of different types of film clubs in Beijing constitutes what I have called the "field of cultural consumption."[16] They differentiate and interrelate to each other according to their internal organization (for example, how they are financed and their membership structure) and the different kinds of films they screen and discuss. Within the field of cultural consumption, I choose the "artistic, commercial film club," Studio Z, as the main focus of my empirical examination in this chapter as it is probably one of the most active, both in terms of frequency and diversity of the events it organizes related to Chinese film in general, and to documentary film in particular.[17]

The Case Study: Studio Z, an Artistic, Commercial Film Club

An artistic, commercial film club, Studio Z was established in the summer of 2002 by a group of recent graduates from Beijing University. The first documentary film event organized by Studio Z was a screening of Du Haibin's *Along the Railway Tracks* (2000) and a post-screening discussion with the director.

Almost all Studio Z activities are related to film, and the club commands the most variety as well as the highest frequency of screenings among all the film clubs. The number of participants varies significantly according to activities. For smaller screenings, it is twenty to thirty people, but for special occasions (such as the domestic premiere of Li Yang's 2003 fiction film *Blind Shaft*), a couple hundred may show up.

In a series called "Conversations with Film Directors," the club usually shows Chinese independent films, many of which are documentaries, and invites directors or other personnel involved for post-screening discussions. The club frequently sponsors lectures on filmmaking, with topics ranging from "How to Become a Film Producer" to "Lighting in DV Filmmaking," as well as academic talks by film scholars and critics. In the past couple of years, the club has begun to produce films, and some of their productions have been featured in international film festivals, illustrating their relatively high quality. More significantly, the club organizes what they call "film exhibitions" (*yingzhan*) and "film exchange weeks" (*dianying jiaoliuzhou*), which are de facto "film festivals" (*dianyingjie*) based on certain themes such as "documentary film" or "young directors' works."[18] "Film exhibitions" and "film exchange weeks" are the culmination of many of the regular activities described above. These special events usually include an opening ceremony, a banquet, and a forum for public discussion on certain themes, in addition to the screenings and post-screening discussions of individual film works.

In the rest of this chapter, I would like to zero in on one specific occasion I participated in and closely observed: a public symposium (*yantaohui*) held during the documentary "film exchange week" organized in the early summer of 2004, by Studio Z. I supplement my discussion in this section with observations and interviews I conducted outside of the symposium and the "film exchange week."

Figure 7.1.   A post-screening Q & A organized by a film club
(November 2003).

The Public Symposium at the Documentary Film Exchange Week Organized by Studio Z

The screening schedule for this film exchange week stretched for seven days, and a total of seventy documentary films, both Chinese and foreign, were on the program.[19] In addition to the film screenings, the film exchange week included an opening ceremony, at which five people, including documentary filmmakers, film critics, and film scholars, were invited to give short speeches, a well-attended banquet, and a symposium on documentary film. The main theme of the symposium was "The Creation and the Development of Chinese Documentary Film" (*Zhongguo jilupian de chuangzuo he fazhan*). The symposium lasted for about three hours with heated discussions, and was attended by more than sixty people. The participants were of very diverse backgrounds, from well-known documentary filmmakers to lesser-known filmmakers, film scholars, and film studies students, as well as interested citizens. At the beginning of the symposium, eight people, including documentary filmmakers, film critics, and film scholars, were invited as panelists to give brief presentations of their observations of the past, present, and future of the documentary film scene in China. After the initial presentations by the panelists, the floor was open to the audience to express their views. As one of the participants in the film exchange week stated proudly: "This event will be a platform for exchanges (*jiaoliu de pingtai*) for the documentary film world in China. More importantly, this kind of activity gives people a space for free exploration (*ziyou de tanfang kongjian*)." In one of the film club organizers' words, it provided a space for the "free exchange" (*ziyou de jiaoliu*) of opinions.

Indeed, both the panelists and the audience presented highly diverse, and sometimes contradictory views on the past, present, and future of Chinese documentaries. In fact, many of the issues that are considered to be crucial to documentary film studies in general were taken as topics of discussion and debate.[20] In addition, some issues that are of particular relevance to the historical and institutional conditions of Chinese documentary were discussed. In this section, I focus on five topic areas: (1) the history of Chinese documentary, (2) the distinction between objectivity and subjectivity, or non-fiction and fiction, (3) the relationship between filmmakers and audiences, (4) ethical issues pertaining to documentary filmmaking, and (5) the impact of the state and politics on Chinese documentary films.

(1) The History of Chinese Documentary

The first example of the diversity and heterogeneity of the views presented at the symposium in the film exchange week pertains to the general history of Chinese documentary film going back to the early twentieth century. During the discussion, one of the panelists presented his view of the history of Chinese documentary, which emphasized the relatively coherent development of the filmmaking practice going back to the state-socialist tradition of "newsreels" (*xinwen jilupian*). He gave a detailed "mini lecture" on the history of the Chinese documentary starting from the 1920s up to the present. In sum, he presented the participants with a clean, evolutionary history of the development of the Chinese documentary over the past one hundred years.

In addition, according to this person's presentation, the history of the development of the Chinese documentary has been a dialectical process between domestic development and foreign influence. He stated:

> In 1991, CCTV [China Central Television] organized an event called "New Documentary Exhibition" (*Xinjilupianzhan*) at the Beijing Broadcasting Institute (*Beijing guangbo xueyuan*).[21] Coincidentally, at about the same time in the U.S., [Amy] Taubin published an article in *The Village Voice* introducing new documentary films emerging in the U.S.[22] Also, in 1993 in *Film Quarterly*, [Linda] Williams published an article entitled "Truth, History, and the New Documentary."[23] Then in China in 1997, Lu Xinyu published an article called "Chinese TV Documentary Movement" (*Zhongguo dianshijilupian yundong*) and later coined the term "new documentary movement" (*xinjilu yundong*).[24]

In other words, according to his interpretation, new Chinese documentary films and filmmakers emerged on the scene as if following the global current of the emergence of new documentary filmmaking in the 1990s.

Suddenly, another panelist interrupted agitatedly: "I don't really understand. I disagree on many points." Then he presented his own understanding of the history of Chinese documentary as multi-causal, and at times accidental. He presented possible causes including the recent introduction of digital video (DV) technology, which individualized documentary filmmaking practice, as well as the newly emerging social issues in today's China and people's increasing awareness of those issues. According to this person, history is not something that can be outlined in a clear-cut manner, but is a messy process of accidents and serendipity. In addition, he emphasized that the development of recent Chinese documentary films was mostly the result of internal developments, relatively isolated from documentary filmmaking practices abroad. According to him, the recent emergence of documentary films in China was a fundamentally Chinese domestic phenomenon:

> Maybe some influence, for example, Wu Wenguang. He'd seen for sure Michelangelo Antonioni's *China* [1972], and he might have been influenced by the documentary filmmaking style of Japan's NHK [Nippon Hōsō Kyōkai]. But I can say with confidence he was not following the most recent Western documentary filmmaking practice.

Moreover, these disagreements detailed above concern not only the different interpretations of the history of the development of Chinese documentary, but also the difference between more academically oriented viewpoints emphasizing the knowledge of documentary film theory and practice in the West, and those grounded in Chinese documentary filmmaking practice. The person who emphasized domestic development emphatically stated:

> You surely know there's a book called *Documenting China*, and the author may have coined the term "new documentary movement." But she didn't start the movement.

Indeed, this person has guided many documentary filmmakers on the pragmatics of filmmaking rather than academic critique and interpretation. He is referred to by some as the "godfather" of Chinese documentary filmmaking.

In sum, both in terms of the character of historical development (linear evolutionary history versus accidental development; foreign influence versus domestic development) and the angle through which to describe the phenomena (academic versus pragmatic), highly contradictory views were presented.

(2) The Distinction between Objectivity and Subjectivity, or Non-Fiction and Fiction

The second example of the diversity of the views presented at the symposium is on the definition of documentary film as it relates to the distinction between objectivity and subjectivity or non-fiction and fiction. A panelist spoke up on the topic:

> I don't think we should have strict criteria for defining documentary films. I think we should throw away those criteria, or even throw away the concept of documentary film. "Document (*jilu*)," this phrase has the connotation of objectively recording or documenting something. But I don't think that's the only way we can conceive of documentary film. There are films which cast doubts on strictly distinguishing among the concepts such as objective and subjective, fiction and non-fiction. For example, I made a film about male prostitutes. In the film, real-life male prostitutes perform the roles of male prostitutes themselves using pseudonyms. They have many different roles to play. They actually act out their dreams and yearnings in real life. They also act out their ideals and dreams in the film.

In other words, this person is opposing the idea of rigidly defining documentary film with strict criteria, and doubts the meaningfulness of the simplistic distinction between objectivity and subjectivity, reality and fiction, or documentary and fiction films. In response to an idea presented by one of the panelists earlier in the symposium of choosing "One Hundred Best Documentary Films," this person goes on to say:

> Someone mentioned about selecting one hundred best documentary films. But this kind of idea is outrageous ... Film festivals like Yamagata, Marseilles, and Cinéma du Réel, they are more traditional. Some other festivals screen films that question

the clear distinction between documentary and fiction ... destroying the traditional concept of documentary. For example, the documentary film section of the Torino Film Festival explores newer conceptualizations of documentary film ... Wang Bing's *West of the Tracks* ... is now widely appreciated. But everyone should have his or her own criteria for deciding what's good. I think his film is very good. But I disagree with promoting very traditional ways of documentary filmmaking. For example, we should not say we should always focus on big social change, or big social problems. So, I don't like Yamagata Film Festival. They promote big stories. We shouldn't have strict rules for giving prizes. We shouldn't have rigid norms.

Then, another panelist interrupted to modify the view presented by the person above.

> You say Yamagata promotes big stories, but that may not always be the case. I've seen rather avant-garde documentary films from the festival. The films I saw question the clear distinction between "objective" and "subjective," or documentary and fiction.

Here, the important thing to note is not that one or the other view is correct, but rather, the fact that very diverse discourses on the very definition of documentary as well as the distinction between such concepts as objectivity and subjectivity, reality and fiction, were presented and debated *in public*.

(3) The Relationship between Filmmakers and Audiences

The third issue which emerged at the film exchange week was the relationship between documentary filmmakers and audiences.

A fissure that sometimes, if not always, exists in the space of consumption in the film clubs is the ambiguous relationship between the directors and the consumers of the films, that is, film club members. On one hand, many of the documentary filmmakers rely on the film clubs as the only domestic outlet for exhibiting their own films to the public. Indeed many of the now classic "new documentaries" had their Chinese premieres in those film clubs. In particular, given the fact that independently produced documentary films are not positively sanctioned by the government, film exchange weeks like the one I am focusing on here are truly rare opportunities for the filmmakers to exhibit their films side by side with those of other filmmakers. Some documentary filmmakers are members of the film clubs and some film club members make their own documentary films. However, the makers and the members do not always coincide and there are sometimes adversarial relations between the two. One example concerns how they manage the "copyright" of independently produced documentary films during the film screenings, including events like the one I participated in. As is well known, piracy of films is rampant in China, especially for Chinese and foreign commercial blockbusters. Although their films are not usually intended for large-scale commercial release, many of the documentary film directors who exhibit their films in the film clubs are concerned about how their film copies are managed. One documentary filmmaker expressed a feeling of disgust about one of the film clubs in Beijing.

> You know, I was really happy when they invited me for a screening of my work and for an opportunity to discuss my film with the audience. That was the first time the film was shown in China ... But later I found out that they were charging fees for people to get into the screening and discussion. They didn't tell me about this, and I wasn't paid a penny. I was mad. Worse still, it turns out that they made a copy of my film without my permission and are showing my film at other occasions like documentary film screenings they organize. In fact, they are showing my film in the documentary film event they are running right now without notifying me [this person is referring to the documentary exchange week I am discussing in this section]. And again, they are charging fees for people to get in. I'm really mad. At first, I thought those film clubs were genuinely interested in promoting documentary films. But I'm now disappointed with them. Not just this club, I heard other film clubs are the same. They just ask for a copy and never return it.[25]

As this example shows clearly, there is a potential divergence of interests between filmmakers and audiences at film clubs.

(4) Ethical Issues Pertaining to Documentary Filmmaking

The fourth issue that I noticed as I participated in and observed the discussions at the film clubs touches upon the ethics of documentary filmmaking. When I asked one of the participants in the documentary film exchange week what, if any, are the problems Chinese documentary is facing today, the person replied:

> There are some good films coming out of China. And there are some exceptional talents out there. But I'm not that optimistic. Just as an example, one problem Chinese filmmakers are facing is how to maintain an appropriate relationship with the subjects of our films. Because we are not very used to the concept of privacy, there seems to be a rising number of disputes between the filmmakers and the people who appear in the films. For example, I heard a female who appeared in a recent documentary film is not happy with the finished product. I heard she's trying to sue the director or something. Well, I'm not perfectly sure about the details, but there is a dispute for sure.[26]

This example shows that there is a potential conflict about how to represent reality as a finished product between the director and the people who appear in the films. Moreover, this issue points to the emerging ethical issue of the protection of the privacy of the people who appear in Chinese documentary films.

(5) The Impact of the State and Politics on Chinese Documentary Films

The fifth issue that emerged in the discourses presented by the film club members relates to the role of the state and politics in influencing documentary filmmaking practice in today's China.

At the symposium in the documentary film exchange week, one panelist presented his view that the state is encroaching on the development of documentary films in China. He mentioned a recently published government notice regarding DV film broadcasts, which requires both the broadcasting units and the filmmakers to report their broadcasting and filmmaking activities to the state authority.[27] According to the notice, filmmakers will be banned from film-related activities for three years if they violate the notice. He expressed a bit of angst:

> My personal view on those regulations is that it is like telling people to always use the crosswalk when you cross the street, and that you will be arrested and won't be allowed to cross the street for three years if you don't [the audience laughs]. It's also like arresting people who don't get off a bike while waiting for friends. If you wait for a friend and don't get off the bike, you will be arrested and banned from riding a bike for three years.

In other words, according to his view, the state is encroaching on the everyday lives of documentary filmmakers. For him, the involvement of the state is inhibiting the development of documentary filmmaking in China. The person continued:

> I admit that the effect of this DV regulation might not be as straightforward as it sounds. It's one thing to put this regulation on paper, but is quite another to implement it. But it definitely affects the dynamics of documentary filmmaking in China. Because, as filmmakers know very well, even if the regulation is not fully enforced, the existence of it creeps into your thinking when you make films. One thing for sure is that this kind of activity [the documentary film exchange week] will become more and more difficult to organize.

Then, another panelist partially countered his view. Although he is also negative about the possible interference by the state in documentary filmmaking, his view is more "pragmatic" than that of the other person who emphasized the encroaching power of the state. This person countered:

> If you are banned by the state from making films, why don't you become an actor? If you are banned from acting, why don't you become a cinematographer? My view is very different from yours. Although I respect your strong stand against the state, the state is not as capable as some people think. We still have lots of ways to develop Chinese documentary films in today's China. You only have to be just a little bit smart, to try to work around and find ways to make good films.

As can be elucidated by this exchange during the symposium, very different views on the role of the state and politics were presented by the participants *in public*.

Film Clubs as Public Sphere?

Now that I have examined in detail the case of Studio Z and its public symposium at the documentary film exchange week, let me go back to the five criteria of the "public sphere" in the ideal-typical Habermasian sense of the term, which can be characterized by (1) disregard of status, (2) problematization of the status quo, (3) inclusiveness, (4) existence outside the spheres of the state and the economy, and (5) consensus and agreement through debate. Again, the goal here is to elucidate the distinctive characteristics of the urban Chinese film clubs by closely comparing the Chinese case with Habermas's notion of the public sphere as an ideal type.

Figure 7.2.   A screening room at a film club (August 2003).

The first criterion of the "disregard of status" seems to hold on the surface. Film clubs include both younger and older participants and they discuss documentary films relatively freely in the film clubs. However, on a closer look, subtle differences exist between more academically oriented participants and participants who emphasize on-the-ground knowledge of filmmaking. Also, as we have seen, there can be an adversarial relation between audiences and filmmakers, who worry about how copyright is handled in those film clubs. In sum, a closer look reveals the subtle, yet strong differentiation in terms of status and corresponding views.

The third criterion of inclusiveness again, on the surface, seems to hold because most of the film clubs do not operate on a strict membership system and as a rule many, if not all, of the activities are open to the public. However, on closer examination, people who participate in those activities are relatively young, educated people with knowledge of documentary films. Thus, although film clubs do not exclude people from any particular social group, they clearly entail a mechanism of exclusion based on the knowledge of Chinese documentary films. In addition, almost no one who appears in documentary films — for example, laid-off workers in the case of Wang Bing's *West of the Tracks* — participates in the film club activities. Indeed, as I have mentioned in the case of a disagreement between a filmmaker and a woman who appears in the film, potential conflicts exist between the filmmakers and the people who appear in their films; this sometimes, if not always, works as one mechanism of exclusion of the subjects of films from the space of consumption. Thus, the empirical case of the film clubs departs from the third criterion of "inclusiveness."

The fourth criterion of existence outside the spheres of the state and the economy does not hold in the case of urban Chinese film clubs. Some of the activities of the film clubs are enabled both by the very existence and development of the state and the economy. For example, some of the film clubs base their film screening activities in museums and exhibition halls established by "cultural industry firms" at least partly owned and managed by the Ministry of Culture, which is the state administrative organization that oversees cultural activities. Recently, the ministry has been actively promoting the development of "cultural industries" (*wenhua chanye*) such as art, film, and music, and is participating in the industry directly or indirectly through establishing firms with various ownership and management structures.

Some film clubs are attached to commercial cafés and bars, which have emerged in the 1990s due to the development of the state's economic policy of marketization. Thus, film clubs exist not outside the spheres of the state and the economy, but enabled by the development of the state and the economy. Indeed, the film exchange week I examined was held in a museum established by the Ministry of Culture, and was run as a commercial activity based on ticket sales.[28] Therefore, the reality of film consumption in film clubs deviates from the fourth criterion of existence outside the spheres of the state and the economy.

As we have seen, very diverse views and discourses can appear even on a single occasion — the film exchange week and its symposium — organized by one film club. Thus, the reality of the urban Chinese film clubs deviates from the fifth criterion of the creation of "consensus and agreement through debate." As I have elaborated in the above section, the main motor of film consumption is not consensus, but discord, disagreement, and differentiation.[29]

In sum, my argument in this chapter is that the film clubs in contemporary urban China do not constitute a public sphere in the Habermasian ideal-typical sense of the term, as the empirical reality of the film clubs departs from at least four of the five institutional criteria for the existence of the public sphere. The only criterion that fits the case of today's world of Chinese documentary films is the second criterion on the "problematization of the status quo." This point requires further reflection.

From Public Sphere to Discourse: Michel Foucault's Notion of Discourse and Counter-Discourse

In this chapter, I contend that Habermas's second criterion of the public sphere, that is, "problematization of the status quo," captures the reality of Chinese film clubs. Moreover, I argue the criterion can elucidate the phenomenon of documentary film viewing by engaging it with the Foucauldian concept of discourse.

According to Stuart Hall:

> A discourse is a group of statements which provide a language for talking about — i.e., a way of representing — a particular kind of knowledge about a topic. When statements about a topic are made within a particular discourse, the discourse makes it possible to construct the topic in a certain way.[30]

One crucial point to remember is that discourse does not exist in isolation from other discourses. Rather, it always draws on the existence of other discourses and makes sense only in relation to other discourses. When the formerly voiceless begin to express their own understandings of a topic differently from the dominant discourse presented by the "authority," what Foucault called a "counter-discourse" emerges.

In a conversation with Gilles Deleuze, Foucault presents his conception of "counter-discourse" in relation to the prison system in France:

> And when the prisoners began to speak, they possessed an individual theory of prisons, the penal system, and justice. It is this form of discourse which ultimately matters, a discourse against power, the counter-discourse of prisoners and those we call delinquents — and not a theory *about* delinquency.[31]

In the case of this study, even if the film club members do not always intend to oppose the party-state authority, by constructing a topic in a certain way that is different from the dominant discourse presented by the government, the discourses enabled by the clubs can function as a "counter-discourse."

Two Kinds of Counter-Discourses Enabled by the Film Club Activities

As I touched upon earlier, the state attempts to construct the social phenomenon of documentary film in a particular way. For example, according to the "Notice on Strengthening the Management of the Broadcast of Digital Video Films in Film-TV Broadcasting Organizations and on Information Networks Such as the Internet" ("Guanyu jiaqiang yingshi bofang jigou he hulianwang deng xinxi wangluo bofang DV pian guanli de tongzhi," hereafter "Notice on DV Broadcast"):

> ... In recent years, with the spread of small digital video (DV) cameras, different types of DV films produced by some social organizations and individuals have already become one of the sources of audio-visual programs for TV stations and information networks. Among these films, the majority of the contents are healthy and beneficial, but there are some DV films whose topics are esoteric, that have negative contents, and some even send these types of DV films abroad to participate in competitions and exhibitions, and they are producing bad effects ...

> ... All DV works that deal with issues related to religion, the nationalities, and sensitive social problems should seek the opinions of the relevant authorities. Of those films, the ones that do not capture the issues precisely, or that may induce negative social influences, should not be broadcast.

Given the existence of such restrictions and censorship by the state on independently produced documentary films, the film clubs provide an important arena for watching films that are either not approved by the state or do not have commercial opportunities for distribution and exhibition because of their low-budget production.

Many documentary films that do not go through official approval for production, distribution, and exhibition have been shown to Chinese domestic audiences for the first time in film club activities like the film exchange week I have examined in detail here. Also, some of the low-budget documentary films (such as those made by students of film schools and art schools) that do not have any commercial opportunities for distribution and exhibition have been shown in these activities.

I contend that film clubs enable two kinds of counter-discourse that have important and real consequences in the transformation of state-society relations in contemporary urban China, in the particular sense that they and their activities problematize the status quo. First, by publicly showing and watching films that depict slices of social reality that the dominant authority such as the party-state is reluctant to acknowledge, they enable a counter-discourse — independently produced documentary films as discourse — through the provision of venues where the public actually gets to see these films in China. Second, by facilitating public discussion of the films and social issues surrounding the films, film clubs make possible the emergence of discourse *on* these independent documentary films. In sum, the film clubs and their activities enable two different orders of counter-discourse: (1) documentary films, as discourse, shown and viewed, and (2) discourses on documentary films.

Productive Power, Appropriation, and Resistance from Within

On the surface, the enablement of these two orders of discourse in film clubs, that is, the screening of documentary films and discussions on them, might seem like trivial matters. But in a society officially preserving political rule by the one party-state, making "public" a film, which is itself a discourse, as well as another order of discourse *on* the film and the issues surrounding the film, is significant. To highlight their importance, I introduce one episode during the documentary film exchange week I have examined here.

The documentary film exchange week was planned to run for seven days, but it was "stopped by the government" on the third day. The main organizer of the club called me that morning and told me that he had been informed by the curator of the venue where the event was being held that they could not continue with the screening. At that time, even the main organizer did not know exactly what had happened because it was not the case that someone from the government had come directly to him and told him to stop the activity. A couple of days later, the main organizer and I found out that it was more a case of self-censorship on the part of the venue rather than any explicit political action by the government. After the first day of screenings, when the curator and her boss found larger audiences than they had anticipated, as well as a great variety of films shown, they became afraid of trouble with the government. Especially because the event was held right after the SARFT (State Administration of Radio, Film, and Television) announced the "Notice on DV Broadcast," they became increasingly cautious. The result was a combination of subtle and indirect pressure from the government — the fact that the "Notice on DV Broadcast" had just been published — and self-censorship on the part of the people working with the film club.

Of interest here is that even after this self-censorship became known to the core organizers of the activity, many people who had attended the exhibition continued to stick to the discourse of "the Film Bureau closed down our activity." To know more about what actually happened in the process, when I interviewed one Film Bureau official on a different research topic, I asked what he thought about the recent publication of the "Notice on DV Broadcast."[32] He appeared to be taken by surprise and told me, "What is that notice? I'm not aware of the publication of that notice."

He asked a younger official who was sitting by us, and after finding out the details of the notice from him, he told me, "Oh, that notice wasn't published by us but by the higher General Administration." It turned out the notice was under the jurisdiction of SARFT, which manages all the media industries including radio, TV, film, and the internet rather than the traditional film bureaucracy exclusively centering on 16mm and 35mm films, which is governed by the Film Bureau, a subordinate division of SARFT. In sum, the "political trouble" the film club experienced was a complex combination of indirect political pressure and self-censorship. Moreover, while the Film Bureau was not directly involved in the process of "closing down" the film exchange week, a number of people, if not all, in the club still thought that the Film Bureau was involved in stopping the activity.

This episode clearly indicates the significance of the enablement of discourses through film club activities in a number of ways. First, as Foucault suggests, power can be "productive."[33] In his own words, "Where there is power, there is resistance, and yet, or rather consequently, this resistance is never in a position of exteriority in relation to power."[34] In other words, the existence of the "powerful" film bureaucracy made possible or produced the discourse that "the Film Bureau shut down our documentary film event," which adds to the film clubs' prestige in the world of audiences for documentary films.

Second, although the Chinese film bureaucracy is "powerful," it is not omnipotent. The fact that many of the participants in the film exchange week thought that the Film Bureau was directly involved in "shutting down" the event might first appear as a naïve misunderstanding or lack of knowledge on the part of the participants about the reality that the Film Bureau's main jurisdiction is over 35mm (and 16mm) films for theatrical release, and not over independently produced DV documentary films. However, on closer examination, the "Notice on DV Broadcast" explicitly mentions the "Film Management Regulations" (*Dianying guanli tiaoli*), which were published in 2002 and administered by the Film Bureau to manage the film industry based on 35mm (and 16mm) films, as one of the regulations to be followed by independent DV filmmakers because there are no comprehensive regulations on independent DV filmmaking comparable to the "Film Management Regulations." For example, the fifth clause of the "Notice on DV Broadcast" explicitly mentions (emphasis added):

> 5. When entering film theaters, popular broadcast media such as TV film channels, and *other public places*, and also *when participating in film festivals (or film exhibitions), etc. both in China and abroad, DV films shot with DV cameras* or film works that are converted to [35mm] films *should be administered by the "Film Management Regulations" and other related laws and regulations.*

Although this clause is also talking about relatively large-budget DV films or films converted from DV to 35mm for theatrical release, it can be read as simultaneously targeting independently produced DV films for relatively small-scale, non-commercial audiences, such as the film exchange week Studio Z was organizing. Hence it is not simply a misunderstanding, but an appropriation of the ambiguities and gaps in the government's ability to micro-manage and administer the rapidly developing world of independent DV filmmaking, including DV documentaries.[35]

Last but not least, this episode shows that independently produced documentary films are "independent" not because they are completely outside of the spheres of the state and the economy, as Habermas's fourth criterion of the public sphere would suggest, but because they engage with the influence emanating from the spheres of the state and the economy. As Foucault argues, "one is always 'inside' power, there is no escaping it, there is no absolute outside where it is concerned."[36]

To conclude, by utilizing Foucauldian notions of discourse and productive power, I have presented the consumption and audiences of documentary films as highly diverse, heterogeneous, and at times conflicting. At the same time, I have tried to show that although the film clubs deviate substantially from the Habermasian ideal type of public sphere, they contribute to an important social critique, or what Habermas himself has described as "the problematization of areas that until then had not been questioned."[37] In other words, the social practice of "watching documentary" in urban Chinese film clubs gives rise to critical public discourses in today's Chinese society.

8   Alternative Archive: China's Independent Documentary Culture

Chris Berry and Lisa Rofel *

In her historical analysis of China's New Documentary Movement in this volume, Lu Xinyu notes that the term "New Documentary Movement" first appeared in 1992, a little while after the first films began to appear. Wu Wenguang's *Bumming in Beijing: The Last Dreamers* (1990), analyzed in Bérénice Reynaud's chapter in this volume, is widely regarded as the first film of the movement. It was shot in 1989 and shown first in 1990. This places the origins of the movement between two crucial dates in Chinese history: 1989 and 1992. Nineteen eighty-nine is the year of the Tiananmen Democracy Movement and its suppression. Nineteen ninety-two is the date that Deng Xiaoping made his famous "Tour to the South," in the course of which he called for increased development of the market economy.[1]

What is the historical significance of these two events, and how has the configuration of power associated with them produced and shaped the New Documentary Movement? This chapter investigates the idea of "alternative" culture to capture the specificity of China's post-1989 culture and explore the New Documentary Movement as part of it. In this introduction, we further examine the stakes of naming post-1989 independent culture as "alternative." In the remainder of the chapter, we examine how alternativeness is manifested in the New Documentary Movement — in its themes, formal properties, spaces of production and viewing, and archiving characteristics.

The 1989/1992 conjuncture has produced a distinctive configuration of power in contemporary China. The year 1989 foreclosed upon the possibility of public and visible oppositional culture in the People's Republic of China.

* This research was made possible with a grant from the University of California Pacific Rim Research Program. We would also like to express our gratitude to all the filmmakers and others involved with the Chinese documentary scene, who were so helpful to us throughout.

The year 1992 foreclosed upon the possibility of a return to the singularity of a hegemonic ideology and command economy that characterized the People's Republic during the Mao era (1949–1976). These two fundamental forces distinguish the post-1989 era not only from the Maoist period, but also from the 1980s, when some anticipated that economic "opening up" might be accompanied by a transition to the liberal democratic culture of the West.

"Marketization" (*shichanghua*) and the rollback of the state have led to terms like "civil society" and "the public sphere" being applied to the contemporary Chinese context.[2] The applicability of these terms even to Western societies can be challenged. They are couched in discourses that define "freedom" to act and speak as absence of state power. This view ignores some crucial problems. First, the so-called "reduction" of state power fails to capture the way in which state power operates strongly in other realms, not the least of which is the market economy itself.[3] Second, the "freedoms" of civil society and the public sphere have not been available equally to all, as the struggles to extend the franchise to those without property, the illiterate, women, and others demonstrate.[4]

Even if we set aside these issues, "civil society" and "the public sphere" are unsuited to the contemporary Chinese context. They only capture the 1992 aspect of the 1989/1992 conjuncture. The same limitation applies to the widely used term "independent."[5] It captures the pluralism (*duoyuanhua*) that constitutes one crucial aspect of the contemporary Chinese condition. But it does not accommodate the foreclosure on a public, visible, and organized opposition that is the other side. In the language of the contemporary Chinese government, this prohibition of public opposition is the promotion of a "harmonious society" (*hexie shehui*). We suggest that the term "alternative" best captures the way in which the 1989/1992 conjuncture shapes the cultural and artistic practices that have developed outside the new state-corporate hegemonic culture of China today.

Some idea of the particular meaning of "alternative" in the contemporary Chinese context can be gleaned from the Alternative Archive website, which includes among its many connections and activities the two documentary films, *Sanyuanli* (2003) and *Meishi Street* (2006).[6] One of the co-founders of the site is Ou Ning, who also co-directed the films, which document urban change and its impact on ordinary citizens in Guangzhou and Beijing respectively. In a recent interview, he traced his interest in the general idea of building alternative archives back to the experience of researching a project on Chinese graphic design. What little historical material he could find was mostly state or government design work kept in state archives. This experience led him to believe in the importance of civilian or popular (*minjian*) collections and archives.[7]

The usual Chinese word for "alternative" is a neologism: *linglei*.[8] However, the Chinese title of the Alternative Archive site is "Bie Guan." This term translates literally as "side building." But, as Ou Ning explained, it is also a homophone or pun for a phrase meaning "don't bother me" or "leave me alone." When it was suggested to him that the term also implies that the alternative does not substitute for or exist in competition with the "main building," but simply grows alongside as something additional, he readily agreed.[9] This interpretation captures the way in which alternativeness can produce significant change but not through the route of direct opposition.

Themes

The themes of various Chinese documentary films readily exemplify their alternative quality. These films address topics that are ignored in official discourse, or marginalized politically because they do not "fit" with the hegemonic approach to post-Mao reforms, or they raise questions about the effects of those reforms on the subjects marginalized by them. These themes include lesbians and gay men, Tibetans, the disabled, the elderly, drug addicts, migrant workers, miners, the building of the Three Gorges Dam, poverty, farmer creativity in the face of adversity, and injured workers, to name just a few. These films further contribute to an alternative archive because even when they address themes that are discussed in public (urban) debates, such as urban renovation, they approach them through an angle that disrupts popular common sense about them.

The subject of people marginalized by the market economy induces a great deal of ambivalence in China, not merely on the part of the party-state, but in scholarly and popular discourses as well. With rural migrant workers for example, one finds reactions among urban residents that resonate with the debates about undocumented immigrants in the United States or the European Union. The residence permit system (*hukou*) established in the 1950s fixed everyone into a permanent residence.[10] In the 1980s market economy, an explosion of migrant workers, sometimes called "the floating population," made their appearance in China's large cities. They are hired to do the construction work that has radically reshaped urban landscapes, or as domestic servants for the urban bourgeoisie. They exist on the margins of urban life, because most of them are "illegal," but at the same time they are crucial to the urban mega-development that has characterized the eastern coastal economy.[11] Urban residents tend to portray these migrants as dirty, criminal, and responsible for social instability.[12] The government has an ambivalent response, for the Communist Party in its official rhetoric still represents itself as speaking for the underprivileged, but in its practical daily activity has the most intimate existence with the globalizing market that creates this underclass.

Li Hong's *Out of Phoenix Bridge* (1997) offers an ethnographic close-up of four migrant women. Her documentary contributes to an alternative archive because she films those who are "out of focus" in the neo-liberal era. They are marginalized not only by the economy and the government's abandonment but also by the current culture that lauds the elite. *Out of Phoenix Bridge* does not directly condemn the government but rather addresses a deeper issue of representational power. Thus Li indirectly counters Beijingers' attitudes by showing these migrant women's articulate critique of their own situation. Living with and filming these women in their one-room apartment for a year, Li uses *cinéma vérité* to show how these women speak back to Beijingers, the media, their landlady, the patriarchal forces in their villages, and even the local Beijing police.

The film opens with a claustrophobic view of four women crowded into what should really be called a one-room hovel, rather than an apartment, on the outskirts of Beijing. The young women recount their terror from their experience earlier in the evening when an unknown man easily entered their room, because their door has been broken for some time. The landlady then appears, only to deny any responsibility by telling the women they have overreacted. This opening scene condenses some of the film's themes: the women's insecure and dehumanizing living conditions and their precarious existence in the city. Li develops these themes by examining the women's arduous work situations and their trans-geographical travels between their home village, Phoenix Bridge, and the city. Li provides occasional voiceovers to mark her own transition from a typical Beijinger's ignorance to one of empathy. But most of the film is given over to the women themselves. "Even prisoners live better than us," comments one of them about the room's lack of heating in the dead cold of the Beijing winter. "Back home I thought Beijing was perfect. It really falls ten thousand miles short," says another.

Yet, this film is not gloomy, because these women, as Li portrays them, are determined and filled with dreams. Li uses a feminist perspective to emphasize that these migrant women are not merely pursuing narrow economic interests, as common stereotypes would have it, but are trying to escape an existence that, back home, is patriarchally defined. Thus, the camera lingers over conversations the women have at night about their mothers' fates, boyfriends, engagement, and marriage. Xiazi is one of the most articulate on these issues. She states categorically, "I'd be better off dead than to live like my mother. Once I said to myself, I'll kill myself if I have to live like her." At another moment, in answer to Li's question about why she wanted to come to Beijing, she responds: "It's so boring if all you ever do is get married and have kids."

Li allows the audience to hear other views less sympathetic to these women, and not only from urbanites like the landlady. She travels to Phoenix Bridge in Anhui Province, one of the poorest areas in China. She films Xiazi's stepfather angrily criticizing Xiazi for running away to Beijing because she wanted to break a marriage engagement he had arranged. Li then shifts back to Xiazi for her side of the story, which includes her preference for another young man whom her parents opposed. The film then cuts back to Phoenix Bridge, where we hear the men in Xiazi's stepfather's barbershop criticizing young women migrants for hoping to marry rich men in Beijing. The latter half of the film increasingly focuses on Xiazi, as she first moves back to her home village for another possible marriage engagement that falls through, then tries a local factory job, and finally decides to move back to Beijing. While back at her ostensible home, Xiazi comments, "I feel I've lost myself."

Figure 8.1. *Out of Phoenix Bridge*. Xiazi returns to the village.

If *Out of Phoenix Bridge* creates an alternative archive by filming subjects who make only intermittent appearances in public debates dominated by urban concerns, *Nostalgia* (2006), by Shu Haolun, addresses a topic that has fueled urban residents' anger for the last decade: the tearing down of old homes in urban centers to make way for more lucrative shopping malls, skyscrapers, and high-rise gated communities for the wealthy. What makes Shu's film, about the Shanghai neighborhood in which he grew up, thematically contribute to an alternative archive is his approach to this topic. The pervasive sentiment among urban residents focuses on local government corruption in turning what had been socialist guaranteed housing into profitable real estate, and on the unfair compensation to former residents. One finds newspaper articles on this topic on a nearly daily basis. Many people we know in China have been affected by this comprehensive razing of the old city centers and complain bitterly of their inability to challenge local officials' warlord-style power.

But *Nostalgia* contributes to an alternative archive by bringing forth the incipient, unspoken critique embedded in discourses of corruption. Shu calls into question the pervasive worship of modernization and profit-seeking that motivates the astonishingly rapid and absolute makeover of China's cities. Shu does so by reminding us that the razing of neighborhoods is not simply about just compensation but more importantly about the destruction of the intimate relationships that once sustained urban social space.

Figure 8.2.   *Nostalgia*. Shu Haolun videos in his childhood neighborhood.

Nostalgia opens with the filmmaker looking at photos of his childhood with his grandmother. Eighty years old at the time of the filming, his grandmother still lives in the *shikumen* home of Shanghai's Dazhongli neighborhood she moved into in the 1930s. (*Shikumen* are colonial-era tenement buildings specific to Shanghai.) Shu moves from filming his grandmother, to her close friends with whom she plays mahjong, to the other neighbors he grew up with: the man who moved into their home during the Cultural Revolution, the crazy woman who talks to herself, the man nicknamed "Tiptoe" because of his bad leg, who sweeps the neighborhood and keeps watch. Shu also points out the homes of his former classmates and childhood friends who have since moved away, as well as his elementary school that has disappeared, the high school about to be redeveloped, the corner grocery store fallen on hard times, and the local cinema torn down to accommodate an expressway. Shu not only figures throughout the film; he has child actors who re-enact his life as a child, in scenes filmed in black and white. Shu then films the skyscrapers that engulf his old neighborhood, but from a perspective down inside the neighborhood. This perspective creates the irony underlying an interview Shu conducts with a five-star hotel manager explaining how the guests love the view of these old homes and how he hopes these neighborhoods will be redeveloped as bars and cafés, like the wildly popular Xintiandi. The latter is a reconstructed *shikumen* neighborhood in which a Hong Kong developer kept the old exterior architecture, but inside are bars, cafés, restaurants, and boutiques, frequented mostly by foreign expats and tourists.

Shu is unapologetically nostalgic. He is nostalgic for a lost way of life, one in which the intimacies of a tightly knit neighborhood have died at the hands of what Shu calls the "iron monster" — the building crane he characterizes as running madly about the city. Shu is not directly critical of the government. Indeed, he lets the government have its say, by filming a banner hung across the homes of Dazhongli: "The new round of 'old town reconstruction' needs the residents' support and cooperation." But his framing of the banner against the "iron monster" is obviously ironic. Still, Shu seeks a deeper critique. He makes this critique most obvious near the end of his film, when he declares in a voiceover: "Do people truly worship these skyscrapers? I doubt it. Do the times really drive everyone to chase so-called fashion, pursue the so-called modern, and love the neon lights at night? I don't believe it." This critique is what makes the film alternative.

The alternative challenge of *Nostalgia* became clear in two showings of the film at university settings. The students loved the filmic innovations of mixing elements of a more conventional documentary with a memoir-like quality that put the filmmaker squarely in the film, along with black-and-white re-enactments. But there were two striking differences in the audience reactions. In the first showing, students vociferously challenged Shu's critique of modernization. They pointedly asked him if he wanted to halt progress and what he would suggest to replace it. Shu deftly responded to these queries by insisting that people should have the right not to be forced from their homes and that we should all ponder where this relentless "progress" is heading. In the second showing, however, the students showered praise on Shu for his critique. Perhaps the separation of one year had made a difference — as more stories of corruption surfaced, the Shanghai stock market took a plunge and China's economy experienced a downturn. In both showings, Shu made audiences confront a critique that implicated the government but also urban culture as a whole.

Form

The forces shaping China's alternative culture not only manifest themselves in themes not dealt with in the mainstream, but also in the formal properties of the documentaries in the New Documentary Movement. As the discussion in the essays collected in this volume attests, those formal properties are complex and have changed over time.

Initially, China's alternative documentary movement defined itself formally in contrast to the established practices of television documentary— the "special topic film" (*zhuantipian*) that took the form of an illustrated lecture. In reaction against that form, the makers of these new documentaries pursued a spontaneous on-the-spot realist style (*jishi zhuyi*). When they went overseas to attend film festivals in the mid-1990s, they were quickly drawn to the *cinéma vérité* tradition of filmmaking. Here, two tendencies were drawn upon. One was the fly-on-the-wall style of American Direct Cinema, which signified an emphasis on objectivity. The other form, in which filmmakers did not disguise their participation in the environment and even acted as provocateurs, is more associated with the French style of *cinéma vérité*. The arrival of the DV camera in the late 1990s made it easier for relatively untrained documentarians to pursue this style, and it also made it possible for filmmakers to act alone, as celebrated in Wu Wenguang's chapter on individual filmmaking and analyzed in Luke Robinson's chapter on "personal" films, both in this volume. Filmmakers became increasingly concerned to avoid exploiting their subjects and also increasingly conscious of the pitfalls of claiming objective recording of truth. In these circumstances, filmmakers also became increasingly present on-screen, making the documentary process more visible — and audible — to the audience, as discussed in Yomi Braester, Bérénice Reynaud, and Yiman Wang's chapters in this volume.

Throughout these various developments, the underlying structure of China's alternative culture has pushed its documentaries in two contrasting formal directions. On one hand, the drive to stand apart from the mainstream has led to forms different from those of both the old socialist *zhuantipian* and the more ratings-driven style of contemporary television. Although Chinese television remains state-owned, today it is funded through advertising. Therefore, it has also been eager to differentiate itself from the lifeless lecturing of the *zhuantipian*. It has crafted this distinction partly by adopting many of the signifiers of spontaneity found in New Documentary Movement films, such as hand-held camerawork, people walking in and out of the frame, partial shadows, and stumbling delivery in interviews. However, like the old *zhuantipian*, it continues to deploy voiceover narration that directs the audience's interpretation of what is seen and heard.[13] This tendency to anchor and limit meanings is avoided by the alternative documentaries, whether or not they use narration. On the other hand, foreclosure on explicit opposition leads the alternative documentaries to avoid any direct criticism of the state. The more sensitive the subject matter to the state, the more likely they are to pursue formal qualities that maximize ambivalence and reticence in regard to judgment. Again, one way in which this reticence is commonly manifested is the avoidance or minimization of voiceover narration that interprets the recorded materials shown in the film, as in *Out of Phoenix Bridge*.

To further demonstrate these formal qualities, we will examine two main examples: Duan Jinchuan's 1996 film *No. 16 Barkhor South Street* and Ou Ning's 2006 film *Meishi Street*. Both cover potentially controversial topics: Tibet and urban redevelopment, respectively. But their formal qualities are quite different. The earlier *No. 16 Barkhor South Street* is a strict example of Direct Cinema that eschews all narration and favors a fly-on-the wall style. In *Meishi Street* the camera is handed over to local resident Zhang Jinli, who records not only the demolition process but also to-camera monologues. However, in both cases the filmmakers avoid displaying any judgment.

No. 16 Barkhor South Street was made after Duan and other pioneering Chinese alternative documentary filmmakers had begun attending international film festivals. As Wu Wenguang recounts in his chapter here, they had been impressed by, among others, the works of Frederick Wiseman. Wiseman is a key exponent of the Direct Cinema style. But instead of following the stories of individuals or events (like elections and rock festivals), Wiseman's focus is usually on social institutions, such as schools and hospitals, conveying his insights through a series of autonomous scenes documenting various kinds of activities and interactions. Bill Nichols has called the combination of these scenes into a meaningful whole a "mosaic" structure.[14] Duan adopted this model for *No. 16 Barkhor South Street*, which was part of a Tibetan trilogy.

No. 16 Barkhor Street South is the address of the courtyard building accommodating the local neighborhood committee offices, as well as those of the local police station and the local party committee. The film alternates between scenes of several minutes' duration set in the offices and shorter montages of street scenes or single shots set in the courtyard of the building. The montages and courtyard shots are used to transition between office scenes. The first and last office scenes are meetings, in which party officials give speeches about the importance of security and order to local residents in anticipation of New Year celebrations and celebrations marking the thirtieth anniversary of the establishment of the Tibetan Autonomous Region. Although this description implies a chronological order from early in the year to September, there is no way of knowing in which order most of the scenes were actually shot, because there is no evident connection between them. This autonomy of scenes is typical of the mosaic structure.

In between the meetings that bookend the film, we see scenes of local officers doing hospital accounts; mediating disputes amongst residents; interrogating suspected criminals; distributing monthly pay to other officers; giving reading lessons and lessons on party history; dealing with distribution of flat-bed tricycles intended to enable the local Tibetan poor to make a living; and making decisions about party membership. Clearly, this film is characterized by alternative subject matter. It is doubtful if any previous film made in China about Tibet has had such direct access to government offices at work or been able to observe ordinary Tibetans in this manner. The use of Tibetan language throughout, except in scenes involving native Mandarin speakers, comes as a surprise to viewers used to Mandarin voiceover in Chinese films about Tibet.

The editing is also alternative. Throughout, in a manner also reminiscent of Wiseman's technique, individual scenes are edited to create the impression of continuity, although they also cut back and forth between speakers and listeners. Unless the filmmakers had multiple cameras, the "reaction" shots were almost certainly recorded later and then the sound from the speakers laid over it. This technique probably also covers ellipses, when the filmmakers have chosen to jump forward from one moment of speech to another. Throughout, there is no narration, mood music, or other intervention. This last quality makes the film not only totally different from the pedagogical *zhuantipian* but also completely different from mainstream television today.

This lack of anchoring the meaning, when combined with the editing, leaves the interpretation of what is shown in *No. 16 Barkhor South Street* very open to the audience. The film cuts back and forth between speakers or teachers and listeners or pupils in meetings and lessons. Some viewers will see the listeners' and pupils' silence and neutral facial expressions as evidence of attentiveness and discipline, whereas others will see them as signs of sullen boredom. This kind of ambivalence runs throughout the film. When we see that a thief has to sign a document with her thumb print, will this gesture confirm for some the impression that Tibet is "backward"? Who will perceive the interrogation as lenient and who will perceive it as evidence of repression? When we see that the local officials are themselves Tibetan, will viewers think this fact means most Tibetans accept that Tibet is part of China and have self-determination, or that some Tibetans are collaborators with the occupying powers?

More recently, Duan Jinchuan has moved away from the Direct Cinema approach. Along with many others in the New Documentary Movement, he has become more interested in closer contact with his subjects, and the adoption of an interview-based form reflects this goal in *The Secret of My Success*, his 2002 film about the processes of local government and local democracy in a village in northeast China. Here again, however, the interpretation of what the interviews reveal is left up to the viewer. The absence of voiceover makes the film different from mainstream documentary and also avoids directing the viewer to any critical interpretation. Where some will see corruption and confirmation of the fraudulence of village democracy, others will see the difficulties of instituting democracy where no one is used to it.

Another filmmaker whose work has followed a similar trajectory away from purely observational forms is Ou Ning. Together with his colleagues in the U-thèque organization based in Guangzhou, Ou made a city documentary in 2003 called *Sanyuanli*. Explicitly modeled on early twentieth-century films like Walter Ruttmann's *Berlin, Symphony of a City* (1927) and Dziga Vertov's *Man with a Movie Camera* (1929), it is set in a section of Guangzhou and documents urban change. Although also observational, the film is formally different from Duan's Wiseman-inspired Tibetan trilogy. Instead of Direct Cinema, it is based on fast-paced montages with music overlaid and no dialogue. However, this approach is also shaped by the drive for difference from mainstream documentary form and avoidance of any direct criticism of the authorities. Although the film may be understood by some viewers to show undesirable developments in Sanyuanli, the film does not direct an interpretation that lays responsibility for them at anyone's door.[15]

More recently, Ou and his colleagues have turned to documenting urban change in Beijing in *Meishi Street*, which is also part of a larger project of documentation detailed at their Alternative Archive website. But this time, like Duan, their filmic form communicates closer connections to their subjects. However, where Duan turns to the interview form, Ou and his colleagues literally turn their camera over to one of their subjects. Otherwise, they continue with the observational form, although they use more titles identifying places and people than Duan does in his Tibetan trilogy. Zhang Jinli, the main subject of their film, lives on Meishi Street, after which the film is named. As part of the redevelopment of the Dazhalan district of the city, the street is to be widened and Zhang's "Jinli Restaurant" is to be demolished. As the discussion of Shu Haolun's *Nostalgia* above indicates, ordinary inner-city residents all over China have found themselves caught in similar circumstances, because marketization has suddenly made the land under their feet commercially valuable.

Zhang is a *dingzihu*. Literally translated, this term means "nail household" and refers to those who refuse to move. It was the Chinese title of one of the earliest independent documentaries on the phenomenon, Zhang Yuan's 1997 film, which is variously translated as *Last House Standing*, *Demolition and Rehousing*, and *Hanging on to the End*. Some believe these people just want more compensation, while others think they really do not want to leave at all. This ambiguity surrounded the family Zhang Yuan followed for his film, and it also surrounds Zhang Jinli. On one hand, the notices plastered all over his restaurant invite developers to negotiate compensation with him. But on the other, when the restaurant is forcibly demolished at the end of the film he is in tears.

What makes *Meishi Street* different from the other films about urban redevelopment (as well as from mainstream television coverage) is the handing of the camera over to Zhang himself. About ten minutes into the film, a title appears: "October 12, Taoranting Park. Zhang Jinli uses the digital video camera we gave him for the first time." We see a shot of the park, presumably filmed by Zhang. From then on, material filmed by Ou and his colleagues is mixed in with material filmed by Zhang. At first, the camera is an unfamiliar thing to him. Presumably associating it with entertainment, he sets it up to perform his exercises in front of or to sing to. But it soon becomes a tool with which he can record what he perceives as the outrages perpetrated by the authorities, a companion he can confide his anxieties and grievances to alone in the night or early morning, and an excuse to talk to his neighbors and attempt to mobilize them.

At the same time as this filming strategy distinguishes *Meishi Street* formally from the mainstream, it also creates strategic ambiguity about the filmmakers' position. First, it is not always clear which shots have been filmed by Zhang and which by Ou and his colleagues. This uncertainty is because Ou and his colleagues film in the observational mode and there is no direct interaction between them and Zhang included in the film. When we see Zhang in his kitchen, has he set the camera up or are they there filming him? This lack of a clear distinction about who is behind the camera suggests a certain shared enterprise. On the other hand, while Zhang is unstinting in his accusations of corruption and illegal procedures directed against the developers and the local authorities, the filmmakers' own reticence leaves it unclear whether they support him and he is their mouthpiece or whether they are more neutral. (Many of Ou Ning's comments and essays at his blog and elsewhere suggest the former, but this viewpoint is not evident in the film itself.)

Furthermore, Zhang Jinli's use of the camera creates a self-reflexive dimension to the film that speaks to the entire documenting process and its role in the construction and negotiation of public space. The use of writing as a part of the contestation of public space is clear from the beginning of the film, as Zhang and his neighbors post their protests on their houses for all to see. The local authorities counter these posters by stringing banners proclaiming the fairness and benefits of redevelopment across the road, and sometimes by tearing down the residents' posters. In the People's Republic, sticking up "big character posters" (*dazibao*) was a legitimate form of public expression throughout events such as the Cultural Revolution and right up until the wake of the 1978 Democracy Wall movement in Beijing, when the constitutional right codified in 1975 was reversed in a measure to control such activities.[16] Indeed, Zhang invokes a certain nostalgia for those old revolutionary days, not only by singing songs from the Maoist era, but also by sticking up posters with pictures of Mao. These posters either take the form of petitions to Mao or mock quotations from him, stating that people must be properly compensated and their rights must be protected. With these actions and also flying the national flag, Zhang contests the legitimacy of the authorities and the developers to the legacy of the revolution and the authority of the state.

Figure 8.3. *Meishi Street*. A local policeman responds to being videoed by Zhang Jinli.

In the final stages of the film, this struggle of the posters and banners extends to encompass film and photography. We see one of Zhang's holdout neighbors not only putting up protest posters on her house before it is pulled down, but also taking pictures of the posters. In the final demolition of Zhang's house, not only are Ou and his colleagues recording the process, but at least two representatives from the police and the local authorities are also recording it. When the house comes down, Zhang has his camera as well. But he is too upset to record, and as Ou and his colleagues film Zhang's tears, the screen goes to black, and the noise of the demolition crashes over the closing credits. This ending communicates very clearly the reticence of Ou and his colleagues and their formal difference from mainstream documentary, as they continue to make no comment. But it also dramatizes the official and alternative archiving processes themselves. We see the police and the authorities focus their cameras on their own procedures, filming the reading out of the order to demolish to Zhang so that they have a record to show that they have done the right thing. Meanwhile, Ou and his colleagues are more concerned with Zhang's reactions and feelings, which would otherwise remain unrecorded because they are of no interest to the official archive.

The formal innovation of turning the subjects of the documentary into documentarians themselves is by no means confined to *Meishi Street*, but is in fact one of the main characteristics of the New Documentary Movement, especially after the arrival of the DV camera. As Yiman Wang has discussed, this relatively easy-to-use technology is closely tied to the conscious espousal of an amateur aesthetic in Chinese documentary and the involvement of growing numbers of professionals outside the media industries in the movement.[17] Another excellent example of this amateur aesthetic is Zheng Dasheng's *DV China* (2003). This documentary follows a citizen of Jingdazhen who buys a video camera and mobilizes his fellow residents to make dramatic videos — which he calls "TV series" — in a variety of popular genre forms ranging from martial arts to revolutionary dramas. Other examples include Hu Xinyu's *The Man* (2003) and Zuo Yixiao's *Losing* (2005), discussed in detail in Luke Robinson's chapter in this volume.

Spaces of Production and Viewing

The spaces in which documentaries as well as non-commercial drama films are shown in China vary a great deal, from neighborhoods that glitter with the lights of the nearby elite shopping malls to areas that are "edgy" and just in transition to commercialized art/café spaces, from university campuses to former farmer villages being absorbed into the urban municipality. What these distinctive venues have in common is their commitment to showing films that are "alternative." The individuals or groups who run these venues differ in their understanding of that term, but all of them place that notion as in conflict with both commercial and governmental pressures and constraints. Their very commitment to these types of films makes the locations of their viewing unstable, not merely because of government disapproval but more importantly because government officials, in seeking profit through real estate, require these film groups to make way for the commercialization of their venues. This commitment signals these venues' contribution to an alternative archive, for their activities do not include direct critiques of political or economic power but rather deeper critiques of the ideologies and values that subtend this power.

A comparison of four different venues in Beijing in 2004, at the time we undertook our fieldwork, is instructive. First, the Cherry Lane Theater. Cherry Lane was located near the Lufthansa Center at the time we visited it in 2004. (It has since moved.) The Lufthansa Center is an expensive shopping mall that caters to foreigners and wealthy Chinese. Cherry Lane also caters to foreigners but enables Chinese to come and view films they might otherwise have difficulty seeing. Cherry Lane is, however, not quite in the thick of things. It is located in a fairly discreet spot on a side street. The inside of the building is stark. It has an enclosed feeling, as the building is without windows and it is impossible to see inside the building if one is standing outside. This venue does not have elaborate design or decoration. It does not have any kind of "hip look" with any particular design statement. Tickets cost 50 yuan (roughly US$6) at the time we visited the theater in 2004. This fee is steep for students and workers, yet there were nearly equal numbers of Chinese and foreigners in the audience. The films all have subtitles in English. Cherry Lane clearly mixes more mainstream Chinese films with others. The night we visited they showed Zhang Yimou's *House of Flying Daggers* (2004), his second epic martial arts film. But its seemingly harmless appearance as a venue for non-Chinese-speaking foreigners also allows them to show films such as Wu Wenguang's *Bumming in Beijing*. While we did not have the opportunity to interview the managers of the venue, it is clear that this space has begun to create a transnational dialogue between China and the West about other ways to view China.

The 22filmcafé is in stark contrast to Cherry Lane. This café is located in the old center of the city, along the path by the artificial lakes built to the west side of the former Imperial Palace grounds, now the seat of the communist party-state, Zhongnanhai. Though seemingly geographically central, in fact the curving path signals an area in transition, from one that used to house industrial equipment to a commercial space. 22filmcafé has three large open windows that patrons can step through to enter, as well as a regular door opening. Its inside is completely open to the outside, so that passersby can view everything inside the café. The café shows films but also has art exhibits. The films, sometimes with English subtitles, are projected onto the back wall. Audiences are a mixture of Chinese and foreigners, with the majority Chinese. There is no fee to watch the films.

Seven young people are involved in running the café, though two are responsible for the film showings. They were all classmates at the Beijing Film Academy. Their goal, as they explained to us, is to encourage everyone to take up a camera in order to make better films in China. For Li, one of the young managers, the café is an alternative space because it tries to support films that are "true" to the filmmakers' own vision, not something dictated by anyone else or by the government. For them, film has become more popular than music for expressing social problems, in part thanks to the practice of copying DVDs. This space is alternative because it wants to encourage a culture of film viewing among Chinese audiences that will develop modes of social critique. It is decidedly focused on domestic audiences, not worrying about how foreigners might view China.

A third venue, Hart Salon, differs yet again from the 22filmcafé and Cherry Lane. At the time we visited, Hart Salon was located in another area frequented by foreigners, the Sanlitun area on the east side of Beijing. (Their building has since been torn down.) In contrast with the Lufthansa Center, this area is young and energetic and has foreigners from all over the world, including Africa and Spanish-speaking countries as well as Europe and the United States. Hart Salon is in a tiny venue, though the space on the second floor for film showings held about fifty people. Tickets cost 30 yuan. What makes this space alternative are the kinds of cultural identifications the husband and wife team who run the Hart Salon wish to foster. As they explained to us, they have two goals. First, they hope to capture "Chinese" culture as opposed to "Western" culture. They want young Chinese people to feel a sense of identification with their own culture. Second, they hope to create south-south transnational networks, through film but also art exhibits and performance art. They have held exhibitions of Mexican art, and art from other Asian countries, not just Korea and Japan but also Southeast Asia. Their goal is to encourage Chinese people to learn about other places besides the United States, especially places in Asia. The wife expressed concern about what she saw as a trend among young people — that they know more about the United States than about China.

Finally, Wu Wenguang has a filmmaking center in Caochangdi, in a farmer village on the northern edge of Beijing that is transitioning into the Beijing municipality. The center is large, with living spaces, editing rooms, offices, and a central area for audience viewing. Wu Wenguang has dedicated this center to teaching rural residents to take up a camera and film their lives. He began this project in 2003, when the European Union offered him and several other filmmakers a grant to film the process of village democracy. Wu Wenguang decided that rather than film these villagers himself, he would teach residents how to film their own villages. Since then, he has instituted a yearly workshop in which young rural residents come to live at this center for two weeks and study filmmaking. They merely pay for the bus or train fee; Wu Wenguang houses and feeds them. Film students from Beijing also come to participate, together with those from the countryside. Its two main features are what make this center alternative. First, putting the camera into the hands of rural residents means not merely teaching them technical methods but encouraging them to think reflexively about their everyday lives and figure out a creative way to comment on them. In other words, film as social critique, not of the "larger" political structures but of the very materiality of quotidian lives that are shaped by those structures. Second, as discussed above, one of the most obvious social divisions in China is that between urban and rural residents. Wu's center self-consciously tries to bridge that division. His goal is not so much to have those from the countryside learn how to mimic urbanites. Rather he is trying to teach urban youth how to respect the intelligence of rural residents and how to understand the circumstances of their lives.

In sum, these spaces vary in what makes them "alternative." Some want to create alternative transnational networks while others focus on domestic alternatives. Since 2004, some have closed, others have moved, and new spaces have opened up. But the patterns we have laid out here in these specific examples persist.

The Archive

The discussion in the previous section of the places where alternative documentary can be seen makes it clear that alternative documentary cinema remains very much a minority and intellectual pursuit. Because these films are available to a very small number of people in China, many others dismiss the phenomenon when asked about it. They may be correct to worry that Western academic focus on alternative documentary might create misapprehension outside China about its immediate social impact. But this dismissal also judges alternative documentary by the standards of the mass market, where significance is determined by the number of tickets or DVDs sold and media exposure. Since these films are deliberately produced and circulated on the edges of or even outside the market system, such standards are inappropriate.

Furthermore, one of the motivations for the production of these materials is archival. The intention is not only to record events and give voice to people normally overlooked in the mainstream official and commercial media, it is also to create a store of these materials for the future. In the introduction to this chapter, we noted Ou Ning's belief in the need for a popular archive as a response to his experiences working on the history of design in China. In her chapter about the history of the New Documentary Movement in this book, Lu Xinyu makes a more general observation that distrust of the official record had already inspired a desire for a popular or civilian process of documentation by the late 1980s.

As our discussion so far has already indicated, almost all the films in the New Documentary Movement constitute original contributions to an alternative archive of topics, voices, and perspectives. In this final section, we will examine the archiving function of the New Documentary Movement further with reference to a genre within the movement that we have not discussed so far — the oral history film. This topic is a particularly sensitive one, and it tests the limits of alternativeness. This is not because the films themselves are explicitly oppositional. Rather, it is because history within living memory is the history of the revolution and of the People's Republic itself.

An indication of just how sensitive recent history is could be gained from watching the opening ceremony of the 2008 Beijing Olympic Games. Choreographed by blockbuster director Zhang Yimou, a large part of the event was given over to a tour through Chinese history. Noticeably absent was all of China's revolutionary history, from the struggles with the Kuomintang and the Japanese through to 1949 and onwards. For those used to the almost liturgical recitation of such glorious events on similar occasions, this lacuna may have come as a surprise. But it demonstrates how difficult it is to narrate a version of recent history acceptable to everyone. Events the mainland authorities deem successful may be seen as disasters by others. In these circumstances, the mere recording of popular oral history is likely to be seen as a challenge, making this an area where the space of the alternative is almost squeezed out of existence.

Two of the earliest alternative documentaries that are more or less impossible to find today are oral histories. This difficulty suggests that even those people who have copies in China may not want to circulate them because they sense danger. The films are Shi Jian and Chen Jue's *I Graduated!* (1992) and Wu Wenguang's rarely seen *1966, My Time in the Red Guards* (1993). The first film, made with a camera shown being smuggled onto Beijing University campus, interviews the survivors from the Tiananmen 1989 generation on their graduation. The second interviews members of Wu's own generation about their Red Guard experiences in the early years of the Cultural Revolution decade (1966–1976). Given the taboo nature of the 1989 events, it is not surprising that the first film is elusive.[18] But the situation with the Cultural Revolution is more complex. In the late 1970s, after Mao's death and the arrest of the Gang of Four, "errors" were acknowledged. The extent of these errors spread until they covered the entire decade. However, after a few years of "scar" literature and films, in 1981 it was decided that the matter had been dealt with and there was no need to delve into it any further.[19]

More recently, some of China's alternative documentary filmmakers — perhaps aware that the generations who can remember revolutionary history are passing — have begun to make oral history films again. For example, Wang Bing has recently made his follow-up to *West of the Tracks* (2003) as an oral history film. In *Fengming: A Chinese Memoir* (2007), the former Rightist He Fengming gives her testimony direct to camera with almost no cuts, and for nearly three hours. She explicitly compares the Anti-Rightist camps to the concentration camps of the Soviet Union and Nazi Germany. However, she has already published a book on the topic, making the film less risky — although no less powerful — than it might seem. Furthermore, Wang confines himself to witnessing her testimony, taking advantage of a rare pause for breath to ask her if he can turn the lights on in her apartment because dusk has fallen as she has spoken.

Another example is Duan Jinchuan and Jiang Yue's 2007 film *The Storm*. They return to the village in the northeast used as the basis for the famous Land Reform novel and film of the same title in the 1950s and interview survivors from the period. This is one of the few episodes of post-revolutionary history that remain heroic, but the testimony suggests a more complex era that was at least as much a reign of terror as a liberation. So far, concerned that foreigners know little about the era and that the topic is too sensitive, they have only shown it in venues like university classrooms.

However, the primary example we will talk about here is Hu Jie and his 2006 film *Though I Am Gone*, also known as *Though I Was Dead*.[20] Hu Jie screened the film in March of 2007 in Hong Kong at various community and academic venues. The Hong Kong International Film Festival was happening at the same time, but the film was not included. When asked about this, Hu acknowledged that he felt it wise to avoid high profile events.[21] Soon after, the inclusion of the film in the schedule for the 2007 Yunnan documentary film festival — itself an alternative event — was commonly believed to have triggered government intervention and the closing of the event.[22]

Though I Am Gone is about an early victim of the Cultural Revolution, Bian Zhongyun. Bian was the vice-principal of the girls' middle school attached to Beijing Normal University, and she was beaten so badly by her students that she had to be taken to hospital, where she died. Her husband Wang Jingyao has kept everything he can from those times, including the tracts she was carrying in her book bag, her watch, her ID card, and her bloodied clothes. Although the film includes interviews with others, his testimony forms its spine. Wang names his wife's attackers and tells how his efforts to bring a case against one of them after the end of the Cultural Revolution were blocked, on the grounds that it was beyond the statute of limitations. Wang also states that the school was a "royal school" attended by many students closely connected to the highest echelons of the party and state apparatus. The implication is that justice has not been done because of party connections, but the statement comes from Wang, not from the filmmaker.

In addition to recording Wang, Hu's film also foregrounds the very idea of archiving and testimony. Even before the title of the film appears, the first shot is a close-up of Wang Jingyao's Seagull-brand camera, which we later find out he used to take photographs of his wife's body the day after she died. The year of the film's production, 2006, is the fortieth anniversary of the outbreak of the Cultural Revolution and of his wife's death. Wang says he has been carrying a cross since then and that he feels it is his responsibility to reveal what happened. The film draws attention to the connection between the archiving of all documents from photographs to bloodstained clothes and the convincing revelation of truth.

Hu's editing of the film and his dual focus on Wang Jingyao's documentation process almost as much as what he has documented suggest a strong sense of affinity with Wang. Indeed, *Though I Am Gone* is not his first documentary using oral history to challenge official accounts. Hu started making documentaries in the mid-1990s in much the same way as others, documenting the stories of marginal peoples and events not shown in mainstream media. But between 1999 and 2004 he completed a film about Lin Zhao. Lin was a student arrested in the 1950s because of some poems she had written. She continued to write poems in jail using her own blood, and later she was executed. According to Hu, his interest in this story caused him to lose his job at the Xinhua News Agency, even before he had begun to make *Looking for Lin Zhao's Soul*. However, he has persisted in making these films about history that the authorities do not like. He says, "Because the Chinese official authority does not want us to remember the history, we non-official people should remember on our own."[23]

This statement is a fitting point at which to end our analysis of China's New Documentary Movement as an alternative culture, for it raises again the relationship of the alternative to the mainstream. Is the supplement merely an added extra, or does it reflect back upon and change the mainstream? No doubt different directors have different motivations for pursuing the alternative, and Hu Jie's position is only one among many.

Part IV

Between Filmmaker and Subject:
Re-creating Realism

9 Translating the Unspeakable: On-Screen and Off-Screen Voices in Wu Wenguang's Documentary Work

Bérénice Reynaud

New Chinese Documentaries have been lauded often enough for "giving the floor" to the subjects of their investigation — allowing them to speak to the camera, in their own words and with their own voices — that such a point has become trivial. What is interesting, on the contrary, in Wu Wenguang's work, is that from the onset, it opens up the possibility of a split between subjects and language; it casts a doubt not only on the nature of the message of the so-called "communication" but also on the identity of the speaker.

For Pascal Bonitzer, what constitutes modern cinema is the "simultaneous questioning of the status of the classical image as a full, centered, deep image and of the use of the voice as homogeneous and in harmony with the image. What is at stake in cinematic modernity, is ... as it has often been said, the effects of rupture, overlapping, the 'noises' of the filmic chain, where a tearing apart of the effect of reality of the filmic image, the effect of mastery of the voice can take place. The relationship between voice, sound, and silence is transformed, becomes musical."[1]

In this chapter, I examine Wu Wenguang's explorations of the aural and his use of it in ways that challenge ontologically and ethically not only the seemingly self-evident veracity of "seeing is believing" that is the foundation of documentary cinema but also the distinctions between self and other, and filmmaker and the filmed that are equally crucial to it. My primary focus is on his first film, *Bumming in Beijing: The Last Dreamers* (1990) and the last film he completed before the writing of this text, *Fuck Cinema* (2005).

"The Sound of Your Own Voice"

In August 1988, Wu Wenguang started working on *Bumming in Beijing* — a piece often described as marking the birth of the New Documentary Movement. A "transitional" work, *Bumming in Beijing* started when Wu was still a television employee — he worked for Kunming Television Station, then for China Central

Television (CCTV) between 1985 and 1989 — and sparked his career as an independent videomaker. It also spans the months preceding, as well as those following, the June Fourth crackdown. *Bumming in Beijing* has become a "classic," a beloved work bringing to mind the bohemian milieu of the late 1980s and early 1990s in Beijing. Much has been written on its cultural and historical importance. Here I want to emphasize a specific aspect of its radicalness: its treatment of the sound, in particular of the voice. While making allusions to other works, I will mostly compare it to what may be Wu's second most controversial video, *Fuck Cinema*.

In its original, 150-minute version, *Bumming in Beijing* is organized into a series of chapters that appear as titles in Chinese and English: "Why come to Beijing?," "Accommodation," and "Lifestyles and Dream." The opening sequence, which lasts about two minutes, is quite remarkable. One after another, the five subjects of the documentary are introduced. There are three men — the experimental theater director Mou Sen ("Mu Sen" in the original subtitles), the painter Zhang Dali, and the photographer Gao Bo — and two women — the painter Zhang Xiaping and the writer Zhang Ci. We see them, in their modest and cluttered dwellings, in the *hutongs* (Beijing alleyways) where they come to do their laundry, and cycling down rainy streets, with a title unfolding a brief biography (birth date, studies, early employment, date of moving to Beijing). They talk, smoke, and gesture with their hands. However, these vignettes unfold in absolute silence. A conventional documentary would have coated the images with an explanatory voiceover, but Wu's much lauded oppositional practice starts in that moment of silence. He actively stands against the authoritarian voiceover, which was prevalent in the *zhuantipian* (special topic programs) produced by state-owned television stations at the time, as well as in Western mainstream documentary. Wu's strategy had long-lasting consequences. In New Chinese Documentary films, it helped to eliminate the voiceover, and fostered reflection about its effect of flattening the soundscape and subjugating all the other noises and voices to the commentary. In Wu's oeuvre, it marked the first step in an aesthetic and ethical investigation into the visual and aural presence of the documentary filmmaker.

Wu's voice is heard throughout *Bumming in Beijing*, but always on the boundary of the image, sometimes barely audible, as if floating in the cinematic field without being anchored. The radicalness of the first few minutes is startling, and some of the first spectators thought that something was wrong. The work was achieved through a series of trials and errors at a time when Wu had never traveled abroad or seen the work of Frederick Wiseman, the Maysles Brothers, Ogawa Shinsuke, and other *vérité* documentarists that he was later to identify as inspiration and mentors.[2] If it is "a mistake," it is a telling one. Here I am reminded of an anecdote once recounted in a private conversation by Indian New Wave director Mani Kaul, who had also studied classical chanting. His voice teacher had told him: "If you make a mistake when you sing, what you hear at this moment is the sound of your own voice." This "mistake" has been beautifully read by Ernest Larsen as a form of resistance against the violence of the state: "The prolonged moments of near silence in *Bumming in Beijing* produce the aesthetic effect of outlasting the remembered roar of government tanks."[3]

A significant proportion of *Bumming in Beijing* is a variation on "talking heads" — the subjects shot in their usual setting addressing the camera, with the questions and comments of the filmmaker missing or reduced to an off-screen mumble. However, the first sound in *Bumming in Beijing* is not the human voice, but some ambient noise as the camera pans into a run-down *hutong*. A printed title informs us that this is "a rented place of Zhang Ci," and then we see the young woman going to the water pump and talking to a female neighbor (or the landlady) as some barely audible off-screen voices are heard. A few scenes later, after being introduced to Zhang Dali, Mou Sen, and Gao Bo's habitats, the first person to speak on camera is Zhang Xiaping. But she is not conveying information; she is uttering sweet nothings to her pet white rabbit. Then the screen fades to black.

Dirty Sound

French film critics like to oppose "clean sound" to "dirty sound," a distinction I find useful here. "Clean sound" means clear sound — sound caught with a high-power microphone that captures the voice of the speaker and is able to filter out ambient noises. More significantly, "clean sound" implies that what matters in sound recording is the meaning of what is being said, and so the viewer cannot be distracted by ancillary or secondary noises. Documentary film or television crews usually attach a lapel microphone to the body of the speakers. This does not happen in Wu's work, which proceeds from another philosophy of "recording reality." This turns out, first by accident, then by design, to be a version of *cinéma vérité*'s fly-on-the-wall approach.

Early *vérité* films strike the viewer with a dense tapestry of sometimes difficult-to-decipher sounds, be they the regional accents in the working-class kitchens where the subjects of the Maysles brothers' film *Salesman* (1968) try to unload their Catholic Bibles, or the confusing roar of a crowd of out-of-control fans heard from backstage in another Maysles's documentary *Gimme Shelter* (1970). On the other hand, mainstream cinema, with its emphasis on "clean sound," tends to overvalue what Michel Chion calls "semantic listening," which is used to "interpret a message."[4] Spectators expect to hear the dialogue, or the words in the interviews or the voiceover, because they are going to give sense to the image. The second — and most important — mode of listening is "casual listening," which "consists of listening to a sound in order to gather information about its cause (or source)."[5] This is what we do when we find ourselves within a texture of ambient sounds. The last listening mode, "reduced listening," consists of paying attention to a sound for its physical or quasi-musical properties, not for the message or information it may convey.

The recording of "dirty sound" produces a specific mode of listening, one that combines "casual" and "reduced" listening. It is the not-so-distant heir of the "city symphonies" of early cinema. Originally silent, these symphonies later became celebrations of the ambient noises caused by urban activities. A new form of documentary, often by filmmakers gracefully treading the line between documentary and fiction, has also explored the potential of this kind of sound. Examples include Ulrike Ottinger's *China. The Arts — The People* (*China. Die Künste — der Alltag. Eine filmische Reisebeschreibung*, Germany, 16mm, 270 min, 1985), or Chantal Akerman's moody trip to the countries of the former Eastern bloc in *From the East* (*D'Est*, France/Belgium, 16mm, 107 min, 1993). In both cases, the filmmakers, who did not speak the language of the countries they were visiting, chose not to translate the dialogue overheard in the streets and public spaces. Equally radical is the solution chosen by Jia Zhangke for *In Public* (2001): while filming people speaking Chinese, albeit local dialects spoken in Datong (Shanxi Province), he often disregards "properly" recording their conversation. For example, a significant portion of an exchange between a young man and a woman who had just missed the bus is inaudible. Or he allows individual voices to be drowned in ambient noise. The film was produced by the Jeonju Film Festival in South Korea, and therefore targeted at the international film circuit, but only parts of the audible dialogue are subtitled. What is really at stake here is not the semantic meaning of what the people are saying, but how they are saying it and the way they position and move their bodies in relation to each other and their surroundings; such is the essence of what it means to be in a public space.

Missing Subtitles

The availability of subtitles has been of crucial importance since the first works of the Sixth Generation, such as Zhang Yuan's *Mama* (1990), and the independent documentary movement, such as Shi Jian and Chen Jue's *Tiananmen Square* (1991). Matthew David Johnson stresses that "international exhibition ... was clearly essential to the process by which independent or non-state perspectives, through the conduits of non-official distribution, first gained a visible foothold as legitimate representation of China abroad."[6] Eager to communicate with audiences abroad, as stated in the "manifesto" of Shi and Chen's SWYC Group ("Structure, Wave, Youth, Cinema Experimental Group"),[7] the artists systematically subtitled their work. Often, as in *Mama* or the original version of *Bumming in Beijing*, the subtitles were rough and imperfect, in both their grammar and layout. Zhang and Wu had barely enough money to complete their work, and certainly no budget to secure the services of a professional translator, transcribe the totality of the soundtrack, do a "spotting," and proofread the titles. An example of *arte povera*, these subtitles were born out of desire and necessity, within the context of the displacement and alienation experienced by independent Chinese filmmakers at the time.[8] As the work was produced outside legal "production units," it officially did not exist and could not be shown in China.[9] The most attractive possibility was for the films to be shown abroad, hence the strategic function of subtitling.

If translating is betrayal, subtitling is abstraction. No matter how well done, subtitles only represent a reduced and minimal approximation of what happens on the soundtrack. A focal point of the theoretical and practical reflection on subtitles has therefore consisted in dealing with them as fragmentary texts. Jean-Marie Straub and Danièle Huillet developed an exemplary practice. Out of respect for both the image and the grain of the voice, and to make the spectator *watch* what was on the screen as well as *listen* to *what* was being uttered (the sound of the voice and the musicality of the specific language used) and *how* it was being said (the delivery, the tone, the relationship between spoken language and body language), Huillet often did not translate all the dialogue, but only fragments. Producing minimalist subtitles is an act of courage, as spectators may get frustrated and feel that something is being hidden from them. Ultimately, they are confronted with the fundamental opacity of any operation of linguistic exchange: *something is always lost.*

The parts of *Bumming in Beijing* that are *not* subtitled in the original version are the rehearsals of Eugene O'Neill's *The Great God Brown* ("The Big God Brown" in the overlaid title introducing the sequence) by Mou Sen's experimental theater group; a song by Cui Jian that Gao Bo listens to; and a moment of crisis in Zhang Xiaping's life. When Wu had the rehearsals translated in the seventy-minute version of the piece, the result was somewhat anti-climactic. We do not need a Chinese film to introduce us to O'Neill's words, and what the theater crew is saying ("Move this to the right!" and so on) is not particularly enlightening. Years later, when working on *Jiang Hu: Life on the Road* (1999), in which the subtitles are professionally done, Wu often refrains from translating the desultory exchanges of the members of the "Far & Wide Song and Dance Troupe" as they set up or dismantle their tent.

Acousmêtre

Cui Jian's song appears twice: first we hear a few lyrics in the section devoted to Gao Bo's habitat. Following a series of vignettes devoted to the daily life routines of Zhang Ci, Zhang Dali, and Mou Sen, in which only ambient sound is recorded, his voice is the first human noise heard clearly in the piece. The same footage is recycled and expanded in the section devoted to the three "dreamers" who stay in Beijing in the fall of 1989. Gao Bo is silent, and looks depressed. At some point, he plays the cassette of Cui Jian's *Start from the Beginning* — a song that encapsulated the mood of Chinese youth at that time. In the original version of *Bumming in Beijing*, the audience listens to the song until Gao Bo decides to switch it off and put a Western classical music tape on instead. The lyrics are not subtitled, but anybody vaguely familiar with Chinese culture will have recognized Cui Jian's raspy voice, and perceived the mood of disillusion and angry disappointment it expresses.[10] In the final months of 1989, Cui's songs were banned, but they could be heard in unexpected places in Beijing — in a noodle shop, at the corner of a *hutong*, or coming from the street. The rock star was nowhere in sight, yet he was ubiquitous. Formally speaking, this voice of an invisible singer recorded on audiotape is a singular case of what Chion calls an *acousmêtre* — the voice of somebody who is not (or not yet) visible on the screen.[11]

Knowingly or not, Wu plays with the three modes of listening defined by Chion. One of the vectors of his exploration of sound is his own voice. When recording his subjects, he does not act as an interviewer, but as a sympathetic friend sharing their lifestyle. He does not so much ask questions as prompt the conversation through comments and reactions to what has just been said. Now, after looking at countless tapes made by Wu and listening to him talk in public, we are able to identify the specific timbre (the musical quality) of this discreet voice, intermittently haunting the borders of the screen. This is what Roland Barthes would call its "grain," or Pascal Bonitzer its "body." Bonitzer has further analyzed the paradox of this body as follows: once the viewer "encounters" the (invisible) body/grain of the voiceover, then he/she "encounters the subject of this voice ... the subject fallen to the status of an object, unmasked."[12]

This is quite different from what happens in Nick Broomfield's documentaries. There, the voice of the filmmaker is foregrounded and attached to a body often at the center of the image. It is a spectacle halfway between the routine of a stand-up comic (look at me as I am goofing up and cannot meet Margaret Thatcher) and a demonstration of narcissistic mastery (look at me as I am skillfully inserting myself within and without tricky documentary situations). Broomfield's performing antics create a hierarchy between him and his subjects — he asks us to identify with *his* plight rather than with *theirs*. In contradistinction, by carefully keeping himself in the margin of the image, by allowing his voice to slip in and out of the soundtrack, Wu puts himself within a cinematic space in continuity/contiguity with that of the people whose lives he documents. He loses his status as a master of the discourse to become one of the objects in the field. He is also one of these young artists who are struggling to make a living and find decent dwellings while producing independent work in Beijing.

At a minimum, this strategy articulates a major contradiction in the work of the documentary filmmaker that Wu has never ceased to address, implicitly or unconsciously, in *Bumming in Beijing*, but then does so head-on in *Fuck Cinema*. Even if a filmmaker comes from the same milieu as his subjects, adopts a position of sympathy and understanding toward them, and shares a common experience with them, once he points a camera and a microphone at them the balance of power is no longer equal and shifts in his favor. The voice of the subjects facing the camera and the voice of the unseen filmmaker do not have the same ontological value.

In *Bumming in Beijing*, the occurrence of Wu's voice is extremely discreet. In the section "Accommodation," as Gao describes the feelings of insecurity caused by moving from sublet to sublet, the filmmaker interjects a sympathetic comment about "living in Beijing without a [residency permit]." Later, we spend a breathtaking amount of time in Zhang Dali's studio, as he is painting, in silence. Off screen, two male voices (one of them probably the filmmaker's) exchange small talk. We can assume these are two friends of the painter, who are close enough to him to be able to drop by while he is absorbed in his work.

The Madness of Zhang Xiaping

The tables are turned when Wu comes to the Exhibition Gallery at Beijing's Central Academy of Fine Arts where Zhang Xiaping has hung a show of her paintings — while she is having a delirious episode. A drama unfolds between the space on screen, in which a disturbed young woman is making a spectacle of herself, and the space off screen, in which a friend of hers is keeping his professional cool while directing his assistant to point a camera at her. In her "madness," Zhang Xiaping performs a number of transgressions that pierce holes in the wall that usually divides the subject from the documentary filmmaker. She addresses him in a manner that borders on hostility (through the use of strong language such as "motherfucker," "fuck," "cunt") and playfulness (as she is trying to enlist him in her delirium). In three instances, Wu is almost forced to verbally interact with her — and, of course, is completely off the mark.

This episode, introduced by a title that says "The Madness of Zhang Xiaping," is strategically inserted after a long and melancholy sequence showing the depressive state of the three artists who stay in Beijing in October 1989, having witnessed the crackdown, repression, and squashing of hopes following the Spring Movement.[13] Two of their friends, Zhang Ci and Zhang Dali, have married foreigners and moved abroad. This is when Gao Bo is listening to and mouthing the lyrics of Cui Jian's song. In his studio, Mou Sen cuts his toenails, looks at pictures of his rehearsals, and listens to Western classical music as well. The two men are silent, and Wu does not engage in a conversation with them. The mood changes in Zhang Xiaping's place; she holds her pet rabbit, and puts on a romantic American pop song. Wu shows his intuitive mastery of the off-screen space in panning from Zhang's face to her tape player, then panning back to an extreme close-up of the face of the young woman: in the time it took for the pan to be completed, she has burst into silent tears, and the change of her mood is all the more powerfully signified in that it happened unseen. Here Wu uses a panning to produce an effect dealt in three shots by Ozu in *Late Spring* (*Banshun*, 1949): in the first shot, Setsuko Hara is smiling; in the third she is crying. The "transitional object" (concealing the arrival of tears on the face of the young woman) is a vase of flowers in Ozu's film and a tape-player in Wu's piece, but the effect is similarly striking – another example of Wu's profound cinematic intuition.

Because of its contextualization, it is tempting and not without grounds to read "The Madness of Zhang Xiaping" as an aftershock of the June Fourth crackdown. However, the scene is so multilayered that it can be viewed through more than one framework. In the original version, the sequence was not subtitled, so a foreign spectator would perceive the violence of the situation with a terrifying impact. The difficulties inherent in this passage are due to the fact that Zhang Xiaping utters a mixture of coherent and incoherent sounds — a texture of sighs, burps, sobs, laughs, cries, onomatopoeia, curse words, metaphysical questions, poetic metaphors, incomplete sentences, and insults. We are entering the domain defined as "the intrusion of the semiotic rhythm within language" by Julia Kristeva, who then quotes, as an example, Stéphane Mallarmé's reflections on his poetry: "a space ... indifferent to language, enigmatic and feminine ... rhythmic, unfettered, irreducible to its intelligible verbal translation; it is musical, anterior to judgment."[14] For professional subtitlers and translators, just to try and *transcribe* "the semiotic" accurately presents specific difficulties. So it is no surprise that the translation I commissioned and the one that appears in the seventy-minute version differ slightly — the second being "more polite," eschewing sexual language and curse words, and omitting Wu Wenguang's brief off-screen interventions.

Here is the translation I commissioned:

Zhang Xiaping: OK, all right. Now God is speaking. This isn't my voice now, it's God's voice. [Pointing at her expressionistically painted self-portrait] Is it a man or a woman?

Wu Wenguang [Off screen]: Does God have a gender?

ZXP: I don't know. Whoever knows, speak up!

WWG [OS]: Can I borrow a light? ["fire" in Chinese]

ZXP: Motherfucker, talking about "fire" all day long … this world lacks fire … motherfucking cunt. I want to start a fire, but the fire wouldn't start.

WWG [OS]: Where's my lighter?

ZXP: Motherfucker, how should I know? My cunt can't feel it!

[Rolling on the floor] Motherfucker, the sky's going to fall. God, oh God, can you hear me God? Who the fuck am I? [Sob] Who the fuck am I? [Laugh] Let me tell you. [She stands up] I was given a fucking wrong last name in this world. Yes, a fucking wrong last name … Who the fuck am I? I fucking don't know! … Let me tell you … I am talking here … Nothing else to say … Motherfucker … [sigh] … [Back on the floor] Eeeyou … urgh … eeeyou … am feeling awful all of a sudden. Listen to me. This is going to be an eye-opener for you … You don't even know shit! You don't even know shit about drama … Just invite them back. Here, come here boy, here … psst … zzzitt [as if calling a dog] … I thought this play was on at 11:30. I was thinking more like 11, but 11:30 at the latest. I thought it was just the two of us here, painting, but who are these people? Why the fuck are they here? [15]

In a later sequence (not included in the seventy-minute version), when talking about this episode, Zhang Xiaping first says she was "directing a play," and then brings in the myth of Nü Wa, the primeval goddess-mother who repaired the sky, adding, "I was doing the same thing for mankind." Restating this important myth and reflecting on its impact on Chinese culture in his 1922 book *Old Tales Retold*, Lu Xun explored its sexual politics as well: Nü Wa dies of exhaustion after mending heaven, which was destroyed in a war between men and giants, and then becomes a victim of the patriarchal system established by the humanity she had created out of clay.[16] The reference to the goddess-mother's body as an object of fascination and abjection (a priest berates Nü Wa's nudity) is very much in line with Kristeva's theses, in particular when she links the "semiotic chora" to the maternal body.[17]

Figure 9.1. *Bumming in Beijing.* "This isn't my voice now, it's God's voice … Is it a man or a woman?"

A self-taught painter, Zhang Xiaping is depicted in the piece as producing visual works and writings that acutely articulate the "contradiction between the semiotic and the symbolic." Mou Sen confesses to an intimate kinship with her "madness," intuiting that she is tapping into sources of creative and poetic energy that he can only dream about. In turn, Zhang Xiaping's psychotic episode is clearly a reply to Mou Sen: she is turning her internal reality into an expressionist spectacle, and enlisting a reluctant Wu Wenguang to be a part of it — as well as the silent young male students of the Central Academy of Fine Arts, who are helping to hang her paintings. The "drama" staged by the young woman is a spatialization (through her body language and writhing on the floor), but also a musicalization (through her burbling, screams, and onomatopoeia) of a double contradiction. First, there is contradiction between the symbolic and the semiotic. However, instead of producing poetry like Mallarmé, she experiences a psychotic breakdown. Second is the contradiction between being an object and a subject of representation. In a patriarchal culture that wants to assign women to the position of "images [while men are the] bearers of the look,"[18] becoming a painter is a form of transgression. This is why the question of the gender of God/the goddess is not a futile discussion about the sex of the angels, but a poignant questioning of identity. As a producer of culture, however, Zhang Xiaping realizes that she is doubly feminized by the gaze of the camera, hence her attempt to engage the filmmaker on a sexual ground, using the hysterical strategy of threatening one's interlocutor's masculinity — asserting bluntly that her "cunt can't feel [his] lighter."

The Presence of the Filmmaker

By keeping his voice on the soundtrack, Wu leaves a mark of his presence in the space-time continuum created between him and his subject. This opens the way for a more radical questioning of the filmmaking contract, as is fully articulated in *Fuck Cinema*. Yet, in spite of its "imperfections," *Bumming in Beijing* already contains insights that put Wu's work at the vanguard of cinematic modernity. The radicalness of the piece does not lie so much in the "uninterrupted filming process,"[19] but in another aspect of Wu's experiment — how to handle the presence of the filmmaker.

Wu has often admitted that when he was working on the piece, he was not fully conscious that he was "making an actual documentary,"[20] and just shot randomly while hanging out with his friends. In subsequent works, it is alluded to that Wu "keeps shooting all the time." A good example of his method is described (and implicitly criticized) by Wang Zhutian, the main protagonist of *Fuck Cinema*:

> When I went to show [Wu] my script, he very eagerly recorded the whole process of our discussion with his digital camera, and afterwards invited me to dinner.

These methods are not exactly *vérité*, because in such films the filmmaker must refrain from any kind of intervention; they also pose a significant problem at the time of editing. Even if the filmmaker has carefully kept himself outside the picture, his voice can be heard throughout. Wu admits that his goal in *Bumming in Beijing* was to "edit out [his] voice,"[21] but it was not entirely possible. As a result, his voice keeps floating on the edge of the image — sometimes no more than a whisper, an offhand remark, or a poorly repressed laugh — constantly frustrating our expectations that the subject of these utterances will appear on screen. Here we have an imperfect *acousmêtre*, since visualization will never take place, and the effect does not indicate a possible threat (as in horror movies), nor a place of mastery (as in Fritz Lang's *Mabuse* films), but a space of uncertainty concerning the subject of enunciation.

It is not because people are speaking "with their own voices" that they are telling "the truth." In Wu's films, they are perfectly capable of producing an elaborate *mise-en-scène*, of lying, of manufacturing complex statements in bad faith, of evading their true feelings, hiding behind embarrassed laughter.

The moments of *Bumming in Beijing* in which we feel some kernel of "truth" is communicated to us are precisely when the subjects are silent (as when Zhang Dali is painting), or not resorting to a "normative" use of language (Zhang Xiaping's onomatopoeia, or Gao Bo's theatrical voicing of Cui Jian's lyrics). On the other hand, this persistent delocalization of the speech act itself (mostly mapped out by the off-screen, whispering voice of the filmmaker, but starting with the unsettling non-synchronized sequences of the beginning, and extending by contagion and contiguity to a number of other situations) suggests Arthur Rimbaud's famous insight: "I is another."[22]

Two Positions

Wu's subsequent work oscillates between these two poles of uncertainty. First, there are the films in which he reintroduces the presence of the filmmaker within the image itself. Most notable is *At Home in the World* (1995), the follow-up to *Bumming in Beijing*, in which he goes to different countries to follow what has happened to his artist friends, five years later. Gao Bo has gone to Paris and married a French woman, and Zhang Xiaping has married an Austrian man and moved to a suburb of Salzburg. The piece starts with Mou Sen, still involved in his experimental theater troupe in Beijing. Wu's presence unfolds as a complete *acousmêtre*. Initially he is an unseen interviewer. Then he is shown from the back in a conversation, explaining to Mou his excitement at starting the second phase of *Bumming in Beijing*. Then, totally visualized, he becomes another protagonist, as he and his girlfriend, modern dancer and choreographer Wen Hui, welcome Zhang Dali, his Italian wife, and their little girl as they arrive at the airport in Beijing. More significantly (and maybe following Zhang Xiaping's prompting), Wu becomes a performer in Mou Sen's new play *File Zero* (*Ling Dang'an*), based on a text by avant-garde poet Yu Jian.[23] On stage, he stands behind a keyboard regulating the sound, and then speaks from this static place — in and out of synch with Wen Hui's choreographed movements. When the play is invited to Brussels, Mou is denied an exit visa, and Wu becomes a sort of substitute for him, explaining to the audience the genesis of the play and the process of his involvement: "I said I'd most like to play myself. I said I'd like to say something about my father."[24]

From then on, Wu keeps appearing in the image in a variety of situations, reversing the traditional position of the *acousmêtre*. Chion's primal situation of "hide-and-seek" is still there, but what we are anticipating now is not so much the moments when Wu will appear, but those in which he will be swallowed back into the off-screen space. He is in numerous airports, waiting for passengers to arrive; making a phone call in the streets of Paris; and talking with Gao Bo in his kitchen. His presence is justified by his friendship with his subjects, as well as by shared concerns and lifestyle, which put it within the field of his study. Yet, treading the line between absence and presence also reveals the growing gap between him and his subjects, the subtle cracks in their friendship. Wu has to explain to them that he has no idea about what it means to live in a foreign country. Moreover, his presence appears to create real discomfort, and even generate hostility, in Gao Bo, as he conducts his everyday business (making portraits for tourists in the streets of Paris), laughing too hard under the gaze of the camera:

Gao Bo: No time for talking shit with you. Go to hell. So, you're Wu Wenguang, so what?

Wu Wenguang [Off screen]: Why do you laugh every time you mention doing portraits?

GB: Everybody thinks that doing portraits is ridiculous.

The Silences of the Filmmaker

The second route taken by Wu in the wake of *Bumming in Beijing* was to edit out the visual and aural traces of his presence. A prime example is *Jiang Hu: Life on the Road*, which was also a piece in which a smaller DV camera (a mini DV, Panasonic EZ-1) replaced the earlier and more cumbersome Betacam cameras borrowed from television stations, allowing him greater mobility and intimacy with his subjects and expanding his visual vocabulary. The piece explores a multi-polar space of several dozen performers living and working under the tattered "Big Tent" of the troupe. While a number of sequences are shot frontally, with the subjects talking to the camera — or at least to the person behind the camera — the majority cover crowd situations. The voices of the subjects come from different corners of the cinematic field — some from the off-screen space — and their source is not always clear. This is true in particular of the moments when the troupe is performing, with the camera shooting the show itself; the backstage area, where some of the actors and singers comment as they watch their colleagues or prepare to go on stage; the spectators; and people standing outside the tent. As noted above, the dialogue is sometimes treated as "ambient noise," not always intelligible (and not subtitled).

In this piece, underlining the gap between him and these poor peasants-turned-impoverished-performers, Wu does not create a situation of continuity and contiguity. Although he is in the same physical space as his subjects, having lived "on the road" with them for months, he is not in the same mental and emotional space as he was with Zhang Xiaping or Zhang Dali. His presence does haunt the image, but it remains constantly on the edge.[25] He is obviously a part of those dinners or drinking bouts where the guests are talking about their lives, complaining about not being paid for months or spilling their guts, but his voice does not appear on the soundtrack. There are a couple of instances in which some of the players address him, once to ask for his advice, and another time a monologue in which a young man describes his destitute situation:

> Is the boss so evil? He seems all right, but you stick around too long, you'll see ... The reason I came to work is ... I don't like farm work. If I worked in a small local factory, I wouldn't make much money ... So I went out full of hope. But I didn't expect ... [turning his head to see if someone is listening] I can't say this to anyone; if I did, I'll get in trouble for it ... Fuck, I don't care if you laugh. I just have one yuan twenty cents in my pocket. You see, someone like me, besides all the mental energy, I also give sweat and blood ... I should have a bit of spending money...

Figure 9.2. *Jiang Hu: Life on the Road*. "Fuck, I don't care if you laugh. I just have one yuan twenty cents in my pocket."

Composed of a large array of short vignettes and divided into chapters introduced by short explanatory titles, the piece unfolds as a rich tapestry of sounds, but is organized around the silences of the filmmaker. His presence in the field, signified by an absence in the image, is what "pierces the screen," as Chion puts it so beautifully.[26] It creates a void within the cinematic field, a negative space. This obliteration is constituted in two stages. At the time of shooting, the cameraman is given instructions to carefully avoid the filmmaker. This operation is reduplicated at the time of the editing, when Wu's aural presence is systematically deleted from the sound material.

The Silences of *Fuck Cinema*

Fuck Cinema occupies a unique place in Wu's oeuvre. A piece that was several years in the making and shelved for a couple of years by the filmmaker himself, it exists in two different versions. Since this film, Wu has virtually stopped making the kind of documentaries he is famous for. Instead, he has dedicated himself to performing and to a series of projects in which he trains peasants and young filmmakers to document their own communities, such as *China Village Self-Governance Film Project* (2006). In the first version of *Fuck Cinema*, Wu had edited out not only every utterance of his voice, but also every allusion to his presence.[27] He later changed his mind, and produced a second version. Here, his presence is readily acknowledged by both the main subject of the film, Wang Zhutian, and the people he encounters while being followed by the camera. However, he remains silent, a fact that becomes more and more meaningful as the piece unfolds. The "sound barrier" is only broken in Wu's final interaction with one of the film's subjects, Xiao Wu.

Fuck Cinema follows two men and a group of women that all have a subservient relationship to the film industry. In various ways, they want "in," but remain outside, in the margins. What has significantly changed from the time of *Bumming in Beijing* is that Wu, now one of the most notorious independent filmmakers in China, is no longer a marginalized figure — he is in the center. People recognize him and are drawn to him. His name can open doors.

In the most complicated set-up, he shoots a film crew as they are video-recording the auditions of young actresses for the part of a hooker. The girls are extremely young, inexperienced, dressed shabbily, and often have bad acne. First they are prompted to talk about themselves, and we learn they all come from the provinces, have very little, if any, acting experience or training, and are quite unsophisticated. They are asked what they think of women who work as "hostesses," and when they misunderstand the word, it is explained that these women are prostitutes. Once their minds have been probed, they are asked to remove their jackets (it is obviously winter outside) and stand against the wall, in various poses, to expose their bodies to the camera. These sequences recur throughout the three-hour piece and present a construction *en abyme*. Wu shoots the film crew at work, his voyeuristic camera lingering on the bodies of the young women duplicates the film crew's camera and the voice of the unseen interviewer becomes a substitute for his own voice. This in turn magnifies some of the features of the audition process (the objectification of the bodies of the applicants, the manipulation they are subjected to, and their willingness to be so commodified) and constitutes an implicit critique of it. By remaining silent and keeping the interviewer off screen, Wu allows us to fantasize the voice we hear as *his*. By doing this, he is clearly putting himself on the same side of the "Great Divide" that occurs in cinema between the people who have access to cameras and shoot others, and those who can only stand in front of the cameras, often for not very long.[28]

Figure 9.3. *Fuck Cinema*. "I studied performing arts. I took piano lessons for seven years when I was younger."

The utter powerlessness of the aspiring actresses is mirrored in reverse by the actual resistance of the second character, Xiao Wu, who sells illegal DVDs. Unlike the young women, he does not depend on the gaze of others — he sells them what they want to see. Neither is he a "wannabe," hoping that his contact with people more powerful than him will help him to "get somewhere." He is the one who resists the filming process, forcing the filmmaker out of his masterful silence.

In the last sequence, Xiao Wu and Wu Wenguang argue about the filming that is about to take place. The documentarist wants to follow his subject as he makes his way through the crowd on his bicycle, his cargo of DVDs in tow. Xiao Wu thinks that, at some point, the camera should stop following him, while Wu Wenguang wants to accompany him much longer. Believing he has won the argument, Wu Wenguang starts shooting, until he loses Xiao Wu in the crowd. The last utterance on the soundtrack is the sound of his voice, calling for the young DVD seller, now missing from the image. Then the screen turns black.

The most compelling and tragic figure is Wang Zhutian, who encapsulates many of Wu's previous "characters." Like *Bumming in Beijing*'s *liulang* (vagabonds), he has come to Beijing to follow his artistic calling. Like the performers in *Jiang Hu: Life on the Road*, he is a displaced peasant. Like Gao Bo, he is followed by Wu during his peregrinations through the city, which makes him uncomfortable. And like Zhang Xiaping, he seizes the opportunity to address the presence behind the camera.

The portion devoted to him, also sliced up into separate sequences that recur through the piece, is bracketed by two monologues in which he reads from a text he has written. At the beginning, he seems to be excerpting a letter sent to him by his brother from the countryside, who has not heard from him since he left to take the entrance exam at the Beijing Film Academy. We later learn that this letter is part of a semi-autobiographical script written by Wang about his experience as a peasant coming to Beijing, taking (and failing) the Beijing Film Academy entrance exam, and eking out a miserable existence while living on the roof of a university.

Wu follows Wang as he meets with producers, television executives, and independent filmmakers to try and get his film made; stands at the door of the Beijing Film Studio looking for work as an extra; attempts to register with talent agencies that demand an exorbitant registration fee; and hangs out with kibbitzers who may or may not have made a film, and may or may not have the phone number of a "potential investor" or good advice to waste on him. When Wang enters offices or hotel suites, film industry people only pay cursory attention to him, but immediately recognize Wu, greet him, comment on the technical prowess of his camera (a 3 CCD, Canon XL), and exchange small talk. It becomes clear that Wu has arranged, or at least facilitated some of these meetings. However, not once does he reply to the words addressed to him.

The cruelty of the situation comes to a climax when Wu organizes a meeting with Sixth Generation filmmaker Zhang Yuan, who used to be a close friend of his in the post-1989 underground circles. Making "overground" cinema since *Seventeen Years* (1999), Zhang Yuan had temporarily moved into a suite in the Beijing Landmark hotel in mid-2002, as he was working on the post-production of two films at the same time. He does not hide his hilarity, laughing uproariously, cracking jokes at Wu, intimating that he is exploiting and manipulating his subject, and telling Wang Zhutian that he would never direct a script he has not written or commissioned himself. Completely star-struck, Wang reacts with a feeble request for a job as a crowd extra, which makes the filmmaker laugh even harder.

The film's *pièce de resistance* is a twelve-minute take of Wang reading a text to Wu — sometimes interrupting himself to venture a comment — who remains absolutely silent in spite of being multiply addressed.

The next bit is a bit negative about you.

I don't know why, but whenever Wu meets me he is always armed with his DV camera, and while talking to him I am always fearfully dodging his lens that he points at me like a gun. I worry I am being rude by doing that, so I feel very awkward ...

I am aware that at times, I am turning some extremely ridiculous and childish behavior into luxury goods for the consumption of others ... I stared angrily at Wu, and said rudely: "It may be fun for you, but it's suffering for me." Wu didn't know what to say, and for the first time he took away that gun-camera of his ...

I felt more and more that I was slicing pieces of flesh from my body, to show to the people around me, but these people thought I wasn't singing the blues good enough, they egged me on to try harder, to do better tricks, to drench the streets with my blood ...

Mr. Wu, I hope you can understand me. I'm really in a difficult position, and I can't find a way out, you see?

In fact, at first I didn't want to read this to you, but I feel we can say anything to each other and that you wouldn't mind if I read it.

Figure 9.4. *Fuck Cinema*. "The next bit is a bit negative about you."

Wu's refusal to speak at this moment echoes another form of institutionalized silence — that of the Freudian analyst. Yes, analysts *do* speak. However, unlike traditional therapists, their role is to not respond to the patient's emotional demands, but to allow him/her to express a discourse of desire. When an analyst interrupts the patient's speech, it is usually not to be "nice" or to say, "I understand what you mean, and you have my sympathy," but to mark a pause on a signifier that may be pregnant with meaning, or stop a logorrhea spewed out by the analyzand and as a smoke screen. Often these interruptions are not well received by the patient, but the analyst's silence is an even worse ordeal.

The issue of how much language the analyst utters is irrelevant. What matters is that the analyst's presence outlines a void within the field of language that defines the subject. Jacques Lacan was fond of defining "the place of the analyst" as *la place du mort*. This can be translated either as "the dummy" in a poker game (the player who folds their cards and decides to remain silent), or as "the place of the dead man" (the passenger's seat in a car). Adding that, "the Freudian field [of the unconscious] is a field which, of its nature, is lost. It is here that the presence of the psychoanalyst as witness of this loss, is irreducible,"[29] he "stressed the importance ... in the misunderstood concept of repetition ... of the ever avoided encounter, of the missed opportunity. The function of missing lies at the heart of the analytical repetition. The appointment is always missed."[30]

And yet, if we take seriously another Lacanian construct — the Real as trauma or leftovers from the two instances of the Symbolic and the Imaginary — the failing (*ratage*), the missed encounter, is the only possible way to have access to the Real. Wu's intuition and increasing rigor — the integration of the filmmaker's silences in the texture of the film — have opened this royal way to the Real, but maybe at a cost.

Empirical studies of linguistic patterns tend to prove that, in the course of everyday conversation, people keep interrupting their interlocutors with comments, questions, even criticisms, or by interjecting information about themselves, as a way of proving their interest in what is being told to them. It is tempting, indeed, to "produce" small talk, and most speakers are implicitly begging for such interruptions, seeking reassurance and a validation of their existence in the field of the Other and interpreting silence as a lack of interest. Yet, is it not the case that we often end a conversation with the feeling that our chatty reaction has prevented our interlocutor from fully expressing something? For a documentary filmmaker whose camera is recording all sorts of material or psychological misery, the temptation to delude yourself into believing that you can "change the life" or "improve the lot" of your subjects is also great — a fallacy that now, after years of filmmaking, Wu steadily refuses.[31] It takes courage to hold a camera for more than ten minutes on a subject talking by himself (or remaining silent), rather than indulging in "sympathetic" interruptions or fast cutting. Wu's silences open a gap in the increasingly garrulous continuum of sound and images with which we are saturated. They bore a (sometimes uncomfortable) hole within the cinematic field, splitting the subject from his/her discourse, and the spectator from an uncritical belief in "the Truth" of what is shown. They open a space in which there is room for unaccounted-for voices, as well as for hard questions about the nature of the filmmaking process, and, ultimately, our role as speaking subjects.

10 From "Public" to "Private": Chinese Documentary and the Logic of *Xianchang*

Luke Robinson

From "Public" to "Private"

If the early years of China's New Documentary Movement were dominated by what has become known as the "public" documentary — films that focused on "public topics" (*gonggong huati*), usually encompassing issues of nation, history, ethnicity, or the functioning of the state, and which were often shot in public or communal spaces — recent interest has largely shifted to what is increasingly described as the *siren*, the "private" documentary. This form concerns itself with topics quite distinct from those of the "public" documentary, focusing on individual, sometimes even autobiographical, emotional experiences; the familial; and internal domestic spaces, as opposed to external public ones. In addition, these films frequently include scenes of a highly private or sensitive nature, such as sexual relations or physical self-harm.[1] Such differences are conscious: the genre is understood as defining itself against the ethos of the "public" documentary and everything it stands for; whilst directors who work within it are seen to be less interested in socially or politically engaged filmmaking than in addressing personal issues and expressing a personal point of view.[2] Documentary, in this formulation, has moved away from concerns about the formation of public life, becoming instead a mode of introspection, concerned solely with the fate of the individual.

Explanations for such changes are various. Some scholars have seen this as part of a generational shift: as a new cohort of directors came to adulthood after *gaige kaifang*,[3] so the rise and fall of the 1980s "Culture Fever" and its associated values, integral to the work of the early New Documentary Movement directors, became ever less of a defining experience for the Chinese documentary as a genre. Sometimes this is seen as a deliberate rejection on the part of a younger generation of those topics, particularly the national and the ethnic, which they believe to have caused individuals who lived through the 1980s so much pain and trouble; at other times it is understood as an almost inevitable consequence of working post-commercialization, in a society where the political has clearly become subordinate to the economic.[4] Some, including directors such as Wu Wenguang, trace the changes to the proliferation of new technology, with DV being seen not only as particularly suited to the production of the personal stories that characterize the "private" documentary, but also crucial to the liberation of documentary directors from the constraints of the state television system.[5] Finally, certain scholars have seen the particular formal characteristics of recent work in China as indicative not simply of the "personal"/"public" divide, but also of a complex dialectic between so-called "amateur" and "professional" filmmaking, one that raises questions about contemporary documentary's position vis-à-vis official culture.[6]

Elegant as this framework is, it raises as many questions as it answers. First, these terms do not exist in a vacuum, but are highly ideological. In the immediate post-revolutionary period, the CCP was closely involved in the creation of a public political culture that incorporated aspects of social life designated as private in Western society, most obviously the sphere of interpersonal relations. This process, and its metamorphosis since the 1980s under the impact of marketization, has been explored in some detail by historians of gender.[7] More recently, scholars have pointed to the government's involvement during the 1990s in the creation — or at least tacit acceptance — of a private realm where the individual is understood in specifically consumer terms, a phenomenon paralleled in the world of artistic production by the rise of a commercial popular culture and literary market.[8] Given this history, the process through which either category is constructed in China is often fraught with implications. Thus, when a film such as Zuo Yixiao's *Losing* (2005) presents a picture of divorce as a purely personal affair, devoid of any relevance beyond its emotional impact on the couple involved, or when Zhang Ming's *Springtime in Wushan* (2003) or Shu Haolun's *Nostalgia* (2006) stakes a claim to the consequences of grand state development projects viewed from the perspective of an individual or a family, such interpretations of what constitutes the private, or what the private individual has a right to comment on, inevitably carry a particular political *frisson* derived from their relationship to, and difference from, state-driven discourses on the subject.

Acknowledging this question, however, raises others. What exactly do we mean when we talk about "constructing" such categories? How do we understand this process to operate? As the brief definitions I have given above may suggest, the emphasis to date has implicitly been on the subject matter presented, and the approach to this material, but always understood in terms of difference. Initially, this was a question of departing from mainstream discourse; increasingly, it has become one of distinctions between older and younger members of the New Documentary Movement. Perhaps this is inevitable: as Matthew David Johnson has noted, the movement was initially both identified by, and valorized on account of, a discourse of "sharing marginal perspectives, reinterpreting history, and testing the mainstream's capacity for 'difference'."[9] Being positioned "outside" the official state-controlled media — whether literally or figuratively — thus functioned both to determine the movement's importance, and to define it as internally coherent. Yet, whilst this move was arguably essential in the post-Tiananmen political environment of the early 1990s, an emphasis on the shared and distinctive character of these early films has, in hindsight, perhaps obscured several significant ways in which the movement did not conform to such a narrative. The first, which has already been addressed by several scholars, is the extent to which, at the beginning of their careers, the early New Documentary Movement directors drew on practices already current, if not widespread, within the official media system.[10] The second is the tensions internal to the movement, both between directors, and, crucially, within the films themselves. Simply put, there are few films that, in purely representational terms, neatly fit the categories "public" or "private," however one chooses to define them. To quote Paul Willemen: "some aspects of a text may pull in one direction, while others pull in a totally different direction, with yet others exerting pressure in diametrically opposite directions, and so on."[11] If Wu Wenguang's *Bumming in Beijing: The Last Dreamers* (1990) is a work of "public" documentary, what are we supposed to make of the famous moment in which the artist Zhang Xiaping, one of the central characters, suffers a nervous breakdown on camera? If Hu Xinyu's *The Man* (2003) is indeed China's first full-length "private" film,[12] how do we relate his subjects' ongoing commentary on gender relations and unemployment to their equally frank discussions of their sexual and physical dysfunctions? Are the distinctions between the earlier and later stages of the movement as clear-cut as they are often made to seem?

My point is that understanding changes of the Chinese documentary genre requires an analysis not simply of how these works may differ from mainstream state discourse in content and style, but also of how their directors have tried to order such naturally heterogeneous material within their documentaries, and the manner in which these efforts too may have diverged since the movement's inception. This realization in turn requires serious consideration of film form and practice; issues that, sadly, have been glossed over in much of the recent literature on Chinese "alternative" film and documentary culture, sometimes to the point of dismissing its products as at best "rough," at worst "forgettable."[13] The aim of this chapter is to address precisely such questions. It argues that the pluralization of the documentary form during the 1990s is not a simple shift from the "public" to the "private": rather, it is also a shift from a metonymic or metaphorical mode, to one of the particular. In the former, the possibility of generalizing from the events depicted is encouraged: in the latter, the specific or the idiosyncratic is given pride of place. However, this distinction stems less from differences in content than from the forms used to frame this material. Crucial in this regard is the unexpected or contingent event, which directors in the early 1990s sought to contain, and those at the end of the decade to embrace. This embrace of the unexpected, I argue, represents a decisive break with socialist realism, which in turn has implicit political undertones; but it is a break manifested to differing degrees by documentaries of various different kinds, rather than being exclusive to any one type. Furthermore, these developments are immanent in the earlier stages of the movement, though never fully developed. The reasons for this pervasiveness lie in the cinematic practice to which all members of the New Documentary Movement share a common commitment: *xianchang*, or shooting live. And so it is to *xianchang* I turn first.

Xianchang and the Unexpected Event

Xianchang is the term for location shooting, a practice codified by Chinese directors, both feature and documentary filmmakers, in the early 1990s. It is closely associated with the new realist aesthetic of *jishi zhuyi* — "documentary realism" — that these artists were seeking to develop as an alternative to the by then discredited *xianshi zhuyi*, or socialist realism, that had characterized studio-based Chinese documentary practice up until the late 1980s.[14] However, whilst *jishi zhuyi* appears to have fallen out of use as an idiom in Chinese documentary circles, the principle of *xianchang* remains seemingly inviolable. It is arguably the thread that binds together an increasingly diverse Chinese documentary scene.

Wu Wenguang's definition of *xianchang* as a filmic practice "in the present and on the spot"[15] has inevitably focused academic attention on issues of space, place, and time in Chinese documentary. Yet, as Chris Berry has noted, one of the ways in which the New Documentary Movement sought to signify this sense of being "on the scene" — and thus by implication differentiate itself from the officially sanctioned, studio-based *zhuantipian* of the 1980s — was by referencing events within their films that suggested uncontrollable spontaneity and a lack of script.[16] That encountering the unexpected was an integral part of shooting on location was recognized by Jia Zhangke who, with reference to the filming of *Xiao Wu* (1997), noted that:

> Experiences told me that when you were shooting on location, many unexpected things would happen. But unexpected possibilities would also arise.[17]

Acknowledging the contingent nature of pro-filmic reality was thus an integral part of both *xianchang* and *jishi zhuyi* as they evolved within the context of China's independent documentary- and feature-filmmaking during the early 1990s.

The result is a tension at the heart of *xianchang* that, ironically, is perhaps best captured by Dai Vaughan in his analysis of the Lumière Brothers' early *actualités*. Vaughan argues that early directors were fascinated by film's capacity to capture the spontaneous event, a capacity that distinguished it from the theater. Yet this potentiality also presented the earliest exponents of the medium with a conundrum, for such moments of spontaneity constituted, in Vaughan's words, "an escape of the represented from the representational act."[18] In other words, incorporating the unexpected pro-filmic event into the documentary diegesis was complicated by the lack of conventions indicating how the unexpected should be represented or interpreted: its inherently asystematic nature defied attempts at capture through traditional, established semiotic codes. The opportunities provided by this new relationship with the pro-filmic were thus counterbalanced by the problems it represented for "making meaning" within the diegetic context of a documentary short.

Clearly this conflict between the desire to embrace the unpredictability of the pro-filmic and the need to systematize it within a structured diegesis is not unique to the New Documentary Movement. Arguably it is as old as cinema itself, as Siegfried Kracauer implicitly recognized in his discussion of editing in the *Theory of Film*: on one hand, the director wishes to assign any given shot a connotation specific to a film's plot; on the other, he or she desires to retain its multiple meanings in order to remain faithful to the nature of physical reality.[19] Yet this problem was perhaps particularly pronounced in 1990s China. The political positioning of the early film directors — their commitment to an ethos of *zhenduixing*, or confrontation with the authorities — resulted in a powerful drive to analyze the function of ideology and the exercise of government power at the grassroots level. Some degree of diegetic coherence was essential if this goal were to be reached. However, the crucible of post-Tiananmen society in which the movement was formed was hardly conducive to explicitly critical works of art; indeed, the director Shi Jian has argued that one of the attractions of the documentary image in the early 1990s was precisely its capacity to support multiple interpretations.[20] Furthermore, the *xianchang* aesthetic was an essential guarantor of a documentary's authenticity to a prospective audience, without which the directors' representation of events on screen as "real" would be seriously compromised. Pro-filmic contingency as a marker of truth, whilst appealing in relation to the immediate political context from which the New Documentary Movement emerged, ran the risk of undermining part of what might be described as the movement's intellectual project: a balance therefore had to be struck between the pro-filmic and the diegetic. In consequence, I would argue that the early New Documentary Movement directors displayed a far more ambivalent relationship with the unexpected than has previously been allowed for. Aspects of the "public" film genre, and the film practices that grew up around it, were in part a response to this ambivalence.

"Public" Documentary between Contingency and Metaphor

The particular form of *xianchang* that the early New Documentary Movement directors are famous for developing — and one that is characteristic of both "public" documentary and certain types of feature filmmaking — is sometimes described as quasi-anthropological. It is almost ethnographic in its use of extensive pre-shoot research, interviews, and careful forward planning: Wu Wenguang has used the term "fieldwork" to describe this process with reference to his earlier films.[21] Perhaps in consequence, this methodology tends to be interpreted as indicative of the movement's "sensitivity toward the relationship between subject and object" — particularly the relationship between director and documentary subject — and its "sense of urgency and social responsibility."[22] *Xianchang* is thus constituted as a question of ethics. It is, however, worthwhile quoting Duan Jinchuan at length on these working methods. Whilst acknowledging the inevitability of change in location shooting — "there will be some discrepancy between what you thought of in advance and the actual process of shooting" — Duan also notes the following:

> As far as documentary filmmakers are concerned, you must also have the vision to be able to see how things will develop; you must plan in advance. Why do I like to shoot films? Because the discrepancy between my understanding of the issues and what I shoot afterwards isn't that great. When conducting research and interviews prior to shooting, I can actually see in advance how certain things are going to pan out; but because during shooting people change, your actual content may change. This happens all the time, it's inevitable. [So you must have a plan] Otherwise you won't be able to shoot your film.[23]

In other words, however unpredictable pro-filmic reality, the impact of such unpredictability can be minimized through proper preparation. The ethnographic aspect of location shooting does not simply reflect a desire to reassess the relationship between the director and his or her subject. It can also be seen as a practical measure to ensure maximum control over pro-filmic material within the limits established by the *xianchang* aesthetic, thus reducing the element of surprise inherent in location work until it is acceptable to the director.

If this "ethnographic" practice is characteristic of the 1990s "public" documentary, its corollary is a formal trope borrowed from the American documentary director Frederick Wiseman, and perfected in the two films that arguably represent the "public" documentary in its purest form: *The Square* (1994), by Duan Jinchuan and Zhang Yuan, and *No. 16 Barkhor South Street* (1997), directed by Duan Jinchuan alone. This mode, christened by Bill Nichols as "metaphoric" or "mosaic," is a particularly extreme example of American Direct Cinema.[24] It is characterized by an absence of commentary and extra-diegetic sound; a refusal to stage or re-enact events; a minimization, wherever possible, of the camera's on-site presence; and a consequent reliance on editing to impose a coherent structure upon the documentary whole. Most importantly, though, its sequences are not organized in an explicitly chronological fashion. Nichols points out that successive images are edited to follow each other consecutively, but without a clearly marked temporal correlation; instead, their relationships are usually one of spatial co-existence. The result is a series of internally coherent scenes that supplement one another, each yielding some sense of the documentary's overall design without ever merging into a single identifiable narrative.[25]

Critics have tended to interpret Duan's adherence to Direct Cinema in relation to his politics, seeing it as a necessary adjunct both to his interest in the analysis of socio-political institutions, and his desire to break with pre-Tiananmen filmic conventions and the intellectual positions with which these were associated.[26] His movement away from the didacticism of voiceover is also invoked as an attempt to force greater critical engagement on the part of the audience, and thus the development of a public in the Western, Habermasian-inflected sense of the term.[27] And yet, as Nichols quotes Wiseman himself as saying, within the context of the latter's oeuvre, the mosaic form constitutes a quite self-conscious theory of the event.[28] By avoiding the use of explicitly temporal structures in his documentaries, Wiseman moves away from suggesting linear causal relationships between the episodes that he portrays on screen. Instead, these are the product of multiple relationships, ultimately shaped by the institutional spaces within which they occur. Events in Wiseman's films, whilst not staged, are therefore understood to be far from accidental. Instead, they are a consequence of the constraints imposed upon individuals by their social and institutional environment.[29] The mosaic or metaphorical mode is key to conveying this view, in that, by linking successive sequences through space rather than time, and presenting each as a facet of a greater whole, it effectively articulates the pro-filmic event in relation to the overall theme of the documentary. The films are edited such that what we see on screen is not suggested as absolutely contingent, being instead the manifestation of social forces invisible to the naked eye.

In effect, Wiseman uses editing to impose a particular structural logic on his pro-filmic material, and Duan does the same. The result is that although *No. 16 Barkhor South Street* and *The Square* appear as studies of the quotidian, it is not the day-to-day activities represented that actually animate the documentaries, but the larger ideological context in which these events take place. I would like to illustrate this argument with reference to a very short sequence that occurs near the beginning of *The Square*. The documentary opens with the filmmakers' observation of an extended live interview, conducted by a China Central Television camera crew in one of the Tiananmen Square police precincts, and featuring some of the officers who work there. After this scene is concluded, the documentary shifts outside, to the external space of the square proper. These spaces are linked, however, by a brief four-shot transition sequence. The final shot of the interview cuts away, not to an image of Tiananmen, but to a close-up of Mao's face, or two-thirds of it: a portrait, slightly off-center, which fills almost half the screen, but framed at either side so that the image is incomplete and almost two-dimensional. The sound of people working can be heard, but it is hard to identify the actual activity. The film then cuts to a close-up of the source of this sound: it is carpenters planing wood. We appear to be in a workshop, but where exactly is difficult to tell. The camera tilts slowly upwards, to reveal behind the workmen the same portrait of Mao's face that we have seen in the first shot. This time, however, we can see that it is framed through an opening in the wall of the workshop. The camera cuts again to a close-up of a carpenter's hands planing, tilting slowly upwards before cutting to the final shot. This is a full shot of the workmen, framed again through an opening in a wall; a smaller segment of the portrait is visible again in the background, thus providing us with the perspective necessary to understand the spatial relationship between the image and the workmen. The camera then cuts to the square itself: in the distance we can see the façade of the Forbidden City, hung with its now barely visible image of Mao.

This sequence is unusual, almost unsettling. It bears no obvious causal or temporal relationship to either the scene that precedes it, or that which follows. When and where it occurs is not immediately clear. Its significance, I would suggest, is simply that it allows the directors to introduce the image of Mao, an image that recurs throughout the film, functioning as a point of visual reference in a documentary that has no clear characters or "storyline."[30] The nature of the activity we see depicted in this brief scene is essentially unimportant: what *is* important is that it takes place under the watchful eyes of the Chairman somewhere near Tiananmen Square, thus hinting at the centrality of ideology and politics to the film's themes. Yet what is most interesting is that through a series of spatial reframings that invert the classical relationship between an establishing shot (which here comes last, as opposed to first) and a close-up (which here comes first, as opposed to last), Zhang and Duan edit this sequence in a manner that mirrors the structure of the entire documentary. We start with a detail, we finish with an overall picture; and the two are connected through spatial proximity. The form of the documentary as a whole — one in which individual, internally coherent sequences are edited such that they build up a broader picture of the documentary's subject matter — is thus replicated over the course of this one short scene.

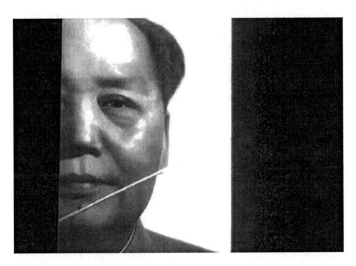

Figure 10.1. *The Square*. Close-up of Mao's portrait.

Figure 10.2. *The Square*. Carpenters working, with Mao's portrait framed through a wall in the background.

Figure 10.3.   *The Square.* Close-up of carpenter's hands, planing wood.

Figure 10.4.   *The Square.* Full shot of carpenters working, with Mao's portrait in the background.

That the "public" documentary as a form is understood to function in this manner is reinforced by the explicitly metaphorical or allegorical language used by early New Documentary Movement directors to describe their work. Wu Wenguang illustrates this point clearly in a discussion of his documentary *Jiang Hu: Life on the Road* (1999), about a Big Top and its traveling company of players. *Jiang Hu*, he insists, should not be understood as a film that is merely about the experience of "other people," namely those without urban residency, who effectively constitute the subjects of the documentary. Rather, it should be understood as a film about everyone in China, urban or rural: now everyone's life is "on the road," in a constant state of flux in which the old rules no longer apply, and the new ones have yet to be created.[31] Through these people, who form a new and distinct social strata that lies somewhere between that of the migrant worker and the farmer, one can analyze broader social change.[32] The metaphorical or allegorical mode thus becomes the form through which the relationship between daily life and more abstract socio-political issues can be traced in a concrete manner, imbuing both with meaning. As Duan Jinchuan has said, without metaphors to connect the sites of his films to everyday activity, shooting such locations would be pointless.[33]

When one talks of "public" documentary, then, one is not merely describing a kind of documentary focused on specific subject matter, nor a genre with a particular political message. One is also talking of a documentary form that developed to mediate the tensions between a particular conceptualization of what documentary is and what it does, and the belief that it should be shot in a certain manner. Whilst far less didactic than the *zhuantipian* of the 1980s, early New Documentary Movement directors sought to shape the events they captured on film to suggest a particular message. In order to achieve this goal, they developed practices and forms that allowed them both to manage the unexpected elements inherent in location shooting, and to curtail the significance of the contingent in relation to the overall diegetic structure of the documentary. They desired the unpredictable to the extent that it signified realism, but not to the degree that it undermined coherence. With the emergence of new genres, however, the delicate balance between these diverse elements is gradually shifting; this is no more apparent than in the attitudes displayed by directors of the "private" documentary genre toward the work of their predecessors.

"Private" Documentary and the Rejection of Metaphor

For many younger directors, the "private" genre is not merely a rejection of social and political ideals; it is a comprehensive refutation of the "metaphorical" or mosaic mode adopted by the early documentary filmmakers. The director Hu Xinyu makes this view abundantly clear in a discussion of the final scene of his film *The Man*. This film chronicles the trials and tribulations of three male friends who share a bed-sit in Taiyuan, Shanxi Province. The final scene, however, is a single, long take of a mouse dying on the floor of their room, having been shot by one of the trio with his air gun. As a conclusion, the significance of this image is hard to decipher. What relationship does it bear to the rest of the material? The obvious answer would be that it is in some way metaphorical or symbolic, as would probably have been the case in the early "public" documentaries. Yet Hu Xinyu rejects this interpretation absolutely: "It's [this shot] not a metaphor. Poetry rejects metaphor: so too does documentary."[34] In this understanding of documentary, an event takes on no significance in relation to the broader picture: it signifies only in and of itself. It is, in other words, singular and particular, with no wider import. This point is made even more forcefully by the poet and filmmaker Yu Jian, when commenting on audience responses to documentary films screened at the 2005 Yunnan Multi Culture Visual Festival in Kunming. Why, he inquired, was every work, every character in a documentary, expected to be "meaningful"? Everyone seemed to think of him or herself as a potential intellectual, always wanting to know "why": "There is no why, it's just like that."[35] Interpretation in a documentary context is thus a meaningless exercise, as the events portrayed speak for, and only for, themselves.

What this approach suggests is a subtle readjustment of the relationship between the pro-filmic and the diegetic. In the "public" documentary, this event, if symbolic, would have derived its significance from its position relative to the other elements of the diegetic structure, and the overall form into which they had been edited. In contrast, in *The Man*, the pro-filmic event is asserted as absolutely contingent, in the sense of being unassimilable to wider meaning. The death of a mouse is simply the death of a mouse: the image derives its resonance less from a framework of broader symbolic significance, than from its place within the daily routine of the three main characters. The primacy of diegetic coherence has thus given way to an assumption that material events are inherently unpredictable, and that the structuring of a documentary should reflect this reality. A film should not seek to frame an event; rather, an event should frame a film.

An extreme example of this approach can be found in Zuo Yixiao's short documentary *Losing*. *Losing* is the chronicle of a divorce. It tracks the day in July 2004 when the director and his wife formally dissolved their marriage. Stylistically it displays many of the traits that have been associated with "private" documentaries: a subjective voiceover, akin to an internal monologue; the on-camera presence of the director as an integral part of the diegesis; the constant questioning of the possibility of capturing a truly objective account of the proceedings on camera. But the film also strongly emphasizes the inherently contingent nature of the film's events. As Zuo's voiceover announces in the prelude to the film, which describes briefly his married life in the run-up to divorce:

> Every day brings change. Some of these changes I liked, some I didn't. Some I expected, some I didn't.

After this statement, which concludes a monologue over photographic and home video images of the director, his wife, and their child, the camera cuts to an image of Zuo, inside his home, camera in hand, facing a mirror. He says: "As I shoot this, I am about to get divorced." The scene then cuts to the film's title. The implication is clear: life is change; many of these changes are unpredictable; and the collapse of a relationship is but one of them.

This position is reinforced by the film's structure. To describe *Losing* as a chronicle of a divorce is perhaps misleading, for it implies a sense of extended temporality that is quite consciously missing from the documentary. The film's short prelude is all we get to hear about the couple's life together prior to the present; similarly, the documentary concludes immediately following the official dissolution of their marriage. In effect, *Losing* is almost entirely dedicated to the actual day on which this event takes place, cutting between Zuo's feelings in the early hours of the morning, and, to a lesser extent, his wife's; their journey across Shanghai to the government office where they will obtain their annulment; and the final confirmation that this has been authorized. Thus, although the divorce does not quite take place in "real time," the relationship of the events on screen is derived from temporal as opposed to spatial proximity. Zuo's interest is in the current moment, not the past; how he feels now, not how he got this way. Thus, he inverts the relationship between time and space implicit within Duan's metaphorical mode to assert the significance of events taking place in the present. Suspended as it is within such a prescribed time frame, *Losing* therefore provides few clues as to why the couple's marriage may actually have broken down: all we know is that now, on this day in July 2004, it has. In consequence, the divorce really does appear contingent, whilst the possibility of generalizing from the couple's experience is limited. In *Losing*, the event does not simply frame the film: to all intents and purposes it *is* the film.

Zuo's film uses editing to define its subject matter as both private and idiosyncratic. Yet even more recent documentaries that touch on issues of history, power, or ideology — all subjects considered to lie at the heart of the "public" documentary — tend to incorporate or highlight the contingency of their subject matter. This effect is often achieved less through technical facility than by incorporating the unexpected pro-filmic event as a fundamental part of their formal architecture. In other words, unexpected events are actually featured as key to the documentary's development. One excellent example is Wang Bing's *West of the Tracks* (2003). Shot on a shoestring budget by a first-time director using a hired DV camera, this nine-hour trilogy garnered domestic and international accolades upon its release. Most of this praise was the result of the unique picture it presents of a particular historical moment: "the dusk of an entire social world," to quote Lu Xinyu, referring to the closure of the Shenyang factories that she sees as the main protagonists of the epic's first section, "Rust," and the socialist ideals that they symbolized.[36] In this sense, *West of the Tracks* shares an affinity with the more metonymic approach of early

New Documentary Movement films. Yet, in his approach to the question of the unexpected pro-filmic event, Wang Bing demonstrates a sensibility subtly different from that of his predecessors. This distinctiveness is illustrated by one particular moment in "Rust" that has received significant critical attention. Wang is filming a maintenance worker in one of the factories recounting his life story, most particularly the disruption to his education that resulted from the Cultural Revolution. Suddenly, one of his co-workers enters the room and announces that the plant will shut in two days: the news has just been broken to them by the factory manager. As Lu Xinyu points out, Wang has caught on film the precise moment at which the factory received its "death sentence."[37] Yet the director's explication of this sequence is also of interest:

> This moment is extremely important. Although when we see it now we are prepared for it, at the time of filming there was no way to know [it was coming]. You [the viewer] and he [the worker] experience the moment together; you will remember it very clearly.[38]

Wang suggests that the significance of this scene — one which is arguably pivotal to the entirety of *West of the Tracks*, in that its consequences play out for the rest of the documentary — derives from its contingency. Its utter unexpectedness, both for those on screen and those watching, ensures its lasting power. Here, the unpredictability of the pro-filmic is no longer a problem or a challenge; instead, it is a quality to be harnessed by the documentary filmmaker.

Toward a Contingent Film Practice

Zuo Yixiao and Wang Bing utilize a sense of events as contingent for slightly different purposes. In *Losing*, the emphasis appears to be on decontextualizing the collapse of a relationship, asserting the specificity of the experience, and (implicitly) exonerating the director from any responsibility. In *West of the Tracks*, the contingent provides an emotional entrée into the world of the film's subjects, supposedly encouraging empathy between the audience and the individuals portrayed on screen. It thus appears as a linking device, an attempt at connecting viewer and subject, individual experience and historical context, without erasing the distinctions between these categories. Yet the fact that both these films seek to make use of the contingent at all is demonstrative both of a change in Chinese documentary film practice and in an understanding of what documentary as a genre is. Increasingly, the extensive pre-shoot preparation preferred by the early directors is being abandoned in favor of a far more laissez-faire approach to filming. Wu Wenguang, for example, now eschews his previous "ethnographic" style altogether: with regard to *Fuck Cinema* (2005), at the time of writing his most recent documentary, he talks about coming across the topic unexpectedly, rather than deliberately selecting or preparing for it.[39] This sense of stumbling across the subject of one's film, sometimes literally, is echoed by other filmmakers.[40] That this, in turn, has been accentuated by the emergence of DV is also clear. Wang Bing only turned to the documentary form when it became evident that the technical, logistical, and financial demands of undertaking a feature film were beyond his means. In consequence, after renting a DV camera and buying around twenty DV cassettes, he says he suddenly found that, camera in hand, he was unsure of what to do next: he had no clear sense of how to go about structuring his film in relation to a potential subject.[41] When uncertainty permeates the filmmaking process at so many different levels, it is hardly surprising that it is also increasingly manifested on screen.

These changes are also intertwined with a reconceptualization of the documentary form that goes beyond the rationalization of a financial or technological imperative. No longer is documentary seen, in almost allegorical terms, as a means whereby broadly applicable truths about society as a whole are conveyed through the observation of a part. Instead, contemporary directors seem to associate it with a quite different experience, pithily summarized by Zhu Chuanming: "the excitement of shooting a documentary lies in never knowing what you will be going to shoot. Sometimes not even you yourself know what you are doing."[42] In this formulation, the fleeting and the contingent are integral to the documentary experience; the *raison d'être* of the director has, in turn, become that of capturing them on film.[43] Rather than seeking to shape their material through editing, contemporary directors therefore talk of responding to the flow of events as they happen, allowing the documentary to evolve. To quote Wang Bing on *West of the Tracks*:

> When you start, you may plan the structure, style, and content of your film, but as you gradually get into it, the point at which the object of your shoot reveals itself is not up to you. In the midst of constant development, things have their own cycle, and you have to slowly wait for this. Only once this cycle has been constituted will you feel that your film is gradually beginning to take shape.[44]

Wang here implies that the structure of *West of the Tracks* was not imposed *a priori*; instead, it evolved out of the process of interaction with his environment and his subject matter. Contingency is thus accepted as pervading the documentary not simply on the level of practice, but also in relation to the theorization of its form and function.

This quotation from Wang Bing, focused as it is on the interplay between director and subject, echoes Zhang Zhen's proposition that *xianchang* is in effect an ethical reformulation of the relationship between subject and object. It thus brings us full circle, in the process suggesting — as I hope I have illustrated — that contemporary Chinese documentary filmmakers are not per se rejecting the basic principles of the early New Documentary Movement. Instead, they are abandoning those methods adopted by the early New Documentary Movement directors in defiance of the dynamic of contingency inherent in location shooting, but necessitated by both circumstance and inclination, thus extending the possibilities of *xianchang* to their logical conclusion. This has helped effect a shift from a metonymic model of documentary toward one more closely associated with specificity and unpredictability. Such developments are not historically unique to China.[45] However, within a Chinese context they carry particular overtones. Socialist realism is noted for its use of "models," the most famous being the model characters that peopled revolutionary opera. Derived from the concept of *dianxing*, or the "typical," outlined by Mao in his *Talks at the Yan'an Conference on Literature and Art* (1942), such characters were broadly imitative, in that they were intended for emulation: they were a key way in which individuals could be instructed in the basic categories of Maoist political thought.[46] But in consequence they were also archetypes, images fashioned from material that was already understood as present within the body politic, but presented in an idealized form.[47] Through such images broader social and political issues could be articulated. Therefore, at their most extreme, socialist realist characters could become stock figures in an allegorization of social processes, the outcome of which was pre-determined: there was little space for development, change, or the unexpected in a narrative where revolutionary history was "epic, futuristic, and always victorious in the end."[48]

Set against such a history, the rejection of the general and the embrace of the particular that is explicit in some contemporary Chinese documentary take on a greater significance.[49] In their deployment of metonymic form and ambivalence toward the contingent, the early works of the New Documentary Movement still bear traces of the socialist realist tradition. This is not to suggest an unbroken connection between the two, but rather to highlight the complexity of periods of aesthetic transition, in which old and new forms of media practice may co-exist simultaneously, often synergistically. Despite their many obvious differences, these documentaries do not depart completely from the practices of the 1980s. Whilst the moral certitude of socialist realist discourse has been abandoned, there is still a desire to view people as representative of broader social and political developments. Thus, the subjects of Duan Jinchuan's early films are important as much because of what they suggest about society at large, as in and of themselves. In contrast, contemporary documentary has broken with this practice in a more decisive way. At one extreme, the "private" documentary emphasizes a complete rupture with the past, and a clearer distinction between the individual and society: Zuo Yixiao's divorce may be personally significant, but its broader social import is hard to assess. At the other, directors like Wang Bing have tried to reconstruct this relationship so that, although the individual is recognized as distinct, he or she is seen as caught up in social and political change, whilst not necessarily symbolic of it. By embracing the possibilities offered by the contingent at a variety of levels, these filmmakers have begun to explore new ways of representing the relationship between "self" and "society." In this sense, these works are perhaps more political than many have so far been prepared to admit.

These issues, though locally specific in their manifestation, are not unique to contemporary China. Indeed, one of the advantages of recognizing their salience in this context is precisely the comparative dimension it adds to any study of Chinese documentary. The problem of the generic and the specific is closely bound up with issues of objectivity, subjectivity, and the power of representation that have bedeviled Euro-American social-scientific thought, as much as socialist realism, for the better part of the last century. These issues in turn have found their own expression in documentary filmmaking. Even as Wiseman was starting to hone his self-consciously objective form of Direct Cinema, these questions — who is representing whom, how, and for what purpose? — had already been broached by his French contemporary, Jean Rouch, in the form of the reflexive documentaries for which he was to become famous. Nor have such questions become less relevant with time. As we watch Chinese documentary filmmakers grapple with the legacy of Maoist positivism, their efforts should perhaps serve as a reminder that the political implications of mediation remain as relevant to us, here and now, as they ever were.

Conclusion

What I have attempted to demonstrate in this chapter is that, although there are indeed differences between more recent Chinese documentary film and that which was shot at the beginning of the 1990s, these distinctions are not perhaps as stark as is sometimes implied. There has been a tendency to see both the emergence and the pluralization of the New Documentary Movement as a consequence of serial polarizations: initially, between the movement and the official state-run media; and subsequently, in the wake of political, technological, and institutional change, between different stages of the movement. In choosing instead to focus on the ordering and understanding of material within the documentaries, and on shooting live as a practice, I have tried to suggest a process which is perhaps less absolute. Thus, although the early directors broke with certain of the practices of official documentary production, others —consciously or unconsciously — were maintained; hence the importance of the metonymic form. More recent directors, with their emphasis on specificity and particularity, have tried far more self-consciously to distance their work from this tradition, although to differing degrees, and in different ways. Yet, whilst these recent films may represent a more obvious rejection of the socialist realist legacy, they cannot be categorized as an absolute break with the work of the early 1990s. Instead, elements of each approach can be identified within the other, not least as a consequence of a continued commitment to *xianchang* on the part of all directors. Although the emergence of the "private" documentary may signify an attempt to rework the relationship between the individual and society, it is consequent upon factors already present, if not always fully developed, in the earliest of the New Documentary Movement films from the 1990s. Both the emergence and pluralization of the movement are perhaps better understood as an ongoing process of negotiation between tradition and innovation, rather than as a series of ruptures whereby the former is abandoned in favor of the latter. Furthermore, given the nature of the tradition concerned, and its particular intellectual inheritance, this negotiation has parallels well beyond the borders of China proper.

What I trust this argument also demonstrates is the extent to which Chinese documentary is the product of an interaction between context, theory, and practice. Academic analysis to date has tended to focus on particular aspects of the New Documentary Movement, most obviously its subject matter, mode of production, and relationship to both mainstream media and political context. In doing so, it has often neglected the ways in which these issues are intimately connected to, indeed mediated through, questions of film form and practice. Yet, as I hope I have made clear, the documentaries addressed in this chapter, and many others that fall outside its scope, are neither crude nor unremarkable. Rather, the generic forms that they exemplify can be understood as sophisticated attempts to navigate the tensions between the various factors noted above. Almost two decades after *Bumming in Beijing* putatively launched the New Documentary Movement, perhaps it is time for a considered reassessment both of how we approach the analysis of Chinese documentary film, and of what we understand its significance to be.

11 Excuse Me, Your Camera Is in My Face: Auteurial Intervention in PRC New Documentary

Yomi Braester

The title of this chapter may be taken as a polite rendering of the answer given by an interviewee in *There Is a Strong Wind in Beijing* (1999, henceforth *Strong Wind*). The filmmakers intrude on a man in a public toilet, literally caught with his pants down, direct the camera and boom at him, and ask, "Is the wind in Beijing strong?" to which he answers, "Damn! I'm squatting here and you're still fuckin' asking?!" (*Wo cao! Zhe'r dunzhe, ni ye tamade wen ya!*). *Strong Wind* is an exceptional documentary by any standards, yet the scene exemplifies the approach of some recent PRC directors, who take a provocative stance vis-à-vis their subjects. The chapter's title is also chosen to contrast the confrontational attitude of *Strong Wind* with the motto of recent documentary filmmakers and fiction directors, "My Camera Doesn't Lie" (*Wode sheyingji bu sahuang*).[1] The so-called New Documentary filmmakers of the 1990s have developed an aesthetics based on unscripted spontaneity that often underplays the filmmaker's presence. The trend has received much attention due to its success in forming a prominent style, to the detriment of critical discussion of both state-sponsored propaganda — still the prevalent mode of documentary production in the PRC — and nuances within independent documentary filmmaking. The focus on the purported objectivity and passivity of the camera may be misleading. In fact, even the phrase "My Camera Doesn't Lie" is originally paired with, "[yet] I am lying."[2] In the context of documentary films, the ostensible ceding of directorial power to the camera has obscured strong tendencies among new filmmakers to intrude upon their subjects, though usually in settings less compromising than the public toilet in *Strong Wind*.

An emphasis in this chapter on films that subscribe to the filmmaker's intrusion upon the scene, especially on instances in which the director's intervention is accompanied by prodding the subject into action, offers a corrective view of New Documentary cinema. First, we should acknowledge variations within the trend and go beyond its current reception, which has tended to generalizations — whether opinionated condemnation or, more often, overenthusiastic glorification as the latest word in world cinema.[3] One should bear in mind that New Documentary filmmakers never formed a movement in the sense of a co-ordinated and uniform group, accompanied by manifestos or prescriptive rules. When Lu Xinyu writes of the "New Documentary Movement,"[4] she does so to set the films apart from Maoist ideology and production patterns. Yet the movement has never committed to a single line, and shades of difference have already been noted, for example in Valerie Jaffe's discussion of conflicting attitudes toward self and other.[5] Moreover, insofar as the intrusive approach breaks away from a main mold that relies on distanced objectivity, the intention behind each case may not be the same. The intervention does not rely on an inherent rapport between the filmmakers and the interviewees. Whereas *Strong Wind* courts defensive and even aggressive responses, the other films discussed here seem to use the intrusion to get closer to, and even intimate with, the filmed subjects.

The cases examined in this chapter might, in a different context, be dismissed as self-indulgent, part of a narcissism of which some independent filmmakers have been accused.[6] The directors discussed here have encountered criticism for extreme self-absorption and accusations (in the case of Yang Lina's *Home Video*) of a patronizing attitude toward their subjects (as I have heard Ning Ying's *Railroad of Hope* described on occasion). Such charges privilege reportage-like exposés of larger social issues and stigmatize any manipulation, which is associated with official propaganda. The intrusive approach has emerged from a perception that current practices are inadequate, at least for some subject matter.

Yiman Wang, in a chapter in this volume, also discerns a recent tendency toward directorial intervention, and links it to a discourse on intimacy and distance from the filmed subjects. Wang points to the tension between the perceptions that identification with the subjects is more ethical and that disaffection supports the film's claim to truth. I claim that the directorial intervention is also motivated by the filmmakers' conception of themselves as auteurs, not simply in the sense of stressing their vision, but more specifically exercising auteurship by being present in their films and even confronting and inconveniencing their subjects.

The nuances in perceiving the documentary filmmaker's relation to the filmed subjects are akin to differences between Frederick Wiseman's Direct Cinema and Jean Rouch's *cinema vérité*, as described by Erik Barnouw: "The direct cinema documentarist took his camera to a situation of tension and waited hopefully for a crisis; the Rouch version of *cinéma vérité* tried to precipitate one. The direct cinema artist aspired to invisibility; the Rouch *cinéma vérité* artist was often an avowed participant. The direct cinema artist played the role of uninvolved bystander; the *cinéma vérité* artist espoused that of provocateur."[7] I suggest that the intrusive approach stems from a reaction to Wiseman's aesthetics, and especially to the analogous concept of *xianchang*, which can be roughly translated as "on site." The turn to directorial intervention may be related to the wish to foreground the alternative to state-sponsored propaganda, yet even more decisive, in my view, is the filmmakers' view of the auteur's role.

I pay particular attention to four films, in chronological order. I start by examining Zhang Yuan and Duan Jinchuan's *The Square* (1994) and comparing it to the precedent set in the TV series *Tiananmen* (1991). *The Square* is a test case for the limits of New Documentary aesthetics. On the one hand, it is in many ways exemplary of the New Documentary principles. It shows how the trend fashions itself as an alternative to official productions and their concealed manipulation of the filmed subjects. On the other hand, *The Square* also points to the limits of non-intervention and the benefits of intruding upon the interviewees. I then turn to *Strong Wind* and demonstrate how it uses the intervention to elicit the performative aspects of the interaction between director and filmed subject. Next I address Yang Lina's *Home Video* (2001), which trains the camera on the director's own family and challenges family members to reveal past actions and present motivations. Finally, I look at Ning Ying's *Railroad of Hope* (2002) as an exploration of the director's latitude of legitimate action in eliciting the interviewees' private thoughts and dreams.[8] These films by no means present a coherent approach to documentary filmmaking, yet they share some important devices. They feature direct questions by the director, often disorienting and even seemingly irrelevant to the situation, and they invade the subjects' personal spaces. The provocation often meets with apprehension, indignation, or outright hostility. The confrontation between camera and subject allows the filmmakers to comment on the uneasy, if not outright manipulative, relationship between the documenting and the documented and give the lie to both the invisibility of the director and the transparency of her message.

From Mao to Wiseman

Practically every account of the New Documentary cinema begins with Wu Wenguang's *Bumming in Beijing: The Last Dreamers* (1990). Wu has been the prime articulator of the movement's history and principles, and *Bumming in Beijing* became the measuring rod for subsequent films. Wu tells how many filmmakers were looking for a way to express themselves in post-1989 China and came together in late 1991, when the TV director Shi Jian organized a workshop in which he showed his eight-chapter TV series *Tiananmen* and Wu's *Bumming in Beijing*.[9] Zhang Yuan and Duan Jinchuan's *The Square*, a one-hundred-minute-long study of Tiananmen Square, can also be traced to that historical juncture, in terms of both personal acquaintance and guiding aesthetics.

As Chris Berry notes, New Documentary films share four common characteristics, all of which are apparent already in *Bumming in Beijing*: an indirect reflection on June Fourth as a "structuring absence"; a focus on urban life, reflecting on the condition of the filmmakers and their social circles; spontaneous shooting in line with "on-the-spot realism" (*jishi zhuyi*); and independent production.[10] These elements are determining factors in *The Square*. The Tiananmen Incident of 1989, although never mentioned in the film, casts its shadow on the location; the square is understood through its urban context and in relation to the people who document it; the film's unscripted nature underlines Tiananmen's use for daily activities; *The Square* was not only made independently of the TV stations and film studios, but also presents itself as the foil to official productions.

The Square sets itself apart from a long tradition of propaganda films that portray Tiananmen as the location of state functions. Starting with *The Birth of New China* (1949), Tiananmen has acquired a specific cinematic iconology, referring back to Mao's declaration of the founding of the PRC from the balcony of Tiananmen Gate and to the spectacles to be viewed by the leaders on the balcony rather than by the people in the square below. The carefully crafted conventions of the official documentaries underline Tiananmen's monumentality and the celebrations' extravagance. Zhang Yuan states explicitly that his film counters practices since 1949, in which documentary films have always been used for political purposes, to the point that cinema circles do not perceive them as bona fide films at all.[11] By contrast, *The Square* shows Tiananmen as a place for popular leisure, a cement-covered park where children fly their kites. Even when a salute to a visiting foreign dignitary takes place, passersby look with disinterest and return to the daily hustle and bustle as soon as the official event is over.

In fact, much of *The Square* is devoted to foregrounding the different aesthetics of the official and independent modes of filmmaking. In contrast with the slick look of propaganda productions, Zhang and Duan use a grainy black-and-white film stock, made for recording scientific experiments, which in Zhang Yuan's words feels "not entirely real" — presumably, the blurry texture counters realistic conventions (the choice of the domestically produced Baoding reels was also guided by financial concerns).[12] Shooting angles of soldiers are awkward and unflattering — for example, a rear view of a receding guard. Entire sequences, such as the flag raising ceremony, have the feel of comical outtakes and stress the highly manipulative selection of images deemed representative in propaganda films.

Zhang and Duan follow two important precedents, both of which lie at the foundation of New Documentary cinema. The first is the TV series *Tiananmen*, which was screened at Shi Jian's abovementioned workshop. *Tiananmen* (directed by Shi Jian and Chen Jue) stands at the transition point between state-sponsored and independent documentary. Commissioned by CCTV (Central Chinese Television), it was shot between 1988 and 1989, yet the occurrence of the June Fourth incident just before the series' scheduled release resulted in the shelving of the official production, which was never aired. The directors completed the project using their own funds in 1991.[13] The series ignores propagandistic, overbearing narratives and creates an oral history of Beijing. It is based mainly on extensive interviews with eyewitnesses to Beijing's transformation, from a former court eunuch to a contemporary fashion model. The eighth and last episode tells the history of Tiananmen. Historical footage, including some from *The Birth of New China*, is interwoven with contemporary interviews, with people such as the woman who, as a girl in 1953, was chosen to hand flowers to Mao during the National Day parade. Yet, rather than present complementary versions, the interviews end up belying the earlier documentaries. Juxtaposing the testimony of a woman who orchestrated the slogan shouting during Mao's review of the Red Guards with the 1966 footage of the event calls into question the ability to glean history from original material alone. When the woman is brought to give her testimony on the balcony of Tiananmen, where she had stood during one of the Cultural Revolution's most notable moments, she cannot relive that experience; instead, she explains how she would now change the slogans. As a documentary, *Tiananmen* does not capture objective history, as state productions before it claimed to do, but rather allows for a reflection on the creation of narratives.

Tiananmen's eighth episode makes an important contribution to rethinking the documentary aesthetic by training the camera on material that had not been considered as legitimate subject matter in official productions. The solemn tone is undercut by a conversation with a young child, who recognizes Chairman Mao's effigy on the gate — but when asked who Mao was, he says, "I don't know." The imposing portrait is literally taken off its pedestal as *Tiananmen* follows the process of painting a fresh replica and hanging it up instead of the dismantled older copy. Providing a stark contrast with the filmed records of state affairs, lengthy sequences show children at the square throwing snowballs, flying kites, and taking photos. Photography is singled out as a way to capture life on the go at Tiananmen. The documentary includes a brief interview with the four Wang brothers, professional photographers who have made it a habit to come down to the square. As they explain, the place "represents the people's joys and sorrows." The experience of being in the square is divested of grand symbolism and is figuratively parceled into short, private moments, as photos by the Wang brothers fill the screen, one at a time.

The TV series *Tiananmen* signals the square's transformation into what Wu Hung calls "a combat zone" — alluding to the violent clashes of June Fourth, but also referring to turning Tiananmen into the site of contesting artistic activities.[14] The filmmakers not only seek to tell a story different from the official line but also invade the square with their own cameras, literally changing the point of view from which the spectacle is seen and toward which it is staged. Whatever the new visions may include, the square is no longer imagined through Mao's omniscient gaze or its replication in propaganda films. The very existence of numerous visualizations of the square and multiple cameras inside the square is at the core of the challenge to the Maoist narrative.

The Square grafts the insights of the TV series onto another main influence for New Documentary cinema, namely Frederick Wiseman's documentaries. Since his 1967 film *Titicut Follies*, Wiseman has inspired filmmakers to make documentaries based on observation with minimal directorial input through score, voiceover narration, or other interpretive additions to the raw footage. Wu Wenguang and Duan Jinchuan were invited to the Yamagata International Documentary Film Festival in 1993, when a Wiseman retrospective was held.[15] Zhang Yuan was inspired by Wu Wenguang and was looking for a topic for a documentary. On the same day that Duan gave Zhang a copy of Wiseman's *Central Park* (1989), Zhang decided to go along with a film on Tiananmen.[16]

Central Park is exemplary of Wiseman's "thematic documentary," which structures unpremeditated footage around a theme. The film shows New Yorkers in the park as they walk, jog, boat, bike, skate, read, bird-watch, and picnic, and as they enjoy music concerts, theater performances, and parades. Zhang Yuan follows Wiseman in claiming that he would let the camera take in any sight and add his narrative only through editing.[17] The director of *Central Park* says: "The final film resembles fiction although it is based on un-staged, un-manipulated actions ... you structure it."[18] Wiseman's structuring device in *Central Park* involves placing citizens' behaviors in the larger context of urban policy, discussing the problems faced by the New York City Parks Department in maintaining the park and keeping it accessible to the public. In light of Wiseman's film, *The Square* not only redefines Tiananmen as an urban park but also challenges any understanding of the square simply through the matrix provided by policymakers.

Unlike Wiseman, who is sympathetic to professional planners, Zhang and Duan look sarcastically on the police station and other elements engaged in regulating the square. The different attitudes to figures of authority in *Central Park* and *The Square* derive from the dissimilar political contexts. Tiananmen's long history as an emblem of the state, and of the People's Republic in particular, endows *The Square* with a sense of irony. The directors' choice of Tiananmen as the location of urban activities aims at a cognitive dissonance. In observing the square — rather than spaces less fraught with symbolism (for example Taoranting Park, a municipal recreation spot landscaped with no monumental function in mind) — Zhang and Duan stress how national politics takes over urban design and how everyday life inevitably presents an alternative to the state's narrative. This nuance, crucial to the project, sets it apart from Wiseman's films. The deviation from Wiseman's model does not, however, amount to challenging the aesthetics of the New Documentary cinema. As Chris Berry notes, the New Documentary films put into action a form of what Lydia Liu calls "translingual practice," that is, a cultural adaptation to China's post-socialist agenda.[19] The deviation from the originary conceptualization is not necessarily an affront. Insofar as *The Square* introduces an alternative aesthetics to the tried formula of New Documentary films, it does so by training the camera on itself and foregrounding the filmmakers' inevitable intrusion into their subjects' space.

From *Xianchang* to *Guangchang*

The Square mostly follows the principles of New Documentary films, but it also calls — perhaps unintentionally — for rethinking the role of the director in ways that stretch the New Documentary aesthetics.

To understand the paradigms of New Documentary cinema, I turn to the term *xianchang*, or "on site," through which Wu Wenguang has formulated his ideas in recent years. Insofar as any coherent vision has been put forth by the New Documentary Movement, it revolved around *xianchang*. Originally the word for live broadcasting, the term refers in Wu's language to the site of production. Wu sees his role as documenting artwork at the time and place of its creation. In a series of books titled *Xianchang*, Wu presents photographs, scripts, oral testimony, and interviews to recreate the moment of origin of art in various media.[20] These so-called "files" are true to Wu's understanding of his role, as filmmaker and book editor alike, in terms of allowing the events to unfold in real time and on site rather than through a distilled narrative injected by the director. As an aesthetic principle, *xianchang* implies that the filmmaker exists in the film only as an archaeologist, a vehicle through which the site is channeled. His presence does not, so to speak, change the site's flow. Some may argue (as the editors of this volume have done in an enlightening correspondence) that *xianchang* includes the potential for directorial intrusion. *Bumming in Beijing*, for example, is based on interviews — but even though Wu Wenguang's presence is implicitly made known, the director makes no attempt to actively intervene, even when one of his subjects suffers a mental breakdown in front of the camera. Insofar as the *xianchang* aesthetics provides an auteurist model, it is for an auteur who stays behind the scenes and aims for objectivity.

Xianchang derives to a large extent from Wiseman's aesthetics of Direct Cinema, which not only emphasizes unscripted observation but also rejects directorial intervention. Although Direct Cinema is associated with the French trend known as *cinéma vérité*, Wiseman reacts against the intrusive practices of his French counterparts such as Jean Rouch, who in *Chronicle of a Summer* (1961) relies on interviews and sometimes uses provocative questioning. Indeed, the films discussed later in this chapter may be described as a return to a *cinéma vérité* approach. Although *The Square* does not fully challenge the Direct Cinema or *xianchang* aesthetics, Zhang and Duan suggest that the directors may in fact benefit from an intervention that changes the course of action around them.

The rupture in the *xianchang*-like position of the filmmakers as observers in *The Square* is subtle. The intrusion is not made directly by Zhang and Duan, but rather through another crew on site, with which a symbiotic relationship ensues. I argue that filming the other crew at work presents a criticism of official documentary practices of manipulating the filmed subject — but at the same time Zhang and Duan also use the other crew's actions to point out how the pretense of remaining objective observers is untenable for any filmmaker.

The coexistence of two crews on site is both the result of necessity and a fortuitous coincidence. To gain access to Tiananmen, the directors of *The Square* took advantage of Duan Jinchuan's connections at CCTV and accompanied a television crew. Since Duan (as soundman) and Zhang (as cinematographer) arrived with the officially approved crew, no one asked for their credentials, and they shot without any hindrance. Yet rather than simply ignore the TV crew, *The Square* often shoots the TV cameraman, soundman, and interviewer. Entire sequences turn into a commentary on filmmaking at Tiananmen. *The Square* must be read at three registers simultaneously — as a study of Tiananmen, as an examination of official documentary practices, and as a testimony to its directors' position as filmmakers.

Watching the TV crew at work underlines the different approach of the independent production. The TV crew is preparing a program celebrating the forty-fifth anniversary of the PRC. The TV director coaxes school children to recite Mao's words at the founding ceremony and thereby replicate the message of propaganda films since *The Birth of New China* and demonstrate the young generation's identification with the symbols of the state. Zhang and Duan expose the official manipulation of the filmed subjects and present their documentary as a foil to the TV program's artificiality. Whereas the TV crew interviews police officers with reverence, Zhang's camera captures the policemen and military personnel in compromising situations, for example when the smartly dressed members of the guard awkwardly straddle the chain surrounding the flagpole and walk through the crowd. The shot questions the borderline, symbolized by the chain, between state-regulated spaces and the people's use of the square for quotidian purposes. The scene is emblematic of the way in which *The Square* marks the fault lines between collective and private spheres, between monumental space and urban daily life, and between propaganda and new documentary. Instead of reaffirming Tiananmen as a monumental space monopolized by state politics and official representation, *The Square* shows the site as given to theatricality and performative manipulation.

Figure 11.1. *The Square.* Two camera crews, two approaches to interviewing.

Zhang says that his interest in Tiananmen comes from the square's use as a stage, by the government and dissident demonstrators alike.[21] The square's theatricality extends to the cinematographers. Zhang felt that the TV crew was acting for his camera, and that if someone were to shoot him, he too would have probably tailored his actions accordingly.[22] By dint of their presence, Zhang and Duan instigate, at least partially, the event that they record. For Zhang, no camera can be present at a site without influencing the outcome, directing and redirecting the actions captured on film. The question, however, is how the camera intrudes and to what effect.

To drive home the cinematographer's — any photographer's — manipulative position, *The Square* portrays the expectations to perform. Zhang's camera lingers, for example, on people taking a photo in front of Tiananmen. The photographer, smartly clad and self-confident, faces the unsure domestic tourists — a man tries in vain to straighten his tie, a woman is told to hide the receipt in her hand behind her back. Like the still photographer, the CCTV crew is shown to induce specific answers from children visiting Tiananmen. On top of Tiananmen's balcony, the TV director attempts to be invisible. "Don't look at me," he says, "don't look at the camera." The director elicits readymade responses and obvious interactions: "Where are you standing?" The children answer as one: "Where Chairman Mao stood." "What did Chairman Mao say?" The children, in unison: "The PRC is founded." "What else?" asks the director, but the children are stumped: "Nothing else." Here the TV director steps in as master of the situation: "Speak out clearly: 'The Chinese people have arisen!' Ready, set, go!" On cue, the children repeat the line made famous in *The Birth of New China*. The already media-savvy children comport with the camera's requirements. The TV director speaks in the voice of the state, and they conform to its demand.

Apart from the inherent theatricality of the situation, Zhang and Duan are not overtly manipulative. Yet since they incorporate the TV crew's camera into their film, *The Square* becomes a document of directorial intrusion, even if not their own. Without a clear disavowal of the TV crew — *The Square* never even explains its relation to the filmed crew — one may even believe that Zhang and Duan are behind the intrusion. This hint of intervention by the directors allows *The Square* to adhere to the *xianchang* aesthetics and at the same time demonstrate its limits. Chris Berry asks about the balcony scene, "Is this just footage of the [CCTV] program makers doing their jobs? Or is it an ironic contrast with the pure observation pursued by Duan and Zhang, exposing the fabricated reality of conventional state-sponsored documentary modes?"[23] I see the situation not only as ironic, but also as an exposé of Zhang and Duan's own artifice — not fabricated but nevertheless acted out. The TV crew's presence is essential in allowing *The Square*'s directors to remain suspended between outside observation and complicity with the TV camera that encourages scripted performance.[24] Zhang and Duan's non-interference is preserved only as long as they intervene vicariously through another's camera.

Extreme Filmmaking: *There Is a Strong Wind in Beijing*

On-the-spot realism gained dominance in the 1990s, and the influence of Wu Wenguang's circle can be traced in almost every documentary film. Other art forms, such as performance art and photography, were rooted in the same milieu. These forms, too, largely concentrated on recording the moment, as if the artist had little latitude for interaction. Yet performance art and digital art also started exploring more involved forms, for example in the works of Feng Mengbo, who created interactive video games that require the spectator's participation.

A case of special relevance to cinema is *A Social Survey* (1998), a seven-minute-long video artwork by Zhao Liang. In the same year that Zhao shot *Paper Airplane*, a study of drug addicts in the New Documentary mode, he also made *A Social Survey*. Throughout the film, the photographer roams through Beijing with a handgun placed directly in front of the camera, pointed at passersby. Walking through a busy shopping street, into a KFC, a shopping mall, and a subway train, the artist fails to elicit any reaction. The crowds are indifferent to the camera and the pistol. The piece draws attention to the aggression inherent in filmmaking, calling to mind Michael Powell's *Peeping Tom* (1960), in which the photographer carries a knife and a mirror attached to his film camera and records his victims' horror as they witness their own violent death. Zhao keeps his finger on the trigger, yet his unsuccessful provocation suggests that it is not the director who remains a bystander but rather the filmed subjects, who prefer to ignore him. Eventually Liang spots a subway rider who is annoyed by his attention. The director intentionally aggravates the situation by lingering on the man, until the latter moves to physically turn the camera and gun away. The piece, which starts with an accelerated shot, ends with a slow-motion shot that further underlines the lack of concern of the passersby. The aptly titled piece indeed functions as a social survey. Much like Zhang Yuan's exploration of ordinary people going through daily routines, Zhao samples everyday activities in the city. Yet by invoking first-person-shooter videogames, in which the gamer operates within a virtual realm, Zhao gives the lie to the implied position of the director as an unobtrusive observer and reverses the roles — the director looks eagerly for action, while the subjects shut him out. Zhao's piece, however, is short and enigmatic, leaving inexplicit any challenge to the accepted practices of documentary filmmaking.

A more comprehensive exploration of confrontational filmmaking is found in *There Is a Strong Wind in Beijing*. *Strong Wind* derives its aesthetics also from being a shoestring production, even by New Documentary standards. The three filmmakers (Ju Anqi, director; Liu Yonghong, cameraman; Wang Yu, soundman) availed themselves of thirteen black-and-white 16mm film rolls, bought cheaply since seven of the rolls had long expired, and a five-yuan microphone mounted on a discarded TV antenna. Using two home-use VCRs to edit the film, Ju excised almost nothing, leaving under- and over-exposed shots, and practically ended up with a 1: 1 ratio of raw footage to used film. Intertitles and black screen time were added to the thirty minutes of footage, resulting in a fifty-minute film.[25] The patently poor quality, the reasons for which are given at the film's end, draws attention to the filmmaking process. The black screen time, often accompanying dialogue among the filmmakers as they move from one site to another, emphasizes the director's presence behind the camera.

Not that the director's intervention is otherwise subtle. The film's premise is simple: the crew goes around Beijing randomly asking the question, "Do you think the wind in Beijing is strong?" The ensuing interaction is best understood at the performative rather than semantic level — not in relation to the inane question about weather, but rather as prompting a social interaction. One may observe how — and not only with what words — various people respond to the unexpected question. People on the street react with varying degrees of media savvy — at times baffled by the non-sequitur, on other occasions trying to come up with a narrative to accommodate the question, for example, "It used to be strong before. The protective forest around Beijing works." The haphazard encounters yield a surprising amount of information about Beijing's streets and present a slice of life. The principle of spontaneous shooting, identified with the *xianchang* aesthetics, shows its advantages toward the end of the movie, when the filmmakers run into the penniless and desperate parents of a child with leukemia. The director reacts quickly and follows the parents to see their child, and a moving human story materializes out of the chance meeting.

The most blatant element of *Strong Wind* remains, however, the filmmakers' repeated challenge to the involuntary interviewees' privacy. Even when they reach out for friendly interaction — "May I eat with you?"; "Have a smoke!" — the interlocutors frown upon the over-familiar approach by total strangers. The subjects' reaction also varies according to their social standing. Residents of an apartment building answer with relative friendliness even when approached at their home. By contrast, a self-appointed vigilante accosts the filmmakers and requires that they first get clearance from the neighborhood committee. The viewer is alerted to the multilayered intrusion to private property as well as to a space regulated by the state apparatus. The most resistant to the filmmakers' efforts at making contact is not even the toilet user discussed above but rather a businessman sitting in a hotel lobby. When asked, "Does your life now give you a sense of superiority?" he retorts, confident of his spatial mastery, "I'd like to answer with my own question — what unit are you from, coming to interview us?" The filmmakers' intrusive position relies on the subjects' willingness to co-operate — or on their inability to protect their privacy.

Ju Anqi may be paying tribute to Zhang Yuan and Duan Jinchuan's *The Square* by talking to a man shooting an upbeat program for CCTV, on new construction in Beijing. The man explains that the film should give Chinese and foreigners alike an occasion to praise the new Beijing. Ju's approach clearly differs from the official line represented by the interviewee. The crew of *Strong Wind* also goes to Tiananmen and records its mundane aspects. One man says: "I have nothing to do so I came to loaf around; I have no work." The dialogue demonstrates the false pretense — what Zhang Yuan identifies as the inherent theatricality — behind supposedly spontaneous interaction in the shadow of Tiananmen's powerful presence as a symbol of the state. The interlocutors, identified by their accents as domestic tourists or migrant workers, blurt out slogan-like phrases: "It's the country's capital, the heart of the PRC. It shows to the world China's strength"; "I hope that China will become even more powerful and prosperous." A man — most likely an illegal migrant — admits to being nervous, at least partly because of the director's presence. The full dialogue gives a sense of the migrant's homesickness, fear of the authorities, and social awkwardness. The director, probably because he holds a camera and speaks in a confident Beijing accent, is inevitably perceived as a menace and identified with the law. Moreover, the scene at Tiananmen is presented almost entirely through blank screens accompanying the off-screen dialogue.[26] The disembodied voices emphasize the underlying tension between the filmmakers and their equipment on the one hand and the filmed subjects on the other. Both *A Social Survey* and *Strong Wind* elicit from the crowd feelings of being threatened, indignation, or outright hostility. Rather than being taken for cheap pranks, they should be understood as comments on how official propaganda can only elicit canned responses — and on the limits of the *xianchang* aesthetics in countering that practice.

Capturing the Yangs: *Home Video*

Whereas *Strong Wind* is interested in the effects of directorial intrusion in public spaces, Yang Lina's *Home Video* literally brings home the approach. Yang is better known for her first film *Old Men* (1999; director credited as Yang Tianyi), welcomed by Wu Wenguang as an exemplary piece in the vein of previous New Documentary films.[27] In her first work, Yang looks at a group of octogenarians who gather daily to catch some sun, shoot the breeze, and keep abreast of who has "moved away." Whereas in *Old Men* the director's role is limited to that of a facilitator who asks disinterested questions, the subject matter of *Home Video* calls for a different approach. The film is motivated by the director's attempt to find out why her parents divorced, at a time when she was away from home. The entire film consists of interviews with Yang's mother, father, and younger brother, mostly in a talking heads format. Yang cannot, and does not pretend to, keep aloof from her subjects. From the very beginning, the director's voice is heard from behind the camera, and the interviewees look at the camera and address the director in intimate terms. They all refer to the film as Lina's personal project. It is precisely by injecting herself into the film that she can elicit a compassionate portrait of each of her family members.

Yang explains that she made both films with little training or systematic knowledge of documentary filmmaking, and that she had no model to follow in shooting *Home Video*. In the process of shooting *Old Men*, she grew wary of advice to render the situations more dramatically. Soon after, she left her position as an actor at the People's Liberation Army Theater, the prime producer of state-sponsored stage propaganda.[28] An alternative approach was hard to find, since few foreign documentaries were available in China at the time. The success of *Old Men* at the Yamagata International Documentary Film Festival opened important venues, yet no paradigm existed for handling the blatantly autobiographical and sensitive material of her parents' divorce. One may cite the taboo-breaking portrayal of a dysfunctional family in Zhang Yuan's *Sons* (1996); years later, Yang was moved by Andrew Jarecki's *Capturing the Friedmans* (2003), which tries to uncover the truth about a father who was charged with pedophilia, through interviews with the offender's family and their 8mm home videos from the time of the trial. Neither film, however, involves the director as a party with personal stakes in the represented situations. Yang, on the other hand, uses the camera to expose the painful truth about her own family.

The result is an exposé of the Yangs, revealing their private thoughts (the first shot significantly shows the mother in a see-through negligee) and emphasizing their different points of view. The details that emerge are painful but banal — the mother had an affair, the father consequently beat her hard; they soon divorced and the father moved to another city. Yet as soon as each family member gives his or her own version, discrepancies emerge. The brother details tearfully how his father mistreated him; the father calmly denies each and every allegation. *Home Video* does not try to reconcile the versions. Instead, toward the end of the film, the father says: "People can decide for themselves how much of what is said in this film is true." Yang Lina regards Akira Kurosawa's *Rashomon* (1950) as a source of inspiration for the film.[29] The film does not aim at fact-finding.

Instead, *Home Video* is a reflection on filmmaking in the absence of any objective viewpoint, even the director's. When the father claims that viewers can decide for themselves, he acknowledges the theatrical situation in which the family members play their *Rashomon*-like roles for an audience. He looks directly at the camera, implying the presence of the director and the spectators as judges. Neither is the director an impartial mediator who simply passes on the information to the viewers. Yang Lina intrudes upon her subjects, sometimes against their express will.

Many scenes emphasize the awkward tension between the director and her subjects. In the opening sequence, the father and brother articulate their objection to the project, placing the director in the position of an intruder. Even as they relent, the intrusion is confined to their homes, and both the father and the brother, in separate scenes, object to being filmed on the street. Moreover, the intervention transforms the family dynamics. Much of the conversation revolves around how the other family members — including the director — may react to the testimony. One realizes that each testimony is acted out with the other participants' future viewing in mind, and that Yang Lina is filming with the intention of using the film to establish a dialogue. In fact, the director states that she likes the film because it has facilitated communication and understanding in her family.[30] Halfway through the film, when all the facts have been told, what remains is to figure out the motivation behind each family member's consent to expose themselves to the camera, and for the brother and mother's reluctance to show the footage to the father. Yang Lina's presence becomes acutely felt, as she tries to ingratiate herself with her mother, brother, and father. It turns out that the mother's attitude is partially motivated by her fear for the children's inheritance. The director must find her position within a battle of wills ostensibly fought with her own good in mind — even when the father objects to the project in the film's beginning and asks Yang Lina to put the camera down, he explains that she would be the one to regret it later. Her directorial intervention is met with raising her personal stakes in the film.

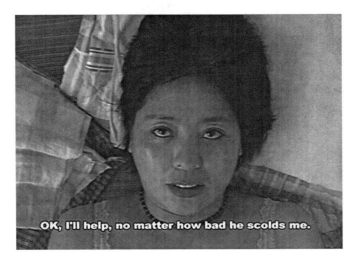

Figure 11.2. *Home Video*. Encroaching on the filmed subject's space.

Although *Home Video* seamlessly edits together the various interviews, the referenced events consistently shift among three temporal registers — the time of the divorce, the present during which the testimonials are given, and the projected time in which the footage will be shown to the other members of the family and to a larger audience. Unlike the *xianchang* aesthetics, which privileges a "site" with clear temporal borders, creating in Zhang Zhen's words "a history of the present,"[31] *Home Video* focuses on subjective, often dislocated perceptions. The past exists not in material records but rather makes itself known through its impact on the present. In this context, *Home Video's* title should be understood as doubly ironic. As a result of the DV movement, it is much like amateur videos celebrating family occasions, yet what is documented is the falling apart of a home. Moreover, a home video constitutes a visual memento; in Yang Lina's film, the camera lens is trained on the present, and the past can only be accessed through current memories. Insofar as Wu Wenguang's *xianchang* relies on live reportage (the original meaning of *xianchang*), *Home Video* suggests an alternative approach, in which the originary moment is deemed inaccessible except through the director's reactivation of the interviewees' memory.

If you don't agree, I'll keep following you around.

Figure 11.3. *Home Video*. Pushing the filmed subject to cooperate.

The principles guiding *Home Video* are similar to those of Claude Lanzmann's *Shoah* (1985), which eschews all footage dating to the Holocaust in favor of reconstructing the experience through memory, jolted by the relentless questioning of the filmmaker. Yang Lina also shares Lanzmann's use of re-enactment in the present as a way to address repressed post-traumatic memories. Yet unlike Lanzmann, who provokes both perpetrators and victims to say more than they intend to reveal, with the remove and irony of an interrogator, Yang Lina is sympathetic to her subjects, crying with her brother and wiping tears off her mother's face while the camera rolls. Her intrusion, even when potentially confrontational, is never intended as an affront. Aptly, the film ends up embracing the director as one of the filmed subjects. During the ending sequence, the father turns to Yang Lina and asks, "How do you feel?" As she explains her viewpoint, the film goes black, as if one is hearing her inner voice. The director never appears on the screen, but the last shot is devoted to her, the film's ultimate protagonist.

Waiting for a Miracle to Happen: *Railroad of Hope*

Experimentation with documentary forms also motivates Ning Ying's *Railroad of Hope*. By 2001, at the time of shooting this film, her first feature-length documentary, Ning Ying was known for her fiction movies, which show everyday life in Beijing. Ning started venturing into documentary films with a series of shorts for UNICEF, and was further pushed in this direction after an exhausting, month-long altercation with censors over *I Love Beijing* (2000). *Railroad of Hope* is as much an auteur piece as Ning's fiction films, guided by the director's off-screen presence, manifested through the persistent question to the interviewees, "What is your dream in life?"

Figure 11.4. *Railroad of Hope.* Asking the filmed subject a question beyond his ability to answer.

Ning's film was made on a train carrying seasonal workers from Sichuan to their destination in the cotton fields of Xinjiang, a three-day journey in what constitutes the most massive yearly inner migration in China, excluding New Year's travels. Thematically, it is what Ning calls "an investigation of the peasant problem," looking at some of China's most urgent plights — economic disparity and a large floating population of migrant workers. Yet the relentless questions turn the film first and foremost into an encounter of minds, and the changing landscape becomes a metaphor for people's journey through life. *Railroad of Hope* synthesizes the spontaneity of the New Documentary cinema with a more intrusive approach, reminiscent in style of *cinéma vérité*.

To some extent, the proactive strategy stemmed from technical necessity. Ning Ying, frustrated with the state-sponsored system, was relying on her own means rather than on studio-funded equipment. The project was made possible once a small SONY digital camera appeared on the market. Affordable, supporting a high resolution, and small enough to carry around the train's congested spaces, it was one of the first of its kind in China. In fact, Ning purchased the exhibition floor model, with a single battery that could last for only ten hours. Since the train ride offered no opportunity to recharge the battery during the three days of travel from Sichuan to Xinjiang, the filmmakers had to be very frugal with shooting time. Similar to the path taken in *Strong Wind*, their solution was to stimulate the subjects with questions that were sure to quickly initiate a dialogue and reveal the interlocutors' thoughts.

The director's intrusion becomes part of the film's subject matter. The largely homogeneous group of Sichuan farmers fails to yield highly personal stories and often concentrates on the moment. "What is your biggest wish in life?" two children are asked, and they reply: "That the train shouldn't be so crowded." In the absence of stirring revelations, the viewer's focus turns to the performative situation and to the overall effect of the conversations. Ning Ying (through the voice of her collaborator, Guo Gang) asks questions, undeterred when the interviewees are visibly embarrassed and even burst into tears. The result is a snapshot of the thoughts guiding the existence of the migrant farmers. Ning Ying claimed later that "whereas in documentary film, you wait for miracles to happen, in fiction film you arrange for the miracles to take place."[32] Yet the director does not wait passively for the situation to occur; she induces the circumstances to which her interviewees react.

Like Zhang and Duan's *The Square*, *Railroad of Hope* shows the touch of a fiction film director and auteur. In a gesture that is rare in Chinese documentaries, the film begins with a title frame, "A film by Ning Ying." Ning, an eloquent interpreter of her movies, explains that she takes issue with many documentary filmmakers who simply place the camera waiting for things to happen. The camera, claims Ning, cannot capture anything that has not already taken place inside the director's mind. Unmotivated filmmaking shows, in her view, "an empty head behind the camera." *Railroad of Hope*, on the other hand, makes use of directorial intervention to produce a highly personal statement. Rather than a *xianchang*-like investigation of a particular site, the film comes close to a fictional account.

Ning readily describes the film as an occasion for making her voice heard through that of others. For the director, the film reflects the quandary of all Chinese citizens, who look for meaning in a society in transition. The questions and the lack of clear answers expose a directionless society, which must awake to its aspirations before everything turns into material pursuit. Ning, who has been accused of asking an overly intellectual and alienated question in "What is your dream in life?", regards it rather as a vehicle for leveling the field and contemplating the moral choices that can be made independently of one's social status. The final destination, the Gobi Desert, becomes for Ning a metaphor for a barren existence — one's inevitable death at the end of life, but also the looming death of social values. At the same time, the final shot, of an austere desert landscape, also redirects the film's focus to the director's inner mindscape.

The film is a road movie; moreover, it is the director's personal journey, continuing ambulations from her earlier life and career. The film is a return to Ning's train ride to the countryside as a child during the Cultural Revolution, when her family was forced out of Beijing. Even though the documentary breaks away from Ning's fiction films, the train ride continues the movement into increasingly larger spaces in Ning's earlier work — from the elderly pedestrians in *For Fun* (1993), through bicycle-riding policemen in *On the Beat* (1995), to the taxi driver in *I Love Beijing*. The title may also refer to Ning's debt to Italian neorealism — Pietro Germi's *The Road to Hope* (1950), with a screenplay by Federico Fellini, also describes a migrant worker's journey (from Sicily to Switzerland) and signals, according to André Bazin, the shift from "a neorealism of war" to "a neorealism of peace."[33] Ning's directorial intrusion introduces interpretive matrices that provide the footage with a storyline. The strong sense of direction — to the cotton fields, to China's uncertain future — imprints the film with an urgency that is rarely seen in Chinese documentaries.

What Is a Documentary Auteur?

The directorial intervention in the films discussed in this chapter evidences how the New Documentary cinema cannot be reduced to a single approach. Wu Wenguang's concept of *xianchang*, influential and instrumental as it has been, should not be given unlimited credit. We may in fact outline an alternative history of New Documentaries cinema — not only translingual adaptations of the principles of Frederick Wiseman, Ogawa Shinsuke, and others, but also idiosyncratic responses developed through independent experimentation. Some filmmakers had little exposure to any theoretical framework or to documentaries made around the world. Yang Lina, for example, says that when she started shooting *Old Men* she did not even know that what she was making was considered a documentary, or that she should be counted as a so-called independent filmmaker. When she learned about documentary films, it was not from watching copies, which were unavailable in China at the time, but rather from Erik Barnouw's textbook *Documentary: A History of the Non-Fiction Film*, which appeared in translation in 1992, significantly retitled as *History of World Documentary Cinema (Shijie jilu dianying shi)*. Even Zhang Yuan and Ning Ying, educated at the Beijing Film Academy and well connected, needed to invent their own documentary film language. Their trial-and-error resulted in various intrusive models.

It does not seem, however, that the filmmakers set out to become agents provocateurs. None of the films, not even *Strong Wind*, aims at creating the kind of disturbance that Michael Moore's work creates — he stalks his interviewees in *Roger and Me* (1989) and approaches congressmen with military enlistment forms in *Fahrenheit 9/11* (2004). Instead, these directors interfere in the recorded situation, and even participate in creating it, to produce more cohesive presentations and focus their highly personal statements.

What is at stake, I argue, is more than the politics of style. In various forms, all the films examined in this chapter address the inherent theatricality in the rapport between filmmakers and interviewees — Zhang Yuan attests explicitly to the effect of the camera on anyone present on site; Ju Anqi reduces interaction to performance rather than content-driven dialogue; *Home Video* foregrounds the nature of the interviews as testimonies acted out for the other participants; *Railroad of Hope* calls on each traveler to stand up to the camera. What seems to motivate the directors is the need to expose the theatricality that remains unacknowledged by the *xianchang* rhetoric of unconcerned observation. Insofar as New Documentary films constitute a reaction to the practices of state-sponsored propaganda, the intrusive approach is a complementary strategy, giving the lie to the purportedly objective official line. Unlike the doctored productions that pretend to represent an unbiased opinion devoid of any personal viewpoint, the intrusive films foreground their debt to the auteurs behind the camera.

The intrusive approach is, at its core, a manifestation of a vision of the documentary director as a proactive and even manipulative auteur. Wu Wenguang exerted his influence again in the late 1990s by shifting to portraying the lives of ordinary people, further bolstering the search for a sense of objectivity in documentary filmmaking.[34] The directors discussed here, on the other hand, embrace an attitude that is unabashedly self-referential.

In an article published in 1998, the film scholar Li Daoxin drew attention to the new documentaries. He claimed that after the so-called Fifth Generation directors, who distinguished themselves through fiction films, the Sixth Generation filmmakers of the 1990s would be able to make themselves known as auteurs only by shooting documentaries.[35] It turned out that there were more ways to leave auteurial fingerprints than Li was envisioning, including through fiction films, yet it is intriguing to note in retrospect what strategies documentary filmmakers have used to assert themselves as unique creators. The prevalent method has been, paradoxically, that of the withdrawing auteur, ceding directorial intent to the camera that purportedly does not lie. To break with accepted norms, documentary filmmakers also seek to go beyond the now-canonized founding fathers of the New Documentary Movement. Given that the Chinese cinema scene is increasingly crowded with powerful generational and individual visions, the *xianchang* aesthetics acts as a source of both inspiration and anxiety of influence. The challenge posed by the intrusive approach attests to the diversity and vitality of documentary filmmaking in China.

12 "I Am One of Them" and "They Are My Actors": Performing, Witnessing, and DV Image-Making in Plebian China

Yiman Wang

Only many years later did people learn to appreciate the year of 1989 — the wake-up call sent from a chaotic denouement. — Wu Wenguang[1]

When I go out, I never forget to bring my DV with me ... It's a habit that resembles a thief always carrying his tools of crime with the mind of stealing something.

— Jiang Zhi[2]

If Wu Wenguang posits a collective genealogy that emerges only in retrospect, a genealogy that traces the beginning of personal documentary making to the loss of idealism in 1989 (or what many critics see as the inception of the post-socialist era), then Jiang Zhi's self-mocking analogy underscores the surreptitious connotations of a special type of personal documentary making, namely digital video (DV) documentary since the mid-1990s. Both Wu and Jiang emphasize the personal turn in documentary making since the 1990s. One identifies the historical imperative; the other describes its unique manner of operation. They invite us (as consumers and critics) to examine the unfolding personal documentary and to properly position it vis-à-vis the current historical conjuncture on the one hand and documentary tradition on the other. A crucial interface between the historical conjuncture and the documentary tradition is the ethics of documentary, which circumscribes not only the content and the form of documentation, but also stipulates the relationship between the documentary maker and his or her subjects. Such ethics of documentary are not fixed, but rather shift with time and place. To assess the significance of personal documentary in post-socialist China, one must therefore examine how DV image-makers negotiate documentary ethics and what new options emerge. This chapter tackles this question by studying some examples of personal DV documentary made in the past decade. Specifically, I analyze how they redefine documentary ethics by configuring new relationships between the documentary maker and his or her subjects.

In an earlier article, entitled "The Amateur's Lightning Rod: DV Documentary in Postsocialist China," dealing with the ramifications of amateur-authorship claimed by a large number of DV image-makers in urban China, I discussed how their negotiations with their subjects necessitate reconceptualization of the long-standing issue of documentary ethics.[3] One of the important discursive maneuvers, I argued, is the DV image-makers' management of "cruelty" inherent in DV documentation. Echoing the familiar formulation of documentary ethics, they readily admit to the intractable power imbalance between them as camera-holders and their subjects. Furthermore, such violence is aggravated by the new technology of DV that easily penetrates into the subjects' private sphere. The "cruelty," however, is inflicted not only on the subjects, who are obviously on the receiving end of the violence of representation. Describing DV as a "double-edged sword," the documentary makers contend that DV hurts themselves as much as their subjects. In a further twist, they contend that only by inscribing cruelty can they be "seared" (*zhuoshao*) by the real, thereby capturing the pulse of raw existence.[4]

To affirm the necessity of documentary cruelty for certain specific agendas (with the possible result of violating documentary ethics) means that we should be attentive to new practices and theorizations, especially when a new media technology (like DV) is involved. This does not mean, however, that DV power should be celebrated unconditionally, or that the ideology and politics of representation can be ignored. Rather, the ideology and politics of representation continue to play a crucial role, even if they adopt new forms that deserve our critical attention. Indeed, the issue of ethics becomes even more urgent due to DV's rapid popularization and apparent ease of operation, which subject it to increasing commercialization, trivialization, and misuse. As Lu Xinyu points out:

> To break away from ideological constraints makes sense only when it aims to critique dictatorship. It does not mean that one can be totally free from any ideological stance, or that one does not need to reflect upon this stance or that it is exempted from ethics ... Chinese documentary must make its ideological commitment — herein lies its significance and power. Without this commitment, it becomes no more than a trivial toy that distracts the player from the goal.[5]

Similarly, Zhang Yingjin points out three major problems that potentially undermine Chinese independent documentary making. They are erasure of the self, blind belief in objectivity, and the exploitation of subjects.[6] Both erasure of the self and blind belief in objectivity assume the documentary maker's ability to transcend his or her subjective position, thereby achieving omnipotence and objectivity. This assumption tends to conceal his or her exploitative relationship with the subject, hence the violation of documentary ethics. Such exploitation, according to Zhang, exists even when the documentary maker admits to his or her guilt and undertakes self-critique, and even if it constitutes the precondition for making an incisive documentary that captures the texture of the subjects' existential experiences.[7]

The diverse discourses on documentary ethics generated by critics as well as the documentary makers suggest the intractable importance of this issue. Its salience is further reflected in a collection of interviews with sixteen independent documentary makers, entitled *Zhongguo duli jilupian dang'an* (Profile of Chinese independent documentary), published in 2004.[8] Half of the interviewees were asked to comment upon documentary ethics in the context of their own work. Despite their varied perspectives, the commonly agreed criterion for judging a violation of documentary ethics consists in whether the act of penetrating into the subjects' private space leads to objectification, voyeurism, and exhibitionism, or whether it generates genuine concern for grassroots interests and thereby delivers a humanist (*renwen*) "thick description" of the subjects' existential life experiences. In other words, the issue of documentary ethics is ultimately bound up with effective presentation and articulation of grassroots reality from a humanist, sympathetic perspective.

The humanist precondition, or humanism (*renwen zhuyi*), evokes diverse historical and political connotations. Developed hand in hand with the Enlightenment (*qimeng*), humanism in China is generally regarded as originating in the early twentieth century from the May Fourth and New Literary Movements, characterized by the iconoclastic rejection of feudalism and the promotion of Western values such as democracy and science. As a (petty-)bourgeois ideology, humanism was soon criticized by Lu Xun and leftists for its elision of class conflict. Following the end of the Cultural Revolution, however, humanism resurfaced in the 1980s as the antidote to the ten-year rampant political prosecution, providing the ideological rationale for restoring human (especially intellectual) dignity. Since the 1989 Tiananmen Incident, the loss of idealism once again submerged humanism, giving way to wholesale commercialism in the 1990s.

The historical and cultural-political rupture in the late 1980s constituted what Wu Wenguang terms the "wake-up call" that spurred the New Documentary generation. From the ruins of official ideology and traditional utopianism arose a new documentary movement in the early 1990s, which initially took the observational stance. The inception of DV in the mid-1990s ushered in a new phase characterized by diversified modes of documentary making. Its dominant style can be described as self-reflexive and performative.[9] What the New Documentary Movement has in common is the attempt to re-energize humanism so as to present a new reality from the perspective of the disenfranchised social sectors, thereby to inject critique, sympathy, and collective concerns into an increasingly atomized, commercialized society. In other words, humanism is revived on the condition that its intellectual elitism and alienation from the masses are sublated, and that it is retooled into a vision that can potentially defy official ideology on one hand and wholesale commercialization on the other. It is a position that both deconstructs and reconstructs. This revised humanist position has contributed to the innovation of the documentary form, which, Lu argues, is manifested in more diverse modes of discourses.[10]

Importantly, the revised documentary perspective that combines humanist and grassroots concerns signals a continuous attempt to negotiate documentary ethics and reconfigure the documentary relationship. To explicate how their negotiation opens up new discourses, I examine two ostensibly opposite statements. The first can be summarized as "I am one of them," and the second as "they are my actors." The apparent contradiction between reality (being) and fictionality (acting) signals the ambiguity inscribed in the documentary aspiration to witness grassroots reality. By juxtaposing the two statements, I suggest that experiencing and witnessing do not always contradict performance or the instigation of performance, if performance is understood as enacting and making visible what is deemed too commonplace or too abject to be noteworthy or newsworthy. The possible continuity, even co-dependence between witnessing and experiencing on one hand, and creating or performing a certain situation on the other offers a new angle for our understanding of the humanist/grassroots DV documentaries' self-positioning vis-à-vis their subjects (i.e., documentary relationship) and vis-à-vis reality (i.e., truth claim).

In his study of video media produced up to the early 1990s, Sean Cubitt argues that electronic media, unlike film and TV, "need to be thought in terms of *relationships* first, and of representations only second."[11] Specifically, the relations obtain "between enunciations, and the subjects of enunciations," or what cultural studies calls "the moment of reception," as opposed to representation that is concerned with "the enunciated, and the subject of the enunciated."[12] This refocus on relationships allows for better comprehension of the "*material aesthetics* of electronic media."[13] Cubitt's premise is that video media has broken away from the burden of representation (i.e., the epistemological task), and is thus able to undertake the "critical" and "negative" work that is the Hegelian philosophical legacy.[14] Specifically, such a philosophical function consists in inviting us to consider the "conditions of enunciation and the active processes of communication."[15] Cubitt's work on video art predates the DV age. His idea that video art has refocused from (transparent) representation to materiality of the form contradicts China's new (DV) documentary impulse. Nevertheless, his emphasis on relationships is instructive for my study. In my analysis of the documentary relationship below, I broaden the notion of relationship to include not only that between the enunciation and the subjects of enunciation, that is the relation in reception, but also that between the enunciator (or the documentary maker) and the enunciated (or the subject of the documentary) that is the relationship in production. Furthermore, the enunciator and the enunciated oftentimes become interchangeable, so much so that the issues of representation/production and reception become interconnected, each reframed in the context of the other.

"I Am One of Them" — Identification and Alienation

Now, let us turn to some concrete articulations of being and acting that emerge from the DV documentary makers' rethinking of documentary ethics. A major independent documentary maker who formulates the idea of "I am one of them" is Wu Wenguang. This stance was already implicit in his first documentary, *Bumming in Beijing: The Last Dreamers* (1990), which is generally considered to be the founding work of China's New Documentary Movement. Since all the subjects, the five roaming avant-garde artists, were his personal friends, the documentation was easy and spontaneous. "I lived a similar life in Beijing, with no local registration [*hukou*] or a stable job."[16]

If Wu's identification with his subjects in this early documentary was confined to his like-minded peers, nearly ten years later, in his documentary *Jiang Hu: Life on the Road* (1999), he comes to identify with a peripatetic peasant troupe who initially had little in common with him. The transition from identifying with roaming artists in Beijing to identifying with the peasant troupe is expressed in the way he "trashes" his earlier documentaries, describing the avant-garde artists he documented as fragile and obsessed with "collective masturbation."[17] According to Lu Xinyu, Wu's transition and self-critique in the late 1990s, along with the rise of a new generation of documentary makers such as Jiang Yue and the locally rooted Kang Jianning, signal precisely a new humanist turn toward the grassroots (*dao diceng qu*), that is, to be concerned with the disenfranchised social sectors.[18]

What enables Wu's grassroots turn, from the technological perspective, was his adoption of DV in place of the chunky Betacam that he used to use. The incisive and penetrating capacity of DV allows him to establish productive interactions with the peasant troupe. Importantly, the intimate observation of the peripatetic peasant troupe is complicated by Wu's two apparently contradictory recognitions. On the one hand, he stresses that what he has documented is not just irrelevant peasant life; rather, "we lived inside there. I even felt I was shooting a sort of autobiography."[19] On the other hand, he admits his inescapable alien status vis-à-vis his subjects. "You remain an outsider even if you live with them, eat with them, have fun with them, and help them through some troubles with local bureaucrats. Sooner or later, you will leave them."[20]

One wonders why Wu describes himself as simultaneously an outside "other" *and* one of them (or them as a mirror of the self and the vehicle of autobiography) in the same process. To understand the disjuncture and the connection between the outside and the inside, between distance and identification, we must consider the expressive capacity of DV. According to Wu, DV not only allows him to penetrate into his subjects' private life, but also enables single-handed shooting.[21] The unprecedented independence (in sharp contrast with the official media institution) leads to a form of "personal writing" (*geren xiezuo*), which in turn facilitates "a grassroots stance" (*minjian lichang*). It "liberates image-making from a group or an institution, making it a genuinely individual work."[22] This leads Wu to break away from his earlier aspirations for professionalization, and to champion "amateur" image-making.[23] The excitement with personal documentary making, and the entailed casualness and intimacy, are manifested in the consistent comparison of DV to the pen.[24]

The privileging of the personal leads to the entanglement of intimate witnessing and self-expression. As Wu breaks away from conventional plot and official coercion, he also folds grassroots reality into his inner world. In this light, a documentary like *On the Road* "is what I wanted to do, and it becomes insignificant to others."[25] To reinforce the intransitive quality of his investment, Wu observes that to hope to change certain things through making a documentary is no more than unrequited love,[26] since "what you have documented cannot change their lives, or help them in any way." A documentary therefore is ultimately premised on the cruel dialectic "between hurting and being hurt."[27] These observations, in combination with the DV-pen analogy, foreground the "self" as the ultimate reference. Thus, what starts out as a personal, intimate witnessing of a peasant troupe, premised upon "I'm one of them," turns out to be a vehicle of self-expression — "I remain myself." The ostensible identification between the documentary maker and the subject flips into distance and alienation. Consequently, the peasant troupe is recognized only as the performers whose acting in the documentary allows Wu to design his self-oriented project.

Wu's vacillation between intimacy and distance is shared by a number of other post-1990s documentary makers. Hu Shu, for instance, describes himself as a friend, even a family member, of the three call girls he documents in his DV film, *Leave Me Alone* (1998–1999). This documentary deals with these call girls in the private as well as public domains during a three-month period when he was invited to live in their apartment. Hu emphasizes that the co-habitation drew them so close that he actually shared their joy and miseries.[28] Hu further indicates that he and they are of the same type. "If I had come from a similar background,

I probably wouldn't have fared much better."[29] Yet at the same time, Hu was fully aware that he was the one who could determine what to document and what to keep in the finished documentary. This power makes him feel like one of their customers (except that he does not even pay them) since he has also prised them open and exposed them to his (DV) gaze.[30] As Zheng Tiantian argues, by enticing the audience with voyeuristic pleasures, Hu has aggravated their actual social exploitation by subjecting them to a second round of exploitation "in the name of humanizing them."[31] The making of the documentary itself thus becomes an ethical paradox.

One way of negotiating this ethical paradox inscribed in "I'm one of them" is to fully acknowledge and understand the documentary maker's subjectivity, and to determine his or her agenda and how the individual documentary maker is related to his or her times. For as Lu Xinyu argues, the reality manifested in the documentary is not objectivity, but the documentary maker's interpretation of and approach to life, determined by his or her subjectivity.[32] Furthermore, such subjectivity leads to individualized and individualistic DV documentary making, which risks becoming trivialized as part of salon activities unless it is articulated with certain social concerns.[33]

Given DV's incisiveness and its capacity for instantly capturing everyday drama (*zhiji xiju xing*),[34] it can potentially subvert the distanced narrative paradigm and help to establish a new relationship between the documentary maker and his or her subjects.[35] In this new relationship, the individual documentary maker is no longer an isolated, individual agent distanced from and feeling guilty about exploiting "them," but rather an agent who not only works with his or her subjects as agents, but also helps to produce more agents.

This new direction in negotiating documentary ethics is borne out in Wu Wenguang's recent project, *China Village Self-Governance Film Project*. Growing out of the Civic Bureau's (*Minzheng bu*) collaboration with the European Union, the project selected ten villagers from a large number of applicants, providing them each with a DV camera and ten tapes, training them to use the equipment, then sending them back to capture ten tapes worth of footage in their villages for one month. They then returned to Caochangdi Workstation, where they each learned to edit their footage into a ten-minute DV documentary, with the help of Wu Wenguang's expert team.[36] These indigenous documentaries are supposed to register the villagers' own grassroots perspectives on rural democratization, which will in turn introduce China's rural situation to an international as well as an urban domestic public. According to Wu Wenguang, the original EU plan was to have him make a long documentary on rural reform; it was Wu who proposed the villager DV project. "After all, it is better to have ten more people make documentaries. Moreover, very few outsiders know much about rural autonomy."[37] Wu's proposal underscores the possibility and necessity of amateur documentary making — possible because DV operation is easy to learn and the cost is relatively low, necessary because the villagers can provide perspectives that no outsider can have access to, and they should be allowed to express their voices and visions. DV provides precisely such a platform.

Here Wu still categorizes himself and others distanced from direct rural experiences as outsiders whose purview differs from that of the villagers. Nonetheless, contrary to his previous feelings of alienation and helplessness, he now sees the grassroots populace as the privileged site of knowledge that they can learn to transmit to the public through a proper conduit (i.e., their personal DV documentaries). Given the crucial role played by Wu and his Caochangdi Workstation in equipping and training villagers, we may argue that this project not only discovers already existing agents, but, more importantly, produces them, or brings them into a self-conscious identification as an agent and a documentary maker. This is illustrated in the experiences of Shao Yuzhen and Jia Zhitan, two fifty-five-year-old villager participants whose ten-minute documentaries were awarded the first and the third prize respectively in the China Village Democracy Videos Competition. For them, obtaining and then learning to use a DV camera is empowering. They not only gained the ability to record detailed everyday happenings in their villages, but also learned to be more perceptive, to defamiliarize routine, to capture mundane details now viewed afresh. Furthermore, their presence with DV allowed them extra power that made them simultaneously insiders and somewhat outsiders in the village.

In Shao Yuzhen's case, her fellow villagers did not always take her DV filming seriously. They carried on their everyday work and quibbling in her presence. Yet, they sometimes viewed the DV camera as a suspicious, alien presence, and inquired about her purpose in filming, to which she consistently responded, "Just for fun." The resulting documentary, entitled *I Film My Village* (2006), edited by Ma Jun, preserves the unstructured, episodic casualness of the footage, contrary to Shao's original proposal to document the rural execution of land allotment. It is precisely the insider's attention to everyday details and her intimate relationships with her fellow villagers that won the documentary the first prize. Antithetical to professional filmmaking, Shao uses DV as if it were "part of her body."[38]

Jia Zhitan's documentary, *The Quarry* (2006), takes a different approach. Zeroing in on the disputed ownership of a quarry, Jia captured the villagers fighting for their ownership rights, an event that unfolded in the present tense. The documentary not only records villagers' multiple voices regarding their need for democracy, but also transmits their voices to the broader public. This effect was facilitated by two factors: the presence of DV and Jia's base-level cadre status as the village party secretary. Jia's DV filmmaking, therefore, directly partook in constructing rural autonomy by tuning the public ear to subaltern speech.[39]

Figure 12.1. Shao Yuzhen carries her "prosthetic" DV camera around the village while participating in communal activities, or in this case, provoking villagers' suspicion and consequently documenting the technological encounter.

Both Shao and Jia have since continued to make locally grown DV documentaries, screened to fellow villagers. In 2006, Jia launched "The Villagers' DV Club," the mission of which is to screen autochthonous DV documentaries and provide a healthy entertainment (in place of mahjong) for villagers.[40] The rudimentary training they received at Caochangdi Workstation certainly does not make them professionals, nor can they really master editing and post-production just through one sitting with the Workstation experts.[41] Nevertheless, these professional skills do not seem crucial to their agendas. Judging from the footage Shao Yuzhen snatches and shows to her fellow villagers, which mostly derives from her everyday work experiences and includes imagery such as the blue sky and the crop field, what seems important is that peasants now are taking an interest in their ordinary lives and feel the importance of archiving a way of life so far either dismissed or misunderstood. In Shao's words, the value of DV is that it allows peasants to voice their opinions and to make visible their own lives through the DV lens.[42] In other words, DV empowerment for the peasants consists in their acquisition of a new purview and a new language, one that is related to, yet not confined by, a new technology.

To the extent that Jia and Shao are now committed to using DV to document and bring into public consciousness a specific mode of collective life and identity that used to be occluded in public media, they become producers and agents in their own right. What is diversified is not only the subject matter of documentaries, but also the types of documentary makers.[43] In this sense, DV amateur-authorship fulfills what Walter Benjamin envisions in his early twentieth-century essay, "The Author as Producer":

> ... a writer's production must have the character of a model: it must be able to instruct other writers in their production and, secondly, it must be able to place an improved apparatus at their disposal. This apparatus will be the better, the more consumers it brings in contact with the production process — in short, the more readers or spectators it turns into collaborators.[44]

In this current context, the apparatus that connects the consumer with the producer and converts the consumer into the producer is none other than the DV camera. Wu's Caochangdi Workstation fulfills precisely the role of setting up a model, and making it appropriable by consumer-producers. This pedagogical setting ultimately leads to a collaborative relationship that problematizes the self-other binary. The result is not just to turn the self into "one of them," but rather to ascribe to them as much agency as to oneself.

Analogously, Cubitt's study of video media also emphasizes the pedagogic context of teaching, learning, and group practice that "insists that everyone is an artist, and consequently that the narrow definitions of art must be done away with."[45] To push it further, not only the notions of art and artist, but also the idea of agent needs to be broadened and democratized. If agency becomes imaginable for each individual, then each individual must work with other individuals, since nobody is to remain only an object of a documentary. In other words, all individuals can potentially be on both sides of the DV camera. Consequently, the conundrum of self vs. other becomes unviable since it loses its premise that the self is an agent while the other is only to be documented, represented, defended, and/or exploited.

The dissolution of the self/other binary allows us to reconceptualize the ethical paradox, which in turn paves the way for a new form of interaction between the documentary maker and his or her subjects, namely co-producership or co-authorship. David MacDougall has theorized multiple authorship in the making of participatory ethnographic documentary films. The potential of such authorship, however, goes beyond ethnographic documentary. To the extent that DV technology democratizes the audio-visual mode of discourse as never before, it facilitates multiple or collaborative authorship, a crucial element of which is improvisation on the part of all participants. This means that what is being documented is volatile and contingent. Thus, the "reality" that is documented does not necessarily pre-exist, but rather develops from the circumstances of the here-and-now, and the way it develops has to do with the specific configuration of co-authorship. Consequently, the process of documenting reality merges with the process of creating and performing a situation into being. This is borne out in the documentary relationship that can be summarized as "they are my actors."[46]

"They Are My Actors" — Co-Authorship and "Becoming" Reality

Lu Xinyu's comments on staging (*baipai*) are instructive here. Instead of objecting to posing as a whole, Lu observes that any form of interview already involves staging and pre-arrangement, and that it serves an important purpose as long as such pre-arrangement follows the natural course of development and fits with the subject's emotional state. "If a documentary looks fake, that is not because it is staged, but rather because the documentary maker's aesthetic conception is flawed." Staging is just one strategy for the documentary maker to "convey to the audience what he/she feels."[47] The justification for staging and realistic construction goes hand in hand with Lu's stress on the documentary maker's subjectivity and the camera's rhetorical capacity. According to Lu, they combine to produce "poetic" documentary.[48]

The "poetic" quality Lu envisions for future documentaries does not mean mere fictionality, but rather a compelling and constructive presentation brought forth by the documentary maker's vision and the camera's rhetorical capacity. A comparison of such "poetic" quality with what Cubitt calls the "Third Video" can provide a clearer sense of its significance. According to Cubitt, contrary to the Third Cinema that tends to be epic national allegories, the "Third Video" is characterized by "the small-scale interventions it makes, the intimacy of its address, the local quality of its speech and techniques, and its ability to address the local through history rather than history through the local."[49] In Cubitt's view, such video is important not because it speaks the "truth," but rather because it forms a "negative relation to philosophical truth," since it critiques the status quo and aims at change.[50] As a means of agitation, it demands "solidarity and support"; its existence both relies upon and helps to produce a new group identity, one that attends to previously occluded social sectors.[51] Such a proactive conception of documentary poetics signals "commitment to the possibility of a future culture." That is, "where the facts don't match the implicit or inherent truth of the medium, then it may be necessary to produce those 'facts' in such a way as to influence the construction of the truth."[52] In brief, the "Third Video" is oppositional, constructive, and agitational rather than reflective, and concerned with occluded localized social sectors. These characteristics, along with its self-conscious differentiation from the epic "Third Cinema," closely parallel the New (DV) Documentary's self-positioning vis-à-vis official Chinese media. The most important common feature I would like to analyze here is their attention to "producing" the facts and "constructing" the truth.

The possibility of producing "facts" that can "influence the construction of the truth" not only enhances but also complicates the documentary maker's agency. The result transcends the conventional association of this agency with individualism. If DV is capable of converting a consumer into an author (to borrow Benjamin's terms), as borne out in Wu Wenguang's Village Video project, then the agency of producing "facts" lies on both sides of the camera. The fact that Lu Xinyu highlighted the camera's rhetorical capacity and the documentary maker's subjectivity in an article written toward the end of 1995, which coincided with the invention of DV, seems to anticipate the important role DV was to play in generating new documentary authorship. This new role is demonstrated by a number of DV documentary makers' emphasis on performance and acting, and even interventions that help to bring certain situations into being.

Before going into more detail, we should note that acting in this context is distinguished from the negative version deployed in conventional, institutionalized documentaries. As Duan Jinchuan observes, the institutionalized television system carries so much political authority that even if the documentary director wants to forge a bond with his or her subjects, the subjects have from the very beginning been deprived of the right to collaborate. The resulting documentary is thus no more than a real-person show staged under direct or indirect pressures.[53]

Contrary to such coerced acting, some recent DV documentaries have mobilized another kind of acting which leads to restructuring the documentary relationship. In *Landlord Mr. Jiang* (2005), the documentary maker, Liang Zi, begins by speaking to her subject/landlord, Mr. Jiang, "I've tried in vain to interview you. I'm very upset." Jiang replies casually, "Look, I've never asked you anything; yet you keep on bugging me." The film goes on to follow how their relationship changes from Jiang's initial rejection, to gradual reconciliation and then communication, until harmonious interaction emerges between Jiang and Liang Zi. During the process, Liang Zi constantly stimulates Mr. Jiang into actions that gradually reveal the history of this sixty-year-old man, who stubbornly clings to his soon-to-be-demolished old house in Shanghai and ritualistically rehearses bits and pieces of colonial legacy (such as making his own lemon tea and sandwich). Importantly, these details would not have been revealed without Liang Zi's intervention, or what her scriptwriter and editor,

Gan Chao, half-jokingly describes as her "violent treatment of an old man."[54] Furthermore, Liang Zi's intervention was effectively agitative because of the dramatic contrast and *lack* of identification between her as an inquisitive northern Chinese woman and Mr. Jiang as a southern Chinese man. This distance allows her to broach issues unimaginable for a local Shanghai filmmaker.[55] Such an interventional relationship forces us to rethink the efficacy of intimacy and identification based upon natural sympathy and consanguinity. It leads us to consider the potentially transformative and productive power of apparent "violence." In Liang Zi's documentary, to the extent that her intervening interview produces the plot, she herself becomes an *actor* and an agitator (in addition to being an observer and an interlocutor) within the documentary. She is both within and outside the frame, trespassing the boundary between the documentary maker and the subject, the self and the other.[56] Meanwhile, she also turns Jiang into an actor who performs his personal life details and micro-history into public consciousness. In this sense, Liang gets Jiang to collaborate with her on developing an audio-visual narrative that is both realistic and constructed.

Like Liang Zi, who stimulates a stranger into acting out and producing his everyday life drama, Jiang Zhi gets his interviewees to co-author or, more precisely, to co-imagine and co-remember a fictional girl named Xiao Hong. The result is a forty-five-minute DV documentary, *Little Red* (2002), composed of interviews with people on what they know about a girl named Xiao Hong. Literally meaning "little red," Jiang says the name "Xiao Hong" is charged with vernacular and political connotations. It is a name people can generally relate to — as a woman who has once appeared in their lives. It could be "your friend, acquaintance, boss, colleague, poor relative, model, sister, daughter, mistress, laid-off wife, clandestine lover, a one-night stand girl, your first lover, etc."[57] Jiang's project is to get randomly selected people to talk about their relationships with the fictional and generic Xiao Hong.

An important feature of *Little Red*, as in *Landlord Mr. Jiang*, is the interviewer's interventional strategy, which provokes a wide range of responses by people caught unawares. The rationale for being interventional, according to Jiang, is that "to make certain things happen, you must prod or stimulate them with your action."[58] Indeed, Jiang's prodding gets responses from some interviewees who actively collaborated *and* co-acted with him. One migrant worker, for instance, provides a vivid description of Xiao Hong only then to tell Jiang that the whole thing is fabricated, because the entire documentary seems like a joke, which Jiang feels to be an accurate summary of his project.[59] Voluntary acting or playing along premised upon the shared "as-if" logic on the part of both Jiang and his subjects becomes constitutive of this documentary. The question of how to comprehensively assess the documentary value of this "joke" is not my concern here. What is important for my purpose is that, along with recent independent DV documentaries like *Landlord Mr. Jiang*, *Little Red* uses acting to explore a dynamic, interactive documentary relationship, which in turn facilitates the notion of "becoming" reality.

Such "becoming" reality hinges upon activating one's memories and fantasies, allowing them to interject into and reshape the present and reality. The generic yet charged name, Xiao Hong, serves precisely as the key toward this substratum of memories and fantasies. To the extent that it galvanizes layers of memories from diverse historical periods and social classes, for an interviewee to recall and describe "Xiao Hong" means to fathom and stage memories that he or she might have subconsciously or deliberately erased. The compilation of various interviewees' accounts amounts to a repertoire of strategies for retrieving memories. The fact that some interviewees deliberately conjure "Xiao Hong" as a joke suggests that the memory involved is necessarily implicated with fictionalization and fantasy, rather than pure facts. David MacDougall summarizes the importance of eliciting memory and fantasy in these terms: "the values of a society lie as much in its dreams as in the reality it has built"; therefore "it is only by introducing new stimuli that the investigator can peel back the layers of a culture and reveal its fundamental assumptions."[60] Such new stimuli, MacDougall continues, sometimes come precisely from role-playing.[61] The quality of playing a game may not pre-exist, but rather develops from the documentary maker and his or her subject's (sometimes violent, sometimes complicit) interactions, as demonstrated in both Jiang Zhi's *Little Red* and Liang Zi's *Landlord Mr. Jiang*.

Now let us turn to an emblematic case that highlights how the interactive relationship not only converts an unwilling subject into an actor of her story, but also into a DV documentary maker in her own right, which in turn leads to the emergence of more voluntary storytellers. Zhang Hua is one such case. Zhang Hua is a single mother from rural Zhejiang Province who completed only a junior high school education. She had opened a hair salon in Shenzhen that went bankrupt in 2001. Fortunately, an old friend, Li Jinghong, had spent three years documenting her difficult enterprise. In 2004, Li finished editing over three hundred hours of footage into a twenty-episode documentary. Entitled *Sisters*, it was aired on several regional TV stations, and instantly attracted the audience's attention nationwide. By then, Zhang Hua, the subject of the documentary, had already participated in the post-production of the documentary, become a legendary figure, and embarked upon her own documentary projects. Her first DV documentary, *Kuang Dan's Secret* (2004), chronicled a high school student Kuang Dan's close relationship with her father, a street-side bike repairman. It won the 2004 grand prize in the contest, "DV 2004: Our Image Story" (DV

2004: *Women de yingxiang gushi*), co-sponsored by China Broadcasting, Film and Television Group and the Social Education Department of China Central Television Station.

Zhang's case illustrates how DV's intervention into her life has had a positive impact on her subject position. In her interview with Shandong Satellite TV on March 3, 2005, Zhang describes herself as initially a selfish person preoccupied with money-making and unhappy with her poor business. When Li Jinghong entered her salon with a DV camera, scaring away her customers, she reacted with distrust and hostility. "He told me he wanted to make a documentary. But I had no clue what he was up to. I'm just an ordinary woman with a hair salon. How could he make a documentary out of me? And how could it possibly be shown on TV? We didn't believe him."[62] Li's persistence and the TV broadcasting of *Sisters* ultimately led Zhang to reflect upon her own weaknesses and to be convinced of DV's power.

As Zhang increasingly became a public figure, representing working-class women who had tried so hard and suffered so much, she was sought out by many women who turned to her to voice their miserable experiences. These reactions prompted Zhang to document their stories, as her own had been documented by Li Jinghong. Now, she has become a close colleague of Li and works full time for Beijng Ling Pindao (Channel Zero Media Inc. http://www.bjdoc.com), a company dedicated to promoting grassroots documentary culture. Zhang's current project is a sequel to *Sisters*, composed of her long-term tracking interviews with a selected number of women throughout China.

Zhang Hua's story has become a media event, celebrated as "life transforming" (*chongsu rensheng*) and "fate changing" in the fashion of the American dream.[63] The ideological implications of tokenizing and celebrating Zhang's case are undoubtedly problematic. Nevertheless, the fact that public media, especially the combination of DV (production) and TV (exhibition), not only effectively make an ordinary hairdresser into a media event, but also empower her by making her an agent *and* a felicitous conduit for women's voices, demonstrates two things. The first is the existence of a market that readily galvanizes real-looking documentaries that feature ordinary people's everyday struggles. The second is the increasing feasibility of the amateur as author/agent. Zhang Hua's case illustrates Benjamin's promotion of the author as producer in that it foregrounds the (re)productive, even contagious power of DV image-making. Not only did Li Jinghong's *Sisters* set a model for Zhang; Zhang also transforms herself from a hostile subject to an actor of her own story, a collaborator of Li's, and finally, a documentary maker in her own right.

The mutually constitutive and transformative relationship between the documentary maker and his or her subjects is carried even further in Zhang's own documentaries. Contrary to the conventional situation in which the documentary maker seeks out, even exploits the subject for a story, Zhang is sought after by women from all over China as a sympathetic listener and witness, whose DV documentaries could become the ideal conduit for their stories. In *Kuang Dan's Secret*, the sixteen-year-old Kuang Dan took the initiative to contact Zhang. She asked Zhang to document her life, especially her relationship with her father, a migrant worker in Shenzhen, shortly before they had to leave the city and go back to their home town. Within the documentary, Kuang Dan is not only the subject framed by Zhang; she also takes up Zhang's DV camera to film her neighbors and her father at work.

A more prominent example is Zhang's other DV documentary, *The Road to Paradise* (2006), edited by Li Jinghong, which won an award at the 2006 International Leipzig Festival for Documentary and Animated Film, and was first shown in China in January 2007. This documentary was also initiated by the subject — a female teacher from Wuhan, recently diagnosed with breast cancer. Meanwhile, her younger sister was experiencing a difficult relationship with their father presumably due to childhood abuse. In response to her phone call, Zhang came into her family with a DV camera and documented the family drama at different stages during the course of one year. The presence of the camera is emphasized throughout the documentary. At one point, it triggers the suspicion of a grocery market manager, who responds by trying to stop the sister's mother from collecting trashed vegetables. At another point, the elder sister urges Zhang to turn off the DV camera to "chat" with her. The camera is seen as blocking the "chatting" relationship because it makes Zhang's eyes invisible. The younger sister, in a fit of violence against her father, challenges DV's witnessing power by shouting, "Go ahead and shoot! I'm dying to appear on TV! Shoot! I won't close my eyes until I'm on TV."

Interestingly, as Zhang got increasingly implicated in the family drama, her DV camera became gradually decoupled from her, so much so that it failed to mark her as an outsider.[64] In several sequences when the younger sister will not stop hitting her father, Zhang gives the DV camera to another person (possibly the elder sister) and jumps into the frame to restrain her. In one sequence, the father is injured and everyone rushes to pull the younger daughter from him, while the camera sits and continues to take in the action through its bloodstained lens. The bloodstain that smears the image underscores the camera's presence in the midst of fighting. On the other hand, the fact that it was shoved aside, un-operated by anyone, suggests that in this case of an emergency, it is nothing more than an inert and befuddled witness, a stand-in for the audience. Meanwhile, Zhang has transgressed the boundary of the documentary frame, leaving the DV camera behind and becoming a character within her own documentary.

你让我们包扎
Let me wrap it up.

Figure 12.2. The camera stained with the father's blood (foreground) coldly keeps on witnessing the domestic violence while the documentary maker, Zhang Hua (at frame left), intervenes and becomes one of the "subjects."

Zhang's dissociation from the DV camera has three important implications. First, it signals her relinquishment of DV's techno-power. Second, being left aside, the DV camera is revealed as nothing but an "eye," one that is susceptible to external interventions (such as the bloodstain), thus a necessary yet fallible conduit. Third, DV's automatic recording function renders it a public resource, amenable to different parties' appropriation, including that of the audience and the ostensible subjects, as well as the initial documentary maker. These implications lead to a reconfiguration of the field of interaction. In MacDougall's terms, as "the filmmaker is drawn further into the subject area of the film, the audience is drawn into the position the filmmaker originally occupied"[65] — in this case, the position behind the DV camera, looking through the bloodstained lens. Given the relaying and reciprocal relationship between Zhang, the subjects and the audience, the documentary becomes what MacDougall calls a depository of "multiple authorship, confrontation, and exchange." It has begun from separate directions, yet ends up converging upon a common subject.[66]

Zhang's intervention into her subjects' space leads her to play multiple roles — the documentary maker, the interlocutor, the financial helper, the arbitrator, *and* the blatant intervener or actor on the site. Whether it is correct (that is, conforming to documentary ethics) to intervene so much is debatable, as Zhang Hua admitted at a press conference.[67] What it highlights is her role as a "quasi-social worker," whose initial plan to document the life of a breast cancer patient turns out to be an exploration into the psychosomatic state of a marginalized, malfunctioning family.[68] Positioned and perceived as a quasi-social worker, a status further enhanced by her DV camera, Zhang cannot possibly stay outside the scene. Her pronounced presence and co-authorship with her subjects derive from the fact that her documentaries are needed and requested by the subjects from the very beginning. They are not irrelevant to the latter, as Wu Wenguang sees to be the case with his documentary *On the Road*. Thus we see another important feature of Zhang's documentaries, namely their practical efficacy. The difference from Wu's earlier perspective is again obvious. Wu emphasizes his inability to change the harsh reality through documentary making. Furthermore, he views the very act of making the documentary as potentially inflicting another layer of exploitation on his subjects — hence the documentary cruelty. Zhang Hua, however, describes her documentaries as a form of consolation. "I don't know what I can do for them. But I want to document them. I'll be very content even if I only get to chat with them and live with them for a while."[69] She sees DV as potentially capable of helping her subjects out of difficult situations just as it once helped her.[70] Change is envisioned not as a major improvement in social status or financial situation or a realization of social justice. Rather, it stays on the microscopic level of getting problems articulated and represented, generating an open-minded exchange of ideas, consoling, and forging a broadly defined sisterhood. In accordance with these goals, the camera style is unprivileged, with the interview format replaced by informal exchanges. These types of informal exchanges, according to MacDougall, characterize multi-authorship.[71]

Indeed, Zhang Hua's case exemplifies the mutually constitutive relationship among three parties: the documentary maker, the subject, and the DV camera. Decoupling the documentary maker and the camera makes the camera a shared tool. Even though conventional documentary ethics are undermined, it is not simply an act of violence, but is rather symptomatic of the documentary maker's difficult negotiation with such ethics. Only by negotiating with these documentary ethics can new configurations of the documentary relationship come into being, making possible the shuttling between the two sides of the DV camera, between being a witness/ documentary maker and an actor/subject. The resultant co-authorship or multiple authorship, developed along with what Lu Xinyu calls the camera's rhetorical capacity, facilitates the grassroots turn at two levels. It documents the grassroots existence from an unprivileged perspective, and it turns the grassroots subject into a producer and author, even if temporarily.

Conclusion — From Documentary Ethics and Politics of Representation to Post-Utopian Documentary Relationship and Grassroots Author-Producer

The increasing value accrued to the "grassroots" since the 1990s stems from the bankruptcy of utopianism and the reaction to wholesale commercialization.[72] The two formulations of the documentary relationship discussed in this chapter ("I am one of them" and "They are my actors") are both driven by the documentary makers' negotiation with post-utopianism, commercialization, and the increasing topicality of the disenfranchised. These factors in turn lead to the desire to reach toward "raw, pristine reality" (*yuan shengtai*), to feel the pulse of a not yet articulated stratum of grassroots sentiment (or what Raymond Williams calls the "structure of feeling"), and more importantly, to present these to the public from a personal (*geren hua*) perspective facilitated by DV technology.

The hard question is how this desire can be realized, and what kind of documentary relationships can be innovative enough to produce new modes of representation. A common strategy is to adopt an unprivileged camera style and a new, counter-official angle. "I am one of them" crystallizes this formulation. Importantly, "I am one of them," as practiced in Wu Wenguang's *On the Road* and Hu Shu's *Leave Me Alone*, is inevitably troubled by the dilemma of documentary ethics, i.e., the documentary maker's schizophrenic sense of simultaneous intimacy with and alienation from, even exploitation of, his or her subjects. The formulation of "They are my actors," however, offers the opportunity to convert the grassroots subjects into author-producers who perform and image their own psychic as well as existential situation into being. This transformation in turn leads to a creative and reconstructive understanding of reality, a reality that is seen as malleable and susceptible to the interventions of the "actors" (including the subjects as well as the documentary makers).

Such post-utopian Chinese documentaries are significant because they actively question accepted authority, documentary ethics, and modes of knowledge production, so as to develop new documentary relationships, thereby fermenting new knowledge and new "reality." The role of DV in this process is to enable a highly personalized, embodied, *and* shareable means of mediation and creation, which challenges the conventional binary of realism and fiction by blurring their boundaries and teasing the real out of the performative. Such new modes of knowledge production build upon yielding, or "yielding-knowing" that does not bend its objects to its will.[73] The resulting documentary relationship attends to documentary ethics without being prudish, produces knowledge without being domineering.

Given the fact that independent Chinese DV documentary making is still at the stage of exploration and trial and error, it is and will continue to be subjected to critique and transformation. In Wu Wenguang's words,

> All is unfolding and in progress, including all documenting methods prior to and following the inception of DV, including all discourses and articulations that are being constructed and deconstructed. At this very early stage of the long journey, image-making as means of self-expression is awaiting further development in both content and form. The fact that an individual is beginning to develop his/her voice is not the end, but rather just the first step made with one's own feet. Nobody can tell what is lying ahead. What is noteworthy is that the image-makers are beginning to show their individuated faces, even though they are still fuzzy, or the signs of persistence may vanish following a brief revelation. Nevertheless, new faces will soon appear. What is important is that our feet are now embarking on the journey, even if the road is dusty, foggy and filled with traps.[74]

Wu's "journey" trope underscores the collective — the continuous emergence of new faces — as opposed to the elitist figure of the lonely hero. It is precisely through constantly reconfiguring the collective, maximizing its egalitarian basis, and intensifying the collaborative interactions between the collective members, that new modes of documentary making may emerge. These in turn allow for grounded and versatile engagement with utopian values in the post-utopian era.

Appendix 1: Biographies of Key Documentarians

Compiled by Chen Ting and Chris Berry

All those filmmakers whose works are discussed in any detail in the book are included in this appendix. Many of them, as noted, also produced experimental films or dramatic films. The listings focus on their documentary output.

Ai Xiaoming

Born in Wuhan in 1953, Ai Xiaoming studied at Central China Normal University and Beijing Normal University. She is a professor in the Department of Chinese Languages and Literature at Zhongshan University in Guangzhou, Guangdong Province, where she has also led the Sex/Gender Education Forum since 2003. She is a feminist academic, human rights activist, and documentarian.

2004	*White Ribbon*
2004	*Vagina Monologues* (co-directed with Song Sufeng)
2005	*Painting for the Revolution: The Peasant Painters of Hu County*
2005	*Tai Shi Village*
2006	*What Are You Doing with That Camera?*
2006	*Epic of Central Plains*
2006	*People's Representative Yao*
2007	*The Garden of Heaven* (co-directed with Hu Jie)
2007	*Care and Love*
2007	*Red Art* (co-directed with Hu Jie)
2008	*The Train to My Hometown* (co-directed with Hu Jie)
2009	*Our Children*

Chen Jue

Chen Jue was born in Beijing in 1961, and studied at the Beijing Broadcasting Institute. He began working for China Central Television (CCTV) in 1985. As a producer and director he has been involved in numerous innovative and award-winning programs and series, and in the early 1990s he was one of the pioneers of the New Documentary Movement within the television system.

1991   *Tiananmen* (TV series)

1992   *I Graduated!* (co-directed with Shi Jian for SWYC Group)

Cui Zi'en

Cui Zi'en is a research fellow at the Beijing Film Academy and a prolific writer of short stories, film criticism, screenplays, and other work, as well as a producer and director of independent dramatic, experimental, and documentary feature and short films. Only those works with documentary elements are listed below.

2003   *Feeding Boys, Ayaya*

2004   *Night Scene*

2007   *We Are the ... of Communism*

2009   *Queer China, "Comrade" China*

Du Haibin

Du Haibin was born in Shanxi Province in 1972 and graduated in still photography from the Beijing Film Academy. His documentary feature, *Along the Railroad Tracks*, won best film at the First Chinese Independent Documentary Festival and also a special prize at the Yamagata International Documentary Film Festival. His most recent film, *1428*, won best documentary at the 2009 Venice International Film Festival.

1998   *Dou Dou*

2000   *Along the Railroad Tracks*

2002   *Underneath the Skyscraper*

2005   *Beautiful Men*

2005   *Movie, Childhood*

2006   *Stone Mountain*

2007   *Umbrella*

2009   *1428*

Duan Jinchuan

Duan Jinchuan was born in Chengdu in Sichuan Province in 1962. He graduated from the Beijing Broadcasting Institute in 1984 and went to work in Tibet for Lhasa Television Station. He returned to Beijing to work as an independent documentary filmmaker in 1992, and established China Memo Films in 1998. One of the films in his Tibet Trilogy, *No. 16 Barkhor South Street*, was the first Chinese film to win the prestigious Grand Prix at the Cinéma du Réel festival in 1996.

1986	*Highland Barley*
1988	*The Blue Mask Consecration*
1991	*Tibet*
1993	*The Sacred Site of Asceticism* (co-directed with Wen Pulin)
1994	*The Square* (co-directed with Zhang Yuan)
1996	*No. 16 Barkhor South Street*
1997	*The Ends of the Earth*
1997	*The Men and Women of Jiada Village*
1999	*Sunken Treasure*
2002	*The Secret of My Success*
2005	*The Storm* (co-directed with Jiang Yue)

Hu Jie

Hu Jie was born in 1958. He served as a soldier for fifteen years and graduated from the Oil Painting Department of the People's Liberation Army Art Academy in 1991. In 1995 he left the army and became an independent documentary maker. Since 2004, he has worked with Ai Xiaoming on various films about women, gender, and human rights education. His films have been shown widely outside China.

1995	*Yuanmingyuan Artist Village*
1996	*Remote Mountains*
1996	*Female Matchmaker*
1998	*The Trash Collector*
1998	*The Janitors*
1998	*Construction Workers*
1998	*The Factory Set Up by the Peasants*
2002	*Bask in Sunshine*
2003	*On the Seaside*

2003	*Folk Song on the Plain*
2004	*Looking for Lin Zhao's Soul*
2004	*The Elected Village Chief*
2006	*The Silent Nu River*
2006	*Though I Am Gone*
2007	*The Garden of Heaven* (co-directed with Ai Xiaoming)
2007	*Red Art* (co-directed with Ai Xiaoming)
2008	*The Train to My Hometown* (co-directed with Ai Xiaoming)
2009	*National East Wind Farm*

Hu Shu

Hu Shu was born in 1967 in Guiyang in Guizhou Province. He graduated from the School of Journalism at Fudan University in Shanghai in 1989, and has worked in Guizhou Satellite Television since 1994.

1998–99 *Leave Me Alone*

Hu Xinyu

Hu Xinyu was born in 1969 and teaches in the Music Department of the Taiyuan Teacher's College in Shanxi Province.

2003	*The Man*
2006	*Zigui*
2009	*Family Phobia*

Huang Weikai

Huang Weikai was born in 1972. He graduated from the Chinese Art Department of the Guangzhou Academy of Fine Arts in 1995. He worked as a cameraman on Ou Ning and Cao Fei's *Meishi Street* and *Sanyuanli*. Since 2002, he has been making experimental films. His documentary films are listed below. Both have been screened widely at international film festivals.

2005	*Floating*
2009	*Disorder*

Ji Dan

Ji Dan began producing independent documentaries in 1994. *Gongbu's Happy Life* was a film shown at the Taiwan International Documentary Festival and Yunfest 2003. *The Elders* was shown at the International Documentary Festival Amsterdam and the Taiwan Ethnographic Film Festival. She has also filmed many documentary programs for NHK Television.

1999	*Gongbu's Happy Life*
1999	*The Elders*
2003	*Wellspring* (co-directed with Sha Qing)
2006	*Spirit Home*
2007	*Dream of the Empty City*
2009	*Spiral Staircase of Harbin*

Jia Zhangke

Jia Zhangke was born in Fenyang in Shanxi Province in 1970, and studied film theory at the Beijing Film Academy in the 1990s. The adoption of a documentary style, with the use of location, hand-held camera, and so forth, has been a major feature of his many award-winning feature films. But he has also made documentary works. At the time of writing, he is working on a documentary about Shanghai.

1994	*One Day in Beijing*
2001	*The Canine Condition*
2001	*In Public*
2006	*Dong*
2007	*Useless*

Jiang Yue

Jiang Yue was born in 1962 and graduated from the China Drama Academy before joining the Beijing Film Studio in 1988. He and Duan Jinchuan set up China Memo Films together in 1998.

1991	*Tibetan Theater Troupe of Lhama Priests*
1992	*The Residents of Lhasa's Potala Square*
1992	*Catholics in Tibet*
1995	*The Other Bank*
1998	*A River Stilled*
2002	*This Happy Life*

2002   *The War of Love*

2005   *The Storm* (directed with Duan Jinchuan)

Jiang Zhi

Jiang Zhi was born in Hunan Province in 1971. He graduated from the Central Academy of Fine Arts in 1995, and lives and works in Shenzhen as a multimedia artist. His output ranges from photography to novels.

1998   *Forefinger*

2005   *The Moments*

2001   *The Empty Cage*

2002   *Little Red*

2004   *Our Love*

2007   *The Nail*

Ju Anqi

Ju Anqi was born in Xinjiang Province in 1975, and graduated from the Directing Department of the Beijing Film Academy in 1999.

1999   *There Is a Strong Wind in Beijing*

2003   *Quilts*

2007   *Night in China*

2009   *Gipsy in the Flower*

Kang Jianning

Born in 1954, Kang Jianning graduated from Beijing Sports College in 1970 and continued there as a teacher for ten years before transferring to work in television. He has worked as the deputy director of Ningxia Television, and has been responsible for pioneering new directions in documentary within the television system. Listed below are just a few of his most important works.

1991   *Sand and Sea*

1994   *Yin Yang*

2000   *Soldier*

2002   *Listen to Mr. Fan*

Li Hong

Li Hong was born in 1967. She studied at the Beijing Broadcasting Institute and works in television.

1997 *Out of Phoenix Bridge*
2002 *Dancing with Myself*

Li Jinghong

Li Jinghong was born in Beijing in 1959, graduated from Tianjin Handicraft University, and ran a clothing factory before becoming involved in documentary production.

2004 *Sisters*

Li Xiao

Li Xiao is head of documentary production for Shanghai TV's Documentary Channel, and an active documentary filmmaker in his own right. He has co-produced films with NHK of Japan, CBS of Canada, and PBS of the United States. The following are his primary works as a documentary director.

1992 *Boatman on Maoyan River*
1996 *Distant Village*
1996 *Strange Homeland*
2000 *Factory Director Zhang Liming*
2007 *Tangshan Earthquake*

Li Yifan

Li Yifan was born in Wuhan in 1966. He studied at the Sichuan Film Arts Institute and the Central Drama Institute in Beijing. He now lives and works in Chongqing, and is also a photographer and video artist. *Before the Flood*, which he directed with Yan Yu, won the best film award at the Yamagata International Documentary Film Festival and numerous other awards.

2004 *Before the Flood*
2007 *The Longwang Chronicles*

Liang Zi

Born in Beijing, Liang Zi entered the army at the age of sixteen and became a documentary photographer. She has also written documentary reportage.

2005   *Landlord Mr. Jiang*

Ning Ying

Ning Ying was born in Beijing. She studied cinema at the Beijing Film Academy and later at Italy's Centro Sperimentale di Cinematografia. She was assistant director for Bernardo Bertolucci on *The Last Emperor* (1987) and has gone on to direct a number of dramatic features, as well as promotional films. Since 2008, she has been head of the Film Department at the Central Academy of Fine Arts.

2001   *In Our Own Words*
2002   *Railroad of Hope*
2003   *Looking for a Job in the City*

Ou Ning

Ou Ning works as an internationally active artist, graphic designer, editor, and event organizer. In Guangzhou, he founded the independent film and video organization, U-thèque. In 2009, he was appointed as the chief curator of the Shenzhen and Hong Kong Biennale of Urbanism and Architecture. He currently lives in Beijing, where he is director of the Shao Foundation.

2003   *Sanyuanli*
2006   *Meishi Street*

Sha Qing

Sha Qing was born in Beijing in 1965. He began working in documentary in Tibet in the late 1990s, and helped to edit Ji Dan's *Gongbu's Happy Life* and *The Elders*. *Wellspring* won the Ogawa Shinsuke Prize at Yamagata in 2003.

2003   *Wellspring* (co-directed with Ji Dan)

Shi Jian

Born in 1963, Shi Jian graduated from the Beijing Broadcasting Institute in 1985 and began working as a director and producer for China Central Television (CCTV), where he continues to work to this day. In 1993, he launched *Oriental Horizon*, a series which became an important site for the development of new documentary within the television system. In 1996, he launched China's first hit talk show, *Tell It Like It Is*. As an independent producer, he helped to establish the Structure Wave Youth Cinema Experimental Group (SWYC Group) at the beginning of the 1990s.

    1991   *Tiananmen* (TV series)
    1992   *I Graduated!* (co-directed with Chen Jue for SWYC Group)

Shi Lihong

Shi Lihong is an environmental activist and filmmaker. She spent ten years working on the film *Mystery of Yunnan Snub-nosed Monkey* with her husband, Xi Zhinong. The film won a TVE Award at the Wildscreen Film Festival. In 2003, they founded China Wild Film together, and in 2004 she made her first solo film, *Voice of the Angry River*, which was screened at the Yamagata International Documentary Film Festival. She has also line-produced numerous environment-themed documentaries for international producers.

    2002   *Mystery of the Yunnan Snub-nosed Monkey*
    2004   *Voice of the Angry River*

Shi Tou

Professional artist Shi Tou graduated from the Guizhou Art Academy. She appeared as a lead actor in China's first lesbian feature film, *Fish and Elephant*, in 2001. Her oeuvre includes documentary video and photography.

    2001   *Living Buddhas*
    2002   *Gangxiang — Call to Spirits*
    2004   *Dyke March*
    2005   *Wenda Gu: Art, Politics, Life, Sexuality*
    2006   *Women Fifty Minutes*
    2007   *We Want to Get Married*

Shu Haolun

Shu Haolun received an MFA in filmmaking at Southern Illinois University in the United States, and has recently been working on dramatic films. His first documentary, *Struggle*, was his graduation work. It focuses on the efforts of a lawyer to represent those injured in industrial accidents in the factories of southern China. He is currently based in Shanghai.

2001 *Struggle*
2006 *Nostalgia*

Wang Bing

Born in Shaanxi Province in 1967, Wang Bing graduated in photography from the Lu Xun Art Academy in Shenyang, Liaoning Province in 1995, and in cinematography from the Beijing Film Academy in 1997. *West of the Tracks* was shown at the Berlin International Film Festival and went on to screen around the world.

2003 *West of the Tracks*
2007 *Fengming, a Chinese Memoir*
2008 *Crude Oil*

Wang Shuibo

Wang Shuibo was born in Shandong Province in 1960. He studied and taught at the Central Academy of Fine Arts in Beijing, before moving to Canada in 1989. He is an artist and filmmaker. His animated documentary *Sunrise over Tiananmen Square* was nominated for an Academy Award.

1998 *Sunrise over Tiananmen Square*
1999 *Swing in Beijing*
2005 *They Chose China*

Wang Wo

Wang Wo is a trained graphic designer. He is also an independent artist. He was born in Hebei Province in northern China in 1967 and studied at the Central Academy of Arts and Design in Beijing.

2006 *Outside*
2007 *Noise*

Wei Xing

Wei Xing was born in 1960. He has worked for Yunnan Television since 1986, where he has been a prolific maker of documentary programs. His best known film, *A Student Village*, was also originally made for the station.

2000   *A Student Village*

Wu Wenguang

Born in Yunnan in 1956, Wu Wenguang was one of the first filmmakers to work in the Chinese New Documentary Movement. He has also written widely about it. Together with his partner Wen Hui, he founded the Living Dance Studio. In 2005, they also established the Caochangdi Workstation Art Centre in Beijing, where he has organized numerous classes, screenings, and other events, including the China Village Documentary Project.

1990   *Bumming in Beijing — The Last Dreamers*
1993   *1966, My Time in the Red Guard*
1995   *At Home in the World*
1999   *Jianghu: Life on the Road*
1998   *Diary: Snow, 21 November 1998*
2001   *Dance with Farm Workers*
2005   *Fuck Cinema*

Yan Yu

Yan Yu was born in Chongqing in 1972. He began his career as a photojournalist at Chongqing Television. He worked there from 1994 to 1998, and then moved to Beijing to work in documentary and advertising photography. He co-founded Fanyu Studio in 2001. *Before the Flood* won the Wolfgang Staudte Award at the Berlin International Film Festival, the Cinéma du Réel Scam International Award, the Yamagata International Documentary Film Festival Grand Prize, and the Yunfest Grand Prize.

2004   *Before the Flood* (co-directed with Li Yifan)
2008   *Before the Flood II*

Yang Lina

Yang Lina was born in Jilin Province in 1972. She graduated from the Acting Department of the People's Liberation Army Art Academy in 1995, and began making documentaries in 1997.

1999   *Old Men*
2001   *Home Video*
2007   *My Neighbors on Japanese Devils*
2008   *The Love of Mr. An*

Ying Weiwei

Also known as Echo Y. Windy, Ying Weiwei has screened *The Box* was at film festivals around the world. She works for Shanghai Television, where she continues to produce documentaries.

2001   *The Box*

Zhang Hua

Born in Zhejiang Province in 1970, Zhang Hua was a professional hairdresser before getting involved in documentary film.

2004 *Kuang Dan's Secret*
2006 *Road to Paradise*

Zhang Yuan

Born in Jiangsu Province in 1963, Zhang Yuan graduated in cinematography from the Beijing Film Academy in 1989. He pioneered independent feature filmmaking in China with his film *Mama*, and in 1997 rejoined the mainstream film system with his feature *Seventeen Years*. Many of his films work at the intersection of documentary and fiction, such as *Sons* (1996), in which the lead actors re-enacted scenes from their real lives. He has also made independent documentaries.

1994   *The Square* (co-directed with Duan Jinchuan)
1999   *Crazy English*
2000   *Miss Jin Xing*

Zhao Gang

Zhao Gang was born in Chengdu in Sichuan Province, and graduated from Sichuan University in 1985. He makes documentary programs for Chengdu Television Station.

2003　*Winter Days*

Zhao Liang

Zhao Liang was born in Dandong on the border with North Korea in 1971. He studied photography at the Beijing Film Academy. He works as an artist, video artist, photographer, and screenwriter, as well as a documentarian.

2001　*Paper Airplane*
2005　*Farewell Yuanmingyuan*
2006　*Return to the Border*
2007　*Crime and Punishment*
2009　*Petition*

Zheng Dasheng

Zheng Dasheng was born in Shanghai in 1968. He graduated from the Directing Department of the Shanghai Drama Academy, and undertook graduate studies at the Chicago Art Institute. Partly funded by China Film Group, *DV China* was aired on China Central Television in 2004. Zheng Dasheng works for the Shanghai Film Studio, and he has also been directing *kunqu* operas.

2003　*DV China*

Zhou Hao

Born in 1968, Zhou Hao is a director with the 21st Century Film Workshop. He has previously worked as a reporter for the Xinhua News Agency and *Southern Weekend*. He is based in Guangzhou.

2002　*Houjie*
2006　*Senior Year*
2007　*Using*
2009　*The Transition Period*

Zhu Chuanming

Zhu Chuanming was born in 1971 on a tea plantation on Lushan, Jiangxi Province. He worked in a petrochemical factory for five years before entering the Photography Department at Beijing Film Academy. Besides his documentary works, Zhu Chuanming also regularly publishes stories, poems, and essays in Chinese literary magazines.

1999   *Beijing Cotton Fluffer*
2001   *Extras*

Zuo Yixiao

Zuo Yixiao was born in Shanghai in 1974 and studied at Shanghai University. He worked as an editor at the Propaganda Department of Shanghai Television for three years, and is currently studying scriptwriting at Beijing Film Academy.

2004   *Losing*

Appendix 2: Sources of Films

Readers may want to know how they can see the films discussed in this book. Unfortunately, most of the independent documentaries discussed in this book are not commercially distributed. This is true in the People's Republic of China, and it is also true overseas. However, in recent years, university libraries have been building collections in response to the attention paid to the Chinese New Documentary Movement. The research collections with major holdings in this area now include the University of California at San Diego Library's Chinese Underground Film Collection, and the collection of the University Services Centre at the Chinese University of Hong Kong.

Readers who wish to encourage libraries at their own institutions to acquire films like those discussed in the book will be pleased to know that more specialist distributors are making films available. Three currently operating are Fanhall Films in Beijing, dGenerate Films in New York, and Visible Record in Hong Kong.

However, this situation is volatile. We are not listing address or contact details for this reason. We also recommend readers to undertake digital searches, using both English and Chinese titles if possible. Readers may not only find some titles freely available online, for example. They may also find new sources, screenings and other ways of accessing films.

Notes

Chapter 1

1   When we originally drafted this introduction, filmmakers, artists, and intellectuals in China were somewhat optimistic about the possibilities for cultural productions and exhibitions in China. There was a more general optimism in China about a shift towards greater freedom of expression. Since then, however, there have been worrisome signs that the Chinese government has stepped up its interventions. These include the temporary closure of a well-known independent film website; the refusal to allow feminist scholar and documentary maker Ai Xiaoming to enter Hong Kong on at least one occasion; the well-publicized struggles with Google over censorship; and the jailing of Tibetan documentary maker Dhongdup Wangchen. It is difficult to predict any particular future scenario and we do not assume linear historical developments in one direction or the other. However, at the very least we imagine the dialectical tensions over non-government-sponsored cultural works will continue.

2   Lu Xinyu, "Dangdai Zhongguo dianshi jilupian yundong" (Contemporary Chinese TV documentary movement), *Dushu*, no. 5 (1999); Lu Xinyu, *Jilu Zhongguo: Dangdai Zhongguo xin jilu yundong* (Documenting China: The New Documentary Movement in China) (Beijing: Sanlian Shudian, 2003).

3   In chronological order, some of the chapters that have appeared are: Bérénice Reynaud, "New Visions/New China: Video-Art, Documentation, and the Chinese Modernity Question," in Michael Renov and Erika Suderburg, eds., *Resolutions: Contemporary Video Practices* (Minneapolis: University of Minnesota Press, 1996), 229–57; Chris Berry, "On Top of the World: An Interview with Duan Jinchuan, Director of *16 Barkhor South Street*," *Film International*, 5, no. 2 (1997): 60–2; Charles Leary, "Performing the Documentary, or Making It to the Other Bank," *Senses of Cinema*, no. 27 (2003), http://archive.sensesofcinema.com/contents/03/27/performing_documentary.html (accessed December 7, 2008); Bérénice Reynaud, "Dancing with Myself, Drifting with My Camera: The Emotional Vagabonds of China's New Documentary," *Senses of Cinema*, no. 28 (2003), http://archive.sensesofcinema.com/contents/03/28/chinas_new_documentary.html (accessed December 7, 2008); Paola Voci, "From the Center to the Periphery: Chinese Documentary's Visual Conjectures," *Modern Chinese Literature and Culture*, 16, no. 1 (2004): 65–113; Zhang Yingjin, "Styles, Subjects, and Special Points of View: A Study of Contemporary Chinese Independent Documentary," *New Cinemas: Journal of Contemporary Film*, 2, no. 2 (2004): 119–35; Maggie Lee, "Behind the Scenes: Documentaries in Mainland China, Taiwan, and Hong Kong," *Documentary Box*, no. 26

(2005), http://www.yidff.jp/docbox/23/box23-2-2-e.html (accessed December 7, 2008); Lin Xudong, "Documentary in Mainland China," translated by Cindy Carter, *Documentary Box*, no. 26 (2005), http://www.yidff.jp/docbox/26/box26-3-e.html (accessed December 7, 2008); Shen Rui, "To Remember History: Hu Jie Talks about His Documentaries," *Senses of Cinema*, no. 35 (2005), http://archive.sensesofcinema.com/contents/05/35/hu_jie_documentaries.html (accessed December 7, 2008); Valerie Jaffee, "Every Man a Star: The Ambivalent Cult of Amateur Art in New Chinese Documentaries," in Paul Pickowicz and Yingjin Zhang, eds., *From Underground to Independent: Alternative Film Culture in Contemporary China* (Lanham, MD: Rowman and Littlefield, 2006), 77–108; Matthew David Johnson, "A Scene beyond Our Line of Sight: Wu Wenguang and New Documentary Cinema's Politics of Independence," in Pickowicz and Zhang, eds., *From Underground to Independent*, 47–76; Chris Berry, "Independently Chinese: Duan Jinchuan, Jiang Yue, and Chinese Documentary," in ibid., 109–22; Wang Qi, "Navigating on the Ruins: Space, Power, and History in Contemporary Chinese Independent Documentaries," *Asian Cinema*, 17, no. 1 (2006): 246–55; Chris Berry, "Getting Real: Chinese Documentary, Chinese Postsocialism," in Zhang Zhen, ed., *The Urban Generation: Chinese Cinema and Society at the Turn of the Twenty-First Century* (Durham, NC: Duke University Press, 2007), 115–34; and Wang Ban, "In Search of Real-Life Images in China: Realism in the Age of Spectacle," *Journal of Contemporary China*, no. 56 (2008): 497–512. In addition to these essays, the impact of independent documentary on feature films means that many essays on contemporary Chinese fiction feature films also deal with documentary.

4   Frances Hoar Foster, "Codification in Post-Mao China," *American Journal of Comparative Law*, 30, no. 3 (1982): 405–7.

5   For more on this era, see Wang Jing, *High Culture Fever: Politics, Aesthetics and Ideology in Deng's China* (Berkeley: University of California Press, 1996).

6   See Wang Hui, "The Year 1989 and the Historical Roots of Neoliberalism in China," *positions: east asia cultures critique*, 12, no. 1 (2004): 7–69, for a full development of this argument.

7   See Jonathan Unger, *The Transformation of Rural China* (Armonk, NY: M. E. Sharpe, 2002), for a more detailed description of these transformations in the rural areas. See Yimin Lin, *Between Politics and Markets: Firms, Competition, and Institutional Change in Post-Mao China* (Cambridge: Cambridge University Press, 2001), for a discussion of urban changes.

8   See Ching Kwan Lee, ed., *Working in China: Ethnographies of Labor and Workplace Transformation* (London and New York: Routledge, 2007), for a discussion of changing labor conditions for urban workers. See Vivienne Shue and Christine Wong, eds., *Paying for Progress in China: Public Finance, Human Welfare and Changing Patterns of Inequality* (London and New York: Routledge, 2007), for a more general discussion of new forms of inequality in China.

9   Zhang Yimou, one of the best known of the Fifth Generation filmmakers, made numerous films that were allegorical critiques of the Cultural Revolution. Most recently, he directed the opening spectacle of the Beijing Olympics.

10 Jia Zhangke, "Yeyu dianying shidai jijiang zaici daolai" (The age of amateur cinema will

return), in Zhang Xianmin and Zhang Yaxuan, eds., *Yigeren de yingxiang: DV wanquan shouce* (Beijing: Zhongguo qingnian chubanshe, 2003), 307–8. On the inside cover, the English title of the book is given as *All about DV*, but the Chinese title could be translated as "The Individual's Image: A Complete DV Handbook."

11 Zhang Xianmin and Zhang Yaxuan's *Yigeren de yingxiang* is a prime example.

12 Lev Manovich, *The Language of New Media* (Cambridge: MIT Press, 2002).

13 See, for example, Michelle Pierson, *Special Effects: Still in Search of Wonder* (New York: Columbia University Press, 2002).

Chapter 2

1 Suisheng Zhao, "Chinese Intellectuals' Quest for National Greatness and Nationalistic Writings in the 1990s," *The China Quarterly*, no. 152 (1997): 725–45; Jiayan Mi, "The Visual Imagined Communities: Media State, Virtual Citizenship and Television in Heshang (River Elegy)," *Quarterly Review of Film and Video*, 22, no. 4 (2005): 327–40; Edward Gunn, "The Rhetoric of River Elegy: From Cultural Criticism to Social Act," in Roger V. Des Forges, Lou Ning, and Wu Yen-bo, eds., *Chinese Democracy and the Crisis of 1989: Chinese and American Reflections* (Buffalo: State University of New York Press, 1993), 247–62.

2 According to Xiaoping Li, by the end of the 1980s nearly every urban household had its own set, with China's television network estimated to reach 78 percent of the population. Li Xiaoping, "The Chinese Television System and Television News," *China Quarterly*, no. 126 (1991): 341–2.

3 Author's interview with Wu Wenguang in "Trends toward the Individualization of Writing," in Lu Xinyu, *Documenting China: The New Documentary Movement in China* (Beijing: Sanlian Shudian, 2003),

4 Jing Wang, *High Culture Fever: Politics, Aesthetics and Ideology in Deng's China* (Berkeley: University of California Press, 1996); Wang Hui, *China's New Order: Society, Politics and Economy in Transition*, edited by Theodore Huters (Cambridge: Harvard University Press, 2003); Lisa Rofel, *Desiring China: Experiments in Sexuality, Public Culture and Neoliberalism* (Durham, NC: Duke University Press, 2007).

5 The 1989 Tiananmen Incident involved hundreds of thousands of students and citizens protesting a range of issues, including students' demands for better university conditions and more democracy in government, as well as citizens' opposition to government corruption. The protests in Beijing centered in Tiananmen Square, where students and some citizens camped out and refused to leave. Protests were also held in all major cities in China. The protests ended on June 4, 1989, when the central government called in the army to shoot down the protesters in Tiananmen Square.

6 Ningxia is a province located in the north central part of China, far from Beijing. The province is rather poor; it is remote from the cultural centers on the coast of China.

7 Zhou Enlai was second in power to Mao, serving as the premier of the People's Republic of China from its founding until Zhou's death in 1976. His efforts to dampen the worst violence of the Cultural Revolution meant that his popularity never waned, and hence the immense outpouring of grief by citizens upon his death. See Dick Wilson, *Zhou Enlai: A Biography* (New York: Viking Press, 1984).

8   Zhang Zhen, "Bearing Witness: Chinese Urban Cinema in the Era of 'Transformation'," in Zhang Zhen, ed., *The Urban Generation: Chinese Cinema and Society at the Turn of the Twenty-First Century* (Durham, NC: Duke University Press, 2007), 1–39.

9   See Hu Ke, "André Bazin's Influence and the Concept of Truth in Chinese Cinema," *Dangdai dianying* (Contemporary China), April 2008.

10 See Guo Qing, "Finding One's Voice through a Thousand Melodies: A Compilation of Research on Recent Cinema," *Dianying yishu* (Film Art), December 1987.

11 See Ren Yuan, "The Use of the Long-Shot in Documentary Film," *Dianying yishu* (Film Art), August 1987; Ren Yuan, "On the Correct Naming of Documentary Film," *Zhongguo guangboshi xuekan* (China Radio and TV Academic Journal), April 1992. Ren Yuan is a professor at Beijing Radio and Television Institute (now called Communication University of China). He is the main advocate of the use of the theory of long shots in television documentaries.

12 See my "Chinese Documentaries: Views and Values," in *Documenting China*, 264–71.

13 See my essay, "Shenme shi jilu jingshen?" (What is the spirit of documentary?), *Shijie* (Horizons), no. 3 (2001). This essay tries to capture conversations that these filmmakers were having at various conferences at the time.

14 In "Documentary Modes of Representation," Nichols outlines the expository, observational, interactive, and reflexive modes of documentary; Bill Nichols, *Representing Reality* (Blomington: Indiana University Press, 1991), 32–76. In "Performing Documentary," Nichols adds the performative mode, something previously included in the reflexive mode, as a mode in its own right; Bill Nichols, *Blurring Boundaries: Questions of Meaning in Contemporary Culture* (Bloomington: Indiana University Press, 1994), 92–106.

15 Zhang Zhen, "Bearing Witness," 15.

16 I participated in the 2005 "Evaluating the City" panel discussion at the Guangzhou International Bi-annual Photography Exhibition. Photography theory and realist photography were the main points of discussion. See my "Chinese Urban Images under the Sign of 'Valuation'," in *Shuxie yu Zhibi* (Writing and What It Obscures) (Guangxi Normal University Press, 2008), and also http://www.gdmoa.org/zhanlan/international/xiangguan/7459.jsp (accessed September 7, 2009).

17 At that time, the production team picked from multiple scripts to work with. The production process and scriptwriting were separated.

18 In the fall of 1994, I interviewed the first producer of Shanghai Television Station's Documentary Editing Room, Liu Jingqi. This interview was aired in 2003 on CCTV's program *Jianzheng* (Witness), in its series called *Shijian de Zhongliang* (The Weight of Time).

19 See my "Why We Need Documentary — Some Thoughts on the Development of China's Television Documentaries," in *Documenting China*, 272–8.

20 CCTV and a Tibetan production house worked together, with most of the funding from CCTV. The version shown internationally did not list CCTV in the credits so that it would not be viewed as a propaganda film. See my interview with Wei Bin in my *Documenting China*, 223–4.

21 See my "From the Ruins of Utopia — China's New Documentary Movement" and "From

the Other Shore — A conversation with Jiang Yue," in *Documenting China*, 1–4, and 101–40.

22 http://beijing.cnex.org.cn/index.php (accessed August 17, 2009).

23 This was not a formal publication but a booklet that accompanied the film at the Venice Biennale Festival.

24 From an interview I conducted with the director at the Shanghai Biennial Festival, on September 28, 2004. I had recommended this film for this festival, under the festival's thematic rubric of "Techniques of the Visible."

25 The debates about the "humanistic spirit" occurred in intellectual circles during 1993 to 1995. In 1994, *Dushu* (Reading), a major scholarly journal, published a series of essays with interviews and conversations with people from the media world, sparking reaction among intellectuals. For further details, see Wang Xiaoming's *Renwen Jingshen Xunzhaolu* (Searching for the Humanistic Spirit) (Shanghai: Wenhui Publishers, 1996).

26 See my "Shenme shi jilu jingshen?," in *Documenting China*, 298.

Chapter 3

1 Wu Wenguang, *Jianghu baogao* (Report from the Jiang Hu) (Beijing: Zhongguo Qingnian Chubanshe, 2001).

Chapter 4

1 Zhang Yaxuan, "Wang Bing: Wo wei xianzai pai dianying" (Wang Bing: I am making films for today), *Yishu shijie* (Art World), no. 8 (2004): 83.

2 Pang Hong, "Jianguoqian Shenyang Tiexiqu de xingcheng" (The formation of Shenyang's Tiexi district before the establishment of the People's Republic), *Lantai shijie* (Lantai World) no. 7 (2005): 137; Su Mei, "Tiexi District of Shenyang, a Frontier of Revitalizing Northeast Traditional Industrial Base," *Guotu zeyuan* (Land and Resources), no. 10 (2004): 6–15.

3 Fan Haitao and Liu Zhiming, "Tiexiqu: Zai zhentong zhong chongxin qitiao" (Tiexi district: Taking off again through the difficulties), *Zhongguo jidian gongye* (China Machinery and Electronics Industry), no. 21 (2003): 21–3.

4 Personal interview with Wang Bing, August 28, 2003; Li Hongyu, "Tiexiqu: Gongchang shi zhurengong" (*West of the Tracks*: The factory is the protagonist), *Nanfang zhoumo* (Southern Weekend), April 17, 2003.

5 Personal interview with Wang Bing, August 28, 2003; Li Hongyu, "Tiexiqu."

6 Zhang Yaxuan, "Wang Bing."

7 Georg Lukács, *History and Class Consciousness*, translated by Rodney Livingstone (Cambridge: MIT Press, 1971), 133.

8 Personal interview with Wang Bing, August 28, 2003; Li Hongyu, "Tiexiqu."

9 Zhang Yaxuan, "Wang Bing," 80.

10 Personal interview with Wang Bing, August 28, 2003.

11 Karl Marx, *Capital*, volume 1, translated by Ben Fowkes (New York: Vintage, 1977), 932.

12 Ibid., 125–31.

13 This effort to relate price to perceived use value originates with the Austrian economist Friedrich von Wieser in *Über den Ursprung und die Hauptgesetze des wirtschaftlichen Wertes* (The Nature and Essence of Theoretical Economics) (Vienna, 1884).

14 A prime example is Jean Baudrillard, *For a Critique of the Political Economy of the Sign* (New York: Semiotext(e), 1983).

15 Georg Lukács, "The Antinomies of Bourgeois Thought," in *History and Class Consciousness: Studies in Marxist Dialectics*, translated by Rodney Livingstone (London: Merlin Press, 1971), 11–149.

16 Karl Marx, "The Dual Character of the Labour Embodied in Commodities," in *Capital*, volume 1, 131–8.

17 Max Horkheimer and Theodor W. Adorno, *Dialectic of Enlightenment* (London: Continuum, 1990), 230.

18 Barbara Demick, "Suicide Puts Face on Farmers' Plight," *Los Angeles Times*, September 19, 2003, http://articles.latimes.com/2003/sep/19/world/fg-suicide19 (accessed October 27, 2008).

19 Walter Benjamin, *The Origin of German Tragic Drama*, translated by John Osborne (London: New Left Books, 1977), 177–8.

20 "Xin Zhongguo shiyou zhanxian de tieren" (Iron man on New China's oil frontline), http://news.xinhuanet.com/ziliao/2003-01/17/content_694588.htm (accessed October 27, 2008).

21 Hu Shi, "Jianguo wenti yinlun" (On building the nation), *Duli pinglun* (Independent Critique), no. 77, November 19, 1933.

22 Immanuel Wallerstein, *After Liberalism* (New York: New Press, 1995).

23 Eric Hobsbawn, *The Age of Revolution*, 1798–1848 (New York: Vintage, 1996), 44.

24 Benjamin, *The Origin of German Tragic Drama*, 151.

25 Lu Xinyu, *Jilu Zhongguo: Dangdai Zhongguo xin jilu yundong* (Documenting China: The New Documentary Movement in China) (Beijing: Sanlian, 2003), 1–23.

26 Personal interview with Wang Bing, August 28, 2003.

27 Ibid.

Chapter 5

1 See Lu Xinyu, "Rethinking China's New Documentary Movement," this volume.

2 Zhang Zhen, "Dai sheyingji de nüren: Dangdai Zhongguo nüxing jilupian paishe huodong yipie" (Women with video cameras: A glimpse of contemporary Chinese women's documentary), *Yishu dangdai* (Modern Arts), 3, no. 1 (2004): 30–3. An extended version of this essay is collected in Ping Jie, ed., *Lingyan xiangkan: Haiwai xuezhe ping dangdai Zhongguo jilupian* (A New Look at Contemporary Chinese Documentary) (Shanghai: Wenhui Chubanshe, 2006), 84–95.

3 In addition to the Elvira Notari Prize at the Venice International Film Festival in 2001, *Fish and Elephant* also won a special mention at the Berlin International Film Festival in 2002. For a review of this film, see Cui Zi'en, *Diyi guanzhong* (The First Audiences) (Beijing: Xiandai Chubanshe, 2003), 94–8.

4 Shi Tou's works have toured several major cities in China, and have been selected for exhibitions in the United States and Europe. More recently, she has been invited by New York University, University of Chicago, Illinois School of Professional Psychology, and San Francisco International Lesbian & Gay Film Festival to show her works. In 2005, she was invited by the University of California, Berkeley, for a one-woman show at the

Berkeley Art Museum, where her paintings, photographs, and new video work, *Women Fifty Minutes*, were exhibited. Mills College Art Museum bought a piece from her photo series *Together* for its permanent collection; Public Art Commission of Silicon Valley chose *Together* as a centerpiece for their annual city exhibition. In 2006, her latest work, a three-piece photo-painting, was part of the exhibition "Jiang Hu" at the Tilton Gallery in both New York and Los Angeles.

5   Shi Tou was also the organizer and host of the first "Chinese Lesbian and Gay Conference" and the first mainland Chinese "Convention of Lesbians" (both held in Beijing in 1998). She also served as the editor of *Tiankong (Sky)*, a community newsletter for Chinese lesbians, and helped set up a telephone hotline to exchange opinions about sexual orientation. Among others, Shi participated in the first and second Beijing International Gay and Lesbian Film Festival (in December 2001 and April 2005) and the Beijing Gay and Lesbian Culture Festival (in December 2005).

6   Entitled "Hezhong qiri" (Seven days in the box), Echo Y. Windy's personal statement can be found in "Jilupian *Hezi*" (Documentary *The Box*), *Nüquan Zhongguo* (Chinese Feminism). See www.feminism.cn (accessed January 28, 2005).

7   Ibid.

8   Harriet Evans, *Women and Sexuality in China: Female Sexuality and Gender since 1949* (New York: Continuum, 1997), 7.

9   Ibid., 27.

10 Quoted from Zhu Jingjian and Cao Kai, "Zhongguo yingxiang dageming de DV shidai lailin" (The advent of the DV era and the great revolution of imaging in China), *Fenghuang zhoukan* (Phoenix Weekly), no. 6 (2005). See www.phoenixtv.com/ phoenixtv/72935047266566144/20050324/524810.shtml (accessed May 2005).

11 Quoted from Li Duoyu, "Cong zuidi de difang kaishi paishe" (Starting filming in the lowest position), *Nanfang zhoumo* (Southern Weekend), http://cn.cl2000.com/film2/dldy/ dldycn1.shtml (accessed May 2005). Wu Wenguang expresses a similar opinion in a short article entitled "Nüxing yu DV shexiangji" (Women and DV cameras), *Xinlang wang* (New Wave Website), http://bn.sina.com.cn/dv/2006-02-03/182414077.html (accessed July 2006).

12 Windy's interaction with A is slightly different from that with B. I assume this difference is related to A's somewhat reticent personality, which sometimes made Windy play a more active part during the interviews. On the other hand, at least twice B seems to be trying to engage Windy in dialogue or conversation, but I do not perceive Windy's responses to B.

13 Bill Nichols, *Introduction to Documentary* (Bloomington: Indiana University Press, 2001), 109–23.

14 Ibid., 116.

15 Ibid.

16 Wu Wenguang, "*Xianchang*: He jilu fangshi youguan de shu" (*Document*: A book about the ways of recording), in Wu Wenguang, ed., *Xianchang, diyi juan* (Document, Volume One) (Tianjin: Tianjin Shehui Kexue Yanjiuyuan, 2000), 274.

17 Chris Berry, "Facing Reality: Chinese Documentary, Chinese Postsocialism," in Wu Hung, Wang Huangsheng, and Feng Boyi, eds., *Reinterpretation: A Decade of Experimental*

Chinese Art: 1990–2000 (Guangdong: Guangdong Museum of Art, 2002), 121–31, esp. 122, 124–5.

18 Lu Xinyu, *Jilu Zhongguo: Dangdai Zhongguo xin jilupian yundong* (Documenting China: The New Documentary Movement in China) (Shanghai: Sanlian Shudian, 2003), 14–15, 335.

19 Zhang Yingjin, "Fengge, zhuti, shijiao: Dangdai Zhongguo duli jilupian yanjiu" (Styles, subject matters, perspectives: A study of contemporary Chinese independent documentary), in Ping Jie, ed., *Lingyan xiangkan*, 55.

20 Bill Nichols, "The Voice of Documentary," in Alan Rosenthal, ed., *New Challenges for Documentary* (Berkeley: University of California Press, 1988), 48–9.

21 Zhang Yingjin, "Fengge, zhuti, shijiao," 57.

22 Windy, "Jilupian *Hezi*."

23 Tze-lan D. Sang, *The Emerging Lesbian: Female Same-Sex Desire in Modern China* (Chicago: University of Chicago Press, 2003), 168.

24 Ibid.

25 *Tongzhi* is one of the most popular contemporary Chinese phrases for lesbian and gay people. It was first translated from a Soviet communist term, "comrade (or cadre)," and was taken up by both the Chinese Communist and Nationalist Parties to refer to comrades struggling for the Communist/Nationalist revolution. After 1949, *tongzhi* became a friendly and politically correct term by which to address everyone in the People's Republic of China. Although "*tongzhi*" has lost its popularity in post-socialist China, the phrase was appropriated in 1989 by Edward Lam, a gay activist from Hong Kong, for the first Lesbian and Gay Film Festival in Hong Kong. Within a few years, "*tongzhi*" was widely used in Hong Kong, Taiwan, and, more recently, major cities in China, to refer to same-sex eroticism. In this chapter I use the word *tongzhi* with some flexibility. When "*tongzhi*" appears unmodified, it mostly refers to LGBT/Q. When it is employed with female and male, the term mainly signifies lesbians and gay men, respectively.

26 Chou Wah-shan, *Tongzhi: Politics of Same-Sex Eroticism in Chinese Societies* (New York: Haworth Press, 2000), 110.

27 Homosexuality as a mental illness was removed in 2001 from the *Categories and Diagnostic Standards of Mental Illness in China* (Third Edition), published by the Chinese Society of Psychiatry. See Cui Zi'en, "Filtered Voices: Representing Gay People in Today's China," translated by Chi Ta-wei, *IIAS* Newsletter, no. 29 (2002): 13.

28 Wan Yanhai, "Becoming a Gay Activist in Contemporary China," edited and translated by Chris Berry, in Gerard Sullivan and Peter A. Jackson, eds., *Gay and Lesbian Asia: Culture, Identity, Community* (New York: Harrington Park Press, 2001), 47.

29 Sang, *The Emerging Lesbian*, 170.

30 See, for instance, Zi Feiyu, "Weimei, gudian, liuchang — zoujin minjian dianyingren de shijie" (Romantic, classic, fluent — entering the world of grassroots filmmakers), *Wenhua xingqiwu* (Cultural Fridays), www.china.org.cn/fribry/2001-12-06/2001-12-06-22.htm (accessed December 5, 2001); Cheng Suqin, "Ling yizhong jiyi — dui duli jilupian de fansi" (Another kind of memory: Rethinking independent documentary), *Zhongguo chuanmeiwang* (Chinese Media website), http://academic.mediachina.net (accessed November 11, 2002).

31 Li Bingqin, "Pingminghua, duli jingshen yu jilupian chuangzuo" (Popularization, independent spirit and documentary creation), *Wuhan Shengping* (Wuhan radio), www. whradio.com.cn/co195/co197/co1126/article.html?id=1536, (accessed May 2005). Zi Feiyu holds a similar opinion. See Zi, "Weimei, gudian, liuchang."

32 See Zi, "Pingminghua" and Cheng, "Ling yizhong jiyi," as well as Li, "Pingminghua."

33 Michel Foucault, *The History of Sexuality, Volume 1: An Introduction*, translated by Robert Hurley (New York: Vintage Books, 1990).

34 Windy, "Jilupian *Hezi*."

35 Zi, "Weimei, gudian, liuchang," and Cheng, "Ling yizhong jiyi."

36 "Di'er jie Zhongguo jilupian jiaoliuzhou jiabin yu guanzhong jiaoliu quanjilu" (A full record of the face-to-face communication between the guests and the audiences during the second week for Chinese documentary communication), http://www.topart.cn/cn/room/show/htm (accessed May 2005).

37 Pierre Bourdieu argues that cultural distinctions support class distinctions. Taste is a highly ideological category: it functions as a marker of class, a double-coded term that refers to both a socio-economic category and a particular level of quality. To consume culture is "predisposed, consciously and deliberately or not, to fulfill a social function of legitimating social differences." See Pierre Bourdieu, *Distinction: A Social Critique of the Judgment of Taste*, translated by Richard Nice (Cambridge, MA: Harvard University Press, 1984), 7.

38 For a debate over the population quality in relation to the education system in present-day China, see Ann Hulbert, "Re-Education," *The New York Times Magazine*, April 1, 2007, 36–43, continued on 56.

39 Lisa Rofel, "Qualities of Desire: Imagining Gay Identities in China," in *Desiring China: Experiments in Neo-liberalism, Sexuality and Public Culture* (Durham, NC: Duke University Press, 2007), 85–110.

40 Windy, "Jilupian *Hezi*."

41 In her statement "Hezhong qiri" (see note 6), Windy chose the perplexing term "shocking" to describe her first impression of A and B, who, according to Windy, were doing nothing but standing in the bright sunshine. She also wondered "if such a pure and beautiful world [the world of A and B] would someday collapse," which, she lamented, made her feel "helpless" and "sentimental." I find those descriptions somehow testify to the romanticized quality of Windy's own imagination projected onto the lesbian couple as her other.

42 Michel Foucault, *Discipline and Punish: The Birth of the Prison*, translated by Alan Sheridan (New York: Vintage Books, 1979), 27.

43 *Dyke March* has been shown in China on various occasions, including the Second China Documentary Film Festival in Beijing, Shanghai, and Nanjing (June 2004) and the Second Beijing International Gay and Lesbian Film Festival (April 2005), among others. In our e-mail exchanges, Shi Tou informed me that the film has been screened at numerous *tongzhi* gatherings, though she is equally interested in showing the film at events that are not specifically for *tongzhi*.

44 Arjun Appadurai, *Modernity at Large: Cultural Dimensions of Globalization* (Minneapolis: University of Minnesota Press, 1996); Lisa Rofel, *Other Modernities: Gendered Yearning*

in *China after Socialism* (Berkeley: University of California Press, 1999). In her essay "From Gender Erasure to Gender Difference," Mayfair Yang also stresses the aspect of imagination in constituting transnational Chinese subjectivities. See Mayfair Yang, ed., *Spaces of Their Own: Women's Public Sphere in Transnational China* (Minneapolis: University of Minnesota Press, 1996), 35–67.

45 I borrow the term "glocal" from Roland Robertson. See Roland Robertson, "Glocalization: Time-Space and Homogeneity-Heterogeneity," in Mike Featherstone, Scott Lash, and Roland Robertson, *Global Modernities* (London: Sage Publications, 1995), 25–44.

46 The "West" itself is also an imaginary location. Essential to such a concept is less geographic locale than the hegemonic power structure embedded in the Eurocentric colonial legacy and the matrix of political, economic, and cultural disparities. When talking about the West, I am fully aware that even within the West there exist layers of unevenness and heterogeneity.

47 Appadurai, *Modernity at Large: Cultural Dimensions of Globalization*, chapter 2.

48 Lydia H. Liu, *Translingual Practice: Literature, National Culture, and Translated Modernity—China, 1900–1937* (Stanford: Stanford University Press, 1995). In her book Liu highlights the vehicle of translation somehow omitted from Edward Said's concept of traveling theory. She traces, for instance, the historical contingency of the discourse of individualism particularly in relation to "the master narrative of the nation-state in the early republican period," where individualism was sought by some Chinese intellectuals, in Liu's words, "not to liberate individuals so much as to constitute them as citizens of the nation-state and members of a modern society" (86 and 95).

49 Rofel, "Qualities of Desire: Imagining Gay Identities in China," 94.

50 Judith Butler, *Gender Trouble: Feminism and the Subversion of Identity* (New York: Routledge, 1990); Eve K. Sedgwick, "Queer Performativity: Henry James's *The Art of the Novel*," *GLQ*, 1, no. 1 (1993): 1–16; Eve K. Sedgwick, "Affect and Queer Performativity," in *Working Papers in Gender/Sexuality Studies*, nos. 3 & 4 (1998): 90–108. (Note: *Working Papers* is a publication by the Center of the Studies of Sexualities at National Central University in Zhongli, Taiwan). Thomas Waugh identifies the performance/performativity tradition in early gay/lesbian documentary filmmaking. See Thomas Waugh, "Walking on Tippy Toes: Lesbian and Gay Liberation Documentary of the Post-Stonewall Period, 1969–84," in Chris Holmlund and Cynthia Fuchs, eds., *Between the Sheets, In the Streets: Queer, Lesbian, Gay Documentary* (Minneapolis: University of Minnesota Press, 1997), 107–24.

51 Lauren Berlant and Elizabeth Freeman, "Queer Nationality," in Michael Warner, ed., *Fear of A Queer Planet: Queer Politics and Social Theory* (Minneapolis: University of Minnesota Press, 1993), 196–7.

52 Thomas Waugh, "Introduction: Why Documentary Filmmakers Keep Trying to Change the World, or Why People Changing the World Keep Making Documentaries," in Waugh, ed., *"Show Us Life": Toward a History and Aesthetics of the Committed Documentary* (Metuchen, NJ: Scarecrow Press, Inc., 1984), xiv.

53 Ibid., xiii.

54 For an excellent examination of AIDS videomaking vis-à-vis AIDS activism and

communal self-empowerment, see Alexandra Juhasz, *AIDS TV: Identity, Community, and Alternative Video* (Durham, NC: Duke University Press, 1995). For an analysis of early feminist documentary filmmaking, see Julia Lesage, "Feminist Documentary: Aesthetics and Politics," in Waugh, *"Show Us Life,"* 223–51, and Patricia Erens, "Women's Documentary Filmmaking: The Personal Is Political," in Rosenthal, *New Challenges for Documentary*, 554–65.

55   Chao Shi-Yan, "Hezi nei wai de qingyu zhengzhi — jian lun Nütongzhi Youxing Ri" (The erotic politics inside and outside of *The Box*, alongside a discussion of *Dyke March*), in Ping Jie, *Lingyan xiangkan*, 143–51.

56   For instance, they portray a group of girls who have "a special liking" for each other and, had they the choice not to marry, would have remained together for life. In another example they show two women in their nineties who have been "really close" to each other since their childhoods but were forced to marry. Now that their husbands have passed away, they once again enjoy each other's company. Even though these girls and women love one another, they do not consider themselves lesbians, in part because they do not have a concrete idea about lesbianism in the first place. Although Shi Tou and Ming Ming are self-identified lesbians, they do not impose a presumed lesbian identity on their subjects. Rather, they respect the varied perceptions of same-sex eroticism played out along the axis of urban/rural difference.

Chapter 6

1   However, Beijing's relevance in the development of contemporary Chinese documentary should not be overemphasized. For instance, Bérénice Reynaud has pointed out how the Tibetan experience has had a significant impact on many Chinese documentarians in "Dancing with Myself, Drifting with My Camera: The Emotional Vagabonds of China's New Documentary," *Senses of Cinema*, no. 28 (2003), http://archive.sensesofcinema. com/contents/03/28/chinas_new_documentary.html (accessed August 14, 2008). The exploration of rural China is another main line of consideration. It has covered issues ranging from political and administrative changes (*Village Head Election*, 1998), to environmental degradation (*Big Tree County*, 1993), inadequacy of education (*Lighting a Candle*, 1999, and *A Student Village*, 2002), and the loss of traditional ways of living among ethnic minorities, especially in Yunnan Province (*The Cormorants and the Lake*, 1998 and *Foggy Valley*, 2003). Furthermore, Yunnan can be considered another important center for documentary as it hosts the YUNFEST (Yunnan Multi Culture Visual Festival), a biennial event organized by the Visual Education Department of the BAMA Mountain Culture Research Institute (an action research team under the supervision of the Yunnan Academy of Social Sciences).

2   Examples of this neo-socialist/capitalist realism include the ten-part series *Song of the Sun*, produced by the General Political Department of the People's Liberation Army in June 1992, and *Journey through the Century*, a TV documentary made in four half-hour episodes in 1989, each focusing on one of the Four Basic Principles (adherence to socialism, the proletarian dictatorship, party leadership, and Marxism-Leninism-Mao Zedong Thought).

3   Even when the focus is on Tiananmen, the square becomes a problematic "center," as in Shi Jian and Chen Jue's television series, *Tiananmen* and *The Square*, directed by Zhang Yuan and Duan Jinchuan in 1994. For an in-depth analysis of *Tiananmen* and a comparative discussion of documentary's subsequent developments produced by both independent documentarians and state-run TV stations, see Paola Voci, "From the Center to the Periphery: Chinese Documentary's Visual Conjectures," *Modern Chinese Literature and Culture*, 16, no. 1 (Spring 2004): 65–113. Tiananmen Square's physical and symbolic space has been the subject of both artistic and theoretical readings, for example in Wu Hung, *Remaking Beijing: Tiananmen Square and the Creation of a Political Space* (Chicago: University of Chicago Press, 2005). For an analysis of the global media depiction of the square, see Gina Marchetti, *From Tiananmen to Times Square: Transnational China and the Chinese Diaspora on Global Screens, 1989–1997* (Philadelphia: Temple University Press, 2006).

4   Besides Chris Berry, Bérénice Reynaud (particularly regarding *Dance with Farm Workers*), and Charles Leary (in his analysis of Jiang Yue's *The Other Bank*) have also noted the importance of the "performative" aspect in the representation of marginal communities. See Chris Berry, "East Palace, West Palace: Staging Gay Life in China," *Jump Cut*, no. 42 (1998): 84–9; Bérénice Reynaud, "Dancing with Myself"; Charles Leary, "Performing the Documentary, or Making it to the Other Bank," *Senses of Cinema*, no. 27 (2003), http://archive.sensesofcinema.com/contents/03/27/performing_documentary.html (accessed August 14, 2008).

5   See Berry, "East Palace, West Palace," 84–9.

6   While in *The Other Bank*, *Life on the Road*, and *Swing in Beijing*, access to a public space is a concern for both the viewing and the viewed subjects, in *Dance with Farm Workers* such a need is mostly reflected in the director's conscious attempt at enabling his actors to become visible.

7   The documentary was produced with the support of the Canada Council for the Arts and never released or broadcast in China. *Swing in Beijing* is distributed by First Run/Icarus Films, http://www.frif.com/subjects/marker.html.

8   *Swing in Beijing* presents other interesting similarities with *Bumming in Beijing*. Both documentaries directly refer to Beijing in their titles and rely on the "talking heads" interview format. Furthermore, both works seem to find their *raison d'être* in the directors' personal connections with the artists they interview. *At Home in the World* (1995) was Wu's follow-up to *Bumming in Beijing*, in which he followed his interviewees to their new homes. For all except one, these were outside China.

9   The song is "Awakening" (*Juexing*). In the documentary, Gao Xing explains that the reference to the flag was deliberately covered with city noise in the video for the song.

10 In his painting, he says, he uses nude women to symbolically uncover and expose the destruction of cultural heritage caused by the Cultural Revolution.

11 Zhang is a sculptor who works in a state-owned studio. He explains that he decided to produce some commercial work to pay the bills, so he does not have to compromise on his creative freedom.

12 At the time *Swing in Beijing* was shot, Jia had just started his directing career. His interview is intercut with scenes from his first film, *Xiao Wu*.

13 Since 1999, Jia Zhangke's film festival prizes have increased in number. Most recently, his 2006 feature film *Still Life* won the Golden Lion at the 63rd Venice Film Festival.

14 In this context, he also refers to an ideal alliance between China and Europe (as equally rich cultural traditions) against Hollywood.

15 Unlike *Bumming in Beijing*, there is no in-depth exploration of the individual human being and their emotional complexity. Each brief interview offers very minimal information about the interviewee from a more personal perspective.

16 Cui has also recently produced a more traditional documentary, *We Are the ... of Communism* (2007), in which he records the story of Beijing's Yuanhai Elementary School for the children of migrants without Beijing residency permits. The school is suddenly closed down, forcing its students and teachers to hold their classes outside the school gates, while struggling to decide what to do next.

17 By using a mix of students, actors and "real" gigolos, Cui has explained that his goal is to displace viewers' preconceptions about what gigolos look like as well as to protect the identities of his subjects. (Personal interview, Sydney, November 24, 2006.)

18 Cui has also noted that he deliberately did not include any captions to identify the experts, because he did not wish them to have a more authoritative voice than his other subjects. (Personal interview, Sydney, November 24, 2006.) While unknown to general audiences, the experts are all researchers who work on sexuality or gay rights, or social workers active in AIDS prevention programs. They include the sociologist Li Yinhe, Wan Yanhai (an HIV-AIDS prevention activist), and Zhang Beichuan (author of a book on the history of homosexuality). In the video, the only explicit reference to a known institution is to the Center for AIDS Prevention Studies (University of California).

19 The tank is later revealed as one of many in the Fish Bar, a gay bar in Beijing. In Chinese the words for fish and desire are close homophones (they are both pronounced *yu* although they have different tones).

20 The director himself performs in front of the camera in one of the many staged encounters.

21 Earlier in the documentary, Liang Yang tries to kill herself. At the end, one of the intertitles mentions that, for fear she might attempt suicide again, "we" decided to give her some money and hoped she would use it for methadone rather than heroin.

22 Besides his short experimental videos, Zhao has shot two other full-length Beijing documentaries *Farewell Yuanmingyuan* (2005) on the government's closing down of one of the Yuanmingyuan artists' communities, which is considered a landmark in contemporary Chinese art history; and *Petition: The Court of the Complainants* (2009) about the people who come to Beijing to submit their complaints and hope to find justice. He has also directed at least one non-Beijing documentary, *Crime and Punishment* (2007).

23 Kees Bakker, *Joris Ivens and the Documentary Context* (Amsterdam: Amsterdam University Press, 1999), 225.

24 In Vertov's own words, the camera does not just observe, but actively exposes meanings: "Our basic, programmatic objective is to aid each oppressed individual and the proletariat as a whole in their effort to understand the phenomena around them ... This objective of ours we call kino-eye. *The decoding of life as it is*" (emphasis added). Dziga Vertov, *Kino-eye: The Writings of Dziga Vertov* (Berkeley: University of California Press, 1984), 49.

25   For a discursive analysis of documentary's formal features and production contexts, see Keith Beattie, *Documentary Screens: Non Fiction Film and Television* (New York: Palgrave McMillan, 2004).

26   On earlier cinema configurations of the city, see Yingjin Zhang, *The City in Modern Chinese Literature and Film: Configurations of Space, Time, and Gender* (Stanford, CA: Stanford University Press, 1996); Andrew Field, "Selling Souls in Sin City: Shanghai Singing and Dancing Hostesses in Print, Film, and Politics, 1920–1949," in Yingjin Zhang, ed. *Cinema and Urban Culture in Shanghai, 1922–1994* (Stanford, CA: Stanford University Press, 1999), 99–127; and Yomi Braester, "A Big Dying Vat: The Vilifying of Shanghai during the Good Eighth Company Campaign," *Modern China*, 31, no. 4 (2005): 411–47. For an analysis of urban culture in contemporary Chinese cinema, see Zhang Zhen, ed., *The Urban Generation: Chinese Cinema and Society at the Turn of the Twenty-First Century* (Durham, NC: Duke University Press, 2005); Harry H. Kuoshu, "Beyond the Yellow Earth: The Postsocialist City as a Cinematic Space of Anxiety," *American Journal of Chinese Studies*, 4, no. 1 (1997): 50–72; and Harry H. Kuoshu, "Filming Marginal Youth: The 'Beyond' Syndrome in the Postsocialist City," in *Lightness of Being in China: Adaptation and Discursive Figuration in Cinema and Theater* (New York: Peter Lang, 1999), 123–52. On the particular trope of Taipei, see Yomi Braester, "Tales of a Porous City: Public Residences and Private Streets in Taipei Films," in Charles Laughlin, ed., *Contested Modernity in Chinese Literature* (New York: Palgrave Macmillan, 2005), 157–70; Lee Ching-Chih, "The Construct and Transformation of Taipei's City Image," in Chen Ruxiu, ed., *Xunzhao dianying zhong de Taibei* (Focus on Taipei through Cinema) (Taipei: Wanxiang, 1995), 27–33; and Mark Abe Nornes and Yueh-yu Yeh, "Taiwanese Cinema: A *City of Sadness* Webproject," http://cinemaspace.berkeley.edu/Papers/CityOfSadness/table.html (accessed August 14, 2008). As for Hong Kong's cinematic space, the main reference remains Ackbar Abbas's *Hong Kong: Culture and the Politics of Disappearance* (Minneapolis: University of Minnesota Press, 1997). See also Lisa Odham Stokes and Michael Hoover, *City on Fire: Hong Kong Cinema* (London and New York: Verso, 1999).

27   Chris Berry has introduced the notion of post-socialism to better describe postmodernity in the Chinese context in "Facing Reality: Chinese Documentary, Chinese Postsocialism," in Wu Hung, Wang Huangsheng, and Feng Boyi, eds., *Reinterpretation: A Decade of Experimental Chinese Art: 1990–2000* (Guangzhou: Guangdong Museum of Art, 2002), 121–31.

28   Ackbar Abbas, *Hong Kong*, 15.

29   Bérénice Reynaud, "New Visions/New Chinas: Video-Art, Documentation, and the Chinese Modernity in Question," in Michael Renov and Erika Suderburg, eds., *Resolutions: Contemporary Video Practices* (Minneapolis: University of Minnesota Press, 1996), 235. Chris Berry's translation, "on-the spot-realism," effectively captures the close link to a very specific temporality that characterizes most of the works that are generally referred to as part of the New Documentary Movement of the 1990s.

30   In 1993, the first Visible Evidence conference took place at Duke University and has been held regularly in different locations both in the Americas and Europe. Over the years, the Visible Evidence conferences and the associated series of books (published by University

of Minnesota Press) have developed an ongoing debate on the role of film, video, and other media as witness and voice of social reality.

31 Jane Gaines and Michael Renov, *Collecting Visible Evidence, Visible Evidence; V. 6* (Minneapolis: University of Minnesota Press, 1999), 323. Renov has further expanded the whole question of subjectivity in documentary film- and videomaking by focusing on autobiographical variations in film and video and tracing the developments of the representation of the self in a broad variety of documentary modes, from war-time reportage, to essay films, ethnographic documentary, and web sites in *The Subject of Documentary* (Minneapolis: University of Minnesota Press, 2004).

32 In *A Man with a Movie Camera* (Dziga Vertov, 1929), the witness is exposed through the reactions of the people to his recording or, even more directly, when a second camera shows the cameraman filming Moscow and its people.

33 On subjectivity in relation to visual authenticity in new Chinese documentaries, see Paola Voci, "From the Center to the Periphery," 102–3.

Chapter 7

1 See, for example, Paul G. Pickowicz and Yingjin Zhang, eds., *From Underground to Independent: Alternative Film Culture in Contemporary China* (Lanham: Rowman & Littlefield Publishers, Inc., 2006). See also Zhang Zhen, ed., *The Urban Generation: Chinese Cinema and Society at the Turn of the Twenty-First Century* (Durham, NC: Duke University Press, 2007).

2 See, for example, Chris Berry, "Independently Chinese: Duan Jinchuan, Jiang Yue, and Chinese Documentary," in Pickowicz and Zhang, eds., *From Underground to Independent*, 109–22.

3 Neglect of the issue of documentary audiences and consumption is not limited to the study of Chinese films. In the General Introduction of the 1988 edition of his *New Challenges for Documentary* (Berkeley: University of California Press, 1988), 5, Alan Rosenthal notes this problem. In the second edition published seventeen years later in 2005, the editors still note the problem. See Alan Rosenthal and John Corner, eds., *New Challenges for Documentary* (Second Edition) (Manchester: Manchester University Press, 2005), 2–3.

4 In addition, I conducted follow-up observation and interviews in the summer of 2005. Since my data comes from Beijing alone, I do not claim this study to be strictly representative of all urban China. However, given the fact that the largest number of film clubs exists in Beijing, this study presents one of the most important cases of the phenomena of documentary audiences and consumption.

5 Hence, my goal in this chapter is not to criticize Habermas's general category of public sphere as it is used by him to historically describe the emergence and disintegration of public sphere in western Europe. My empirical evidence from Chinese society neither contradicts nor confirms Habermas's notion of public sphere in this sense. What I attempt to do in this chapter is to take his notion of public sphere as an "ideal type" (Max Weber), an abstracted category we can compare with reality to highlight the different aspects of actually existing social phenomena. For the concept of the ideal type, see Max Weber, *The Methodology of the Social Sciences*, translated by Edward A. Shils and Henry Finch (Glencoe: The Free Press, 1949), 89–105.

6   Jürgen Habermas, *The Structural Transformation of the Public Sphere: An Inquiry into a Category of Bourgeois Society*, translated by Thomas Burger with the assistance of Frederick Lawrence (Cambridge: MIT Press, 1989), 36.

7   Ibid.

8   Ibid.

9   Ibid., 37.

10   Jürgen Habermas, *The Theory of Communicative Action vol. 1: Reason and the Rationalization of Society*, translated by Thomas McCarthy (Cambridge: Polity Press, 1984); *The Theory of Communicative Action vol. 2: Lifeworld and System: A Critique of Functionalist Reason*, translated by Thomas McCarthy (Cambridge: Polity Press, 1987).

11   To protect privacy and ensure the anonymity of the people whom I communicated with, all the names of the film clubs in this chapter are pseudonyms.

12   Seio Nakajima, "Film Clubs in Beijing: The Cultural Consumption of Chinese Independent Films," in Pickowicz and Zhang, eds., *From Underground to Independent*, 161–208.

13   Author's interview, June 15, 2005.

14   Author's interview, June 18, 2005.

15   Author's interview, February 18, 2005.

16   Along the lines of Pierre Bourdieu's concept of the field of cultural production. See Pierre Bourdieu, *The Field of Cultural Production: Essays on Art and Literature*, edited by Randall Johnson (New York: Columbia University Press, 1993).

17   The precise reasons for the case selection are as follows. Compared to other film clubs, which emphasize one primary orientation, whether political, economic, or artistic, Studio Z's focus on multiple logics potentially attracts the most diverse range of people to the film club. This has affinity to the first and the third of Habermas's institutional criteria for the existence of the public sphere, i.e., disregard of status and inclusiveness. Moreover, both in terms of the types of film shown and the discussions of them, Studio Z is the most diverse. Although it is not as "politically-oriented" as some, this diversity resulted in showing many documentary films that potentially problematize the status quo by depicting the slices of social reality that the government might not openly acknowledge, or acknowledge only in certain ways, for example unemployment, minority nationalities, and environmental problems. Thus, Studio Z has affinity to the second institutional criterion, that is, the problematization of the status quo. In terms of the fourth criterion, that is, "existence outside the spheres of the state and the economy," Studio Z is not necessarily the most ideal case as it is at least partly based on "commercial" logic. In terms of the fifth criterion of "consensus through debate," Studio Z has potential affinity. The already mentioned diversity of opinions expressed suggests I should observe this process — starting from differences of opinions but converging on consensus — most clearly in this film club. Overall, then, Studio Z is the "most likely" case for the existence of the public sphere in the Habermasian ideal-typical sense among the film clubs in Beijing. For the notion of the "most likely" case, see Alexander L. George and Andrew Bennett, *Case Studies and Theory Development in the Social Sciences* (Cambridge: MIT Press, 2004), 120–3. See table for more clarification.

Potential Fit between Four Types of Film Clubs and Habermas's Five Institutional Criteria

	Disregard of Status	Problematization of the Status Quo	Inclusiveness	Existence outside the State and Economy	Consensus through Debate
Politically Oriented Film Club	×	☐	×	☐	×
Commercially Oriented Film Club	×	×	×	×	×
Art for Art's Sake Film Club	×	×	×	☐	×
Artistic, Commercial (= the most likely case = Studio Z)	☐	☐ / ×	☐	☐ / ×	☐

Notes: The top row is Habermas's five criteria of the public sphere. The far-left column is different types of film clubs. ☐ signifies that the club fits the criterion. × signifies it does not. ☐ / × means it partially fits the criterion.

18   To avoid trouble with the state authorities, film clubs often use the terms "film exhibitions" and "film exchange weeks" rather than "film festivals" to emphasize their "non-political" nature. According to a person who has organized a series of film events in Beijing, "The word 'festival' is only allowed for a government-sponsored event, like the Shanghai International Film Festival or the Changchun Film Festival. When we organize a de facto festival, we use the term 'film exhibition' to avoid political trouble." (Author's interview, June 18, 2005.)

19   The film exchange week was to be run for seven days, but was canceled on the third day due to a combination of political pressure and self-censorship. For the details of how it was canceled, see the section, "Productive Power, Appropriation, and Resistance from Within."

20   For a concise introduction to key issues facing documentary film studies, see Paul Ward, *Documentary: The Margins of Reality* (London and New York: Wallflower Press, 2005).

21 The speaker here is referring to an academic symposium on documentary film held at the Beijing Broadcasting Institute (renamed as Communication University of China in August 2004) in the winter of 1991. According to an article published by Lin Xudong, the symposium "marked the first time in mainland China that so many of these new documentaries were brought together in one place." See "Documentary in Mainland China," *Documentary Box*, no. 26 (2005), http://www.yidff.jp/docbox/26/box26-3-e. html (accessed December 6, 2007). According to the article, the films screened included: *Bumming in Beijing: The Last Dreamers* (Wu Wenguang, 1990), *The Great Wall* (CCTV-TBS [Tokyo Broadcasting System, Inc.] co-production, 1991), *Sand and Sea* (Kang Jianning and Gao Guodong, 1991), *A Family in Northern Tibet* (Wang Haibin and Han Hui, 1991), and *Tiananmen* (Shi Jian and Chen Jue, 1991).

22 Amy Taubin, "Oscar's Docudrama," *The Village Voice*, March 31, 1992, 62.

23 This person only mentioned the subtitle of the article in his actual speech. The full citation is: Linda Williams, "Mirrors without Memories: Truth, History, and the New Documentary," *Film Quarterly*, 46, no. 3 (1993): 9–21.

24 Lu Xinyu, "Dangdai Zhongguo dianshi jilupian yundong" (Contemporary Chinese TV documentary movement), *Dushu*, no. 5 (1999). The article was reprinted in Lu Xinyu, *Jilu Zhongguo: Dangdai Zhongguo xin jilu yundong* (Documenting China: The New Documentary Movement in China) (Beijing: Sanlian Shudian, 2003).

25 Author's interview, June 24, 2004.

26 Author's interview, May 26, 2004.

27 The State Administration of Radio, Film, and Television (SARFT) announced the "Notice on Strengthening the Management of Broadcast of Digital Video Films in Film-TV Broadcasting Organizations and on Information Networks Such as the Internet" (*Guanyu jiaqiang yingshi bofang jigou he hulianwang deng xinxi wangluo bofang DV pian guanli tongzhi*) on May 24, 2004. In terms of the three-level hierarchy of laws and regulations that pertain to the administration of radio, film, and TV industries, this "notice" (*tongzhi*) is in the category of the "prescriptive documents" (*guifanxing wenjian*), which is the least effective after the most important "administrative laws and regulations" (*xingzheng fagui*) and the second most important "ministry regulations and rules" (*bumen guizhang*). However, it did include clauses that directly target the management of broadcasting and the production of independently produced documentary films, and hence was a topic of heated discussion among the participants in the film clubs. The full notice can be accessed at http://news. xinhuanet.com/newmedia/2004-06/04/content_1507415.htm (accessed November 11, 2007).

28 The ticket price was 20 yuan (about US$3) per day, which allowed one to watch around ten documentary films on the day of ticket purchase.

29 Maybe it is not surprising that the one-time discussion in the symposium, which lasted only for about three hours, did not reach any consensus. However, given that Habermas sees this kind of public discussion as the birthplace of the public sphere, I contend that this observation of the actual discussions that took place in bounded time and space gives us a clue for understanding the nature of film clubs in urban China. In order to expand the time and space of observation, I supplemented my study by conducting interviews and participated in activities outside of the symposium and the film exhibition week. However,

fully comparative (i.e., multiple film clubs in multiple cities) and historical (i.e., time frame longer than my fieldwork of a year and a half) examination is beyond the scope of this chapter.

30 Stuart Hall, "The West and the Rest: Discourse and Power," in Stuart Hall, David Held, Don Hubert, and Kenneth Thompson, *Modernity: An Introduction to Modern Societies* (Cambridge: Polity Press, 1995), 201.

31 Michel Foucault and Gilles Deleuze, "Intellectuals and Power: A Conversation between Michel Foucault and Gilles Deleuze," in Donald F. Bouchard, ed., *Michel Foucault: Language, Counter-Memory, Practice: Selected Essays and Interviews* (Ithaca: Cornell University Press, 1977), 209.

32 Author's interview, July 30, 2004.

33 My argument here draws on Chris Berry's utilization of the Foucauldian approach to "power as productive" to the case of the production of independent Chinese documentary films. I extend his observation to the case of consumption of films in urban Chinese film clubs. See Berry, "Independently Chinese," in Pickowicz and Zhang, eds., *From Underground to Independent*, 111.

34 See Foucault's definition of power in Michel Foucault, *The History of Sexuality vol. 1: An Introduction*, translated by Robert Hurley (New York: Vintage Books, 1978), 95.

35 Here I am using the term "appropriation" in the way suggested by cultural historian Roger Chartier when he analyzes the social practice of book reading in *Ancien Régime* France. Appropriation can be defined as a process of social practice in which a social actor, though conditioned by social structural limits, actively reads and uses texts and discourses in his or her own way. According to Chartier:

> In my own perspective, appropriation involves a social history of the various uses (which are not necessarily interpretations) of discourses and models, brought back to their fundamental social and institutional determinants and lodged in the specific practices that produce them. To concentrate on the concrete conditions and processes that construct meaning is to recognize, unlike traditional intellectual history, that minds are not disincarnated, and unlike hermeneutics, that the categories which engender experiences and interpretations are historical, discontinuous, and differentiated. (Roger Chartier, "Popular Appropriation: The Reader and Their Books," in *Forms and Meanings: Texts, Performances, and Audiences from Codex to Computer* [Philadelphia: University of Pennsylvania Press, 1995], 89.)

36 Foucault, *The History of Sexuality vol. 1*, 95.

37 Habermas, *The Structural Transformation of the Public Sphere*, 36. Here, by pointing out a possible parallel between Habermas and Foucault on the importance of critique of the status quo, I am not suggesting a simplistic reconciliation of their very different conceptualizations of the critique. For a perceptive treatment of this issue, see David Couzens Hoy, "Conflicting Conceptions of Critique: Foucault versus Habermas," in David Couzens Hoy and Thomas McCarthy, eds., *Critical Theory* (Cambridge: Blackwell Publishers, 1994), 144–71. However, in agreement with Hoy, I contend that the critique or the problematization of the status quo is an important point of contact between Habermas's and Foucault's otherwise highly divergent theories.

Chapter 8

1   Suisheng Zhao, "Deng Xiaoping's Southern Tour: Elite Politics in Post-Tiananmen China," *Asian Survey*, 33, no. 8 (1993): 739–56.

2   He Baogang details the debates of the 1990s in *The Democratic Implications of Civil Society in China* (New York: St. Martin's Press, 1997). See also Chris Berry, "New Documentary in China: *Public Space*, Public Television," in Chris Berry, Soyoung Kim, and Lynn Spigel, eds., *Electronic Elsewheres: Media, Technology, and the Experience of Social Space* (Minneapolis: University of Minnesota Press, 2010), 95–116.

3   See Wendy Brown, "Neo-Liberalism and the End of Liberal Democracy," *Theory and Event*, 7, no. 1 (2003): 1–25; and Nikolas Rose, *Powers of Freedom: Reframing Political Thought* (Cambridge: Cambridge University Press, 1999). They add to this classic insight that the state itself has been marketized.

4   Nancy Fraser, "Rethinking the Public Sphere: A Contribution to the Critique of Actually Existing Democracy," in Craig Calhoun, ed., *Habermas and the Public Sphere* (Cambridge: MIT Press, 1992), 109–42. Fraser's main focus is on gender. David Morley writes about "the whiteness of the public sphere" in *Home Territories: Media, Mobility and Identity* (London: Routledge, 2000), 118–24.

5   For the Chinese film world, see Paul G. Pickowicz and Yingjin Zhang, eds., *From Underground to Independent: Alternative Film Culture in Contemporary China* (Lanham, MD: Rowman and Littlefield, 2006), especially Pickowicz's discussion of the meaning of the term in the Chinese context in his essay, 2–3.

6   http://www.alternativearchive.com/ (accessed August 13, 2008).

7   Interview with Chris Berry and Laikwan Pang, Beijing, July 9, 2008. This work was partially supported by a grant from the Research Grants Council of the Hong Kong Special Administrative Region, China (Project no. CUHK4552/06H). Thank you to Laikwan Pang for allowing us to quote from it here.

8   Its recent origin is the first thing noted in the entry for the term at the online encyclopedia belonging to the Chinese equivalent of Google, Baidu: http://baike.baidu.com/view/27684.htm (accessed July 29, 2008).

9   Interview with Chris Berry and Laikwan Pang.

10   The *hukou* system was first established in cities in 1951 and in the rural areas in 1955. See Kam Wing Chan and Li Zhang, "The *Hu-kou* System and Rural-Urban Migration in China: Processes and Changes," *The China Quarterly*, no. 160 (1999): 818–55.

11   In recent years the regulations concerning migrants have relaxed somewhat — now migrants who have lived in the cities for a certain period of years can get legal residency, though the route is not easy.

12   Li Zhang, "Migration and Privatization of Space and Power in Late Socialist China," *American Ethnologist*, 28, no. 1 (2001): 179–205.

13   See Chris Berry, "New Documentary in China: *Public Space*, Public Television," and "Shanghai Television's Documentary Channel: Chinese Television as Public Space," in Chris Berry and Ying Zhu, eds., *TV China* (Bloomington: Indiana University Press, 2009), 71–89.

14   Bill Nichols, "Frederick Wiseman's Documentaries: Theory and Structure," *in Ideology*

and the Image: Social Representation in the Cinema and Other Media (Bloomington: Indiana University Press, 1981), 208–36.

15   For further discussion of *Sanyuanli*, see Chris Berry, "Imaging the Globalized City: Rem Koolhaas, U-thèque, and the Pearl River Delta," in Yomi Braester and James Tweedie, eds., *Cinema at the City's Edge* (Hong Kong: Hong Kong University Press, July 2010).

16   Frances Hoar Foster, "Codification in Post-Mao China," *American Journal of Comparative Law*, 30, no. 3 (1982): 405–7.

17   Yiman Wang, "The Amateur's Lightning Rod: DV Documentary in Postsocialist China," *Film Quarterly*, 58, no. 4 (2005): 16–26.

18   For further discussion of *I Graduated!*, see Bérénice Reynaud, "Dancing with Myself, Drifting with My Camera: The Emotional Vagabonds of China's New Documentary," *Senses of Cinema*, no. 28 (2003), http://archive.sensesofcinema.com/contents/03/28/chinas_new_documentary.html (accessed August 15, 2008).

19   The watershed event was the anti–Bai Hua campaign. See Merle Goldman, "The Campaign against Bai Hua and Other Writers," in *Sewing the Seeds of Democracy in China: Political Reform in the Deng Xiaoping Era* (Cambridge, MA: Harvard University Press, 1994), 88–112.

20   At the time of writing, the film was available online at http://voyage.typepad.com/china/2007/04/the_first_casua.html (accessed August 5, 2008).

21   Conversation, Hong Kong, March 26, 2007.

22   "The First Casualty of the Cultural Revolution," uploaded April 7, 2007, http://voyage.typepad.com/china/2007/04/the_first_casua.html, (accessed August 9, 2008).

23   Shen Rui, "To Remember History: Hu Jie Talks about His Documentaries," *Senses of Cinema*, no. 35 (2005), http://archive.sensesofcinema.com/contents/05/35/hu_jie_documentaries.html (accessed January 4, 2008).

Chapter 9

1   Pascal Bonitzer, *Le Regard et la Voix* (Paris: UGE, 1976), 44, translation mine.

2   About the relationship between Wu and Ogawa, see Abé Mark Nornes, *Forest of Pressure — Ogawa Shinsuke and Postwar Japanese Documentary* (Minneapolis: University of Minnesota Press, 2007), 227.

3   Ernest Larsen, "Video Vérité from Beijing," *Art in America*, 86, no. 9 (1998): 55.

4   Michel Chion, *Audio-Vision* (New York: Columbia Press, 1994), 28.

5   Ibid., 25.

6   Matthew David Johnson, "'A Scene beyond Our Line of Sight': Wu Wenguang and New Documentary Cinema's Politics of Independence," in Paul G. Pickowicz and Yingjin Zhang, eds., *From Underground to Independent — Alternative Film Culture in Contemporary China* (Lanham, MD: Rowman & Littlefield, 2006), 56.

7   See *The 16th Hong Kong International Film Festival* (Hong Kong: Urban Council, 1992), 98.

8   See Bérénice Reynaud, "Crying Chinese Women: New Chinese Video and the Post-Tiananmen Square Generation," published in German as "Crying Chinese Women. Der Chinesische Dokumentarfilm und die Generation nach Tiananmen," *Meteor*, no. 7 (Vienna, 1997): 50–8.

9 The Chinese government has relaxed its policy about the illegality of independent work, with the adoption of new regulations at the end of 2001 — and the DVD revolution makes all sorts of work, legal or illegal, available to all.

10 The subtitles that accompany the song in the seventy-minute version read as follows:

> I step on the ground with my head against the sun.
>
> I pretend I am alone in this world.
>
> I close my eyes tightly with my body against the wall.
>
> I pretend that there is not a head on these shoulders ... La la la...
>
> I don't want to leave. I don't want to exist.
>
> I don't want to live too realistically.
>
> I want to leave. I want to exist.
>
> I want to die and then start from the beginning.

11 Michel Chion, *The Voice in Cinema*, translated by Claudia Gorbman (New York: Columbia University Press, 1999), 17–29. Chion states that "the radio is acousmatic by nature. People speaking on the radio are *acousmêtres* in that there is no possibility of seeing them" (21). This commentary applies to the human voice recorded on tape or disk as well. However, it is not, for Chion, a "*complete acousmêtre*, the one who is not-yet-seen, but who remains liable to appear in the visual field at any moment" (ibid.).

12 Pascal Bonitzer, *Le Regard et la Voix*, 42–4, translation mine.

13 The "movement" remains off screen. Wu later confessed that he was "too busy" at the time to even think of shooting what was happening around him.

14 Julia Kristeva, *Revolution in Poetic Language*, translated by Margaret Waller (New York: Columbia University Press, 1984), 97.

15 Translation: Marie Chao.

16 Lu Xun, "Mending Heaven," in *Old Tales Retold* (Beijing: Foreign Language Press, 1961), 13.

17 Julia Kristeva, "The Semiotic Chora Ordering the Drives," in *Revolution in Poetic. Language* (New York: Columbia University Press, 1984), 25–30.

18 Laura Mulvey, "Visual Pleasure and Narrative Cinema," in Constance Penley, ed., *Feminism and Film Theory* (New York: Routledge, 1988), 62.

19 Matthew David Johnson, "'A Scene beyond Our Line of Sight'," 51

20 Ibid.

21 Presentation of *Bumming in Beijing*, University of Michigan, Ann Arbor, December 3, 2007.

22 "Lettre à Paul Demeny du 15 mai 1871," in Arthur Rimbaud, *Œuvres Complètes. Correspondance*, ed. Louis Forestier (Paris: Robert Laffont, 1992), 231–8.

23 For a description of the play, and related bibliographical material, see Shiao-ling Yu, "Chinese Drama in the Post-Mao Period," http://oregonstate.edu/dept/foreign_lang/ chinese/yu/postmao.html (accessed October 2, 2008).

24 This performance marked the beginning of another phase of Wu Wenguang's artistic career. In 1994, he and Wen Hui founded The Living Dance Studio (*wudao shenghuo*) and they have been performing multimedia pieces together since.

25 In *West of the Tracks* (*Tiexi Qu*, 2002), Wang Bing, also armed with a small DV camera, uses a similar strategy.

26 This alludes to the title of yet another of Chion's books, *La Toile Trouée* (*The Pierced Screen*) (Paris: Cahiers du Cinéma, 1988).

27 Wu Wenguang, Center for Chinese Studies, University of Michigan, Ann Arbor, December 2, 2007.

28 Wu shot 85 percent of *Fuck Cinema* himself, but asked his two assistants to shoot the audition scene. However, he designed the shots, and is responsible for the *mise-en-scène* of this sequence. Private communication, December 2007

29 Jacques Lacan, *The Four Fundamental Concepts of Psycho-Analysis* (New York: Norton, 1974), 127, translated by Alan Sheridan from *Le Séminaire XI — Les quatre concepts de la psychanalyse* (Paris: Seuil, 1973).

30 Ibid.

31 Wu Wenguang, Q & A after the presentation of *Fuck Cinema* at the California Institute of the Arts, January 30, 2007.

Chapter 10

1 Examples might include Wang Fen's *Unhappiness Does Not Stop at One* (2001), about her parents' relationship; Yang Lina's *Home Video* (2001), also about her family; Zuo Yixiao's *Losing* (2005), which is focused on his divorce; or Wu Wenguang's *Fuck Cinema* (2005), which follows one man in his quest to get his film script produced in Beijing. Hu Xinyu's *The Man* (2005) is shot almost entirely in the director's single-bedroom flat in Taiyuan, rarely straying outside the room, whilst Hu Shu's *Leave Me Alone* (2001) features a scene in which a bar girl stubs out cigarettes on her arms.

2 Lu Xinyu, personal interview, Shanghai, June 8, 2005.

3 "Reform and opening," the term used to describe the policies of gradual liberalization pursued by Deng Xiaoping from the late 1970s through the 1980s.

4 Zhang Xianmin, personal interview, Beijing, June 21, 2005; Lu Xinyu, roundtable discussion, Yunnan Multi Culture Visual Festival, Kunming, March 23, 2005.

5 Zhu Jingjiang and Mei Bing, *Zhongguo duli jilupian dang'an* (A Dossier on Chinese Independent Documentary) (Xi'an: Sha'anxi shifan daxue chubanshe, 2004), 11–2; Du Haibin, "Ganxie daoban, ganxie DV" (Thank you, pirate copies, thank you, digital video), *Jinri xianfeng* (Avant-Garde Today), no. 12 (2002): 2–3. For Wu Wenguang's views on DV, see, for example, his chapter in this volume.

6 Zhang Yingjin, "Styles, Subjects, and Special Points of View: A Study of Contemporary Chinese Independent Documentary," *New Cinemas: Journal of Contemporary Film*, 2, no. 2 (2004): 130–2.

7 For a cogent overview of these developments, see Harriet Evans, *Women and Sexuality in China: Dominant Discourses of Female Sexuality since 1949* (Cambridge: Polity Press, 1997), 1–32.

8 See, for example, Jing Wang, "Culture as Leisure and Culture as Capital," *positions: east asia cultures critique*, 9, no. 1 (2001): 69–104; Dai Jinhua, "Dazhong wenhua de yinxing zhengzhixue" (Studying the invisible politics of mass culture), *Tianya*, 2 (1999): 32–41.

9 Matthew David Johnson, "'A Scene beyond Our Line of Sight': Wu Wenguang and New Documentary Cinema's Politics of Independence," in Paul G. Pickowicz and Zhang Yingjin, eds., *From Underground to Independent: Alternative Film Culture in Contemporary China* (Lanham, MD: Rowman and Littlefield, 2006), 65.

10 For example, both Chris Berry, "Facing Reality: Chinese Documentary, Chinese Postsocialism," in Wu Hung, Wang Huangsheng, and Feng Boyi, eds., *Reinterpretation: A Decade of Experimental Chinese Art* (Guangzhou: Guangdong Museum of Modern Art, 2002), 125, and Johnson, "A Scene beyond Our Line of Sight'," 53–4, have directly addressed the extent to which the early New Documentary Movement films are stylistically indebted to the influence of foreign film crews working with CCTV on jointly produced television documentaries in the 1980s. For a narrative of these developments, see Fang Fang, *Zhongguo jilupian fazhanshi* (A History of the Development of Chinese Documentary) (Beijing: Zhongguo xiju chubanshe, 2003), 311–26.

11 Paul Willemen, "The National," in *Looks and Frictions: Essays in Cultural Studies and Film Theory* (London: BFI, 1994), 217.

12 Zhang Xianmin, personal interview, Beijing, June 21, 2005.

13 Paul G. Pickowicz, "Social and Political Dynamics of Underground Filmmaking in China," in Pickowicz and Zhang, eds., *From Underground to Independent*, 19.

14 For more detailed discussion of *xianchang* and *jishi zhuyi* in context, see Zhang Zhen, "Building on the Ruins: The Exploration of New Urban Cinema of the 1990s," in Wu, Wang, and Feng, eds., *Reinterpretation*, 116; Berry, "Facing Reality," 124–9.

15 Wu Wenguang, "*Xianchang:* He jilupian fangshi youguan de shu" (Document: A book about the "documentary mode"), in Wu Wenguang, ed., *Xianchang*, no. 1 (Tianjin: Tianjin shehui kexueyuan chubanshe, 2000), 274.

16 Berry, "Facing Reality," 124. *Zhuantipian* is the term for the state-produced, made-for-television, pre-scripted illustrated lectures that constituted the dominant Chinese documentary format in the 1980s.

17 Quoted in Zhang Zhen, "Building on the Ruins," 117. Original quotation from Lin Xudong and Jia Zhangke, "Yige laizi Zhongguo jiceng de minjian daoyan" (A people's director, from China's grassroots), *Jintian* (Today), no. 3 (1999): 2–20.

18 Dai Vaughan, "Let There Be Lumière," in *For Documentary: Twelve Essays* (Berkeley and Los Angeles: University of California Press, 1999), 6.

19 Siegfried Kracauer, *Theory of Film: The Redemption of Physical Reality* (Princeton: Princeton University Press, 1997 [1960]), 69.

20 Lu Xinyu, *Jilu Zhongguo: Dangdai Zhongguo xin jilu yundong* (Documenting China: The New Documentary Movement in China) (Beijing: Sanlian, 2003), 152.

21 Wu Wenguang, personal interview, Beijing, May 28, 2005; Wu Wenguang, "Paishe 'Da Peng'" (Shooting the Big Top), in Wu Wenguang, ed., *Jingtou xiang ziji de yanjing yiyang* (The Camera Lens Is Like One's Eye: Documentaries and People) (Shanghai: Shanghai Yishu chubanshe, 2001 [2000]), 236.

22 Zhang Zhen, "Building on the Ruins," 116.

23 Wang Weici, *Jilu yu tansuo: Yu dalu jilupian gongzuozhe de shiji duihua* (Documenting and Exploring: Conversations with Mainland Chinese Documentary-Makers) (Taipei: Yuanliu, 2000), 132.

24 Bill Nichols, *Ideology and the Image: Social Representation in the Cinema and Other Media* (Bloomington: University of Indiana Press, 1981), 233–4.

25 Ibid., 211–2.

26 See, for example, Berry, "Facing Reality," 125–6; Paola Voci, "From the Centre to the Periphery: Chinese Documentary's Visual Conjectures," *Modern Chinese Literature and Culture*, 16, no. 1 (2004), 99–100; Zhang Yingjin, "Styles, Subjects," 125.

27 Lu Xinyu, personal interview. This is supported by Duan's own comments on the subject — see, for example, Zhu and Mei, *Jilupian dang'an*, 130–1 — which also reflects academic commentary on the relationship Wiseman appears to encourage between the viewer and the screen through use of this form (see for example Thomas Benson and Carolyn Anderson, *Reality Fictions: The Films of Frederick Wiseman* [Carbondale: Southern Illinois University Press, 2002], 136).

28 Nichols, *Ideology and the Image*, 209.

29 Ibid., 216–7.

30 Mao's Tiananmen portrait recurs as the dominant focus of at least six shots over the course of the film, and appears in the background of many more. In addition, the film includes footage of the police chief discussing his time as a Maoist Red Guard with the CCTV crew outside in the square.

31 Wang Weici, *Jilu yu tansuo*, 108; Lu Xinyu, *Jilu Zhongguo*, 14–5.

32 Lu Xinyu, *Jilu Zhongguo*, 12–3.

33 Duan Jinchuan, personal interview, Beijing, August 14, 2005.

34 Cui Zhen, "*Jilupian* Nanren: *Hu Xinyu fangtan*" (The documentary *The Man*: An interview with Hu Xinyu), 22film, 2005, http://www.22film.com/ultracms/content/857/1.htm (accessed August 10, 2005).

35 Yu Jian, "Jilupian biji zhi er" (Notes on documentary Part Two), *Yunnan Multi Culture Visual Festival Kuaibao* (Bulletin), no. 4 (2005): 6.

36 Lu Xinyu, "Ruins of the Future: Class and History in Wang Bing's *Tiexi District*," translated by J. X. Zhang, *New Left Review*, 31 (2005): 126. This is the short version of the full essay re-translated for this volume.

37 Lu Xinyu, "Ruins of the Future," 128.

38 Zhang Yaxuan, "Jilupian *Tiexiqu* daoyan fangtan" (An interview with the director of the documentary *West of the Tracks*), 22film, 2005, http://www.22film.com/ultracms/content/743/1.htm (accessed August 10, 2005).

39 Zhu and Mei, *Jilupian dang'an*, 75; Wu Wenguang, personal interview. This was in fact literally the case with *Fuck Cinema*. The subject of the documentary originally approached Wu to help him find a director or producer for a screenplay he had written. Wu agreed, but ended up shooting a documentary about the process himself.

40 Du Haibin and Hu Xinyu would be two examples, among others. See Wu Wenguang, "Du Haibin fangwen" (An interview with Du Haibin), in Wu Wenguang, ed., *Xianchang*, no. 2 (Tianjin: Tianjin shehui kexueyuan chubanshe, 2001), 213; Cui, "*Jilupian* Nanren."

41 Zhang Yaxuan, "Jilupian *Tiexiqu*."

42 Zhu and Mei, *Jilupian dang'an*, 329.

43 This may perhaps explain why the director and artist Ou Ning has compared the documentary filmmaker to the flâneur. See Ou Ning, "Lishi zhi zhai" (The debt of history), in *The Sanyuanli Project* (Shenzhen: U-thèque Organisation, 2003), 35. It may also explain why Wu Wenguang has argued that such a role is essential if the instinctual, as opposed to intellectual, aspects of the form are to be preserved (Lu Xinyu, *Jilu Zhongguo*, 19).

44 Zhang Yaxuan, "Jilupian *Tiexiqu*."

45 It is precisely such a shift that Gilles Deleuze has argued characterizes European cinema in the wake of World War II, when he suggests directors abandon metaphor and metonymy in favor of a cinema characterized by the linking of independent, unconnected images. See Gilles Deleuze, *Cinema 2: The Time-Image*, translated by H. Tomlinson and R. Galeta (London: The Athlone Press, 2000 [1985]), 214. It is also similar to the departure from the neo-realist "generic" that Ivone Margulies proposes is represented in the work of avant-garde filmmakers such as Andy Warhol and Chantal Akerman. See Ivone Margulies, *Nothing Happens: Chantal Akerman's Hyperrealist Everyday* (Durham, NC and London: Duke University Press, 1996), 40–1.

46 *Mao Zedong's Talks at the Yan'an Conference on Literature and Art: A Translation of the 1943 Text with Commentary*, edited and translated by Bonnie S. McDougall (Ann Arbor: University of Michigan, 1992 [1980]), 70. For discussion of the proleptic function of socialist realism, see Ann Anagnost, *National Past-Times: Narrative, Representation and Power in Modern China* (Durham, NC and London: Duke University Press, 1997), 17–44; Theodore Huters, "Ideologies of Realism in Modern China: The Hard Imperatives of Imported Theory," in Liu Kang and Tang Xiaobing, eds., *Politics, Ideology and Literary Discourse in Modern China* (Durham, NC and London: Duke University Press, 1993), 150–68.

47 Wang Ban, *The Sublime Figure of History: Aesthetics and Politics in Twentieth-Century China* (Stanford, CA: Stanford University Press, 1997), 211.

48 Ibid., 27.

49 Although not a significance necessarily unique to documentary. Xudong Zhang argues that it was precisely such a privileging of "monolithic, transparent political meaning" on the part of socialist realism that the feature filmmakers of the early 1980s attempted to subvert. See Zhang Xudong, *Chinese Modernism in the Era of Reforms: Cultural Fever, Avant-Garde Fiction and the New Chinese Cinema* (Durham, NC and London: Duke University Press, 1997), 241. In turn, those of the early 1990s rejected what they saw as the "grand panoramic film" of the previous decade, with its ambitions to a "Balzacian omniscience" in its subject matter. See Zhang Ming, *Zhaodao yi zhong dianying fangfa* (Searching for a Film Method) (Beijing: Zhongguo Guangbo Dianshi Chubanshe, 2003), 9.

Chapter 11

1 The phrase, taken from Lou Ye's *Suzhou River* (2000), is also the title of Cheng Qingsong and Huang Ou's book on young film directors: *Wode sheyingji bu sahuang* (My Camera Doesn't Lie) (Beijing: Zhongguo youyi chuban gongsi, 2002).

2 *Suzhou River*.

3 The reception of Wu Wenguang has followed this pattern and is discussed in detail in

Matthew David Johnson, "'A Scene beyond Our Line of Sight': Wu Wenguang and New Documentary Cinema's Politics of Independence," in Paul Pickowicz and Yingjin Zhang, eds., *From Underground to Independent: Alternative Film Culture in Contemporary China* (Lanham, MD: Rowman and Littlefield, 2006), 47–76.

4   Lu Xinyu, *Jilu Zhongguo: Dangdai Zhongguo xin jilu yundong* (Documenting China: The New Documentary Movement in China) (Beijing: Sanlian Shudian, 2003).

5   Valerie Jaffee, "'Every Man a Star': The Ambivalent Cult of Amateur Art in New Chinese Documentaries," in Pickowicz and Zhang, eds., *From Underground to Independent*, 77–108.

6   On the alleged "me-me-ism" (*wowo zhuyi*) of recent filmmakers, see Chen Mo and Zhiwei Xiao, "Chinese Underground Films: Critical Views from China," in Pickowicz and Zhang, eds., *From Underground to Independent*, 148.

7   Erik Barnouw, *Documentary: A History of the Non-Fiction Film* (New York: Oxford University Press, 1993), 254–5.

8   My thanks to Zhang Yuan, Yang Lina, and Ning Ying for providing film copies and allowing me and my students to interview them. I also thank Paola Voci, who shared with me her copies of *Tiananmen* and of *A Social Survey*.

9   Wu Wenguang, "Just on the Road: A Description of the Individual Way of Recording Images in the 1990s," in Wu Hung, Wang Huangsheng, and Feng Boyi, eds., *Reinterpretation: A Decade of Experimental Chinese Art (1990–2000)* (Guangzhou: Chuangdong Museum of Art: 2002), 132.

10   Ibid.

11   Li Xin, Liu Xiaoxi, and Wang Jifang, *Bei yiwang de yingxiang* (Forgotten Images) (Beijing: Zhongguo Shehui Kexue chubanshe, 2006), 78.

12   Zhang Yuan, talk at the University of Washington Summer Program at the Beijing Film Academy, July 2006.

13   Li, Liu, and Wang, *Bei yiwang de yingxiang*, 246–396.

14   Wu Hung, *Remaking Beijing: Tiananmen Square and the Creation of a Political Space* (Chicago: Chicago University Press, 2005), 165–7.

15   Chris Berry, "Facing Reality: Chinese Documentary, Chinese Postsocialism," in Wu, Wang, and Feng, eds., *Reinterpretation*, 132.

16   Li, Liu, and Wang, *Bei yiwang de yingxiang*, 210–4.

17   Zhang Yuan, talk at the University of Washington Summer Program at the Beijing Film Academy, July 2006.

18   Kaleem Aftab and Alexandra Weltz, interview with Frederick Wiseman. http://www.iol.ie/~galfilm/filmwest/40wiseman.htm (accessed August 28, 2006).

19   Chris Berry, "Facing Reality: Chinese Documentary, Chinese Postsocialism." See Lydia H. Liu, *Translingual Practice: Literature, National Culture, and Translated Modernity—China, 1900–1937* (Stanford, CA: Stanford University Press, 1995).

20   *Xianchang*, edited by Wu Wenguang (Tianjin: Shehui Kexueyuan chubanshe, 2000); *Xianchang 2*, edited by Wu Wenguang (Tianjin: Shehui Kexueyuan chubanshe, 2001); *Xianchang 3*, edited by Wu Wenguang (Guilin: Guangxi Shifan Daxue chubanshe, 2005). See especially Wu Wenguang, "*Xianchang*: He jilu fangshi yuguan de shu" (*Xianchang*: A book concerning methods of documentation), in *Xianchang*, 274–5.

21 Talk at the University of Washington Summer Program at the Beijing Film Academy, July 2006.

22 Li, Liu, and Wang, *Bei yiwang de yingxiang*, 81.

23 Chris Berry, "Independently Chinese: Duan Jinchuan, Jiang Yue, and Chinese Documentary," in Pickowicz and Zhang, eds., *From Underground to Independent*, 114.

24 Zhang Yuan returns to explore manipulative subjects in *Crazy English* (1999), which also documents the English lessons given by Li Yang. Li's unusual method of "Crazy English" encourages students to shout out loud to lose their inhibitions. The film shows the students, sometimes a stadium-full, as they repeat almost nonsensical English phrases that Li roars into his microphone.

25 Cao Kai, *Jilu yu shiyan: DV yingxiang qianshi* (Documentation and Experimentation: A Prehistory of the DV Movement) (Beijing: Zhongguo Renmin Daxue chubanshe, 2005), 108–10.

26 Cui Zi'en comments on the black shots that it is as if the speakers' faces were blown away by the wind and their voices remained recorded on an answering machine. See Cui Zi'en, *Diyi guanzhong* (The First Spectator) (Beijing: Xiandai chubanshe, 2003), 64.

27 See Wu Wenguang, *Jingtou xiang ziji de yanjing yiyang* (The Lens Is Like My Eyes) (Shanghai: Shanghai Yishu chubanshe, 2001).

28 On *Old Men*, see Wang Weizi, *Jilu yu tansuo: 1990–2000 dalu jilupian de fazhan yu koushu jilu* (Documentation and Experimentation: The Development and Oral Records of Mainland Documentary Film in 1990–2000) (Taipei: Guojia Dianying ziliaoguan, 2001), 165–80.

29 Yang Lina, personal correspondence, August 2006.

30 Ibid.

31 Zhang Zhen, "Bearing Witness: Chinese Urban Cinema in the Era of 'Transformation' (*Zhuanxing*)," in Zhang Zhen, ed., *The Urban Generation: Chinese Cinema and Society at the Turn of the Twenty-First Century* (Durham, NC: Duke University Press, 2007), 18.

32 All quotes and paraphrases of Ning Ying's words are based on a talk at the University of Washington Summer Program at the Beijing Film Academy, July 2006.

33 André Bazin, *Bazin at Work: Major Essays and Reviews from the Forties and Fifties*, edited by Bert Cardullo, translated by Alain Piette and Bert Cardullo (New York: Routledge, 1997), 194. Ning also sees the train theme as a tribute to Krzysztof Kieślowski, probably to *The Railway Station* (1980).

34 Valerie Jaffee, "'Every Man a Star'," 84–5, based on Lu Xinyu, *Jilu Zhongguo*, 3–34.

35 Li Daoxin, "Xin jilu dianying: Zouxiang Zhongguo 'zuozhe dianying'" (New Documentary cinema: Toward Chinese "auteur films"), *Dianying wenxue*, no. 2 (1998): 23–4.

Chapter 12

1 Wu Wenguang, "Ganggang zai lushang: Fasheng zai jiushi niandai de geren yingxiang jilu fangshi de miaosu" (On the road: A description of personal documentary making in the 1990s), May 3, 2003, http://www.chinadocu.com/cms/2005/12-2/211721.htm (accessed August 25, 2006).

2 Jiang Zhi, "DV shi yizhong xuyao" (DV is a need), *Yishu shijie* (The World of Art), May 22, 2005, http://www.22film.com/ultracms/content/744/1.htm (accessed August 25, 2006).

3 Yiman Wang, "The Amateur's Lightning Rod: DV Documentary in Postsocialist China," *Film Quarterly*, 58, no. 4 (2005): 16–26.

4 See Jun Fu, "Jia Zhangke: Wo duli biaoda wo suo kandao de shijie" (Jia Zhangke: I, as myself, express what I see), *Xin kuaibao*, 2003, http://ent.tom.com/1002/1011/20031111-59933.html (accessed July 10, 2004). Jia's notion of being "seared" by reality is reminiscent of Walter Benjamin's description of a photograph as being "seared" by its context. Both underscore the necessity of cruelty, that is, the *wounding* imprint of reality on representation. See Walter Benjamin, "A Small History of Photography," in his *One-way Street and Other Writings*, translated by Edmund Jephcott and Kinsley Shorter (London: NLB, 1979), 242, 243. For more detailed analysis of the parallel use of "searing," see Wang, "The Amateur's Lightning Rod," 22–3.

5 Lu Xinyu, *Jilu Zhongguo: Dangdai Zhongguo xin jilu yundong* (Documenting China: The New Documentary Movement in China) (Beijing: Sanlian Bookstore, 2003), 15.

6 Yingjin Zhang, "Fengge, zhuti yu shijiao: Dangdai Zhongguo duli jilupian yanjiu" (Style, theme, and viewpoint: A study on contemporary Chinese independent documentary), http://www.reelchina.net/articles2/02.htm (accessed April 14, 2006).

7 Zhang, "Fengge, zhuti yu shijiao."

8 Mei Bing and Zhu Jinjiang, *Zhongguo duli jilupian dang'an* (Profile of Chinese Independent Documentary) (Xi'an: Shanxi Normal University Press, 2004).

9 Lu Xinyu, "Xin jilu de li yu tong" (The strength and growing pains of New Documentary), *Dushu*, no. 5 (2006), http://www.xschina.org/show.php?id=6840 (accessed August 29, 2006).

10 Lu Xinyu, "Jintian, renwen jilu yiyu hewei?" (What can humanist documentary do today?), *Dushu*, no. 10 (2006), http://www.xschina.org/show.php?id=7716 (accessed August 29, 2006).

11 Sean Cubitt, *Videography: Video Media as Art and Culture* (New York: St. Martin's Press, 1993), 202, emphasis added.

12 Ibid., 203.

13 Ibid., emphasis added.

14 Ibid., 205.

15 Ibid., 204.

16 Mei and Zhu, "Shenghuo changju li de yige douhao — Wu Wenguang fangtan" (A comma in the long sentence of life — interview with Wu Wenguang), in Mei and Zhu, *Zhongguo duli jilupian dang'an*, 66, 68.

17 Lu, *Jilu Zhongguo*, 6.

18 Ibid., 5.

19 Mei and Zhu, *Zhongguo duli jilupian dang'an*, 91.

20 Ibid., 88.

21 Lu, *Jilu Zhongguo*, 8.

22 Wu's speech at a group meeting of the "DV Documentary Caucus," August 2000. Quoted in Mei and Zhu, *Zhongguo duli jilupian*, 11.

23 Importantly, his turn to DV was partially inspired by the amateur documentary maker,

Yang Tianyi's first DV documentary *Old Men* (1999). Wu was initially invited by Yang to help her with editing. However, he ended up learning from Yang's DV camera's "quiet presence" on the site. See Wu, "On the Road."

24 See Wang, "The Amateur's Lightning Rod." Wu's passion for DV is also expressed in his chapter, "DV: Individual Filmmaking," included in this volume. He observes that DV saves him from staid professionalism and intention-driven narrativization, allowing him to construct a personal relationship with documentary making, one that exceeds simple identity politics. He describes the personal quality in two details: holding the soup ladle in one hand, the DV camera in the other; doing the editing at home with no voice speaking over his shoulder.

25 Quoted in Mei and Zhu, *Zhongguo duli jilupian dang'an*, 12.

26 Ibid., 71.

27 Ibid., 95.

28 Ibid., 387.

29 Ibid., 394.

30 Ibid., 389, 395.

31 See Zheng, "The Tip of the Hostesses' Iceberg — On *Leave Me Alone* by Hu Shu," http://www.reelchina.net/articles/04.htm (accessed July 15, 2006); "Ba wo dang 'matong' — Hu Shu fangtan" (Treat me as a "toilet" — interview with Hu Shu), in Mei and Zhu, *Zhongguo duli jilupian dang'an*, 384–401.

32 Lu, *Jilu Zhongguo*, 262.

33 Lu, quoted in Mei and Zhu, *Zhongguo duli jilupian dang'an*, 46.

34 Ren Ping, "Yu yang chao yiqi tantao — jiaopian yu DV" (Film vs. DV — dialogue with Yang Chao), March 10, 2006, www.cool8.tv (accessed March 10, 2006).

35 Qiu Baolin, "Qingnian DV yingxiang: Wuji de qingchun biaoda yu qianfu de chuanbo weiji" (Youth DV image: Unconstrained youthful expression and latent communication crises), *Shanghai University Journal: Social Science*, no. 2 (2005), http://bbs.chinalabs.com/print.asp?id=25857 (accessed August 11, 2006).

36 For more details of the whole process, see the publicity materials of Caochangdi Workstation at http://www.ccdworkstation.com/english/The20Process20of20The20Ten20Filmmakers20intro.html (accessed June 25, 2006).

37 Zhou Wenhan, "DV jingtou duizhun cunmin zizhi jincheng: Wu Wenguang ren zong cehua, Zhongguo Cunmin Zizhi Yingxiang Chuanbo Jihua qidong" (DV aimed at the unfolding rural autonomy: Wu Wenguang as the general executive, launching the China Village Film Project), *Xin jingbao* (New Beijing Paper), September 7, 2005, http://www.ccdworkstation.com/cgi-bin/topic.cgi?forum=6&topic=5&changemode=1 (accessed June 25, 2006).

38 For extended Chinese and English descriptions of Shao's shooting process, see Dong Yueling's profile of Shao in *Zhongguo qingnian bao* (China Youth Paper), June 24, 2006, http://www.ccdworkstation.com/cgi-bin/topic.cgi?forum=6&topic=25 (accessed June 24, 2006) and Caochangdi Workshop publicity materials at http://www.ccdworkstation.com/english/The20Process20of20The20Ten20Filmmakers20intro.html (accessed June 25, 2006).

39 For a description of Jia's documentary, see Caochangdi Workstation publicity

materials at http://www.ccdworkstation.com/english/The20Process20of20The20Ten 20Filmmakers20intro.html (accessed June 25, 2006).

40 See http://www.ccdworkstation.com/cgi-bin/topic.cgi?forum=6&topic=24&show=0 (accessed June 25, 2006).

41 Indeed, the editing of the villagers' documentaries involved some conflicts in that Wu Wenguang and other Workstation editors seemed to take charge of the final shaping of the projects, which potentially contradicted some of the villager participants' intentions. I thank the editors for urging me to consider the implicit power disparity in the collaborative project.

42 See http://www.ccdworkstation.com/cgi-bin/topic.cgi?forum=6&topic=25.

43 Mei and Zhu, *Zhongguo duli jilupian*, 13.

44 Walter Benjamin, *Understanding Brecht*, translated by Anna Bostock (London: New Left Books, 1973), 98.

45 Cubitt, *Videography*, 52.

46 Yomi Braester's chapter, "Excuse Me, Your Camera Is in My Face," included in this volume, provides a very useful analysis of an important mode of Chinese New Documentary. He calls this mode "auteurial intervention," characterized by the documentary maker's emphasis on his/her presence, and more importantly, his/her intrusion into the situation and manipulation of the subjects' responses. Whereas Braester's article focuses on the encounter and violence between the documentary maker and the subjects, I consider how such a relationship of encounter and violence can potentially be transformed so that the subject comes to need the documentary and his/her technology in order to become an author of his/her own story. Consequently, a collaborative relationship, premised upon each participant's agency, becomes possible, albeit provisional and contingent.

47 Lu, *Jilu Zhongguo*, 262.

48 Ibid., 263.

49 Cubitt, *Videography*, 173.

50 Ibid., 138.

51 Ibid.

52 Ibid., 206.

53 Mei and Zhu, *Zhongguo duli jilupian dang'an*, 7.

54 For comments by Gan Chao, a director of Shanghai TV station, see "Liang Zi de jilu pian: *Fangdong Jiang Xianzheng*" (Liang Zi's documentary: *The Landlord Mr. Jiang*), *Dazhong DV* (Popular DV), July 25, 2005, http://www.22film.com/ultracms/content/1044/1.htm (accessed June 15, 2006).

55 For Liu Jingqi's comments, see ibid.

56 For comments by Shi Jian, the associate director of the column of Social Topics of CCTV (Central China TV Station), see "Liang Zi's Documentary." Shi Jian was among the four pioneering documentary makers who founded SWYC (Structure, Wave, Young, Cinema) and promoted the "New Documentary Movement" in June 1991.

57 Mei and Zhu, *Zhongguo duli jilupian dang'an*, 379.

58 Ibid., 380.

59   Ibid., 381.

60   David MacDougall, *Transcultural Cinema* (Princeton: Princeton University Press, 1998), 135. This argument concerns Jean Rouch and Edgar Morin's participatory documentary, *Chronique d'un été* (1961).

61   MacDougall, *Transcultural Cinema*, 136.

62   Transcription of Shantong Satellite Television Station's interview with Zhang Hua, March 3, 2005, http://bn.sina.com.cn/tv/2005-03-03/17004907.html (accessed June 25, 2006).

63   Chen Xiaobo, "DV gaibian le shui de mingyun?" (Whose fate has been changed by DV?), *Dazhong DV* (Popular DV), February 22, 2006, http://chenxiaobo.blshe.com/post/35/1516 (accessed June 20, 2006).

64   A number of male DV documentary makers, including Wu Wenguang and Zhu Chuanming, have seen their possession of the DV camera as the origin of their inevitable alienation from their subjects. Zhu's vacillation between being an alienated outsider and being "one of them," discussed in the previous part, testifies to the ambiguous position of the documentary maker. For Zhu's reflection on his alienation from his subjects, see Wang, "The Amateur's Lightning Rod: DV Documentary in Postsocialist China."

65   MacDougall, *Transcultural Cinema*, 207.

66   Ibid., 149.

67   Chen Dongtu, "Yong DV jujue shenghuo" (Savor life through DV), *He'nan Ribao* (He'nan Daily), January 5, 2007, http://epaper.dahe.cn/jrxf/t20070105_794475.htm (accessed February 25, 2007).

68   Ibid.

69   Shandong Satellite TV's Interview with Zhang Hua, http://bn.sina.com.cn/tv/2005-03-03/17004907.html (accessed June 25, 2006).

70   Symposium on *Sisters*, sponsored by *Dazhong DV* and Beijing Zero Channel, at http://www.sina.com.cn/tv/2005-07-02/05198413 (accessed August 26, 2006).

71   MacDougall, *Transcultural Cinema*, 207.

72   Lu, *Jilu Zhongguo*, 5.

73   Laura Marks, *The Skin of the Film: Intercultural Cinema, Embodiment, and the Senses* (Durham, NC: Duke University Press, 2000), 191.

74   Wu Wenguang, "*Ganggang zai lushang:* Fasheng zai jiushi niandai de geren yingxiang jilu fangshi de miaosu" (On the Road: A description of personal documentary making in the 1990s), May 3, 2003, http://www.chinadocu.com/cms/2005/12-2/211721.htm (accessed August 25, 2006).

List of Chinese Names

This list contains the roman letter version of Chinese names or the translations of music band names as they appear in chapters in the book, along with the original Chinese characters. It does not contain the names of authors whose works appear in the notes.

Ai Xiaoming	艾晓明	Hu Xinyu	胡新宇
The Bad Boys of Anarchism	无政府主义男孩	Huang Jing	黄静
		Huang Weikai	黄伟凯
Bi Jianfeng	毕鉴峰	Ji Dan	季丹
Cao Fei	曹斐	Ji Jianghong	吉江红
Chen Jue	陈爵	Jia Zhangke	贾樟柯
Chen Kaige	陈凯歌	Jia Zhitan	贾之坦
Chen Meng	陈虻	Jiang Yue	蒋樾
Chen Zhen	陈真	Jiang Zhi	蒋志
Cui Zi'en	崔子恩	Ju Anqi	雎安奇
Deng Xiaoping	邓小平	Kang Jianning	康健宁
Du Haibin	杜海滨	Kuang Dan	邝丹
Du Xiyun	杜锡云	Li Bai	李白
Du Yang	杜洋	Li Daoxin	李道新
Duan Jinchuan	段锦川	Li Hong	李红
Fu Hongxing	傅红星	Li Jinghong	李京红
Gan Chao	甘超	Li Xiao	李晓
Gao Bo	高搏	Li Yang	李扬
Gao Weijin	高维进	Li Yifan	李一凡
Gao Xing	高幸	Li Yinhe	李银河
Guo Gang	郭刚	Li Yu	李玉
Hao Zhiqiang	郝智强	Liang Zi	梁子
He Fengming	和凤鸣	Lin Xudong	林旭东
Hu Jie	胡杰	Lin Zexu	林则徐
Hu Jingcao	胡劲草	Liu Jingqi	刘景锜
Hu Shi	胡适	Liu Xiaojin	刘晓津
Hu Shu	胡庶		

Liu Yonghong	刘勇宏
Lu Wangping	卢望平
Lu Xinyu	吕新雨
Lu Xun	鲁迅
Mao Zedong	毛泽东
Meng Jinghui	孟京辉
Ming Ming	明明
Mou Sen	牟森
Ni Tracy	栀子白
Ning Ying	宁瀛
Ou Ning	欧宁
Sha Qing	沙青
Shao Yuzhen	邵玉珍
Shen Yue	沈岳
Shi Jian	时间
Shi Lihong	史立红
Shi Tou	石头
Shu Haolun	舒浩仑
Su Dongpo	苏东坡
Sun Zhigang	孙志刚
Tang Danhong	唐丹鸿
Tian Jude	田磊
Tian Zhuangzhuang	田壮壮
Underbaby	地下婴儿
Wan Yanhai	万延海
Wang Bing	王兵
Wang Fen	王芬
Wang Guangli	王光利
Wang Jinxi	王进喜
Wang Shuibo	王水泊
Wang Wo	王我
Wang Xiaoshuai	王小帅
Wang Yu	王域
Wang Zhutian	王诛天
Wang Zijun	王子军
Wei Dong	魏东
Wei Xing	魏星
Wen Hui	文慧
Wen Pulin	温普林
Echo Y. Windy	英未未
Wu Tianming	吴天明
Wu Wenguang	吴文光
Wu Yigong	吴贻弓
Xiao Peng	晓鹏
Xie Fei	谢飞
Xu Bin	徐玢
Yan Yu	鄢雨
Yang Lina	杨荔娜
Yang Tianyi	杨天乙
Ying Weiwei	英未未
Yu Jian	于坚
Zhang Beichuan	张北川
Zhang Ci	张慈
Zhang Dali	张大力
Zhang Hua	章桦
Zhang Jinli	张金利
Zhang Junzhao	张军钊
Zhang Liming	张黎明
Zhang Ming	章明
Zhang Nuanxin	张暖忻
Zhang Shadow	张颖
Zhang Wang	张望
Zhang Xiaping	张夏平
Zhang Xinmin	张新民
Zhang Yimou	张艺谋
Zhang Yuan	张元
Zhang Zhen	张真
Zhao Gang	赵刚
Zhao Liang	赵亮
Zhao Yanying	赵燕英
Zheng Dasheng	郑大圣
Zheng Dongtian	郑洞天
Zhi Zibai	栀子白
Zhou Enlai	周恩来
Zhou Hao	周浩
Zhou Yuejun	周岳軍
Zhu Chuanming	朱传明
Zuo Yixiao	左益虓

List of Chinese Film and Video Titles

This list contains the English titles of all the Chinese documentary and feature films and television series mentioned in the book, together with the Chinese original titles, the names of the filmmakers or the television production company, and the year of release. The Chinese characters for the directors' names can be found in the list of Chinese names.

English Title	Chinese Title	Filmmaker/ Production Company	Year of Release
1428	1428	Du Haibin	2009
1966, My Time in the Red Guards	1966，我的红卫兵时代	Wu Wenguang	1993
Along the Railroad Tracks (a.k.a. *Along the Railway Tracks*)	铁路沿线	Du Haibin	2000
Ancient Road of Tangbo	唐蕃古道	CCTV	1985
At Home in the World	四海为家	Wu Wenguang	1995
Bask in Sunshine	圣光	Hu Jie	2002
Beautiful Men	人面桃花	Du Haibin	2005
Before the Flood	淹没	Li Yifan, Yan Yu	2005
Before the Flood II	淹没II，龚滩	Yan Yu	2008
Beijing Bastards	北京杂种	Zhang Yuan	1993
Beijing Bicycle	十七岁的单车	Wang Xiaoshuai	2001
Beijing Cotton Fluffer	北京弹匠	Zhu Chuanming	1999
Big Tree County	大树乡	Hao Zhiqiang	1993
The Birth of New China	新中国的诞生	Gao Weijin	1949
Blind Shaft	盲井	Li Yang	2003
The Blue Kite	蓝风筝	Tian Zhuanzhuang	1993
The Blue Mask Consecration	蓝面具供养	Duan Jinchuan	1988
Boatman on Maoyan River	茅岩河船夫	Li Xiao	1992
The Box	盒子	Ying Weiwei (a.k.a. Echo Y. Windy)	2001
Bumming in Beijing: The Last Dreamers	流浪北京：最后的梦想者	Wu Wenguang	1990
The Canine Condition	狗的状况	Jia Zhangke	2001

English Title	Chinese Title	Filmmaker/ Production Company	Year of Release
Care and Love	关爱	Ai Xiaoming	2007
Catholics in Tibet	天主在西藏	Jiang Yue	1992
China Village Self-Governance Film Project	中国村民自治影像计划	Wu Wenguang (and the directors of the individual short films)	2006
Construction Workers	拆房工	Hu Jie	1998
The Cormorants and the Lake	鱼鹰	Zhou Yuejun	1998
Crazy English	疯狂英语	Zhang Yuan	1999
Crime and Punishment	罪与罚	Zhao Liang	2007
Crude Oil	采油日记	Wang Bing	2008
Dance with Farm Workers	和民工跳舞	Wu Wenguang	2001
Dancing with Myself	和自己跳舞	Li Hong	2002
Delamu	茶马古道：德拉姆	Tian Zhuangzhuang	2004
Demolition and Rehousing	钉子户	Zhang Yuan	1997
Diary: Snow, 21 November 1998	日记：雪，1998年，11月21日	Wu Wenguang	1998
Disorder	现实是过去的未来	Huang Weikai	2009
Distant Village	远去的村庄	Li Xiao	1996
Documentary Editing Room	纪录片编辑室	Shanghai TV	since 1993
Dong	东	Jia Zhangke	2006
Dou Dou	窦豆	Du Haibin	1998
Dream of the Empty City	空城一梦	Ji Dan	2007
DV China	DV中国	Zheng Dasheng	2003
Dyke March	女同志游行日	Shi Tou, Ming Ming	2004
East Palace, West Palace	东宫西宫	Zhang Yuan	1996
The Elders	老人们	Ji Dan	1999
The Elected Village Chief	民选村长	Hu Jie	2004
The Empty Cage	空笼	Jiang Zhi	2001
The Ends of the Earth	天边	Duan Jinchuan	1997
Epic of Central Plains	中原纪事	Ai Xiaoming	2006
Extras	群众演员	Zhu Chuanming	2001
Factory Director Zhang Liming	厂长张黎明	Li Xiao	2000
The Factory Set Up by the Peasants	农民办工厂	Hu Jie	1998
A Family in Northern Tibet	藏北人家	Wang Haibin, Han Hui	1991
Family Phobia	我的父亲母亲和我的兄弟姐妹	Hu Xinyu	2009
Farewell Yuanmingyuan	告别圆明园	Zhao Liang	2005
Feeding Boys, Ayaya	哎呀呀，去哺乳	Cui Zi'en	2003
Female Matchmaker	媒婆	Hu Jie	1996
Fengming: A Chinese Memoir	和凤鸣	Wang Bing	2007

English Title	Chinese Title	Filmmaker/ Production Company	Year of Release
Fish and Elephant	今年夏天	Li Yu	2001
Floating	飘	Huang Weikai	2005
Foggy Valley	雾谷	Zhou Yuejun	2003
Folk Song on the Plain	平原上的山歌	Hu Jie	2003
For Fun	找乐	Ning ying	1993
Forbidden City	紫禁城	Xinying Studio	1987
The Forbidden Palace	故宫	CCTV	2005
Forefinger	食指	Jiang Zhi	1998
Fuck Cinema	操他妈的电影	Wu Wenguang	2005
Gangxiang — Call to Spirits	杠香—请灵	Shi Tou	2002
The Garden of Heaven	天堂花园	Ai Xiaoming, Hu Jie	2007
Gender Game	伤花	Ni Tracey (a.k.a. Zhi Zibai)	2006
Gipsy in the Flower	采花大盗	Ju Anqi	2009
The Girls That Way	别样女孩	Zhang Shadow, Tian Jude	2005
Gongbu's Happy Life	贡布的幸福生活	Ji Dan	1999
Good Morning, Beijing	你早，北京	Zhao Liang	1998
Hanging on to the End	钉子户	Zhang Yuan	1997
Highland Barley	青稞	Duan Jinchuan	1986
Home Video	家庭录像带	Yang Lina	2001
Houjie	厚街	Zhou Hao, Ji Jianghong	2002
House of Flying Daggers	十面埋伏	Zhang Yimou	2004
How Long Can You Stand It?	看看你能忍多久	Zhao Liang	1998
Hui Prefecture	徽州	CCTV	2003
I Film My Village	我拍我村子	Shu Yaozhen	2006
I Graduated!	我毕业了	SWYC Group	1992
I Love Beijing	夏日暖洋洋	Ning Ying	2000
In Our Own Words	让我们自己说	Ning Ying	2001
In Public	公共场所	Jia Zhangke	2001
The Janitors	清洁工	Hu Jie	1998
Jiang Hu: Life on the Road	江湖	Wu Wenguang	1999
Jiang Nan	江南	CCTV	2002
Journey through the Century	世纪行	The Propaganda Department of Shenzhen Municipal Committee	1989
Kuang Dan's Secret	邝丹的秘密	Zhang Hua	2004
Landlord Mr. Jiang	房东蒋先生	Liang Zi	2005
Last House Standing	钉子户	Zhang Yuan	1997
Leave Me Alone	我不要你管	Hu Shu	1998–99

English Title	Chinese Title	Filmmaker/ Production Company	Year of Release
Life on the Road (see also *Jianghu: Life on the Road*)	江湖	Wu Wenguang	1999
Life Space	生活空间	CCTV	Since 1993
Lighting a Candle	烛光	Zhao Yanying	1999
Listen to Mr. Fan	听樊先生讲过去事情	Kang Jianning	2002
Little Red	小红	Jiang Zhi	2002
Living Buddhas	活佛	Shi Tou	2001
The Longwang Chronicles	乡村档案	Li Yifan	2007
Looking for a Job in the City	进城打工	Ning Ying	2003
Looking for Lin Zhao's Soul	寻找林昭的灵魂	Hu Jie	2004
Losing	失散	Zuo Yixiao	2005
The Love of Mr. An	老安的爱情	Yang Lina	2008
Mama	妈妈	Zhang Yuan	1990
The Man	男人	Hu Xinyu	2003
Meishi Street	煤市街	Ou Ning, Cao Fei	2006
The Men and Women of Jiada Village	加达村的男人和女人	Duan Jinchuan	1997
Merchants of Hui	徽商	CCTV	2005
Merchants of Jin County	晋商	Shanxi Television Station	2003
Mine No. 8	八矿	Xiao Peng	2003
Miss Jin Xing	金星小姐	Zhang Yuan	2000
The Moments	片刻	Jiang Zhi	2005
Movie, Childhood	电影·童年	Du Hiabin	2005
My Neighbors on Japanese Devils	我的邻居說鬼子	Yang Lina	2007
Mystery of the Yunnan Snub-nosed Monkey	神秘滇金丝猴	Shi Lihong	2002
The Nail	钉子	Jiang Zhi	2007
National East Wind Farm	国营东风农场	Hu Jie	2009
Night in China	中国之夜	Ju Anqi	2007
Night Scene	夜景	Cui Zi'en	2004
Noise	热闹	Wang Wo	2007
No. 16 Barkhor South Street	八廓南街16号	Duan Jinchuan	1996
Nostalgia	乡愁	Shu Haolun	2006
Odyssey of the Great Wall	望长城	CCTV/TBS	1990
Old Men	老头	Yang Lina (a.k.a. Yang Tianyi)	1999
On the Beat	民警故事	Ning Ying	1995
On the Seaside	在海边	Hu Jie	2003
One and Eight	一个和八个	Zhang Junzhao	1983
One Day in Beijing	有一天，在北京	Jia Zhangke	1994
Oriental Horizon	东方时空	CCTV	Since 1993

English Title	Chinese Title	Filmmaker/ Production Company	Year of Release
The Other Bank (a.k.a. *The Other Shore*)	彼岸	Jiang Yue	1995
Our Children	我们的娃娃	Ai Xiaoming	2009
Our Love	香平丽	Jiang zhi	2004
Out of Phoenix Bridge	回到凤凰桥	Li Hong	1997
Outside	外面	Wang Wo	2006
Painting for the Revolution: The Peasant Painters of Hu County	为革命画画：户县农民画	Ai Xiaoming	2005
Paper Airplane	纸飞机	Zhao Liang, Fan Junyi	2001
People's Representative Yao	人民代表姚立法	Ai Xiaoming	2006
Petition	上访	Zhao Liang	2009
The Quarry	采石场	Jia Zhitan	2006
Queer China, "Comrade" China	誌同志	Cui Zi'en	2009
Quilts	被子	Ju Anqi	2003
Railroad of Hope	希望之旅	Ning Ying	2002
Red Art	红色美术	Ai Xiaoming, Hu Jie	2007
Remote Mountains	远山	Hu Jie	1996
The Residents of Lhasa's Potala Square	拉萨雪居民	Jiang Yue	1992
Return to the Border	在江边	Zhao Liang	2007
River Elegy	河殇	Su Xiaokang (writer)	1988
A River Stilled	静止的河	Jiang Yue	1998
Road to Paradise	天堂之路	Zhang Hua	2006
The Sacred Site of Asceticism	青朴——苦修者的圣地	Wen Pulin, Duan Jinchuan	1993
Sand and Sea	沙与海	Kang Jianning	1991
Sanyuanli	三元里	Ou Ning, Cao Fei	2003
The Secret of My Success	拎起大舌头	Jiang Yue	2002
Senior Year	高三	Zhou Hao	2006
Seventeen Years	过年回家	Zhang Yuan	1997
The Silent Nu River	沉默的怒江	Hu Jie	2006
Silk Road	丝绸之路	CCTV	1980
Sisters	姐妹	Li Jinghong	2004
A Social Survey	一次社会调查	Zhao Liang	1998
Soldier	当兵	Kang Jianning	2000
Song of the Sun	太阳之歌	The General Political Department of the People's Liberation Army	1992
Sons	儿子	Zhang Yuan	1996
Spiral Staircase of Harbin	哈尔滨的楼梯	Ji Dan	2009
Spirit Home	地上流云	Ji Dan	2006

English Title	Chinese Title	Filmmaker/ Production Company	Year of Release
Springtime in Wushan	巫山之春	Zhang Ming	2003
The Square	广场	Duan Jinchuan, Zhang Yuan	1994
Still Life	三峡好人	Jia Zhangke	2006
Stone Mountain	石山	Du Haibin	2006
The Storm	暴风骤雨	Duan Jinchuan, Jiang Yue	2005
The Story of Qiu Ju	秋菊打官司	Zhang Yimou	1992
Strange Homeland	陌生的家园	Li Xiao	1996
Struggle	挣扎	Shu Haolun	2001
A Student Village	学生村	Wei Xing	2002
Sunken Treasure	沉船——97年的故事	Duan Jinchuan	1999
Sunrise over Tiananmen Square	天安门上太阳升	Wang Shuibo	1998
Swing in Beijing	悠哉，北京	Wang Shuibo	1999
Taishi Village	太石村	Ai Xiaoming	2005
Tangshan Earthquake	唐山大地震	Li Xiao	2007
There Is a Strong Wind in Beijing	北京的风很大	Ju Anqi	1999
They Chose China	他们选择了中国	Wang Shuibo	2005
This Happy Life	幸福生活	Jiang Yue	2002
Though I Am Gone (a.k.a. Though I Was Dead)	我虽死去	Hu Jie	2006
Thousand Miles of Coastline	万里海疆	CCTV	1988
Tiananmen	天安门	CCTV	1991
Tibet	西藏	Duan Jinchuan	1991
Tibetan Theater Troupe	甘孜藏戏团	Fu Hongxing	1993
Tibetan Theater Troupe of Lhama Priests	喇嘛藏戏团	Jiang Yue	1991
The Train to My Hometown	开往家乡的列车	Ai Xiaoming, Hu Jie	2008
The Transition Period	冬月	Zhou Hao	2009
The Trash Collector	架子工	Hu Jie	1998
Umbrella	伞	Du Haibin	2007
Under the Skyscraper	高楼下面	Du Haibin	2002
Unhappiness Does Not Stop at One	不快乐的不只一个	Wang Fen	2001
Useless	无用	Jia Zhangke	2007
Using	龙哥	Zhou Hao	2007
Vagina Monologues	阴道独白	Ai Xiaoming	2004
Village Head Election	海选	Hu Jingcao	1998
Voice of the Angry River	怒江之声	Shi Lihong	2004
The War of Love	爱情战争	Jiang Yue	2002
We Are the … of Communism	我们是共产主义省略号	Cui Zi'en	2007
We Want to Get Married	我们要结婚	Shi Tou	2007

English Title	Chinese Title	Filmmaker/ Production Company	Year of Release
Wellspring	在一起的时光	Sha Qing, Ji Dan	2002
Wenda Gu: Art, Politics, Life, Sexuality	谷文达访谈：艺术，政治，人生，性倾向	Shi Tou	2005
West of the Tracks	铁西区	Wang Bing	2003
What Are You Doing with That Camera?	你拿摄影机干什么	Ai Xiaoming	2006
White Ribbon	白丝带	Ai Xiaoming	2004
Winter Days	冬日	Zhao Gang	2003
Witness	目击者	Zhao Liang	1998
Women Fifty Minutes	女人50分钟	Shi Tou, Ming Ming	2006
Xiao Wu	小武	Jia Zhangke	1997
Yangtze River	话说长江	CCTV	1983
Yellow Earth	黄土地	Chen Kaige	1984
Yinyang	阴阳	Kang Jianning	1994
Yuanmingyuan Artist Village	圆明园的艺术家们	Hu Jie	1995
Zigui	姊贵	Hu Xinyu	2006

Index

CPSIA information can be obtained at www.ICGtesting.com
Printed in the USA
LVOW080804240712

291151LV00002BA/1/P